Anglo-Chinese Encounters Before the Opium War

Anglo-Chinese Encounters Before the Opium War: A Tale of Two Empires Over Two Centuries studies the fascinating encounters between the two historic empires from Queen Elizabeth I's first letter to the Ming Emperor Wanli in 1583, to Lord Palmerston's letter to the Minister of China in 1840.

Starting with Queen Elizabeth I's letter to the Chinese Emperor and ending with the letter from Lord Palmerston to the Minister of China just before the Opium War, this book explores the long journey in between from cultural diplomacy to gunboat diplomacy. It interweaves the most known diplomatic efforts at the official level with the much unknown intellectual interactions at the people-to-people level, from missionaries to scholars, from merchants to travellers and from artists to scientists. This book adopts a novel "mirror" approach by pairing and comparing people, texts, commodities, artworks, architecture, ideologies, operating systems and world views of the two empires. Using letters, gifts and traded goods as fulcrums, and by adopting these unique lenses, it puts China into the world history narratives to contextualise Anglo-Chinese relations, thus providing a fresh analysis of the surviving evidence. Xin Liu casts a new light on understanding the Sino-centric and Anglo-centric world views in driving the complex relations between the two empires, and the reversals of power shifts that are still unfolding today.

The book is not intended for specialists in history, but a general audience wishing to learn more about China's historical engagement with the world.

Xin Liu is a Senior Lecturer and Chair of the China Research Center at the University of Central Lancashire. She received her PhD and MBA from the same university. Her other monograph, *China's Cultural Diplomacy: A Great Leap Outward?,* was published by Routledge in 2020.

Routledge Studies in Modern History

The City and the Railway in the World from the Nineteenth Century to the Present
Edited by Ralf Roth and Paul van Heesvelde

Displaced Persons, Resettlement and the Legacies of War
From War Zones to New Homes
Jessica Stroja

Citizens and Refugees
Stories from Afghanistan and Syria to Germany
Joachim C. Häberlen

Anglo-Chinese Encounters Before the Opium War
A Tale of Two Empires Over Two Centuries
Xin Liu

The History and Politics of Star Wars
Death Stars and Democracy
Chris Kempshall

Christianity, the Sovereign Subject, and Ethnic Nationalism in Colonial Korea: Specters of Western Metaphysics
Hannah Amaris Roh

Missionaries and the Colonial State
Radicalism and Governance in Rwanda and Burundi, 1900–1972
David Whitehouse

Jewish Self-Defense in South America
Facing Anti-Semitism with a Club in Hand
Raanan Rein

For more information about this series, please visit: https://www.routledge.com/Routledge-Research-in-Modern-History/book-series/MODHIST

Anglo-Chinese Encounters Before the Opium War

A Tale of Two Empires Over Two Centuries

Xin Liu

NEW YORK AND LONDON

First published 2023
by Routledge
605 Third Avenue, New York, NY 10158

and by Routledge
4 Park Square, Milton Park, Abingdon, Oxon, OX14 4RN

Routledge is an imprint of the Taylor & Francis Group, an informa business

Library of Congress Cataloguing-in-Publication Data
A catalog record for this title has been requested

ISBN: 978-0-367-74167-9 (hbk)
ISBN: 978-0-367-74170-9 (pbk)
ISBN: 978-1-003-15638-3 (ebk)

DOI: 10.4324/9781003156383

Typeset in Times New Roman
by MPS Limited, Dehradun

For Ben and Angi, my eternal inspirations

Contents

Illustrations

Acknowledgements

To me, writing this book is a wonderful journey of discovery. I have so many people to thank that I decide to follow the time sequence that they appeared on this journey.

The journey started on the day in November 2019 when I found where the Queen Elizabeth I's letter to the Chinese emperor was kept. I read about these letters a few years ago, but the different source texts I came across provided vague and varied versions of where the last letter is being kept today, which triggered my curiosity. I decided to dig it out. To my great surprise, in the book *Elizabeth I's Foreign Correspondence*, I read "the third letter, dated 1602, survives in its stunning original form in the Lancashire Record Office (UK)" (Allinson, 2014: 210). I could not believe my eyes as the Lancashire Record Office was the former name of the Lancashire Archives, which is literally 10 minutes' walk from my office at the university! I immediately went there to make the inquiry, and five minutes later, I laid my eyes in amazement on this hidden gem, which then unlocked the door to a whole host of hidden treasures that are now shining in every chapter of the book.

I am extremely grateful to the peer reviewer for the very constructive feedback to my book proposal and the reference list for me to consult; I then made contacts with a number of scholars who have done research in this area and received enormous help. For example, William Poole from the Oxford University, not only answered my questions in detail but also sent me a copy of his new book published about Thomas Hyde. Mr. Guo Fuxiang, a researcher from Beijing's Palace Museum, has become my first point of contact for any questions related to this period of history in the Forbidden City; and Mr. Wang Zhiwei, head of the Imperial History Editorial Office at the Palace Museum Press, while providing me access to many valuable archival materials, also gave me a copy of the book *The Qianlong Emperor and Lord Macartney* published in 1998 that is out of print today.

What is worth special mentioning is that the start of writing the book coincided with the outbreak of Covid-19. The bulk of the book was completed during the on-and-off lockdowns when we could not go to places, I decided to go back to history and go deep into research. I am lucky to have unreserved support and encouragement from my husband and daughter throughout the two years that this book was in preparation. My husband played an instrumental role in being my critical listener on a daily basis, and in inspiring me with his knowledge and insight that pushed me to generate "new" insight from re-reading history. My daughter is always the first reader of my writings. When I managed to fly to Beijing over summer in 2021, the most dreadful three-week hotel quarantine was made amazingly productive as I went through the draft chapters with her on a daily basis. Her candid and sharp comments and feedback from a reader's perspective kept on pushing me to bring the ideas into full articulation and clarity.

I am also deeply indebted to Frank Pearson and Ma Xi for providing the translations for the three letters of Queen Elizabeth I (Appendix 1 to 3). Being a translator myself, I lack the expertise of handling ancient texts in English, thus unable to do justice to the historical documents. Frank added detailed annotations while Ma gave a talented rendering that captured the full beauty and style of classic English and Chinese. I cannot appreciate more their generosity with their time and contributions.

I must acknowledge the Faculty research fund provided by the University of Central Lancashire and an external grant awarded by the Universities' China Committee in London (UCCL), which enabled me to complete the field trips in the UK and China respectively. During my time in Beijing, I visited the Anton Library housed in the Beijing Centre for Chinese Studies, which granted me every facility to access their historical collections, and continued to offer me assistance after I came back to the UK and requested some further materials. I then received more funding from the University to pay for the license fees to use many of the historical images as illustrations in the book. My special thanks also go to Andrea Evans at the University library for making special orders for the books I needed, and to Simon Folwer, for his professional archive search and conscientious work that saved me time from getting drowned in the sea of source materials. Without the generosity of these scholars and institutions, this book could not have reached the breadth and standard.

Last but not least, huge thanks go to Max Novick, my series editor from Routledge, whose efficiency and professionalism impressed me since day one I started working with him. Without his prompt communication, this book will not be able to come out in such a quick turnaround of time. My heartfelt thanks go to Emily Irvine, my copy editor, and Neha Shrivastava, my book project manager, for their patience and professionalism in guiding me through the production process.

This book has been made possible and better because of each and every one of you.

Thank you all.

Introduction: 1583–1840, from cultural diplomacy to gunboat diplomacy

What is history? An echo of the past in the future; a reflex from the future on the past.

– Victor Hugo

A common Chinese saying is to describe history as a "long course of river". If the two historic empires of Britain and China are like vessels navigating on this river, this book tries to chart the people and incidents that played critical roles in steering them to those encounters and conflicts throughout the two and half centuries, from 1583 to 1840. Although the British engagement with the Chinese Empire can be dated back to Queen Elizabeth I's reign, when the history of Anglo-Chinese relations is discussed in the UK, it normally starts with the two failed embassies sent to China in 1793 and 1816, which has become a humiliating memory in Britain's glorious past on its way to conquer the world; while in China, the first phrase that comes to people's minds is probably the "century of humiliations", from 1840[1] when the first Opium War broke out till the founding of the People's Republic of China in 1949. This was a century of "painful Chinese weakness in the face of Western imperialism, territorial division, unequal treaties, invasion, anti-Chinese racism, and social chaos" (Zhao, 2004: 84) that had ripped apart China's cultural superiority, and was later taught in schools as an "enduring narrative of modern Chinese history and identity" (Callahan, 2006: 187). I think "historical trauma" is perhaps a better word to describe the deepest and most recurring traumatic memories of the Western forces who invaded, exploited, carved up China and forced a series of subjugations on a once-proud civilisation. This made me wonder, why do both countries choose to start their story of the relationship with bitterness? Why do they both want to claim victimhood in their encounters? And what is the interplay between historical changes beyond these events?

In the standard frame of modern Chinese history, the First Opium War is treated as the event marking its very beginning. In this sense, we may argue that there is no other country as deeply embedded in Chinese history as Great Britain. However, much fewer people may realise that it

DOI: 10.4324/9781003156383-1

is equally true that China is also deeply embedded in the British identity as a "a tea-drinking nation", as for nearly two centuries time, the only place in the world where the British could obtain their tea was from China, and the first two embassies were sent to China to expand their tea trade. Tea served in Chinoiserie chinaware blended the visions of otherness with the feelings of the nationalist self, and nurtured Britain's complex attitude towards China. The intertwined story of tea and opium run through the intertwined fate of the two countries, with the mutual embedments still having a lasting legacy till today.

0.1 The old tale and a new narrative

This book takes the story back to the very beginning of early interactions between the two empires prior to those milestone events, starting a fascinating journey of inquiry and discovery by documenting the earliest exchanges and movements of people, commodities, ideas and imaginaries that have been understudied in those grand narratives, thus kept in a much more isolated scholarship space so far. Starting from 1583 when Queen Elizabeth I wrote a letter to the Ming Emperor Wanli and ending with a letter from Lord Palmerston to the Minister of the Emperor of China in 1840, what happened between these two letters was a long journey from cultural diplomacy to gunboat diplomacy. Early interactions occurred in three broad categories that were of unequal importance to the two empires: intellectual exchanges, trade and diplomacy. Using letters, gifts and traded goods as fulcrums, and by adopting these unique lenses to re-examine the Anglo-Chinese encounters, this book seeks to cast a new light on our understanding of the complex historical, cultural, trade and political relations between two of the world's most powerful historic empires, and what drove the historical course of the two empires that hold fundamentally different world views.

The main story line of the book is the intriguing dynamics of the relative power shifts between the two empires, driven by the economic and technological advances at both ends and the interactions between the two, as well as other variables in the broader historical and international contexts. By interweaving the most known diplomatic efforts at the official level with the much unknown intellectual interactions at the people-to-people level, from missionaries to scholars, from merchants to travellers and from artists to scientists, this book probes some areas of more intimate encounters, as what the historian Zhang Longxi (1988) has deemed, an essential aspect of the demythologization of another culture is the full recognition of the "other" as a "person", therefore, we need to look at stories of real people that made history. It aims to establish a continuum during the over two centuries time by connecting dots through the manifold intellectual, cultural, economic and political encounters, as no matter how significant and critical those mega events are, history is always a continuum of moments when dynamics of different forces are constantly evolving. Instead of repeating the narratives of the key events and endeavouring to provide a comprehensive history from 1583 to 1840, this book distinguishes itself from other works by adopting a novel "mirror effect" approach by pairing and comparing people, texts, commodities, artworks, architecture, ideologies, operating systems and world views of the two empires. This approach allows me to put China back into world history narratives to contextualise Anglo-Chinese relations, thus providing a fresh analysis of the surviving evidence and offering new interpretations of how the two empires created frameworks for understanding "the other" from an Anglo-centric and Sino-centric points of departure.

Under this framework, archival sources, historical records and accounts from both countries are carefully analysed to decipher what the letters, gifts and products exchanged reveal about the two empires' perceptions of "self and other", and the power relationality between them, specifically, the alterity in the historical cultural relations and connectivity in the global trade context. It explores questions such as: Why the British and the Chinese were treated by "the other" the way they did? How do these mutual perceptions reflect the different assumptions about how trade and diplomatic relations should be carried out between countries? What subtle shifts in tone and rhetorical emphasis can be found between Queen Elizabeth I's letters and King George III's, between the British monarchs' and the Chinese Emperors', and between the original letters and their translations? What do these differences and shifts reveal? How does the fact that there was no resident British missionary sent to China until 1807 (centuries after Marco Polo's arrival in 1275 and Matteo Ricci's residence in Beijing in 1601) affect their understanding of China? Similarly, how does the fact that there are no Chinese records of those early travellers to the Far West affect the Chinese understanding of the West? and finally, how different world views and trade practices shape different civilisations and lead to the power dynamics over history? Apart from better understanding what drove the historical courses in the past, an overarching question this book seeks to address is what nourishments we can get from history to nurture a more harmonious and constructive bilateral relationship today, and how we can use the hindsight to generate foresight to steer future relations between the two countries.

While there have been substantial books about China's interactions with the West published in English, most were written in the Eurocentric framework of "Western impact and Chinese response", while using the "West" as a generalised concept suggesting homogeneousness. As a matter of fact, one of the lessons Qing China learned from interacting with the British Empire was its distinctive Englishness that put its relationship with China in a league of its own. Despite its belatedness in trading with China, it was no ordinary "Western Ocean country" but a modern power that not only wished to *exchange* goods with China, but also to *change* its ways of exchange and the fundamental Sino-centric world view, to the extent of eventually resorting to military forces. I argue this wish to "change" China is also a "British response to the Chinese impact" on its trade relations and mercantile interests. Even the term "gunboat diplomacy" reveals this: It was considered a cheeky term to the Chinese as diplomacy is defined as dealing with international relations via non-violent means, for the British however, it showed the original intention of establishing diplomatic relations, and the subsequent evolvement of the means from failed attempts of peaceful diplomatic missions to military intervention.

There has been extensive research exclusively focusing on the two embassies, such as edited volumes of papers commemorating their 200th anniversaries in 1993 and 2016. Peyrefitte's (1992) *The Immobile Empire* recaptured Macartney's grand and ill-fated mission as the "first great collision of East and West" and Hevia's (1995) *Cherishing Men from Afar* offered excellent scholarly treatments of the Macartney Embassy from a historical perspective informed by Chinese sources, leading to his argument that the failed mission was not so much impaired by the cultural misunderstandings that have often been attributed but by differing ideas about constructing relations of sovereignty and power. There were also a number of books focusing on the violent collisions and incidents *after* the First Opium War, such as *The Clash of Empires* (Liu, 2006). Another recent scholarship assessing China's nineteenth-century history and its place in the global political, economic and cultural networks of the time is Waley-Cohen's (2000) *Sextants of Beijing.* Though she made some good points in putting forward arguments against the long-held myth that Chinese civilisation was inward-looking and perennially isolated from the rest of the world, and described Qing China as more open than most think, I will challenge her by raising domestic governance as endogenous restraints of Qing's openness to modernity and innovation: the deeply embedded concepts of "ancestral precedents" that were considered sacred and immutable, the reactionary role of ministers to serve the Emperor as "minions" and the common practice of "court artifice" as manifested in the negotiations, as well as "literary inquisition" where scholars would be executed for any slight indication of criticism of the government or holding different opinions. These angles were rarely taken before by the English writings to examine the effects they had on those interactions, partly due to the language barrier to handle sources in both old English and classic Chinese[2] at the same time.

As someone who straddles over conceptual, cultural and linguistic boundaries, I am in a privileged position to bridge this gap. My background of being educated in both China (BA in English and Bachelor of Laws in International Law) and the UK (MBA in Change Management and PhD in China's Cultural Diplomacy), with a career route evolving from being an interpreter/translator to a scholar of Chinese Studies, makes me well placed to remedy this issue. While using my ability to wade through the proliferation of materials in both English and Chinese languages to search for truth among competing accounts, I also endeavour to use my vantage point as being both an insider and outsider of Chinese culture to add more insight by synthesising the knowledge produced at both ends. My training and experience in working as a professional interpreter/translator has conditioned me to keep emotional detachment in approaching materials from a neutral perspective. This book happened to be written at a midpoint of my career path—after spending 15 years working in China and the UK—which allows me to not only see different things but also see things differently. While moving between the British and Chinese contexts in the past three decades, I am deeply aware of the cultural distance between the two countries. If the phrases of "iron curtain" and "bamboo curtain" refer to the demarcation marked by ideology during the Cold War, I argue there has always existed a translucent "silk curtain" between China and the West culturally, leaving each other with either a fanciful exotic impression or a clouded image that invites imagination. This means there is often a gap between the reality of China and the perception of China. If reading the other is to see it through the authors' lens that may be tinted with their own perceptions, meeting face-to-face with the other, but with language barriers in between like the two British embassies, is like seeing something under the water, refracted in some form even if the water is clear. I hope this book can lend readers yet another pair of lenses to read China and understand it on its own terms.

What particularly triggered my interest in writing this book is an observation: China did not change drastically during these two centuries, even infamous for being stagnant and immobile as an antiquated empire from the seventeenth to nineteenth century, yet its image in the West had gone through a 180-degree drastic turn: from a most sophisticated civilisation to despotic barbarianism. In other words, the change of China's image was due to its lack of change when tremendous changes took place in the West that made itself the definition of modernity. Then why today, when China *did* go through a comparable magnitude of transformation and modernization in a compressed timeframe of half a century, its image in the West is not reversed, but only added new biases to the old stereotype? Dawson (1964: 4) wrote in the *Legacy of China* that "old misconceptions of her civilisation live long and die hard, for there is a certain inertia in our historical beliefs, so that they tend to be retained until they are ruthlessly questioned by original minds perhaps centuries after they have ceased to be true". Yet, centuries after the Opium War, stale misconceptions of China still tint many people's views of China today. Although the two sides can now negotiate in English with no language barriers, the world views held by each still yield to the long-cast shadows of history, which may hold answers to many of the issues we face today.

For example, the flashpoints of Huawei and Hong Kong in the bilateral relations today show the modern resonance the book has and its relevance to today's world. For China, they represent a microcosm of its views towards the "outside and inside"; for the British, they could serve as reminders of how high nationalist sentiment may rise when a country is in the rise, to the point of easily becoming belligerent as the British did before the Opium War. An observation of Chinese history shows that China expanded "not by conquering, but by being conquered" (Medhurst, 1890: 15) under the non-Han rulings of the Mongols (the Yuan Dynasty) and Manchus (the Qing Dynasty), the Ming China in between (and the Song China before the Yuan) never sought to conquer other lands or to threat its smaller neighbours with invasions. They want to be admired but not feared. Similarly, China today is not interested in threatening other country's national security; it may be perceived to have the ability to invade, but it does not have the intention to do so. Domestic control remains to be the driving concern of the government, and China is far more interested in the politics of placating domestic rule. Wrongly minded accusations only irritate China and show a lack of understanding of its so-called "core interests", which has always been gravitated towards maintaining stability within its own borders and sovereignty over its own territory.

Hong Kong as part of China represents one of such "core interests" that may turn any friend to an enemy if meddling in; its historical legacy from the Opium War as the scar of China makes Hong Kong a particularly sensitive issue for the UK to handle with special care. We can still see the old emperor's worry about the connection between foreign influence and domestic instability today. As the world's No. 1 trading nation, China surely permits the circulation of foreign goods, but not a free rein to foreign ideology, which is considered an invisible threat that might come to prevail over Chinese values, thus must be contained. Meanwhile, the highly invested nationalist sentiment in the much stronger China today means that it would not leave any room for the British to have a say in the future of Hong Kong. They did not even respond to the British questioning but simply asked back: Who do you think you are to lecture us on how to govern Hong Kong? It is no longer 1840! Therefore, looking back beyond 1793 and 1840 allows us to see the imprints of the entangled history on the political, cultural and economic dynamics of our own age. As the world shrinks and China grows, and when the two countries celebrate its fiftieth anniversary of formal establishment of full diplomatic relations in 2022,[3] it is more imperative than ever for a reconsideration of the lasting legacies of these encounters on the modern-day interactions between a post-Brexit UK and a globalising China.

0.2 Structure of the book

Since the intention of the book is not just to tell a fascinating tale but to underscore a lesson that can be learned by reflecting, rethinking and reconceptualising them in relation to contemporary frames of reference, the structure of the book is a combination of thematic and chronological. It narrates the stories of how the early interactions navigated the conceptual and physical space of a land with little first-hand knowledge, and how Britain's increasing knowledge of China and power shifts eventually led to its decision to alter the course of engagement with China from using letters, gifts and diplomats to military might.

This book opens with the three letters written by Queen Elizabeth I to the Ming Emperor Wanli from 1583–1602, when the British lagged behind the Portuguese, Spanish and Dutch in trading with China, but the three attempts to deliver the letter via explorations seeking sea route shortcuts all failed miserably. It situates the start of Anglo-Chinese contact in international histories to set the scene for a better understanding of what drives the evolvement of the bilateral relations. After presenting the full text and picture of the highly ornamented 1602 letter, it explains why with four different language versions provided, its purpose would not be able to be understood by the Chinese emperor, and why the underlying world views of the two empires were incompatible from the very start, which is further illustrated by a set of mirror images of the two monarchs and what symbolises their power. It also highlights an erroneous image of the Chinese Emperor Shunzhi that is still in wide circulation today.

Chapter 2 explains the unique Chinese Tributary System and its underpinning philosophies and ancient beliefs, which had bred a whole host of Sino-speak vocabulary of outsiders and foreigners. It then draws a profile of the Ming China, seen, presented and influenced by Western missionaries, which also helped shape the image of a Utopian China in the West. Then it explains the Ming views of foreign trade and finishes with the actual first Anglo-Chinese encounter in 1637, when the British entered the picture with its first expedition to Canton. This little-known attempt to establish commercial relations and a permanent trading station in China, long before Macartney's famously disappointing embassy to Beijing, foreshadowed the conflict when it ended in a military skirmish taking place in the same waters that would stage the consequential Opium War two centuries later.

Chapter 3 tells four stories of the earliest Chinese travellers to the British Empire by pairing each visitor with a Briton they interacted with, and the legacies left behind that blend elements of cultural, intellectual, political, commercial and artistic aspects of Chinese civilisation. It elaborates the important roles they played as the first-generation cultural ambassadors in knowledge production and dissemination between the two empires. The stories include Shen Fuzong and Thomas Hyde: the first exchanges of a learned nature; Loum Kiqua and William Hickey: the first taste of Chinese music and Chinese food; Tan Che-Qua and William Chambers: the first Chinese artistic legacy that can still be seen in the British Museum today; and Huang Yadong and William Jones: the first English letter exchanged between the two peoples. It then finishes with the first Chinese travelogues about Europe and Britain, but only circulated in a limited circle and produced little impact on Chinese society at the time, and still remain largely unknown today.

Chapter 4 changes from narrating people-to-people contacts to presenting the mirror effects in material culture by comparing Chinoiserie with Euroiserie, using gardens, porcelain and clock making as examples. A short-lived period of Yin-Yang flow was created by cultural inspirations and intellectual exchanges between the two empires in the mid-eighteenth century, in that they not only learned from each other but improved the learned technique by innovative applications of their own creations, such as Wedgwood jasperware and the water fountains in the Chinese Yuanming Yuan. The mutual stimulations suggest a relationship between selves in relation to, rather than in opposition to, the other. The chapter then constructs the background to the Macartney Embassy through a bifocal lens: the mutual perception gaps to the real "other" between the two empires. The mixed writings with both awe and frustrations represent a shift in European views of China from admiration and idealisation to disillusion and degradation by the time of the Macartney Embassy.

Chapter 5 recounts the failed Macartney Embassy by putting it into the global historical context with changing dynamics in the East and the West when both empires considered themselves to be the most civilised. With the king's letter of credential and carefully selected gifts showcasing accomplishments from the ground-breaking Industrial Revolution, it failed miserably in achieving its aims. Reading the British requests alongside the emperor's responses provides a perfect example of the two incompatible world views and different ideas of commerce, civility and diplomacy that were utterly disparate and beyond translation. It uses the Chinese Tributary System and Westphalian System as mirrors to make the point that the famous question of "to kowtow or not to kowtow" was not the key question, nor the root cause of the failure of the two embassies. It then finishes with a discussion of the change of mutual perceptions and the significant new knowledge produced, but also identifies the historically and culturally specific conditions of those knowledge production.

Chapter 6 starts with the negative assets from the Macartney Embassy and the further shifting of power balance between the two empires when Qing was declining from previous prosperous reigns while the British emerged as the century's No. 1 superpower on the global stage. All these mean the generation gap between the two embassies ended up in a deeper gulf that cannot be bridged with language communications. The conflicting testimonies regarding Macartney's reception provided by the Jiaqing Emperor and George Staunton further explained why the embassy was doomed from its very start and why all historical texts need to be read with caution as the official accounts of the British embassy could be just as self-interested as Chinese entries in the archives as a court artifice. It then discusses the minion culture in the Qing court that has been ignored so far in the analysis. It finishes with a renewed mutual knowledge and understanding between the two empires and explains why it was another missed opportunity for the Qing China to engage with the world.

Chapter 7 recounts the stories of tea and opium and compares the opium debates taking place in London and Beijing. It provides different angles of looking at the Opium War as a trade war for commercial interests, a rhetoric war for civilisation and barbarism, and a power shift war for world order dominance. For the latter, the book takes a grander historical and global angle by adopting the lens of the Thucydides Trap to look at the two empires at both their own historical trajectories in the changing global political, economic and cultural landscape, and the merging trend of globalisation that brought the two to collide. As the last chapter of the book, it finishes with a postscript of what happened immediately before and after the Opium War to correct some inaccurate understandings and provide some missing pieces to the giant jigsaw puzzle of what led to the Opium War and its impact on China that has been worked on by previous scholars.

The conclusion tries to reveal the "see-saw of history" (Dawson, 1967: 30) between the two empires by staging the two great reversals: one happened when China' s door was forced open with British gunboats, which reduced it from an admirable wealthy power to a backward "sick man of Asia"; the other is happening today when China opens its door to become the world's No. 1 trading nation. We can see the trajectory of China's movement from splendour to decay then to regeneration, while the British remains proud to be the advocate for liberal trade but still has morality as a recurrent theme in its debates about balancing its economic and political relations with the "Communist China" today. Over four centuries on from the earliest letter correspondence, Britain is still trying to forge a satisfactory relationship with China, and the question of "British response to the Chinese impact" is still relevant, only in a new challenging terrain beyond Orientalism and Occidentalism as living contemporary and global partners.

In the Appendix of the book are 10 letters of historical significance with some translations done and published for the first time. This rare collection itself offers valuable text-based insights to understanding how translation is a political process and how the deeply embedded conflicting world views is beyond translation. A comparison of the original texts and their translated versions shows noteworthy problems of addition, omission, distortion and misinterpretation, which further allows us to form a critical understanding of historical knowledge production by carefully analysing how cultural assumptions and political rhetoric shape both the writing of these texts and the reading and translation of them.

For all Chinese terms included in the book, I have added both Chinese characters and the standard pinyin, the contemporary phonetic system of the language, with a view to clarify the confusions that may have been caused by many variations of spellings and translations throughout history from different language versions. They will appear in italicised form, such as *Tlanxlu*, as a consistent marker to distinguish them. I have also corrected some mistakes in previous studies, including both inaccurate translations and mistaken illustrations, such as that of the Chinese emperor (Figure 1.5 in Chapter 1) used in both the English and Chinese translations of *China Illustrata* and Dawson's famous book, *The Chinese Chameleon* (1967: 40). With altogether 32 illustrations included, the book brings history alive in words and pictures.

To me, the writing process feels like working on a giant jigsaw puzzle, the pieces this book provides will connect with other pieces already provided by other scholars to help reveal the overall picture. The conventional interpretation of Anglo-Chinese encounters as a modernised West crumpling a stagnant yet arrogant Chinese Empire is like judging the size and character of an iceberg by its tip. If the Opium War is the tip of the iceberg, many scholarly efforts have been made to reveal the parts under the waterline, but since this part is so gigantic, this book represents another effort from a different angle. Like Churchill had insightfully said, "the longer you can look back, the farther you can look forward". It is with this hope that the book is written with a view to form a more reasoned understanding of how we have come to this point in our relationship, and how we can move forward in the future.

Notes

1 The Chinese narrative normally puts 1840 as the start of the Opium War, when the British naval force arrived off Canton; while in the UK, it normally puts the start time as 1839, when a skirmish occurred between British and Chinese vessels after Chinese troops were ordered to board British ships to destroy the opium. China's military threat against defenceless British civilians was used to justify the government decision made in October 1939 to send gunboats to China. The different starting time of the Opium War set in the official narratives of the two countries also indicated that both want to claim victimhood in this clash.

2 There were no punctuations in classic Chinese texts, only circles to mark pauses, making them hard to follow and open to different interpretations. Standard Western style punctuations were only introduced to Chinese texts during the Westernization Movement after the Opium War. Circle is still used as the Chinese full stop today instead of a dot.

3 On 6 January 1950, Britain became the first Western country that recognised the People's Republic of China, but since it still maintained relationship with the Republic of China (Taiwan), it took another 22 years of negotiations for the two countries to formally establish full diplomatic relations at ambassadorial level on 13 March 1972.

References

Callahan, W. (2006) 'History, identity, and security: Producing and consuming nationalism in China', *Critical Asian Studies*, 38(2), pp. 179–208.

Dawson, R. (ed.) (1964) *The Legacy of China*. Oxford: Oxford University Press.

Dawson, R. (1967) *The Chinese Chameleon: An Analysis of European Conceptions of Chinese Civilisation*. Oxford: Oxford University Press.

Hevia, J. (1995) *Cherishing Men from Afar, Qing Guest Ritual and the Macartney Embassy of 1793*. Durham and London: Duke University Press Books.

Liu, L.H. (2006). *The Clash of Empires, the Invention of China in Modern World Making*. Cambridge, MA and London, England: Harvard University Press.

Medhurst, W.H. (1890) *China – Its State and Prospects*. The Perfect Library, printed in Great Britain by Amazon (originally published in 1838). Boston: Crocker & Brewster.

Peyrefitte, A. (1992) *The Immobile Empire*. Translated by Rothschild, J. New York: Alfred Knopf.

Waley-Cohen, J. (2000) *Sextants of Beijing, Global Currents in Chinese History*. New York: Norton.

Zhang, L. (1988) 'The myth of the other: China in the eyes of the West', *Critical Inquiry*, 15(1) (Autumn), pp. 108–131. The University of Chicago Press, Stable. http://www.jstor.org/stable/1343606

Zhao, S. (2004) 'Chinese nationalism and pragmatic foreign policy behavior', Chapter 4, in Zhao, S. (ed.) *Chinese Foreign Policy, Pragmatism and Strategic Behavior*. New York: An East Gate Book, pp. 66–88.

1 Where the tale of the two empires began

By this means our countries can exchange commodities for our mutual benefit and as a result, friendship may grow

– Elizabeth I, 1602

This chapter will take us back to where the tale of the two empires began, during the reign of Elizabeth I as the Queen of England and Ireland from 1558 to 1603 and the Wanli Emperor who reigned the Ming China from 1572 to 1620 on the other side of the globe.

However, to tell the whole story, we need to start with the legendary Marco Polo who travelled to China in the 1270s, as English interest in China can find its roots in his published adventures, particularly after the English translation of *The Most Noble and Famous Travels of Marco Polo* became available in 1579. China had occupied an anomalous space in the Western imagination as a distant land of "otherness", and Polo's encyclopaedic account offered numerous references for European readers, although its credibility was often questioned. When placed in synchronic comparison with medieval Europe, Polo's China appeared as the very pinnacle of civilisation. Everything in China amazed him: "Its palaces was the best in the world and its rulers the richest ... Most amazing of all, though, was China's commerce. 'I can tell you in all truthfulness that the business ... is on such a stupendous scale that no one who hears tell of it without seeing it for himself can possibly credit it'" (cited in Morris, 2011: 384).

Polo's pioneering journey to China was also a powerful precursor for the Age of Discoveries. It inspired many people to explore the exotic East, including Christopher Columbus[1] and Vasco da Gama who set sails for their explorations in 1492 and 1498 respectively. According to Davidson (1997: 203), Columbus took letters of credence to any head of states he might encounter, including one for the Grand Khan, although at that time the Grand Khan was no longer the Chinese emperor and China had prospered in the Ming Dynasty (1368–1644) for over a century already.[2] Both explorations aimed at reaching the Middle Kingdom but never did, using the map that positioned Europe itself as the centre of the world.

DOI: 10.4324/9781003156383-2

However, they served as a useful prologue to the Portuguese merchants and missionaries who eventually set foot on Chinese soil in 1514, followed by the first Western embassy sent to China in 1516 led by Tome Pires. Though he failed to meet the Ming emperor in Beijing, the Portuguese managed to establish a trading port of Macau in Southern China in 1557 and held both trade and missionary monopolies there for much of the sixteenth century.

England appeared relatively late in the theatre of trading in the East. It was after the defeat of the Spanish Armada in 1588 that the captured Spanish and Portuguese ships with their cargoes enabled English explorers to vie for fortune and influence in the Far East. We can see an interesting comparison that the ascent of the British was driven by a clear focus on trade, in contrast to other European powers such as France and Italy, who grew their influence by sending Jesuit missions. As a matter of fact, Italy started to receive regular reports about China from its first generation of Jesuit missionaries who arrived and resided in China in the late sixteenth century, while knowledge about China came not as eyewitness accounts but second-hand sources for the British.

So what kind of empire was China at this period of time? In Kennedy's (1989: 5) *The Rise and Fall of the Great Powers*, which traced the economic change and military conflict from 1500 to 2000, Ming China (1368–1644) was presented at the outset as "of all the civilisations of premodern times, none appeared more advanced, none felt more superior, than that of China". He cited its superiority with considerable population, remarkable culture, fertile plains linked by splendid canals, and unified, hierarchic administration run by a well-educated Confucian bureaucracy. He also explained how the four classic inventions contributed to the Ming prosperity: movable-type printing produced large volumes of books; paper money expedited the flow of commerce and the growth of markets; gunpower strengthened the relatively weak Ming army in fighting the Mongol rivalries[3] and the magnetic compass helped navigate the maritime silk road. All these had made China an exemplary empire in the richness of its wealth and culture, development in its technology and refinement of its civilisation.

1.1 Once upon a time, a British monarch wrote a letter to a Chinese emperor

As a relatively late arrival on the world stage, the British were keen to discover a direct maritime route to China, to both shorten the voyage and break the Portuguese monopoly at that time, which required all nationalities travelling to Asia to depart via Lisbon with the specific approval of the Portuguese crown. The Dutch companies also started to trade in China from 1595 and effectively blocked the passage of the small English fleet by having command of the normal trade routes via India and the Malacca Strait. China's exclusive production of silk, tea and porcelain fetched high prices, both from the value in their intrinsic physical and aesthetic qualities, and the long distance they had come from. The underglazed fine porcelain produced in the late Ming was so desired in Europe that they came to be known as "china". Perhaps impressed by the Portuguese and Dutch imports to England as luxury gifts that flourished in the 1580s, Queen Elizabeth I made three attempts in writing to the Chinese emperor in 1583 and 1596, and finally in 1602. She also granted the East India Company (EIC) a Royal Charter on 31 December 1600. History had now come to a point when the British felt they must change the rules of the game to compete, starting with exploring a new route to enable England to trade with China without interference from the European pioneers.

Each of the three letters was carried by a different crew of English merchant adventurers, determined to tap into the lucrative trade that flowed from the fabled land of Cathay, but none was successfully delivered. The first two letters were both intercepted by the Portuguese. Copies and translations were published by the English writer Richard Hakluyt in his three-volume work *The Principall Navigations, Voiages, Traffiques and Discoueries of the English Nation* (1589–1600).[4] Hakluyt also became an adviser to the newly founded EIC. In 1602, George Weymouth (1587–1611), an experienced navigator from Devon, approached EIC to propose another voyage via the Northwest Passage to Asia. Given the failed previous attempts due to the treacherous conditions, EIC was taking a big gamble in accepting Weymouth's proposal. The EIC sponsorship was offered on the condition that Weymouth and his crew "bestowed one yeare att the least from the time of their dep[ar]ture in going forward seeking sounding and attemptynge the p[er]form[an]ce of this intended voyage" (Allinson, 2014: 210). Captain Weymouth agreed and received the letter from Queen Elizabeth I to hand to the Chinese emperor if he should successfully reach Cathey. He set sail from Ratcliff, England on 2 May 1602, with 35 men in two pinnaces, *Discovery* (70 ton) and *God Speed* (60 ton) and provisions to last for just 18 months. Throughout the journey, bad weather accompanied the expedition. After sailing 300 miles into Hudson Strait on 26 July, both ships were hit by another ferocious storm, preventing them to progress further West and many men were ill by the time. His crew mutinied and forced Weymouth to turn back home after exploring part of the Labrador Coast and reached Dartmouth on 5 September 1602.

So the letter was also brought back, but it is a complete mystery how it is now resting quietly at the Lancashire Archives in England today[5] (see Figure 1.1).

As we can see, the letter was exquisitely ornamented, penned on vellum and signed by the Queen, representing the highest quality of workmanship and the finest parchment, as befitted one monarch writing to another, as well as showing off the skills of British workmanship to potential trade

ELIZABETH, BY THE GRACE OF GOD QUEEN

Elizabeth

Figure 1.1 Queen Elizabeth I's letter to the Wanli Emperor. Courtesy of the Lancashire Archives. Document reference: Crosse of Shaw Hill Collections DDSH 15/3, dimension: 433 mm × 517 mm.

partners in the East. Indeed, "it costs £6.13s. 4d" for "writing her Maiestie's lettres to the Emperor of China and Cathay" (Allinson, 2014: pp. 219–220). Taking a closer look, we can see that every time "Your Majesty" appeared, the M is elevated above the rest of the text and gilded in gold, an ornate pageantry both to show the skilled craftsmanship and loftiest respect.

The letter was also accompanied by three translated versions on plain paper, in Latin, Portuguese and Italian,[6] so that if no one at the Emperor's court could read English, then perhaps they could read one of these alternative languages. If Latin was the standard language of international diplomacy at the time, and Portuguese was the lingua franca of China trade due to the fact that they established the first settlement in Macau in 1557, an educated guess for why the Italian version was provided was probably because of the Italian Jesuit Matteo Ricci, who became the first European to enter the Forbidden City in January 1601. His services in matters such as court astronomy and calendrical science became highly sought after to the point that the imperial government allowed him to establish a missionary residence in Beijing. He already started sending back regular reports about

China to Europe since he arrived in Macau in 1583, the same year when Queen Elizabeth I wrote her first letter.

We do not know if the Queen had ever read Ricci's reports from China, but we do know that she is a multilinguist, which may help explain the mystery of her "misspelled" signature of "Elizabetta R" on the letter, "as if to provide an international version of her name, which would, of course, attune to the Romance language texts which accompanied the beautifully penned missive" (Bajetta, 2017: 253). As described by Hurst (2012), a collections archivist at Shakespeare Birthplace Trust, Queen Elizabeth I's signatures featured as being large (several inches across) and ornate. Its grandiosity is certainly in keeping with her royal status, not only an indication of her wealth and authority but also as a method to make the signature more difficult to forge. However, a closer look at the signature seems to show "Elizabetty R", with her usual grandiosely ornamented "b", but the last letter can hardly pass as an "a", especially in comparison with the former "a" in the same signature. It is more likely to be either "h" or "y", in other words, there is either a redundant "t" in her name, or a variance of spelling the latter part of her name as "betty". Another possible explanation for this "misspell" is that as a very frail old lady at the age of 69 – months before her death – she might have been half-conscious in the moment and lost control of her pen, but the missive on vellum is simply too precious to be reproduced. To me, a more important question to answer than solving this signature mystery is what was written in the letter, and why its purpose would not make sense to the Chinese emperor even if it can arrive in Beijing, where there were missionaries who can assist with the translation?

1.2 The incomprehensible letters

The full texts of the three letters, in both medieval English and modern translation with annotations, as well as a Chinese version, can be found in Appendix 1–3. The most striking difference is the way the Chinese emperor was addressed, from the "Most imperial and invincible Prince" in the 1583 letter, to "the highest and sovereign prince, the most powerful governor of the great kingdom of China, the chief Emperor in those parts of Asia and of the adjoining lands, and the great monarch of the oriental regions of the world" in 1596, and "the great, mighty and invincible Emperor of Cathay"[7] in 1602. Along with the increasingly respectful tone of the letter was the increased length and more extravagant presentation of it, showing a growing level of knowledge and admiration of the Chinese Empire, and a stronger desire to develop ties with this kingdom "so strongly and well governed, and so widely known across the face of the whole earth" (1596 letter). Similarly, the way the Queen addressed herself also evolved from the very plain title of "Elizabeth by the grace of God Queen of England, etc." in 1583 to "Elizabeth, by the grace of God,

Queen of England, France, and Ireland, the mightiest defender of the true and Christian faith against all who falsely profess the name of Christ, etc." in 1596, showing off her many titles, territories and dominions. What remained unchanged was the "only purpose" of the mission, to "present their diverse products and examples and specimens of merchandise in the regions of your dominions, to your Highness and to your subjects" (1596 letter).

In fact, the key message put across in the Queen's three letters remained very similar, including key words such as "mutual trade", "profit", "benefit" and "reciprocate" appearing in the 1583 letter, which also claimed that "the benefit they shall all share consists in the exporting of such things we have in abundance and in the importing of things we have need of. It cannot be otherwise that by seeing we are born and made to have need of one another, and bound to aid one another". This "mutual need" we were born with, and "mutual aid" we were cultivated to offer, not only indicated equality among countries but also explained the principle of reciprocity as an indisputable creed. All these remained the key theme in the letter finally successfully delivered to the Chinese emperor by Lord Macartney over two centuries later in 1793. From the most infamous reply (Appendix 5 and 6) he received from the Qianlong Emperor, which we will look at in detail in Chapter 5, perhaps we can well imagine why these modern terms were utter "nonsense" to the Sinocentric world in the sixteenth century.

Now let us use the 1602 letter as an example:

> *Elizabeth, by the grace of God, Queen of England, France and Ireland, Defender of the Faith to the great, mighty and invincible Emperor of Cathay, greetings.*
>
> *We have received divers and sundry reports both by our own subjects and others, who have visited some parts of Your Majesty's empire. They have told us of your greatness and your kind usage of strangers, who come to your kingdom with* ***merchandise to trade****. This has encouraged us to find a shorter route by sea from us to your country than the usual course that involves encompassing the greatest part of the world. This nearer passage may provide* ***opportunity for trade*** *between the subjects of both our countries and also* ***amity*** *may grow between us, due to the navigation of a closer route. With this in mind, we have many times in the past encouraged some of our pioneering subjects to find this nearer passage through the north. Some of their ships didn't return again and nothing was ever heard of them, presumably because of frozen seas and intolerable cold.*
>
> *However, we wish to try again and have prepared and set forth two small ships under the direction of our subject, George Waymouth, employed as principal pilot for his knowledge and experience in*

> *navigation. We hope your Majesty will look kindly on them and give them encouragement to make this new discovered passage, which hitherto has not been frequented or known as a usual* ***trade*** *route. By this means our countries can* ***exchange commodities for our mutual benefit*** *and as a result,* ***friendship*** *may grow. We decided for this first passage not to burden your Majesty with great quantities of* ***commodities*** *as the ships were venturing on a previously unknown route and would need such* ***necessities*** *as required for their discovery. It may please your Majesty to observe, on the ships,* ***samples*** *available from our country of many diverse materials which we can* ***supply most amply*** *and may it please your Majesty to enquire of the said George Waymouth what may be* ***supplied*** *by the next fleet.*
>
> *In the meantime, we commend Your Majesty to the protection of the Eternal God, who providence guides and follows all kings and kingdoms. From our Royal Palace of Greenwich, the fourth of May anno Domini 1602 and of our reign 44.*
>
> Elizabeth R

As we can see from above, the letter was addressed to "the great, mighty and invincible Emperor of Cathay", about which "divers and sundry reports" have been received. Examples of such reports can be found in Hakluyt's book (1589–1600), which also included A *Description of China*, and *Reports of China* learned through the Portuguese, as well as *Certain Notes or References Taken Out of the Large Map of China*, brought home by M. Thomas Candish in 1588. These may help the Queen realise that "her counterpart" was a monarch ruling over a vast and powerful empire rather than a kingdom. However, the Westerners' reports on this empire called Cathey mainly stayed on the level of individual travel records which tend to have an "utopic quality". For example, Marco Polo's account of China was such a prototype of a Utopia where people enjoyed a sophisticated intellectual life in flourishing material abundances. In a strict sense, it cannot be called a report as it was produced in collaboration with a professional romance writer, and the diversity among the approximately 150 manuscripts demonstrated that individual scribers and translators often made free with the text and inserted editorial comments that there was no single manuscript could represent a "definitive version". In comparison, accounts written by the Spanish Augustinian Martin de Rada showed a sense of responsibility for the correctness of the information provided to educate the reader. His book started a tradition of purposeful introduction of China that profoundly influenced the West's understanding and knowledge of the empire. As a member of the first Spanish Embassy who studied Chinese in 1574 and arrived in Fujian on the southeast coast of China in 1575, he stated in the Preface of *Diplomatic Mission to Fujian* and *Notes of Ming Dynasty* that his observations on China and the people's way of life were based on both first-hand travelling and also reading Spanish translations of Chinese books and literature (Liu and Wang, 2017). Very much like Macartney's embassy over two centuries later, the Spanish embassy failed to achieve their primary goals to secure permission for Spain to trade with China and preach Christianity, but succeeded in achieving the secondary goal of transmitting knowledge between nations by recording China and introducing Europe to the oriental culture of the sixteenth century. Juan González de Mendoza's *The History of the Great and Mighty Kingdom of China and the Situation Thereof* was largely based on de Rada's account of his expedition to China and the materials he had brought back. Published first in 1585 in Spanish, this was one of the earliest Western histories of China. It was translated into seven different languages in less than 10 years and 46 editions were published, with its first English translation by Robert Parke appeared in 1588.[8] Another significant source of knowledge about China was reports from Jesuit missionaries who resided in the Middle Kingdom from the late sixteenth century, represented by Matteo Ricci as mentioned earlier, extending Anglophone knowledge of China and anything Chinese.

As for those from her "own subjects", the only recorded English merchant who came close to China's trading zone during the sixteenth century was Ralph Fitch, who travelled to Malacca in 1583 and became one of the most celebrated Elizabethan adventurers. It was in this year that the Queen wrote her first letter to the Ming Emperor. When Ralph Fitch returned to England in 1591, his experience was greatly valued by the founders of the EIC. A necessary note to add here, especially to Chinese readers, is that EIC is no ordinary company in the modern sense with a simple mission of trade and making money, but an organization interested in a broader exchange between the East and West, a "great company whose object is not confined to the pursuit of gain but extends to the general benefits of humanity" (Williams, 2014: 10). They took on a mixed mission to reach out into the world both acquisitively and inquisitively, especially after the establishment of the Royal Society in 1663 with a motto of "Nullius in verba", which means "take nobody's word for it". According to Mungello (1985: 37), the Society's leading lights at that time "were not professional academics or scientists, but enthusiastic amateurs whose backgrounds were often commercial". They assigned a set of 22 queries about foreign lands to the EIC agent.[9] These inquisitions reflected the broad range of interest in China held by the most eminent scholarly bodies in England at the time, and the exploration is a means to seek first-hand knowledge about China, its cultures, products and peoples.

Now let us move on to look at the main body of the letter and try to understand why in four different language versions provided, it would still be hard for the Chinese emperor to make sense of the British requests. It is clear that the main purpose of establishing contacts with

China was to seek "opportunity for trade" with "samples" of "commodities" that can be "supplied" amply, which had remained unchanged since the Queen's first letter in 1583. We can see the repeated use of the key word "trade" and the modern concept of "mutual benefit" employed by the Queen for the exchange of commodities and the equal status suggested between the two monarchs and empires when "friendship" and "amity" were used in the 1602 letter. No gifts (let alone attributes) were packed as they were not considered as "necessities".

We can read a few layers of reasons why there is no common language between the two empires from this. First is the Confucian's scornful view of commerce and the profit motive, while scholarship is valued a lot higher than wealth: "the mind of the superior man is conversant with righteousness; the mind of the mean man is conversant with gain"[10] (Confucius, *Analects*). Profit-seeking was despised as against morality and merchants were placed as a profession of low social status in China. On the other extreme, Adam Smith called the British "a nation of shopkeepers" in his seminar book *Inquiry into the Nature and Causes of the Wealth of Nations* published in 1776. He pointed that Britain's regard for their own well-being was making everyone richer. Another difference related to the Confucian value is the ideology of governance. As pointed by Armitage (2000: 194), "Britain was the only nation in Europe whose constitution as constructed to promote liberty – just as Rome was built for expansion, Sparta for war, Israel for religion, China for natural tranquillity". The British values was in direct contradiction to China's as Yan Fu claimed: "Liberty is a principle profoundly mistrusted by the saints and sages of China ever since ancient times" (cited in Peyrefitte, 1992: 537). Even in modern time today, maintaining stability has always been the top priority of the government. When the British wanted to apply its liberty idea to a global scale of free circulation of goods, it inevitably clashed with the Chinese rule of control of order.

Then there is the contrast in geographical dimension. Smith (1776: 865–866) argued China's geography deterred it from foreign trade because its neighbours were not rich; and the great extent of the empire of China, the vast multitude of its inhabitants, the variety of climate and consequently of productions in different provinces, and easy communication by means of water carriage between the greater part of them render the home market of China of so great extent, as to be alone sufficient to support very great manufactures, and to admit of very considerable subdivisions of labour. This is very true, as internal exchanges between northern and southern China were facilitated by the Grand Canal from Hangzhou all the way to Beijing since the Yuan Dynasty.[11] This point was also raised earlier by Du Halde (1738: 334), who compared the vastness of China's domestic trade to that of the whole Europe: "The inland trade of China is so great, that the commerce of all Europe is not to be compar'd therewith; the princes like so many kingdoms, which communicate to each other their respective productions". Therefore, Millar (2011: 214) argued that China's restricting foreign trade should be understood as being more complex than "ignorant, arrogant isolationism", as it had an "unusual ability to garner significant wealth from internal commerce. China offered a different model for growth that depended almost entirely on domestic consumption and production".

However, I would like to add a more important geographical dimension that put the two empires in stark contrast apart from the sheer size: their relationship with the sea, and the different national characters conditioned by this relationship. Boorstin (1983: 154) had well said that before the fifteenth century, "the ocean led nowhere, in the next centuries people would see it led everywhere". Except that the "people" in this statement were mostly Europeans, who regarded the ocean as a transcontinental contact zone after the Age of Discovery rather than a barrier to communication. In Armitage's book *The Ideological Origins of the British Empire*, he quoted Montesquieu that "a naval empire has always given the people who have possessed it a natural pride, because, feeling themselves able to insult others everywhere, they believe that their power is as boundless as the ocean", in contrast to elsewhere if its terrain were fertile, then the people would be self-sufficient, not ambitious for conquest (Armitage, 2000: 195). China is lucky to be bestowed with such a fertile terrain, but it is not the right soil for liberal trade to germinate. This geographical contrast helps us understand that as a completely self-sufficient agrarian economy, trade had never been a cornerstone for a huge land empire like China, while for an island nation like Britain, trading was in its bloodline, and the whole world can be its market. Besides, what added to the low priority of trade to the Ming was its deep sense of insecurity after defeating the militarily strong Yuan. Indeed, there was constant fear of invasions from the menacing Northern Yuan along its land border and threats from pirates on the south-east sea front. It thus resorted to a defensive military strategy, consolidating the Great Wall to defend its northern border and building a "Maritime Great Wall" to impose a ban on overseas trade by its founding Emperor Hongwu in 1371.

Almost on the opposite of withdrawing behind walls, the British lived in a world of constantly shifting balances of power, each vying for expanded territory or influence, thus shaping the enterprising and adventurous qualities as the Queen's letter embodied: It was a heroic journey of thousands of miles into an unknown territory through an unexplored route, after some earlier attempts which "didn't return again and nothing was ever heard of them", yet they "wish to try again" by "venturing on a previously unknown route". Indeed, the constant search for knowledge lies at the heart of modern European civilisation. On the other hand, the Chinese national character was shaped by its legislators who only had "two objects: they have wanted the people to be both submissive and tranquil" (Montesquieu, cited in Peyrefitte, 1992: 27). The

British enthusiasm for long-distance commerce and the faith in the value of reciprocal discovery reaped from exchanges between distant cultures was in contrast to the Chinese mentality of self-sufficient in economy, self-cultivation in enlightenment and self-contained attitude with little reciprocal curiosity about the West. In a way, in the letter we can see the innate character of an island nation as being outward-looking for exchanges, contrasted to a vast continental power that is naturally inward-looking for being self-contained.

A ready example to demonstrate this contrast is the Chinese Admiral Zheng He's seven naval expeditions between 1405 and 1433. Though much earlier than Christopher Columbus and Vasco da Gama's voyages, and in a much grander scale of fleet, they are much less known to the Western world. Even the official archives went missing, or were destroyed on purpose according to some historians, by the Ming Court itself after the death of Zheng He and a change of emperor. Unlike the two European explorers who made history for their discoveries of the New World and India, trade and discovery were not the main driving forces behind Zheng He's expeditions: there was no such inner drive from the Chinese society or people, instead, they were dispatched by the emperor to display the glory of Ming China and extend the empire's Tributary System[12] to countries that they already knew of, along an established sea route. Therefore, it was not meant to be a voyage of discovery, what they brought back was numerous exotic tributes to please the emperor, not samples for trade or ground-breaking new knowledge to influence the Chinese society and inform its world view.

Then the last dimension of contrast can be seen from the portraits of the two protagonists of our story below (see Figures 1.2 and 1.3).

The two monarchs lived as contemporaries with oceans apart; interesting comparisons can be made in their achievements: both monarchs reigned over their empires for more than four decades and witnessed several successes. Elizabeth I won one of the greatest military victories in English history by defeating the Spanish Armada in 1588, while the Wanli Emperor had successfully defended China against the Mongols and the Japanese invasions by 1596. Another common theme in both empires was the golden age of literature and drama during their reigns. Shakespeare's plays of *Henry V, Julius Caesar* and *Hamlet* were watched by Londoners, while Tang Xianzu's *Peony Pavilion* was performed in traditional opera houses in Beijing. What set them apart was the Queen Elizabeth's embracement of mercantilism and desire to expand trade globally as a means to accumulate national wealth and power. She developed a naval capable of challenging the Portuguese and Spanish monopoly on trade as captured by this most iconic portrait painted to commemorate the most celebrated military achievement in her reign: to the left, we can see the English fleet sailing towards the Spanish; and to the right, Spanish ships dashed against the west coast of Ireland in a storm. The Queen was

Figure 1.2 The Armada Portrait of Elizabeth I (1533–1603). Courtesy of the Royal Museum of Greenwich.

depicted as resting one hand on the globe with her finger pointing precisely at Virginia, named after her,[13] while holding a sceptre in the other hand, an insignia signifying royal or imperial authority. The globe embodied England's colonial and trading ambitions while the crown referred to England's quest for overseas dominion, with the cross above the crown indicating her sovereign was "by the grace of God", being the queen by divine right as God's representative on Earth. And we must not forget that, having a female monarch itself is a "modern concept" unimaginable in a male-dominated society indoctrinated by Confucianism in China.

In comparison, the Chinese emperor was holding nothing in his hands, but with embroidered images of clouds and dragons on the imperial robe. If the British power was as boundless as the ocean, the imperial China claimed to be a "Celestial Empire", whose sway was even more boundless than the ocean. Just like their symbols of a lion and dragon, the former is the most powerful according to the Law of the Jungle, while dragon has superpower as a mythical animal. Since ancient times, the emperor was believed to be the "Son of Heaven" (*Tianzi*, 天子), mandated to rule all

Figure 1.3 Portrait of the Wanli Emperor (1563–1620). Courtesy of the National Palace Museum in Taipei.

subjects "Under Heaven" (*Tianxia*, 天下). His empire was known as the "Middle Kingdom" (*Zhongguo*, 中国), the "the Divine Land" (*Shenzhou*, 神州) governed by the "Celestial Court" (*Tianchao*, 天朝). These indigenous Chinese phrases represented the cornerstone of traditional Chinese political culture that can be found in historical books such as *Lüshi Chunqiu* (*Master Lu's Spring and Autumn Annals*), composed around 239 BC on the eve of the first imperial dynasty of Qin (221–206 BC): "There is no turmoil greater than the absence of the son of heaven; without the son of heaven, the strong overcame the weak, the many lords over the few, they incessantly use arms to harm each other. From the earliest generations, multiple states were extinguished in all under heaven, but the way of the ruler did not decline: this is because it benefits all under heaven" (cited in Pines, 2012: 44).

Before the first map of the world appeared in front of the eyes of a Chinese emperor in 1602, the year when the Queen's last letter was written, *Tianxia* represented a China-centred geographical view of itself as the Middle Kingdom, surrounded by other smaller nations.[14] This ideology encoded China and its surrounding states as superior centre vs.

inferior periphery. Such traditional Chinese beliefs had both an internal and external dimension. Internally, at the apex of the Chinese hierarchy was the emperor who also represented the highest moral standard, an embodiment of virtue that attracted all to be submissive to. The sage-like emperor was thus more than human, named "ten-thousand-year-old" (*Wansui*, 万岁), just like the omnipotent mythical being of a dragon. Externally, as Mancall (1970: 63) explained: "the emperor, far from being the ruler of one state among many, was the mediator between heaven and earth, a cardinal point in the universal continuum, the apex of civilisation, unique in the universe. In other words, the emperor was not only a temporal political ruler but a figure of cosmic dimensions". Obedience to him was to follow "the Way of Heaven" (*Tiandao*, 天道). This was supported by a whole set of vocabulary that rendered other expressions alien and unacceptable. Therefore, although the Wanli Emperor lifted the ban on maritime trade that had been imposed for nearly 200 years (1371–1567), trade was only considered a part of its magnanimous relationship with other states under the architecture of the Tributary System. There was no such thing as "samples of commodities" in the Chinese court vocabulary to refer to anything from a foreign land at the time. As explained by Fairbank (1968: 2), from the Chinese perspective, they "tended to think of their foreign relations as giving expression externally to the same principles of social and political order that were manifested internally within the Chinese state and society. China's foreign relations were accordingly hierarchic and non-egalitarian, like Chinese society itself", while Europe "saw the development of a number of nation-states theoretically equal in sovereignty and mutually independent within the cultural area of Christendom" (ibid: 9). In other words, while China views its relations with the West as of a hierarchical one between the Chinese Empire and its tributary states, the West believed they embarked on "journeys of reciprocity or mutual diplomacy" (Keevak, 2017: 152). So, a translator may help bridge the language barrier but would not be able to find equivalent expressions of the incompatible world views, which are beyond translation.

When viewed from a global macroeconomic context, we can see England during Queen Elizabeth I's reign still occupied a peripheral position in what, until 1800 or so, was a largely Sinocentric world system (Frank, 1998; Pomeranz, 2000). However, they shared a pride in their unparalleled prosperity in Europe and a similar sense of superiority against "foreigners" as evidenced in some reports of European visitors to England. For example, the following was from an account of Duke of Wurttemberg's visit to London in 1592:

> London is a large, excellent, and mighty city of business, and the most important in the whole kingdom; most of the inhabitants are employed in buying and selling merchandise and trading in almost every corner of the world, since the river is most useful and convenient for this

> purpose, considering that ships from France, the Netherlands, Sweden, Denmark, Hamburg, and other kingdoms come almost up to the city, to which they convey goods and receive and take away others in exchange.
>
> ……
>
> The inhabitants are magnificently apparelled, and are extremely proud and overbearing; and because the greater part, especially the tradespeople, seldom go into other countries, but always remain in their houses in the city attending to their business, they care little for foreigners, but scoff and laugh at them; and moreover one dare not oppose them, … .. because they are the strongest, one is obliged to put up with the insult as well as the injury.
>
> (Derry and Blakeway, 1969: 327)

This was echoed by another account by two Italians who toured southern England in 1669, one of them corresponded with Isaac Newton:

> From abundance of all things arises in the English nation that contemptuous disposition which it entertains towards other countries, thinking them unprovided with the advantages which it finds in its own; and on this account the common people treat foreigners with little respect and even with haughtiness, and are scarcely induced to relax by any act of civility whatever that is shown to them on the part of the latter. (ibid: 328)

We can well imagine the kind of clash it trigged when the proud lion eventually met with the even haughtier dragon, first unofficially in 1637 and then officially in 1793. What this book unveils in the following chapters is the encounters between a Sinocentric and a Eurocentric world system that took place on all fronts – trade, intellectual, diplomatic and military, and how such encounters often led to clashes: clashes of ideas, national interests and systematic orbits.

1.3 European sceptre vs. Chinese dragon

Before we move onto Chapter 2, I would like to use a few more images to show how deeply embedded the Europeanised perceptions and understandings of the Middle Kingdom had been, even after a number of embassies had successfully arrived in China, received a reception by the emperor, and came back with first-hand reports published with illustrations from the seventeenth to eighteenth century.

In the first half of the seventeenth century when China had already entered the Qing Dynasty (1644–1911), the Dutch East India Company tried to break the Portuguese monopoly on trade by sending six embassies to Beijing between 1655 and 1685, with an aim to convince the Qing emperor to open up trade relations on the southern coast, but ultimately failed. Johan Nieuhof was appointed to the position of steward on one of these embassies and travelled from Canton to Beijing between 1655 and 1658. Apart from being in charge of ceremonial matters, he was specifically appointed to observe and illustrate all the buildings and landscape along the journey in their true to nature forms. This helped him gain the reputation of producing the first work on China that contained images which were based on eyewitness, as opposed to previous romanticised travel literature where fact and fiction were hardly discernible. The embassy arrived at the emperor's court in July 1656 and was received by the Shunzhi Emperor on 24 September. Nieuhof's manuscript was eventually published in 1665 with 149 images,[15] many of which were based on illustrations done by artists in China. The accurate and detailed illustrations of Chinese architecture in the book, especially pagodas and temples, served as a prized source book with major influence on the rise of Chinoiserie in the early eighteenth century.

The English translation of his book came out first in 1669 and then a second edition in 1673,[16] named *An Embassy from the East India Company of the United Provinces, to the Grand Tartar Cham, Emperor of China, wherein the cities, towns, villages, ports, rivers, &c., in their passages from Canton to Peking are ingeniously describ'd.* Its author John Ogilby, a Scottish translator and cartographer noted for publishing works in handsomely illustrated editions, decided to combine Nieuhof's original written account of the embassy and letters from the Jesuit father John Adams, as well as his own partial translation of another book, Athanasius Kircher's *China Illustrata* (Szczesniak, 1952: 388). First published in 1667 in Latin, *China Illustrata* was a comprehensive encyclopaedia about the Chinese Empire produced from a compilation of written reports sent back to the Jesuits' College in Rome from China-based missionaries, as well as oral accounts by returning missionaries and a variety of western sources. It contained accurate cartography and illustrations that elucidated the vivid descriptions found in the text, representing "an important source of information on the beginnings of western sinology and sinophilism in Europe" (ibid:392). However, an "accident" occurred when Ogilby had many of the illustrations copied for the English version. It may be hard for us to imagine today that before camera and photocopy machines were invented, re-drawing the illustrations was the standard practice at the time. These copied images were then included in the English print of Nieuhof's work – there were around twenty-five illustrations in Ogilby's English edition that were not included in the Dutch original, including the Qing Emperor's full-length portrait, which was copied from *China Illustrata*. Here comes the most intriguing part of the story: a perhaps "innocent" distortion took place when a sceptre was added to the original print in Latin (see Figure 1.4), and Figure 1.5 was the image appeared in the English edition! We can even

Figure 1.4 Portrait of the Supreme Monarch of the Sino-Tartar Empire, in the original Latin version of Athanasius Kircher's *China Illustrata* published in 1667. Available at: https://commons.wikimedia.org/wiki/File:Athanasii_Kircheri..._China_monumentis_(1667)_%22Impery_sino-Tartarici_Supremus_Monarcha%22_(22466895540).jpg.

identify whose mysterious hand this was, as we can clearly see the original artist's autograph of "A a" was replaced by Wenceslaus Hollar's[17] signature showing on the bottom right corner of the picture, while a legible note of "Ker: Folio 69" was also added at the bottom margin. Of course, the original Latin title of the illustration was changed into English: The Supreme MONARCH of the CHINA-TARTARIAN Empire, clearly distinguishing the Qing as a Tartarian empire beyond the Ming China. But

Figure 1.5 Portrait of the Supreme Monarch of the Sino-Tartar Empire, in the 1673 English edition of Johan Nieuhof's account, *An Embassy from the East India Company of the United Provinces, to the Grand Tartar Cham, Emperor of China,* Courtesy of the British Library. Available at: https://digital.library.cornell.edu/catalog/ss:550024.

the image itself was also transliterated, applying the method of domestication,[18] in an unintentionally unethical way. As explained before, since Nieuhof's work was considered to have marked a milestone in the history of the genre because the images of China were dominated by fantasy illustrations in Europe prior to this period; and because the English version circulated more extensively than the original print, this "finishing touch" on the emperor's portrait had had an indelible impact. When a complete English translation of *China Illustrata* eventually came out in 1986, the wrong image was still showing, in yet another different version of the emperor holding a sceptre,[19] and it did not stop here: a Chinese version translated from it (by Zhang et al.) was published in 2010, recycling the erroneous image again, which was then included in a permenant exhibition at the Imperial Archives in Beijing that can still be seen today.

Compared with the official portrait of the same Emperor kept at the Palace Museum (see Figure 1.6), we can easily see this Europeanised portrait is not a good resemblance at all, particularly disclosed in the details of the imperial robe and sceptre. While the sceptre was a symbol of power of the sovereignty in Europe, in the Celestial Court, the symbol of the emperor's superpower was the "dragon over clouds", both embroidered in the "dragon robe" (*Longpao*, 龙袍) and carved in the "dragon throne" (*Longyi,* 龙椅) as shown in Figure 1.6, though the monstrous-looking creature in Figures 1.4 and 1.5 were also supposed to

Figure 1.6 Official portrait of the Shunzhi Emperor. Courtesy of the Palace Museum of Beijing.

represent a dragon. In Nieuhoff's book, there was also a detailed picture of the "dragon boat" (*Longzhou*, 龙舟), but with the caption of a "snake boat", showing his ignorance of "dragon" being a Chinese totem. The frontispiece in Nieuhof's book was another image of the emperor – appeared in both the original Dutch version and the English edition, this time with his hand resting on the globe, yet another indication of the Europeanised view of the world in contrast to the metaphysical, cosmic concept of *Tianxia* held by the Chinese emperor.[20]

Following the steps of the Dutch, the British also made repeated attempts at establishing trade contacts with China. After Queen Elizabeth I died, King James I also sent two letters to China in 1610 and 1613, but again to no avail. After 180 years, the first British embassy arrived in Beijing in September 1793. This will be the main theme in Chapter 5, but I just want to use a picture here from its official report to show the continued Europeanised understanding of the Chinese emperor. Figure 1.7 was an illustration from the official account about the most famous gifts received from the Qianlong Emperor, which were mentioned in almost all the historical records and later writings about the mission, and the caption read "Sceptre and Purse".

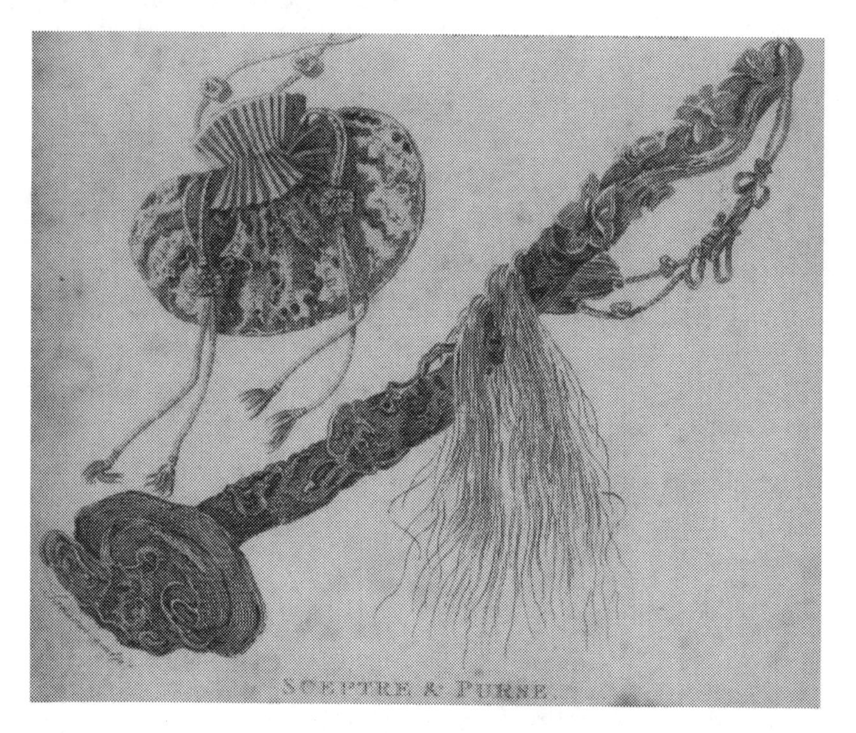

Figure 1.7 Sceptre and Purse, from George Staunton (1797), *An Authentic Account of an Embassy form the King of Great Britain to the Emperor of China,* Vol. 2, p. 115. Courtesy of the British Library, digitised by Google Books project.

The translation strategy of domestication was adopted again when the Chinese item of *ruyi* (literally means "as you wish") was translated into a sceptre, which is rather misleading. Unlike the sceptre that was held in the hand by a ruling monarch as a symbol of imperial authority in Europe, *ruyi*, as the name suggests, is more of a good-luck charm in China that is given as a goodwill present on special occasions such as weddings, birthdays and farewell gatherings. It did become associated with power and wealth when it became more and more lavishly decorated in the Ming and Qing dynasties, and often given to foreign envoys as a friendly gesture, but the auspicious meaning of the object makes it remain popular among the general commoners in a less extravagant form. The original use of it as a back scratcher[21] makes it even more odd to be translated and understood as a "sceptre".

The above shows the Europeanised perception of China and Chinese people that the story of the early encounters of the two empires hung. In order to form a reasoned understanding of how the Wanli Emperor would respond to Queen Elizabeth I if the letter was delivered, or, if he would even bother to write back, we need to understand what kind of Empire Ming China was during his reign – in China's own eyes and through Westerners' eyes. The next chapter describes the Tributary System and Ming China's view of foreign trade and foreign relations, before narrating the first unofficial encounter between the two empires happened in 1637.

Notes

1 The original copy of Polo's Travel read by Columbus is kept at the Christopher Columbus Monument in Sevilla, Spain. It was densely annotated with hundreds of hand-written notes by Columbus.

2 That might because the last legate sent by the Papacy to China was received by the last Yuan Emperor. In his diary dated 21 October 1492, Columbus stated that "I have already decided to go to the mainland and to the city of Quinsay and to give Your Highnesses' letters to the Grand Khan and to ask for, and to come with, a reply" (Dunn and Kelly, 1989: 109).

3 Kennedy's claim (1989: 5) that "cannon were used by the Ming to overthrow their Mongol rulers" exaggerated its power in an oversimplified and inaccurate manner. Firstly, what were used in this period of time were mortars rather than cannons, and the most famous battle employing mortars were against other Han rebels and warlords, not the Mongols. That is why a deep fear for domestic uprisings and court disorder persisted throughout the Ming, which will be discussed in Chapter 2. Secondly, cannons were actually introduced to China from Europe, either purchased from Portugal (including those made in England and Dutch) or made by the Portuguese in Macau, representing one of the few things that both Ming and Qing China recognised as being less developed than Europe. Thirdly, this statement was also a bit misleading in indicating that Ming's overthrowing of the Mongol rulers was a military victory. As a matter of fact, the downfall of Yuan was much more due to its internal decay from poor governance and power struggle, and the Mongols remained a strong military threat to Ming and even captured its emperor at some point. This incident will be discussed in Chapter 2.

4 They were further translated into modern English and annotated by Dr Frank Pearson, which can be found in Appendix 1 and 2, along with the Chinese translations.
5 According to the information provided by the Lancashire Archives, nothing is known about the fate of the letter after its return to England in September 1602, until it was discovered among the papers of the Crosse family of Shaw Hill, near Chorley, which were deposited in the Lancashire Record Office in 1946. There is no known link between the family and the Queen or George Weymouth. There is a possibility that the letter was bought by a family member in the nineteenth century who collected "interesting old documents".
6 These translated versions are hand-written on plain paper, which are also kept at the Lancashire Archives.
7 It was addressed this way because China was referred to as Cathay in Marco Polo's book; it was later confirmed by Matteo Ricci that Cathay *was* China in one of his letters sent back to Europe. This will be explained in Chapter 2.
8 It is worth mentioning that the 1853 reprint of this English translation was edited by Sir George Thomas Staunton, who later became the only member who joined both the Macartney and Amherst's embassies to China and played a critical role as a China hand in the conceiving of gunboat diplomacy in 1840.
9 For other European countries, they have been using diplomats and missionaries to collect such information. For example, when the Manuel I of Portugal sent its first embassy to Malacca in as early as 1508, he also set them a list of very detailed questions to answer about China. Similarly, the French Académie des Sciences composed a list of 35 questions about China to Philippe Couplet, a Jesuit who arrived in China in 1659. When he returned to Europe in 1682, he not only brought back answers but also a Chinese convert who later became the first Chinese visitor to the British Empire. We will look at his story in Chapter 3.
10 The Confucian influence is deep going and long lasting. It was until China's economic reform in the early 1980s when Deng Xiaoping made the revolutionary slogan that "It is glorious to be rich".
11 The Grand Canal was drenched as early as 486 BC, but only connected Hangzhou with Luoyang during the Sui Dynasty. When the capital city was moved to Beijing during the Yuan Dynasty, the Grand Canal was also extended from Hangzhou to Beijing as an artery of waterway transport connecting the northern and southern China since 1293.
12 Some Chinese historians argued that these voyages were initially launched as the emperor's attempt to capture the escaped predecessor following the coup, which will not be explored in this book.
13 The Roanoke Colony was the first English colony in the New World. It was established at Roanoke Island in 1584, which was named "Virginia" in honour of Queen Elizabeth "the Virgin Queen" in 1585.
14 The old Korean atlas is an interesting example as such: the Cheonhado in the seventeenth century was a circular pictorial map that was centred on China.
15 This 574-page-long original Dutch version is now digitalised and available at: https://archive.org/details/gezantschapderN00Nieu/page/n3/mode/2up. Digitizing sponsor: Metropolitan New York Library Council; Contributor: Smithsonian Libraries.
16 This second edition of the English version is available at the British Library and Bodleian Library.
17 Wenceslaus Hollar (1607–1677) was a prolific and accomplished graphic artist of the seventeenth century, who spent much of his life in England. His work

includes about 400 drawings and 3000 etchings. Some are kept in the British Museum and the British Library today.

18 Domestication and foreignization are strategies used in translation, regarding the degree to which translators make a text conform to the target culture. Domestication is the strategy of making text closely conform to the target culture being translated to, which may involve addition or deletion of information from the source text, while foreignization is the strategy of retaining information from the source text, and involves deliberately breaking the conventions of the target culture to preserve its meaning.

19 Copied again by another illustrator. The complete translation of the 1986 version is available at: https://htext.stanford.edu/content/kircher/china/kircher.pdf. The emperor's portrait is on p. 103 and the description on p. 100 did state that "The royal dress is decorated with dragons".

20 There was a very similar portrait of "The Young Emperor K'ang-His" in an empty-handed posture in Alphonse Favier's book of *Peking, Histoire et Description*, published in 1902 (p. 154). It was then used as a cover image in Nigel Cameron's book (1970: 239), *Barbarians and Mandarins, Thirteen Centuries of Wester Travelers in China*, New York and Tokyo: John Weatherhill, Inc.

21 The back scratcher is a tool used for relieving an itch in the back that cannot be reached easily by one's own hands. Not as commonly seen in Europe, a backscratcher is a very common household item in China, even in modern day today.

References

Allinson, R. (2014) 'The Virgin Queen and the Son of Heaven: Elizabeth I's letters to Wanli, emperor of China', in Bajetta, C.M., Coatalen, G., Gibson, J. (eds.) *Elizabeth I's Foreign Correspondence. Queenship and Power*. New York: Palgrave Macmillan.

Armitage, D. (2000) *The Ideological Origins of the British Empire*. Cambridge: Cambridge University Press.

Bajetta, C.M. (2017) *Elizabeth I's Italian Letters*. New York: Palgrave Macmillan.

Boorstin, D. (1983) *The Discoverers: A History of Man's Search to Know His World and Himself*. New York: Random House.

Davidson, M. (1997) *Columbus Then and Now: A Life Reexamined*. Norman: The University of Oklahoma Press.

Derry, T.K. and Blakeway, M.G. (1969) *The Making of Britain 2, Life and Work Between the Renaissance and the Industrial Revolution*. London: John Murray.

Du Halde, J.-B. (1738) *The General History of China*. London: J. Watts.

Dunn, O. and Kelly, J.E. Jr. (1989) *The Diary of Christopher Columbus's First Voyage to America*, 1492–1493. Norman: The University of Oklahoma Press.

Fairbank, J.(ed.) (1968) *The Chinese World Order*. Cambridge, MA: Harvard University Press.

Frank, A.G. (1998) *ReOrient: Global Economy in the Asian Age*. Berkeley: University of California Press.

Hakluyt, R. (1589) *The Principall Navigations, Voiages, Traffiques and Discoueries of the English Nation*. Edinburgh: E. and G. Goldsmid.

Hurst, A. (2012) Royal signatures: Queens Elizabeth. Available at: https://www.shakespeare.org.uk/explore-shakespeare/blogs/royal-signatures-queens-elizabeth/

Keevak, M. (2017) *Embassies to China: Diplomacy and Cultural Encounters Before the Opium Wars*. Singapore: Palgrave Macmillan.

Kennedy, P. (1989) *The Rise and Fall of the Great Powers*. London: William Collins.

Kircher, A. (1667). *China Illustrata*. Translated by Van Tuyl, C.D. in 1986. Available at: https://htext.stanford.edu/content/kircher/china/kircher.pdf

Liu, J. and Wang, Yu (2017). 'On transmission of Chinese culture to the West during the Late Ming and Early Qing', *Canadian Social Science*, 13(12), pp. 52–60.

Mancall, M. (1970) 'The Ching Tributary System: An interpretive essay', in Fairbank, J. (ed.) *The Chinese World Order*. Cambridge, MA: Harvard University Press.

Millar, A.E. (2011) 'Your beggarly commerce! Enlightenment European views of the China trade', in Abbattista, G. (ed.) *Encountering Otherness. Diversities and Transcultural Experiences in Early Modern European Culture*. Trieste: Edizioni Università di Trieste, pp. 205–222.

Morris, I. (2011) *Why the West Rules for Now, the Patterns of History and What They Reveal about the Future*. London: Profile Books.

Mungello, D.E. (1985) *Curious Land, Jesuit Accommodation and the Origins of Sinology*. Honolulu: University of Hawaii Press.

Nieuhof, J. (1673) *An Embassy from the East India Company of the United Provinces, to the Grand Tartar Cham, Emperor of China. wherein the Cities, Towns, Villages, Ports, Rivers, &c., in their Passages from Canton to Peking Are Ingeniously Describ'd*. London: printed by the author [John Ogilby].

Peyrefitte, A. (1992) *The Immobile Empire*. Translated by Rothschild, J. New York: Alfred Knopf.

Pines, Yuri (2012) *The Everlasting Empire: The Political Culture of Ancient China and Its Imperial Legacy*. New Jersey: Princeton University Press.

Pomeranz, K. (2000) *The Great Divergence: Europe, China and the Making of the Modern World Economy*. Princeton: Princeton university Press.

Smith, A. (1776) *Inquiry into the Nature and Causes of the Wealth of Nations*. London: W. Strahan and T. Cadell. Available at: https://www.gutenberg.org/ebooks/3300

Staunton, G. (1797) *An Authentic Account of an Embassy Form the King of Great Britain to the Emperor of China*, Vol 2. London: W. Bulmer & Co. for George Nicol.

Szczesniak, B. (1952) 'Athanasius Kircher's China illustrata', *History of Science Society*, 10, pp. 385–411.

Williams, L. (2014) 'Anglo-Chinese caresses: Civility, friendship and trade in English representations of China, 1760–1800', *Journal for Eighteenth-Century Studies*, 38(2), pp. 277–296. 10.1111/1754-0208.12208

Zhang, X., Huiling, Y. and Xianmo, M. (trans.) (2010) 《中国图说》 [*China Illustrata*]. Zhengzhou: Elephant Publishing House.

2 The Tributary System and the first Anglo-Chinese encounters

In the East and West, there is but one mind and one reason.
– Preface to the Complete Map of the Ten Thousand Countries of the World, 1602

This chapter describes what kind of empire the Ming China was, and what implications the Tributary System had on its interactions with the European powers, which set the scene for the first physical Anglo-Chinese encounters. Britain was still a long way from commercial dominance in Asia at this stage. Chinese commodities were in high demand and British merchants had to compete with many other European nations to get them. China was also perfectly capable of trading on its own terms during the Ming Dynasty, holding onto the largely unchallenged worldview of *Hua-Yi* axis, or China as the superior centre and foreign states as the inferior periphery by this time.

2.1 The Tributary System and its implications on China's foreign relations

The so-called "Tributary System" (*Chaogong Tixi*, 朝贡体系) is a term that describes the Chinese method of dealing with foreign relations that evolved over centuries of Chinese domination in Asia, as "an empire without neighbours" (Elisseeff, 1963). Being isolated from other great centres of civilisation, an "entrenched culturalism" was developed into a sinocentric world view (Levenson, 1968; Hevia, 1995: 11). The "entrenched" Chinese phrase is the notion of *Tianxia* as explained in Chapter 1. Tributary System was first elaborated by Fairbank (1968) in addressing China's historical legacy of dealing with foreigners in his edited seminal book *The Chinese World Order: Traditional China's Foreign Relations*, although the idea was already formulated in his work *Trade and Diplomacy on the China Coast* (1953), which was dedicated to Morse, author of the *International Relations of the Chinese Empire: the Period of Conflict, 1834–1860* (1910). Later scholars such as Perkins (1999: 533) defined it as "a system under which

DOI: 10.4324/9781003156383-3

foreign states submitted to Chinese suzerainty by exchanging gifts for trading privileges in China", where the emperor as the Son of Heaven demanded "submission from those outside the empire who were considered barbarians". Chinese historian Jiang (1996: 3–4) explained it plainly: "whoever wished to enter relations with China must do so as China's vassal, acknowledging the supremacy of the Chinese emperor".

So the system was based on the assertion of China's supremacy that rendered foreign merchants to present their goods as "tributes". Indeed, the word "tribute" (*Gong,* 贡) is one of the "historical legacies" of China, an inherent Chinese term with an embedded hierarchical indication that is clearly defined as offering something to one's king or court to pledge allegiance: all provincial officials were required to bring local produce as tributes whenever they visited the emperor at the impeiral court. They had to perform a rite called *kowtow* (three separate prostrations, with the forehead touching the ground three times with each prostration), the etiquette prescribed between the emperor and the rest. Externally, the same ceremony applied to the relationship between China and the rest: the tributary ruler or their representative also had to *kowtow* before the Chinese emperor as a ritual acknowledgement of their vassal status when they sent tributes of their native goods. As Hevia explained (1995: 65), "the emperor constantly used the terminology expressive of his relationship to his Chinese subjects to describe his relationships with the tributary states or peoples. He showed them compassion, encouraged them, nourished them". In return, "entry into the emperor's presence or court required recognition of these principles through the correct performance of the rituals of tribute presentation" (ibid: 64). As a matter of fact, the first Chinese pictorial book to describe foreigners dated as early as 526–539 was called *Tributary Envoys Illustration* (*Zhi Gong Tu,* 《职贡图》), which was produced in each ensuing dynasties until the Qing. By recognising the supremacy of the Chinese emperor, the tributary states received multiple returns, including gifts of higher value than the tributes, trading privileges, honours and titles, resolving border issues, protection from invasions of other powers, although actual military intervention tended to depend on China's stake in the tributary's stability.

From a Western point of view that regards international relations in terms of "equality" and assumes that commerce was inherently beneficial to both sides, they may find it hard to understand what China gains from this clearly unequal economic transaction if the value of everything given back outweighed the value of the tributes? As Kang (2006: 179) explained with an example, "reciprocating a tribute usually exceeded the tribute itself, which was a profitable government trade to the small nation but a big burden for China. Therefore, China requested for Joseon to send tribute only 'once every three years', but in contrast, Joseon requested to send a tribute 'thrice each year' or 'four times per year' instead and achieved it". A common explanation given by Western scholars often resides on the "prestige value" tribute had for China where "prestige was an all-important tool of government" (Fairbank, 1942: 135), or "tribute expressed or communicated submission" (Hevia, 1995). True, but it can be perhaps better understood by looking at the two cornerstones of Confucianism, namely hierarchy and benevolence. The Confucius saying that "there cannot be two kings for the people just as there cannot be two suns in the sky" (*tian wu er ri, min wu er wang*, 天无二日，民无二王) also indicated that there was only one sovereign in this hierarchy. The underlying Chinese assumption was that the emperor was considered at the apex of the centralised ruling, while China was believed to be at the apex of world civilisations, so the outsiders all aspired to become assimilated and civilised, or longed to revolve in China's political and cultural orbit. It was simply out of the Chinese vision to rationalise a cosmology with multi-centred orbits as "Chinese culture was central to the self-identification of many elite groups in the surrounding Asian countries. China was a constant reference point in their orientation" (Westad, 2013: 10), and their acceptance of Chinese culture throughout history "has served to confirm a cosmology in which China always stands at the centre" (ibid: 5). In the *Doctrine of the Mean*, Confucius was preaching the nine principles of rulership. The last two were "pacify people of remote places" (*rou yuan ren*, 柔远人) and "appease the lords and vassals" (*huai zhuhou*, 怀诸侯). Given that there was no equal status in this hierarchy, of course there should be no exchange of items of "equal" values, it is only fair for the superior being to give more than receiving from the inferior, and the sage ruler would always show compassion to those who travelled great distance to pay homage to him. In this sense, both the Tributary System and the ritual of *kowtow* can be understood as China simply projecting its internal order outward, while using the external submission to justify its domestic ruling legitimacy and maintain a sense of superiority and stability, thus work both ways. This worldview had been many centuries in the making, and became an embedded belief of the Chinese civilisation, under which the Tributary System offered a multilateral approach that involved developing cultural affinity, economic attachment, national security dependence as well as political submission to China.

The value of cultural affinity was elaborated by Confucius: "If such a [well-ordered] state of affairs exists, yet the people of far-off lands still do not submit, then the ruler must attract them by enhancing the prestige [*de*] of his culture; and when they have been truly attracted, he contents them. And where there is contentment there will be no upheavals" (cited in Stevenson, 2021: 2). In modern day language, the Chinese Tributary System is built on soft power attraction than hard power coercion, with its sources of attraction coming from cultural superiority, political system sophistication and prosperous trading opportunities. Though some may argue that the attraction lies more in the latter than former, and the "unequal" economic returns constitute more of an allurement than attraction, few would deny that it does not rely on using military power to annex or conquer the tributary states. This is particularly intentional for the Ming after the fall of Yuan, the most militarily powerful dynasty in Chinese history that conquered the largest expanse of territory but only existed for 98 years, while both Tang and Song Dynasties before Yuan lasted for about three centuries. The lesson that the Ming Empire learned was that as an agrarian civilisation, China's prosperity should be based on the traditional Han core area, the centralised ruling will lose its grip and face challenges when stretched to the nomadic and maritime regions. Internal decay would result from overexpansion, which was again proved true by the Qing Dynasty established by the Manchus. Therefore, as a Han-ruling agrarian civilisation between the Mongol and the Manchu Dynasties, Ming China was clearly distinguished from its predecessor and successor as being a peaceful hegemon: it is hierarchical but not expansional.

This inward-looking gravity made the Ming China see potential benefits associated with overseas trade outweighed by the perceived risk and drew them to the "dogma that asserted that national security could only be found in isolation" and in suzerain-vassal relations (Tsiang, 1936: 3–4). The maritime trade ban, albeit initially put in place for domestic security, had led to the result that any type of "foreign trade" lost its legality and could only be carried out under the name of "paying tributes". This defines the biggest difference of the Tributary System in the Ming compared with previous dynasties as it merged the two separate channels of paying tribute and conducting trade into one, giving it a dualistic nature through the use of tribute and trade, ritual and diplomacy, ideology and pragmatism, cultural and practical reasons (Wills, 1984). Mancall (1970: 75) described the relationship between tribute and trade as being "neither synonymous nor completely independent activities. They were intricately, but not necessarily directly, interrelated". Some scholars argue that the maritime trade ban policy was to support tributary trade, I somehow, believe it is the other way round simply because domestic affairs and national security always hold the centre stage for policy-making in China throughout Chinese history, particularly during early Ming for the reasons explained above. The Tributary System was mainly a political framework for China to establish and manage its regional order, and the maritime trade ban should not be understood as a decision with a primary purpose to close overseas trade but must be understood through multiple lens of geography, history, culture and ideology.

Since the Tributary System is not built on mutual profits on an equal footing, it is only sustainable and stable when both sides get what they want, and when they do, it is a win-win situation with China receiving the acknowledgement of its supreme lordship and tributary states gaining protection, enlightenment and trade benefits in return for their symbolic allegiance. However, this also means it is very expensive to maintain[1] and eventually became unaffordable and unsustainable when the power of Ming deteriorated. When its emperor was captured by the Mongols at the infamous Battle of Tumu in 1449, the Ming lost enormous prestige. Although the Mongols released the emperor a year later, this event marked a turning point of Ming's power and an impetus to refocus its attention on the inland frontier to the north. It was not until 1567 that the maritime trade ban was lifted, when Zhangzhou in Fujian was made the only port trading with overseas, and non-governmental trade slowly replaced the Tributary System to become the mainstream form of trade with China. This marked a new era with a shifting policy towards normal trade.

However, if we put it into a global context, we can see the time for Ming to turn inward-looking coincided with the start of the European Age of Exploration. In 1498, the Portuguese explorer Vasco da Gama became the first European to reach India by sea. In 1511, Malacca was conquered by the Portuguese and became a strategic base for it to expand trade with Southeast Asia. Malacca had been the tributary state that most frequently visited Beijing and used as the base and warehouse for Zheng He's voyages due to its geographic location on the sea route. The Portuguese control of this strategic point started a chain reaction with many smaller tribute states in Southeast Asia, which either chose to sever its relations with Ming, or forced to switch to Portugal for trade and protection with its sea route being cut off. This was followed by the Spanish control of Manila in 1571 and the Dutch arrival in Java in 1619. So when the Ming maritime trade ban was lifted, the seascape of trading had dramatically evolved, and it is significant to note that the rip in the tributary circle was made by external forces from the Far West, which encroached slowly into the heart of the whole ruling system of imperial China over the next two centuries. This eventually led to inevitable clashes staged in the Qing Dynasty that will be discussed after Chapter 4. Although the military conflicts between China and the West only took place during the Qing, the seed was already planted during the Ming, when the Sino-centrism viewed the rest of the world as an extension of its grace while the Euro-centrism viewed the rest of the world as an extension of its market.

2.2 Ming China: Seen, presented and influenced by Westerners

Ming China lasted for nearly 300 years from 1368–1644. This was a time when European knowledge about China started to come directly from the Jesuit missionaries, who often stayed for years and even the rest of their lives in China. However, their accounts were not always objective or accurate. This was partly due to the intention of the missions that framed their information about China. As Mungello (1985: 14) explained, they sent back information to secure and foster support for the China mission, and "the framework of the Jesuits' Confucian-Christian blending became the intellectual funnel through which most information from the Jesuits about China flowed. This framework influenced the selection of information which the Jesuits presented to Europe as well as their interpretation of it", thus "this integration of Chinese culture into Biblical experience had deep-seated influences in European thinking about the 'curious land' of China" (ibid: 358). In other words, both the purpose and strategy of Jesuits missionaries resulted in their writings about China often filled with romantic exaggerations. Meanwhile, there was hardly any second source of information that could offer alternative views or counterevidence. As explained earlier, the Ming court only allowed diplomatic relations within the traditional Tributary System. Aside from a handful of foreigners who lived permanently in Beijing and served the emperor like Matteo Ricci, also only a handful of foreigners could visit the capital on tributary missions. They were permitted to engage in carefully controlled trade for a few days before being sent away, so they only interacted with officials and nobles from the imperial clan but did not have much chance to mingle with ordinary people.

The first generation of Jesuit missions arrived at Macau in 1577, after Alessandro Valignano was appointed to be the first superior of all Jesuit missions in the East Indies in 1573. His steps were followed by Michele Ruggieri and Matteo Ricci, who established a small church west of Canton. Both of them changed into Chinese robes, learned Chinese language and manners, and studied Confucianism. They were keen to find a synthesis embracing Chinese and European cultures and win intellectual acceptance among the Chinese elites through their skills in mathematics, astronomy and geography. Mungello (1985) described Ricci's accommodation method as "intellectually flavoured Christianity", and the flavouring took the form of those aspects of European science developed during the Renaissance. On 24 January 1601, Matteo Ricci (1552–1610) became one of the few earliest westerners who reached Beijing and was allowed to live permanently in the capital with access to the Forbidden City, till the end of his life in 1610. He sent back narratives of his experiences and observations of the country and its people, as well as translations of its philosophy in the forms of letters, official reports and published works. A collection of his letters titled *Matteo Ricci: Letters from China, A Revised English Translation with Commentary* was published in 2019. They were highly informative works interwoven with respect and admiration for the Chinese society and culture.

In one of the letters, Ricci confirmed the relationship between the legendary Cathay and China: "since meeting with Muslims in Beijing in 1601, Ricci was convinced that Cathay (*Qidan,* 契丹), a term introduced for the first time to the West by Marco Polo,[2] was China, and Beijing was Kambaliq (*Hanbali*, 汗八里),[3] and accordingly he had informed his confreres both in India and in Europe" (Gottschall et al., 2019: 116). Other sources mentioned that Ricci informed Europe of this in his letters written in 1607 to "dispel all doubts" (Wiest, 2019: 66).[4] However, despite this written confirmation and the first map of the world Ricci produced for the Chinese emperor in 1602, some geographers and cartographers seemed to be reluctant to accept this identification. For example, the Jean Guerard Map of 1625, the Keppler Map and the Mercator Atlas (10th edition) of 1630 and the Nicholas Berey Map of I650 all showed both Cathay and China separately (Chang, 1970: 494). Even John Milton, one of the best-informed men of his day as Latin Secretary to the Committee of Foreign Affairs of the British government in charge of diplomatic correspondence and foreign relations, also presented the two Chinas in his book *Paradise Lost* in 1667. Chang's (ibid: 495) analysis is because "pictures of life in China and Cathay obtained from a study of materials available to seventeenth-century readers reveal far more differences than similarities", especially after China came under the Manchu ruling after 1644. For instance, it was reported that the Tartars of Cathay held white as a colour of good luck; therefore, white garments were worn on New Year's Day, but in China, white was the colour of mourning. The Tartar women of Cathay participated in feasts in which men were present; but the Chinese women sat in separate apartments from men at feasts. In Cathay, leopards, wolves and even lions were trained to assist men in hunting, but in China, people trained cormorants or sea-ravens to assist in fishing. They appeared more likely to be the different racial characteristics of two neighbouring countries. We can imagine just how difficult it was for the British to grasp the notion that one country as vast, diverse and populous as China could be centrally ruled as one empire.[5] This concept was particularly inconceivable as Europe was never politically centralised in its history. Therefore, Chang's conclusion was that "Milton certainly was not ignorant of the fact that Jesuit writers had for some time claimed that China and Cathay were one and the same country. He had simply ignored the identification because it did not seem to be the truth and because the idea did not appeal to him".

In a way, Cathey represented the Utopianised China, "the mightiest Empire" of wealth, magnificence and romance. Indeed, as Ricci described in his 1583 letter: "Concerning the greatness of China, it's certain that the world does not have a greater King, as we can see from the many parts of the world that he owns, and which are so fertile", and "in sum, they have an abundance of many goods" (Gottschall et al., 2019: 78–79). In his 1584 letter, Ricci highly praised China's statecraft as something "into which they have put all their effort and achieved such brilliance that they leave all other nations behind ……. it would seem to me that Plato could imagine no better republic than what exists in reality in China" (ibid: 123). Kircher's (1667: iii) book further consolidated this: "this great and almost immeasurable empire of the Tartars and Chinese, ruled by an absolute monarchy and administration, which almost anyone would find marvellous. It is so large that you can't find a more powerful or populous nation anywhere on earth". For the British, the quest for a trade route to Cathay was a subject of fascination throughout the seventeenth century, they continued to cherish the dream of finding an unimpeded trade route to Cathay, be it Yuan in Marco Polo's time when first accounts about China were read, or Ming during Elizabeth I's reign when first letters to China dispatched, or Qing when the first British embassy eventually reached China with gifts. Exactly because it was an Utopianised version of China, even when the Macartney Embassy finally arrived in Beijing, they could not believe they were already in Cathay, the legendary dreamland whose splendour only existed in European's imaginations seemed still far to seek.

Ricci's observations of China were often expressed in a comparative way. For example, the biggest difference he noticed was that the Chinese "are quite content with what they have and are not ambitious of conquest. In this respect they are much different from the people of Europe, who are frequently discounted with their own governments and covetous of what others enjoy" (cited in Dawson, 1967: 184). He also elaborated the Chinese elevation of the literati over the military class in that "another remarkable fact and quite worthy of note as marking a difference from the West, is that the entire kingdom is administered by the Order of the Learned, commonly known as the Philosophers. The responsibility for orderly management of the entire realm is wholly and completely committed to their charge and care" (ibid: 184). This was also elaborated in his 1584 letter that "the power and state of China is founded more on the large population, numerous cities, and good governance rather than on walls, fortifications, and the indigenous ability for war. The Chinese are little trained in war and in military arts, and they hold [soldiers] in low esteem" (Gottschall et al., 2019: 124).

This had an enormous effect upon idealising China in the eyes of European learned society. However, the reality of Ming shows great discrepancy as we know today: the founding emperor not only resorted to fortifying the Great Wall that still stands in China today,[6] but also built a "Maritime Great Wall" that was in place for nearly 200 years. Even the reigning Wanli Emperor (1563–1620) during Ricci's time in China was not a good example of the governance model highlighted by him. After 1586, Wanli retreated into the pleasure of palace life, ended his contact with the Hanlin scholars, an academy of preeminent scholars who normally advised the emperor, leaving court eunuchs and civil servants to run the country. He only held six interviews with his grand secretary during his last years from 1591 to his death in 1620, and communicated with his ministers almost exclusively through the eunuchs. Wanli's infamous use of eunuchs in administrative duties in the place of scholar-officials was commonly considered as one of the key contributing causes to the fall of Ming. Therefore, even if Queen Elizabeth I's letter arrived in

Beijing in 1602, though Ricci could have helped with translation and communication, he had very little contact with the recluse Emperor. As a matter of fact, Ricci had never met the Wanli Emperor in person.

The first time Ricci wrote about China's perception of trading with foreigners was in his 1599 letter from Nanjing, an ancient capital city in the middle of Chinese mainland[7]: "The Chinese had always little commerce with foreigners and never wanted to have commercial relations with them. The Chinese people are very fearful of foreigners, especially the king, who is a kind of tyrant, whose ancestors usurped the kingdom by force of arms, and is afraid that someone might take it from them …… After all, China is China, and there is no record that any foreigner stayed here as we are" (Gottschall et al., 2019: 94).

As one of the few foreigners who managed to stay, Ricci's biggest legacy was the first map of the world he produced for the Chinese emperor in 1602, *Complete Map of the Ten Thousand Countries of the World* (*Kunyu Wanguo Quantu,* 《坤舆万国全图》).[8] Precise astronomical measurements were used to construct the map, but Ricci's reading of longitude and latitude for China were said to have been derived from maps found in the Chinese atlas *Kuang Yutu*(《广舆图》), originally composed by Zhu Siben (朱思本) in 1320 and later edited by Luo Hongxian (罗洪先) in 1555.[9] Ricci changed traditional European mapmaking in this world map by placing Asia and the Pacific Ocean, instead of Europe, in the central position. As well put by Westad (2013: 32), "as in the West, mapmaking in imperial China was not just about accurate renditions but about centrality, culture and power". Maps are political than just representational. Some may argue that Ricci made adjustments within the scope of acceptable cartography of the time to elevate the status of China on the map, which can be understood as representation of his accommodation and admiration for the empire as declared in one of his commentaries, written on the map: "Filled with admiration for the great Chinese Empire, whose fame extended over ten thousand li, I came from the West on a floating raft" (Giles, 1918: 367). England was indicated on the map with its Latin name of "Anglia" transliterated into Chinese as "An e li ya" (谙厄利亚).

Although Ricci introduced the concepts of "five continents" and "ten thousand countries" for the first time to the Chinese, he presented the world as one under China's Tributary System in the explanatory note on the map: "The Middle Kingdom is renowned for the greatness of its civilisation. It comprises all between the 15th and 42nd parallels, *and the other parts of the world that are tributary to it include a very large number of states*" (Giles, 1918: 384, emphasis added by the author). That is why I do not agree when many argued that the map shattered the Chinese cosmology of being the centre of the world, nor do I agree with Ricci's own portrayal of the Chinese not being closed-minded in their sense of cultural superiority as based on his record, after being presented with the world map, "the Chinese, for the most part, acknowledge their former error and make it a source of no little mirth" (Mungello, 1985: 72). I would argue the map did not uproot China's belief as the Middle Kingdom as it was still positioned in the middle to please the Ming emperor, and the concept of "ten thousand countries" was simply adopted in the notion of "ten thousand nations coming to pay tribute" as depicted in the picture below during the Qianlong's reign of the Qing Dynasty (see Figure 2.1). We can clearly see the names of those nations on the banners, including England (the grey-purplish banner on the right bottom corner). I therefore argue that what shattered the *Tianxia* mentality for China was actually the Opium War: it took China another two and half centuries to be awakened from this long dream, and eventually joined the modern world as one of the "ten thousand countries".

However, the map did present the new concept of a physical "world" vs. the old shapeless and boundless imagination of *Tianxia*. This contested the old Chinse belief that the earth was flat and square; it also demonstrated an expanded connotation of the "West": since India was where Buddhism was originated from and spread to China during the Han Dynasty, the ancient Chinese concept of the "West" normally referred to the Islam

Figure 2.1 "Ten Thousand Nations Coming to Pay Tribute" scroll. Courtesy of the Palace Museum of Beijing.

World (*Xiyu*, 西域, a shifting geographical concept meaning "the Western Regions") and India (*Xitian*, 西天, both a religious and geographical concept meaning "the Western Heaven"), while the so-called "Western Ocean" (*Xiyang*, 西洋) that Zheng He had explored only reached the east coast of Africa. Now Europe and America were brought on the horizon, making this world map the most significant contribution of Ricci. As Joseph Needham (1954) had rightfully commended on the contributions made by Jesuits in the history of Sino-West cultural encounters, they were not only full of religious passion but well versed in science – as mathematicians, astronomers, geographers, translators and interpreters, experts in artillery, clock makers, artists and musicians. Much of what the Jesuits taught was new in China and this novelty was greatly appreciated by many, including the Wanli Emperor himself, who showed great interests in the map.

I believe the utmost significance of this map lies in its achievement as a cross-fertilization of European and Chinese geographical and cartographical knowledge. In the words of Father Pasquale D'elia (1961: 161), "in Ricci the civilisation of the Far West was for the first time meeting that of the Far East". Yet nothing captures this better than what was written in the Preface by Ricci's Chinese collaborator Li Zhizao (李之藻): "In the East and the West, there is but one mind and reason" (*Dong hai xi hai, xin tong li tong*, 东海西海，心同理同), putting the East and West on an equal scale of civilisation. Ricci also used "us" in referring to the making of the map, giving credits to Li: In his 1605 letter sent from Beijing, he mentioned that "the Map of the World which I sent two years ago has been reprinted more than 10 times, and it does us much credit as it is a work never before seen to China. Many write and print the books about us, and this is because they have never known another kingdom than this one" (Gottschall et al., 2019: 106).

By 1608, Ricci became "the only one left of the first to enter this kingdom" (ibid: 113). Indeed, his first fellow missionaries on the great adventure in the Chinese Empire had either returned to Italy, or sent to Japan, or passed away in China by this time. In his last letter in 1609 from Beijing, Ricci wrote: "even though there are many learned men and theologians among us here, none of them has achieved even a mediocre command of Chinese letters – and knowing our own language without knowing theirs accomplishes nothing" (Gottschall et al., 2019: 138). This represents another dimension of Ricci's tremendous contributions. He created the vocabulary of God (*Shangdi*, 上帝) and Angels (*Tianshen*, 天神) in Chinese and Romanised the Chinese philosopher Kongzi's name as Confucius. He collaborated with Xu Guangqi (徐光启), a learned Chinese intellectual in the field of agriculture, mathematics and astronomy who held high position at court and passionate about introducing European knowledge to China, in translating several Western scientific classics into Chinese, including *Euclid's Elements*. He also compiled the Portuguese-Chinese dictionary with other Jesuits.

Since Ricci admired China so ardently, it is particularly interesting to see his comments on the aspects where China was considered inferior in his observations: one is "ocean-going vessels, the Chinese ships were said to be few in number and inferior to their Western counterparts"; and the other is saltpetre, unlike in Europe, it was "little used in preparing gunpowder and the Chinese state of weapon technology was described as deficient" (Mungello, 1985: 53). He was not very complimentary on Chinese music and painting either, and attributed the "minimally developed Chinese tradition of portraiture, defects in statuary and lack of use of oil paints" to the fact that "they have never come into intimate contact with the nations beyond their border" (ibid: 54). In a way, this can be seen in the gifts Ricci prepared for the Wanli Emperor, representing what he believed China was lacking. Apart from a breviary and a crucifix, two mechanical chime clocks and two sand clocks, two prisms, eight pieces of mirrors and glass vases, and a Western style clavichord, there were three oil paintings of Christ and Virgin Mary. The visual realism of European oil painting immediately caught the attention of Chinese audiences, including the eye of the Wanli Emperor. An interesting anecdote was that the Wanli Emperor had two full-length portraits made for Ricci and his companion, the Spaniard Diego Pantoja, by eunuch court artists. However, according to Pantoja, neither of them were recognizable in these paintings (Guillen-Nuñez, 2014: 443). The only known authentic likeness of Ricci was created before he passed away in 1610 by You Wenhui (alias Manuel Pereira),[10] a Chinese Jesuit brother born in Macau. This is also the earliest oil painting produced by a Chinese artist, a direct legacy inspired by Western style painting. Wanli also liked other gifts brought by Ricci so much that he granted Ricci permanent stay in Beijing and paid him a monthly salary, with the main task of coming to the Forbidden City four times a year to tune and maintain the chime clocks. The emperor was also curious about western music performed on the clavichord. Pantoja became master to four eunuch musicians, and Ricci translated eight European songs into Chinese to be played with these instruments.

Another legacy with long-lasting influence from Ricci was when his manuscripts were brought back to Europe by Nicolas Trigault (1577–1628), another Jesuit missionary who arrived in China following his death. Trigault extended and translated it from Italian into Latin: *De Christiana expeditione apud Sinas (The Journals of Matteo Ricci),* which caused a sensation when published in Europe in 1615. It was regarded as one of the first books that introduced China systematically and accurately by a Westerner and became one of the most widely cited early modern primary accounts of China. It had four Latin editions, three French editions and one edition, respectively, in German, Spanish, Italian and English. In the book, Ming China was known as Ciumquo (*Zhongguo,* 中国) or Ciumhoa (*Zhonghua,*中华[11]) as Chinese people believed their country was the "Middle Kingdom", but Ricci and Trigault concluded that "[Chinese] pride, it would seem, arises from an ignorance of the existence of higher things and from the fact that they find themselves far superior to the barbarous nations by which they are surrounded" (cited in Gallagher, 1953: 23). If these Western missionaries did not eradicate such "ignorance", they had definitely started the flow of mutual influence by infiltrating Western ideas into China and initiating changes in the fabric of Chinese thoughts and worldview.

In comparison, we can see the knowledge gap between Britain and its European neighbours at the time due to the lack of resident missions in China – Britain was two centuries behind in this regard. It was of vital importance to have missionaries representing one's own country in China, as they regularly sent back reports of their experiences and observations of the country as well as translations of its literature and philosophy,[12] while gaining knowledge second-handedly and in translations affected the accuracy of information the British had access to, which has been showcased by the sceptre story in Chapter 1; what added further to the distortion of information was when England had to rely on another country that had a potential conflict of national interests for its dealings with China, as missionaries were involved in almost all affairs related to the West, acting as diplomatic interpreters or advisors to the emperors. This gave them a considerable measure of influence, which could adversely affect the British when they were competing with or even at wars with those European neighbours, such as what happened to the first British Expedition to Canton in 1637 and the first Embassy to Beijing in 1793. This will be looked at in detail in later sections of the book. The next section explores the Chinese views of foreigners and merchants during the Ming Dynasty, which also shows the limitations of depending on English translations as a source of information about China.

2.3 The Sino-speak vocabulary of outsiders and foreigners

As already explained, before the first map of the world was presented to Chinese people, they used to believe that the Middle Kingdom *was* the centre of the world, and there was a whole set of vocabulary to support this knowledge architecture that Perdue (2015: 1002) named it "a basic component of 'Sinospeak'": Beyond this vast Middle Kingdom, people from its east were called *Yi,* south *Man*, north *Di*, and west *Rong*, sometimes collectively known as the *Four Yi. Yi* initially referred to the "non-Han people" when the first Emperor Qin Shi Huang unified China. In the first complete Chinese language dictionary *Shuowen Jiezi* [*An Etymology of the Chinese Language,* 《说文解字》] compiled by Xu Shen in 100 A.D., *Yi* simply referred to "the people from the east" and bore no negative connotations. When China expanded, many of the tribes became part of China, hence the *Four Yi* referred to "foreigners", with its antithesis being *Hua*, the "glorious nation". The Chinese map made in 801 was called the *Hua Yi Atlas* (《海内华夷图》). Chinese historical accounts compiled during the Tang Dynasty such as *Beishi* (*Northern Annals of the Six Dynasties,* 《北史》) and *Tangshu* (*Tang History,* 《唐书》) demonstrated how, in the traditional Chinese perception, heaven had separated the Middle Kingdom from outer regions inhabited by *Yi* peoples; Heaven had given this privileged land good government and social order, guarding its territory by a frontier of natural barriers. In this sense, even if *Yi* simply means "foreigner", being non-Chinese already had this inferior association as it was underpinned by a sense of Sinocentism that both shaped and expressed a cultural superiority: "Beyond these lived the savage tribes devoid of morality and intellectual light; they could be only lifted from their degraded condition by the enlightened government of the Middle Kingdom" (Basu, 2014: 935). There were three circles defined: at the centre, it was a hierarchical system of the "Celestial Court" and "Heavenly Kingdom" (*Tianchao Shangguo*, 天朝上国), which was extended to its peripheral "Vassal States" (*Fanshu guo*, 藩属国) and "Barbarian States" at the outer fringes of civilisation (*Huawi Manyi Gebang*, 化外蛮夷各邦).[13]

Under the ancient Tributary System, *Hua* was the synonym of being civilised and *Yi* as its antithesis took on the meaning of being inferior. Its geographical and ethnical connotations of "foreign" and the culturally charged meaning of "uncivilised" can be considered the two sides of one coin. In essence, the so-called *Hua-Yi Distinction* (*Hua Yi Zhibian*, 华夷之辨) set the frame of a fundamental polarity. Already established by the Warring-States period (475–221BC), I would argue that it was the Chinese form of the philosophical notion of "the same and other" postulated by Plato (429–347 BC), which evolved into the "Self and Other", and then "Orient and Occident" as polarised cultural entities – only that the representations were reversed, with *Yi* as "*the Other*" and China as "*the Self*". The *Hua-Yi* concept had the same underlying structural principle of dichotomy, with the very existence of *Yi* functioning as the antithesis for *Hua* to define its own superior identity. In other words, the predecessor of "the West and the Rest" world view was "the Middle Kingdom and the Rest". One difference is that the Confucian social order required everyone to accept its own place in the hierarchy, so China did not try to convert the rest or to "civilise" them, nor did they use the *Yi* as a mirror to scrutinise themselves. There was little serious curiosity concerning these foreign nations, let alone desire to learn from them. Rather, they were merely expected to pay homage and tributes to the Chinese Empire.

However, since *Yi* had been used through China's historic encounters with those less culturally developed neighbours on its peripheries, a different term *Yang* (Oceans) should have been created to accommodate the expanded horizon as a designated name for the European states beyond the seas to distinguish them from the traditional *Yi*. Perhaps partly due to the Jesuits' accommodating approach to China and partly due to the respect they received at the Ming courts, they did not attempt to change their own designations as being *Yi.* Even the government department of translation during the Ming Dynasty was called the "Four Yi House" (*Si Yi Guan*, 四夷馆). Interestingly, after Ming was subjugated by the Manchus, who were part of *Yi* in its origin and far less civilised but far more aggressive militarily than the Han, they were subdued by the Chinese civilisation and adopted the Han government structure. Both the Chinese language Mandarin and Chinese ministers[14] were kept along with the Manchus, but the "Four Yi House" was renamed to "Four Translations House"[15] (*Si Yi Guan*, 四译馆) in 1644, a homophone of Yi that has a completely different meaning. A conscious decision made by the, father of Qianlong, Yongzheng Emperor was to undermine the credibility of the *Hua-Yi* distinction. As he put in *Awakening to Supreme Justice*:

> The seditious rebels make the suggestion that we were the sovereign of Manchuria and later entered the Central States to become its ruler. Their prejudices about the territorial division between this land and that land have led to hateful lies and fabrications. What they have failed to understand is that Manchuria is to the Manchus what the *jiguan* [birthplace or ancestral place] to the people of the Central States. Shun was a man of the eastern Yi and King Wen was a man of the western Yi. Did that diminish their *shengde* [sagely virtue]? (cited in Liu, 2006: 84)

As pointed by Liu (2006), he shifted the contested ground of his sovereign claims to moral integrity and benevolent leadership and argued that the mandate of heaven had rightfully passed into the hands of the Manchus, not because of where they came from but because of what and who they were: men of virtue. Also, he further shifted the meaning of *Yi* from ethnicity to geographic area to dissolve the subversive potential of the *Hua-Yi* distinction.

Before the 1720s during the reigns of the Kangxi and Yongzheng emperors, the neutral term *Xiyang* (*Western Ocean*, 西洋), together with its two variations, *Xi* (west) and *Yang* (ocean) as a prefix in making a compound, were commonly used to refer to European people and objects. For example, when a missionary who lived in Canton presented "Western wines" (*Yangjiu*, 洋酒) to the Kangxi Emperor in 1710, he was referred to as a "Western Ocean person" (*Xiyang ren*, 西洋人) (Chen, 2017: 94). Every year when the trading season started, the Canton governor-general would organise memorials to report the number of European ships that had arrived and the types of goods they carried. In these reports, the merchants and the staff of the EIC were referred to as "Western Ocean people"; their ships were named "ocean ships" (*Yangchuan*, 洋船); their writing system, "Western Ocean words" (*Xiyang zi*, 西洋字); the enamel they carried to China were called "Western Ocean enamel" (*Xiyang Falang,* 西洋珐琅); their European cloth, *Yangbu* (洋布); and their unspecified cargo *Xiyang wujian* (西洋物件) (ibid: 93–94).

However, the term *Xiyang* seemed to be only used to designate the group of nations in their geographical locations but not to distinguish their status from other tributary states. If *Gong* was used to mean offerings from tributary states, then a new term should also be created for offerings from *Xiyang guo*, in recognition of a new type of relationship with these foreign nations. Without it, *Xiyang* had no significant difference from *Yi*. For example, the picture below (see Figure 2.2 and Figure 2.3) was a clock jointly made[16] by the British clockmaker Timothy Williamson and Swiss watchmaker Jaquet Droz, allegedly procured to please the Qianlong Emperor. It was an ingenious example showing that the Western technology was merely used as a new form to display the antiquated Sino-centric world view that drew all nations to it as the centre of universe. This three-tier, 231 cm-tall automata clock moves a *Xiyang ren* in Georgian court suits, holding a Chinese brush in a half-kneeing

Figure 2.2 Writing Man Automata Clock. Courtesy of the Palace Museum of Beijing.

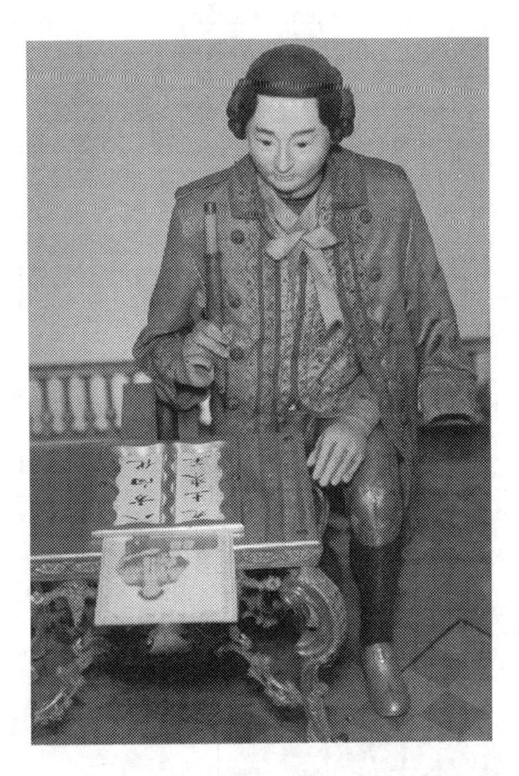

Figure 2.3 Close-up of the writing man inside the frame. Courtesy of the Palace Museum of Beijing.

position. When it is wound, the man dips in the ink well upon moving to a new line, and his head follows the text as he writes the eight characters in Chinese calligraphy style that read: "*Ba Fang Xiang Hua, Jiu Tu Lai Wang*" (八方向化、九土来王), which literally means "countries from all eight directions are drawn to this highly civilised empire; people from all over the world ('nine lands') come to pay tribute to its emperor". This piece had been Qianlong's favourite, there were other automata clocks displaying similar messages such as "ten thousand nations coming to pay tribute" (*Wan Guo Lai Chao,* 万国来朝). In essence, this means China should not be merely described as *being civilised*, but it was *civilisation per se*, radiating like light outward to shine on those living beyond its sway in the uncivilised darkness.

From the above we can see, even after the first map of the world was produced for the Chinese emperor during the Ming Dynasty, it did not bring fundamental changes to the *Tianxia* world view, which was even further strengthened during the Qing around the 1750s, when *Yi* started to replace *Xiyang ren* as the standard bureaucratic language to refer to the Europeans, coinciding with the tightening of controls on Europeans in China (Chen, 2017: 82–83). After examining the extensive records of Chinese correspondence between the Qing authority and the EIC's supercargoes in Canton during 1760–1810, Basu (2014: 930) found that "the term *Yi* is the standard technical expression when referring to the Europeans in all these records, whether used by the Chinese or the supercargoes. No one seemed to have minded the term nor was it translated as "barbarian" in the English language records". Well, no one minded except the British afterwards, whose rise challenged the traditions of the imperial Chinese political thought as well as its discourse. In fact, as strongly argued by Liu in her book *The Clash of Empires* (2006: 31), "never has a lone word among the myriad languages of humanity made so much history as the Chinese character *Yi* (夷), in its uncanny ability to arouse confusion, anxiety and war". It is one of the most tragic and costly fabrications in modern diplomatic history as a quibble over this word transgressed from a clash of principles to a state of war. The conflicts over the two Chinese terms of *Gong* and *Yi* will be looked at in Chapters 4 to 7. Even in today's China, when *Yi* was replaced by a neutral term of *wai guo ren* (outside country person, 外国人), the propensity of viewing the world as "China and the rest" makes the binary division almost perennial and still dominate most people's mindset and world view.

2.4 Exchange ideas, goods or fire?

The early Ming Dynasty had witnessed China's own version of Age of Exploration with Admiral Zheng He's voyages, however, as described earlier, these voyages were not for exchange of goods or exchange of ideas. One of the few essays from the Ming Dynasty that dealt with the trade theme was "On Merchants"(《商贾纪》) written by Zhang Han, 张瀚), a scholar official who was later banished to retirement from the position of Minister of the Board of Civil Official during Wanli's reign. He spent the rest of his life in writing and completed an eight-volume work entitled *Dream Essays at the Pine Window* (*Songchuang Mengyu,* 《松窗梦语》) in 1593. The essay "On Merchants" was a chapter in the book with the greater part as a descriptive economic geography of sixteenth century China on a macro scale. It contained many criticisms of the government policies and arguments for enhancing overseas trade, which could function as an example of the Ming Dynasty's relative openness to different ideas compared with Qing. The most relevant part to our story was the dissident views he put forward in the 10 pages on Ming's foreign trade (pp. 226–236). Interestingly, the English versions I found in two sources were published in the same year, but unfortunately, both versions included some inaccurate and even misleading translations: one was included in *Chinese Civilisation and Society, A Sourcebook* (Ebrey, 1981) and one was included in Brook's special paper (1981: 165) that was dedicated to the discussion and translation of the essay as he believed "this essay has not been translated".

The translation of the first paragraph (by Lily Hwa) in the *Sourcebook* (1981: 156) was a relatively faithful rendering: "As to the foreign trade on the North-western frontier and the foreign sea trade in the Southeast, if we compare their advantages and disadvantages with respect to our nation's wealth and the people's wellbeing, we will discover that they are *as different as black and white"*. In comparison, Brook translated the italicised parts as "*this is not a black and white issue*", which could be due to a misreading of the literary expression of *bu chi* (不啻), meaning "no less than". A full translation of the original sentence is: "the difference is as poles apart as between heaven and earth, black and white" (my translation).

However, Hwa's translation also contained major misinterpretations when she obscured the two groups of "foreigners" that Zhang meant to contrast: the Northern barbarians or "tribal chieftains" (*Lu,* 虜) in the Northwest frontier, to foreigners that approached China from the sea route in southeast (*Yi*, 夷); or foreigners along the land border vs. the maritime border. Because of the historical incursions penetrating the northern borders, the former group was considered a much more serious threat than the latter, as one wanted land while the other only wanted to trade. It was elaborated by Zhang:

> Northern barbarians (*Lu*)[17] are recalcitrant and their greed knows no bounds. At the present time our nation spends over one million cash yearly from our treasury on these foreigners, still we cannot rid ourselves of their demands. What is more, their greedy heart is unpredictable. If one day they break the treaties and invade our frontiers, who will be able to defend us against them? I do not think our present trade with them will ensure us a century of peace. (cited in *Chinese Civilisation and Society, A Sourcebook*, 1981: 157)

Therefore, Zhang's original text argued for the benefits of overseas trade along the coast against "barter trade" along the northwest border in three points: 1) The overseas trade with China was under the name of tributary contributions. That means China's authority is established and the foreigners are compliant; 2) Even if the gifts we grant them are greater in value than the tribute they send us, the costs are still less than one ten-thousandth of the expenses in the Northwest. Moreover, the *Yi* foreigners are more interested in trading with China than gaining gifts; 3) In addition, trading with them can generate wealth among our people. So why do we refrain from it?

For the second point, Hwa's translation compared "our expenses" with "the benefit we gain from trading with them", while Brook's translation compared "the payment of tribute" with "what is transacted in trade". Both translations did not capture it was the two trading exchanges that

Zhang meant to contrast, the frontier market in the Northwest (*Xibei Hushi,* 西北互市) that drained China's national treasury for useless horses in return, and the sea trade in Southeast (*Dongnan Haishi,* 东南海市) that used what one has to exchange for what one lacks. Therefore, the conclusion reached in the essay was that there were only benefits from expanding trade on the Southeast sea route with *Yi* merchants, while there were nothing but harm from trading on the Northwest frontier market with the northern *Lu* barbarians. Another ground-breaking point Zhang made was the "mutual benefit" nature of trade: the *Yi* cannot afford to lose the profits from trading with China, just as China cannot lose the benefits from trading with them. He also used a series of rhetorical questions to urge the court to think wisely: how could the court not see the benefits and detriments? If we prohibit the natural flow of trade out of mutual demand, how can we prevent them from turning to piracy? If sea trade is opened, the trouble with foreign pirates would naturally cease. However, as explained earlier, during the later reign of the Wanli Emperor, the court did not listen to the expert advice of scholars, whose words could have saved the military skirmish resulted from the first British and Chinese encounter in 1637.

The first British attempt to establish commercial relations and a permanent trade station in China,[18] long before Lord Macartney's famous embassy to Beijing, is often forgotten in the story of Anglo-Chinese relations. As the first physical encounter between the two peoples, it is surprisingly understudied and underdocumented in both countries, and worse still, even wrongly recorded in various Chinese texts, such as *History of Ming Dynasty* (1739), *A Brief History of Macau* (1800) and *History of Guangzhou Custom Administration* (1839). These Chinese authors mistakenly believed that their countrymen were fighting against the Dutch,[19] which was not corrected until Xia Xie published his *Event Notes of China's Diplomacy* in 1865, almost 230 years later (Gong, 1998: 237–238). This not only exposed China's very limited knowledge of Britain at the time, the failure of the ill-fated first expedition also exposed the little knowledge the British had about China. English References to the expedition can be found in "Journal of a voyage to Acheen, Macau and Canton Captain John Weddell 6 April 1637–4 February 1638" in *EAST MEETS WEST, Original Records of Western Traders, Travellers, Missionaries and Diplomats to 1852* kept at the Oxford Bodleian Library; *The English Factories in India 1618–1669* by Sir William Foster (1906), and *The English in China, 1600–1843* by James Bromley Eames (1909). The most comprehensive account is *The Travels of Peter Mundy in Europe and Asia, 1608–1667*, edited by Richard Carnac Temple in 1919, as it not only included a detailed journal kept by Mundy, the chief commercial officer of the voyage and the most travelled Englishmen at the time, but also collated a whole range of documents from the official account kept at the Public Record Office MSS, to Weddell's own account of the incident; from the voyage of Weddell's fleet preserved at the India Office, to records of the transactions from the expedition, as well as key documents kept in *Lisbon Transcripts,* including copies of letters exchanged between the British and the Portuguese, between the Portuguese and the Mandarins, and the undertaking signed by Weddell to leave China. The only modern study narrating the event I can find is Austin Coates's *Macau and the British, 1637–1842: Prelude to Hong Kong,* first published in 1966, which also drew heavily on Mundy's book. There was also a very brief mentioning of it in Dawson's book in 1967.[20]

From the Chinese side, a more recent piece of research done by Wan (2011) provided a most critical source of this historic event by joining together records from China (the Ming Archives), British and Portuguese archives as well as the eyewitness's personal account produced by Mundy. From these accounts, we can see the conflicting interests of the three parties: the British simply wanted to trade with China, but as a latecomer, they were met with obstructions from the Portuguese authorities in Macau whose interests were already in conflicts with the vying Spanish and Dutch, who all viewed the British as a new competitor to share "a slice of the cake", while China wanted to expel any invasions and threat to its national security, adopting a restrictive policy and a suspicious attitude towards foreigners and foreign influence. This had largely reduced the British chances of success and even led to the first unofficial encounter between the two empires in the form of a military collision.

On 27 June 1637, Captain John Weddell led the first English expedition to China and arrived at Macau with four heavily armed ships. They were not backed by the EIC but rather by a private group led by Sir William Courteen and included King Charles I's personal interest of £10,000. The British were very eager to start trading with China but found that they could not count on the Portuguese to introduce them as it was against their interests, as they "report us to bee pirattes and thatt wee came only to robbe and spoile, bringuing Neither Mony nor goodes" (Mundy, 1919: 175), so they decided to establish contacts with the Chinese directly. However, they only got half of the story here. They did not realise that the Portuguese monopoly of the China trade was also in the interest of the Chinese government, who initially allowed the Portuguese to settle in Macau to keep the Pearl River free of pirates, then developed the idea of "playing off foreigners against foreigners" (*Yi Yi Zhi Yi*, 以夷制夷), using them to keep other seafaring foreigners away, as they were considered a dangerous disturbance to the central order by Beijing.

When the British ships left Macau on 29 July towards Canton, it immediately alarmed the Ming officials who ordered them to stop moving ahead. The British explained to the messenger that all they wanted was the permit to trade with China like the Portuguese: "we wished them no hurt, but Desired their Freindshippe and goodwill to have Merchandize For our Mony and then wee would depart" (Mundy, 1919: 185). The messenger then agreed to report their requests for approval and asked them to wait eight days to receive the reply from Canton. However, Weddell did not wait for the eight days as requested and approached further up near the Bogue forts, where he was promised by the Ming official (according to the interpreter) that they would get the permit to trade in Canton within 10 days, but if they move further to the fort during the waiting period, they would be encircled and attacked. Weddell, who was impatient and suspected the waiting meant interference by the Portuguese, sent a barge to take surroundings further up near the forts on 12 August, when cannons fired three times at the barge from the forts but missed. At the order of Weddell, the British ships fought back and captured one of the Bogue forts, even hoisting the flag of Great Britain above it before taking back some abandoned cannons from the deserted fort. On 15 August, an interpreter from Canton came to find out the purpose and requests of the British, and Weddell "told him wee were English men and Came to seeke a trade with them in a faire way of merchandizing, but wee had beene abused by some of the under Mandereens and some of our men slayne by them, and for that Cause wee were Constrayned to doe what wee had done" (Mundy, 1919: 207). On 21 August, the same interpreter came back to the British ships with a signed letter of approval from the Mandarin and took three Englishmen with him to the suburbs of Canton with money and goods for sale, and discreetly purchased two junks full of sugar. However, it later turned out that the interpreter wanted to profit from engaging them in illegal trade; he was "Most Falce (as afterward appeared)", telling Weddell they "should have Free trade For 4 shippes yearly, with a covenientt place to inhabit and to secure our shippes. Itt being all contrary as aforesaid". Then the falsely interpreted document had been correctly "expounded by a Jesuitt skillfull in the tongue", who told them the Chinese viewed the British as "being stiled redhaired barbarians, etts", and "they would use all the Force they could to expel us" (ibid: 260).

Indeed, seeing the British ships ignore their warnings and orders to leave, a fleet of Chinese fire-ships was dispatched in the middle of the night to annihilate the British fleet, but did not succeed due to the unfavourable wind. The British ships took revenge by looting some local villages and captured the Bogue fort again. Casualties and deaths were suffered by both Chinese and British in several such engagements, though the Ming record tried to gloss it over. During this process, half a dozen British merchants were detained and imprisoned in the suburbs of Canton. The British was forced to seek Portuguese help, who signed a statement with the Ming officials, stating that the British entered the Chinese territory "being ignorance of the laws of China", and they would not "transgress in the future" (Mundy, 1919: 250). On 9 October, Weddell signed on the undertaking that "if the Aytao of Canton, or his Mandarins, deliver to me my six men who are imprisoned by their authority in Canton, and the silver and merchandise they had with them, or any specimens of the products of China in exchange, that I will depart peacefully from Chinese waters, without injuring anyone, and will never return to those shores" (ibid: 264). Two days later, they signed an official document to pledge again that they would obey the Chinese order and would never break the Chinese laws again. The British eventually sailed off the Pearl River on 27 December 1637, exactly six months after their first arrival in China. By the time they were expelled "outt off the Citty and Country, even by Fire and sword as one May well say" (Coates, 1966: 25), they were still baffled at the contradiction that "existed between the eagerness of local merchants to trade with foreigners and the official unwillingness of the mandarins to permit such trade" (ibid: 26). But during these six months, they also accumulated some basic knowledge about the Chinese coast, whose position was expressed using longitude point of Greenwich. As Mundy (1919: 486) wrote: "if Wee continue the China Trade, it's probable that within few years Wee shall have the full knowledge of the North East and North West passages".

Indeed the British never returned to Ming China again, which fell to the Qing ruling in only six years' time in 1644 after the Chongzhen Emperor hung himself. This was followed by the execution of King Charles I in 1649, closing the curtain of the first encounters between the British Empire and Ming China. However, it only lifted the curtain to the turbulent relationship between the two empires in the next two centuries, although it was hard to imagine at this point that the same waters would stage the consequential Opium War. Mundy's records showed that at least he left China with some splendid descriptions of a Utopia: "This country May bee said to excel in these particulers: Antiquity, largenesse, Ritchenesse, healthynesse, Plentiffullnesse. For Arts and manner off government I thinck noe Kingdome in the world Comparable to it, Considered altogether" (cited in Dawson, 1967: 32). What is worth special mentioning is the first record of British tea drinking in his book: "the people there gave us a certaine Drinke called Chaa, which is only water with a king of herbe boyled in itt. It must bee Drancke warme and is accompted wholesome" (cited in Coates, 1966: 8). Again, at that moment, he had little idea of the part that "Chaa" was destined to play in the future relations between the two empires, that the brew "would alter the social life of nations, providing the lure which was to bring foreigners ever more imperatively to pound upon China's doors" (ibid: 8). Trade between the two countries started to thrive in the Qing and the British overtook other European powers to secure the largest market share by 1670 during the Kangxi Emperor's reign. The EIC finally secured a trading post in Taiwan in 1670 and gained its first foothold on mainland China at Amoy in 1675, and finally in Canton in 1713, representing the official recognition of trade relations between the two empires.

We have opened this chapter with the exchange of ideas between China and the West during the Ming Dynasty, facilitated by the first-generation missionaries, and accompanied by an exchange of commodities operated under the Tributary System, all dominated by the European powers on the continent. When the British appeared on the stage as a latecomer, its first commercial expedition to China ended in an exchange of fire. It exposed the illusory security of the Ming policy of "playing off foreigners against foreigners", and how ill-prepared China was to deal with the British when they eventually decided to prise open China's door by force. If the Opium War is the long shadow it cast on the bilateral relations, this first encounter had foreshadowed the failure of the first British embassy. As Coates (1966:26) commented, although commercially insignificant, Weddell's expedition "is important due to the conclusions about the British which were drawn from it by Chinese officialdom, of which the most salient was that red barbarians were particularly dangerous". This negative impression was so long-lasting that by the Macartney Embassy's visit to China over a century later, to improve the British image was still listed as one of the goals of the mission. The sabotage role played by the interpreter in this first Anglo-Chinese encounter also showed the price of knowledge deficit that the British paid and continued to pay during its first ambassy to China. It is the same lesson for Lord Macartney that was not learned by Weddell: "the British looked upon China as a foreign nation like any other, to be dealt with as other nations were dealt with, while to the Chinese, their country was like none other, being unique and superior, the sole point and centre of human civilisation, beyond the frontiers of which existed nothing that was either interesting or desirable" (ibid: 26).

The following Chapters 3 and 4 will trace the long journey of mutual discoveries in the seventeenth and eighteenth centuries, a journey when the Euro-centric view and the Sino-centric view crossed paths, and a journey when mutual knowledge is gradually increased through dispelling mutual imaginations and reducing mutual misperceptions.

Notes

1 Ming records speak of over 100 tributary states, but China's relationships with its different neighbouring states were different and dynamic, so this number fluctuates from time to time.

2 Originally, Cathay was a name for a northern tribe, then used to refer to the northern area though the kingdom they established was called Liao. Since Polo came to China via the land route along the silkroad, he arrived at the Yuan China through Cathay, while Ricci came to China via the sea route and arrived at Macau as the first point of entry.

3 This is Beijing's old name in Turkish. Another spelling is Khanbaliq, where "baliq" means city and the whole word means "the city of Khan". In Chinese language, it was known as Dadu (大都) during the Yuan Dynasty when Marco Polo visited.

4 According to Wiest (2019), another Portuguese Jesuit, Friar Benedict Goes who travelled from India to Cathay in 1605, had found that Cathay and China were the same country.
5 Matteo Ripa, an Italian priest who spent over 10 years in China presented a copperplate set of Kangxi atlas to King George I on 9 September 1724 when he visited London on his way back from China. On this map, names of places were printed in Manchu north of the Great Wall and in Mandarin south of the Great Wall, indicating the origins of the Manchus and Han.
6 The Great Wall of China started to be built from as early as the seventh century BC, with selective stretches later joined together by the first emperor of China, Qin Shi Huang (220–206 BC). However, little of the Qin wall remains today, the most well-known sections that can be visited now are legacies from the Ming Dynasty.
7 Nanjing was also the founding capital of Ming from 1368–1421 before it was moved to Beijing.
8 There are altogether six known complete examples of the 1602 printing, being kept at: Vatican Apostolic Library Collection I; James Ford Bell Library at the University of Minnesota; Japan Kyoto University Collection; collection of Japan Miyagi Prefecture Library; Collection of the Library of the Japanese Cabinet; Paris, France (in private hands).
9 There are scholars such as Lee (2016) who argued that the map was not produced by Matteo Ricci but Ming cartographers.
10 The painting is now kept in the Jesuit Archives in Rome.
11 The original meaning of *Hua* (华) is gorgeous costume, representing the standard of civilisation, and *Huaxia* (华夏) is the name of a pre-historic tribe nation that is considered a common cultural ancestry of Chinese civilisation.
12 Apart from Ricci, a number of early accounts about China were written by Spanish and Portuguese, such as *A suma Oriental*, written by Thome Pires in Malacca who was the first envoy sent to China by Portugal; and *Letter from Portuguese Captive in Caton,* written by his colleague, Cristqvao Vieiro and Vasco Calvo when they were put in prison in Canton. S. Franciscus Xaverius, one of the founders of Jesuits, was the first man who reported the Chinese ideologies to the West. Another book of great significance was Alvare de Semedo's *Imperio de la China* published in 1638. This book used two chapters to introduce provinces in Southern China and Northern China separately. The book also recorded events like the Ming government purchased western artillery from Macau in 1621. Other influential books include Martin Martini's *Sinicae Historiak Decus Prima* and *De Bello Tartarico Histotia, Antverpiae.* The former verified to the Westerners that besides the civilisation of Christianity, there was Chinese civilisation with even longer history; while the latter was an eyewitness record of how the Ming Dynasty was conquered by Qing based on his own experience in China throughout the transition. It was considered the first book in the West on modern history of China. *An Account of the Empire of China, Historical, Political, Moral and Religions* written by the Spanish missionary Domingo Fernández Navarrete (1610–1689) and published in 1767, was another important magnum opus of Jesuits in China to introduce Chinese philosophy and religion to the West.
13 "People from the outer fringes of civilisation" (*Huawai ren*, 化外人) was a term first appeared in the *Legal Code of the Tang Dynasty* dated as early as 652.
14 It was also Matteo Ricci who first translated the standard Chinese language into "Mandarin" because through travelling his way to Beijing from Macau, he experienced different dialects spoken in different regions in this vast country, thus named the official language used in court by the official's name, Mandarin.

15 "Four Yi House" and "Four Translations House" are homophones in Chinese, "four" indicating the four directions means all over the world.

16 Rather than being jointly made by the two clockmakers, it was more likely to be joined by the workshop inside the Forbidden City after they were procured around 1780. The clock frame was autographed by British clockmaker Timothy Williamson, but the automation part was designed and manufactured by the renowned Swiss watchmaker, the Jaquet-Droz family.

17 Originally translated as "foreigners" in the *Sourcebook* (1981: 157) for both groups of *Lu* and *Yi.* I changed it into the "Northern barbarians (Lu)" here to clarify the meaning.

18 An English ship, *the London,* called at Macau two years before Weddell's visit, but it was under charter to the Portuguese. As Pritchard (1970: 54–55) indicated in his *Anglo-Chinese Relations during the Seventeenth and Eighteenth Centuries,* the first English ship at Canton was sent from India by the British EIC under a "Truce and Free Trade" with Portugal in 1635. However, due to the Portuguese' hostility towards the English, the merchants of this ship did not have successful dealings with Chinese merchants during her short stay in China. There was no record of this British ship in any Chinese writings either as the local Chinese had no idea at all that they were doing business with the British, instead of the frequently-seen Portuguese or Dutch.

19 Britain was still believed to be a vassal state of Holland as described in Fu Heng's *Huangqing Zhigong Tu* (*The August Qing's Illustrated Accounts of Tribute-bearing Domains,* 《皇清职贡图》) in 1751. In the *Hongmao Fan Yingjili Kaolue* (*A Study of the Red-haired Foreigners Called English*, 《红毛番英吉利考略》), compiled by Wang Wentai in 1843, it was partially corrected as a "former vassal state of Holland" (Wang, 1843: 1), and England later "invaded Holland" to refer to the change of power between the two countries. It also explained that the English looked similar to the Dutch in Chinese eyes who viewed both as redhaired barbarians. However, it stated that England never traded with China until the Kangxi's reign (ibid: 11), which also proved that they were not aware of the British expedition during the Ming Dynasty.

20 Dawson's description of Weddell had to "depart empty-handed" (1967: 30) is not very accurate according to other research findings as detailed later in this section. Besides, according to an entry in Historica Wiki regarding Weddell's adventure: "although he failed to trade in Canton in the Ming Empire due to Portuguese intrigues, he was, however, able to deliver 38,421 pairs of eyeglasses to the Chinese in June of 1637 in the first Chinese usage of glasses. That same year, he supplied firearms to Assassin Ma Jianguo, who was in need of his help in taking down the Templar Order-backed Manchus. Weddell gave him the recipes for crafting European firearms and bombs, before leaving for England in 1640." Available at: https://historica.fandom.com/wiki/John_Weddell

References

Basu, D.K. (2014) 'Chinese xenology and the Opium War: Reflections on sinocentrism', *The Journal of Asian Studies*, 73(4) (Nov.), pp. 927–940.

Brook, T. (1981) 'The merchant network in 16th century China: A discussion and translation of Zhang Han's 'On Merchants', *Journal of the Economic and Social History of the Orient*, 24(2) (May), pp. 165–214.

Chang, Y.Z. (1970) 'Why did Milton err on two Chinas?', *The Modern Language Review*, 65(3), (Jul.), pp. 493–498. Modern Humanities Research Association.

Chen, S.-C. (2017) *Merchants of War and Peace: British Knowledge of China in the Making of the Opium War*. Hong Kong: Hong Kong University Press.

Coates, A. (1966) *Macau and the British, 1637–1842: Prelude to Hong Kong*. Hong Kong: Hong Kong University Press.

Dawson, R. (1967) *The Chinese Chameleon: An Analysis of European Conceptions of Chinese Civilisation*. Oxford: Oxford University Press.

D'elia, P.M. (1961) 'Recent discoveries and new studies (1938–1960) on the World Map in Chinese of Father Matteo Ricci SJ', *Monumenta Serica*, 20, pp. 82–164.

Eames, J. B. (1909) *The English in China, 1600–1843: Being an Account of the Intercourse and Relations Between England and China from the Year 1600 to the Year 1843 and a Summary of Later Developments*. London: Sir I. Pitman and Sons. Available at: https://onlinebooks.library.upenn.edu/webbin/book/lookupid?key=ha001257802

Ebrey, P.B. (ed.) (1981) *Chinese Civilisation and Society, A Sourcebook*. New York: The Free Press.

Elisseeff, V. (1963) 'The middle empire, a distant empire, an empire without neighbours', *Diogenes*, 42, pp. 60–64.

Fairbank, J.K. (1942) 'Tributary trade and China's relations with the West', *Far Eastern Quarterly*, 1(2), pp. 129–149.

Fairbank, J.K. (ed.) (1968) *The Chinese World Order, Traditional China's Foreign Relations*. Cambridge, MA: Harvard University Press.

Gallagher, L.J. (1953) Translated from the Latin, *N. Trigault and M. Ricci, China in the Sixteenth Century: The Journals of Matthew Ricci: 1583–1610* [The compilation by N. Trigault]. New York: Random House.

Giles, L. (1918) 'Translations from the Chinese world map of Father Ricci'. *The Geographical Journal*, 52(6), pp. 367–385. Available at: https://zenodo.org/record/2054791#.YMui-ehKjZs

Gong, Y. (1998)《鸦片战争前中国对英国的认识》[*Chinese People's Knowledge about Britain before the Opium War*] in Huang, S. (ed.) *Dongxi Jiaoliu Luntan (Forum of East-West Exchange)*. Shanghai: Shanghai Wenyi Publishing House.

Gottschall, B., Hannafey, F.T., Koo, S.G.M. and Criveller, G. (eds.) (2019) *Matteo Ricci: Letters from China* (A Revised English Translation with Commentary). Beijing: The Beijing Centre Press.

Guillen-Nuñez, C. (2014) 'The portrait of Matteo Ricci, a mirror of Western religious and Chinese literati portrait painting', *Journal of Jesuit Studies*, 1(3), pp. 443–464.

Hevia, J. (1995) *Cherishing Men from Afar, Qing Guest Ritual and the Macartney Embassy of 1793*. Durham and London: Duke University Press.

Jiang, T. (1996)《中国近代史大纲》[*Outline of Modern Chinese History*]. Beijing: Dongfang Chubanshe.

Kang, J.-E. (2006) *The Land of Scholars: Two Thousand Years of Korean Confucianism*. New Jersey: Homa & Sekey Books.

Kircher, A. (1667). *China Illustrata*. Translated by Dr. Charles D. Van Tuyl 1986. Available at: https://htext.stanford.edu/content/kircher/china/kircher.pdf

Lee, S.L. (2016) 'Kunyu Wanguo Quantu, a Chinese World Map, not authored by Matteo Ricci and European cartographer', *Science of Surveying and Mapping*, 41(7), July, pp. 59–66.

Levenson, J.R. (1968) *Confucian China and its Modern Fate: A Trilogy*. Berkeley and Los Angeles: University of California Press.

Liu, L.H. (2006) *The Clash of Empires, the Invention of China in Modern World Making*. Cambridge, MA and London, England: Harvard University Press.

Mancall, M. (1970) 'The Ching Tributary System: An interpretive essay', in Fairbank, J. (ed.) *The Chinese World Order*. Cambridge, MA: Harvard University Press.

Morse, H.B. (1910) *International Relations of the Chinese Empire: The Period of Conflict, 1834–1860*. Longmans, Green and Co.

Mundy, P. (1919) *The Travels of Peter Mundy in Europe and Asia, 1608–1667*. Temple, R.C. (ed.). London: Printed for the Hakluyt Society.

Mungello, D.E. (1985) *Curious Land, Jesuit Accommodation and the Origins of Sinology*. Honolulu: University of Hawaii Press.

Needham, J. (1954–present) *Science and Civilisation in China*, 7 vols. Cambridge: Cambridge University Press.

Perdue, P. (2015) 'The tenacious Tributary System', *Journal of Contemporary China*, 24(6), pp. 1002–1014.

Perkins, D. (1999) *Encyclopaedia of China, The Essential Reference to China, Its History and Culture*. New York, NY: Checkmark Books.

Pritchard, E.H. (1970) *Anglo-Chinese Relations during the Seventeenth and Eighteenth Centuries*. New York: Octagon.

Stevenson, C.M. (2021) *Britain's Second Embassy to China, Lord Amherst's Special Mission to the Jiaqing Emperor in 1816*. Acton: Australian National University Press.

Tsiang, T.-F. (1936) 'China and European expansion', *Politica*, 2, pp. 1–18.

Wan, M. (2011)《明代中外关系史论稿》[*China's Foreign Relations in the Ming Dynasty*]. Beijing: China Social Sciences Press.

Wang, W. (1843)《红毛番英吉利考略》[*A Study of the Red-haired Foreigners Called English*] printed in Beijing by Huang Pengnian, editor of the Imperial Academy.

Westad, O.A. (2013) *Restless Empire, China and the World since 1759*. London: Vintage Books.

Wiest, J.-P. (2019) 'Matteo Ricci: Pioneer of Chinese-Western dialogues and cultural exchange', in *Matteo Ricci: Letters from China* (A Revised English Translation with Commentary). Beijing: The Beijing Centre Press.

Wills, J.E. Jr. (1984) *Embassies and Illusions: Dutch and Portuguese Envoys to Kang-his, 1666–1687*. Cambridge, MA: Harvard University Press.

Xia, X. (1865)《中西紀事》[*Event Notes of China's Diplomacy*]. Available at: https://ctext.org/library.pl?if=gb&res=1891&remap=gb

Zhang, H. (1593)《松窗梦语》[*Dream Essays at the Pine Window*]. Available at: https://ctext.org/wiki.pl?if=gb&res=640532&remap=gb

3 The earliest Chinese travellers to the Far West

> The Chinese and we are pretty much alike. Different degrees of refinement, and not of distance, mark the distinctions among mankind.
>
> – Goldsmith, 1762

By the seventeenth to the eighteenth centuries, the English interest in China had grown into a fascination that flourished with the inflow of more abundant travellers' accounts and Chinese imports. Porter (2010: 21) argued that the resulting dissemination of knowledge about a distant culture "stamped the European imagination with the indelible, and, I think, deeply transformative awareness that there existed, on the far end of the globe, a highly advanced civilisation with a rich and unbroken cultural heritage of over four thousand years". However, it was not matched by a similar level of curiosity towards Europe on that far end of the globe. Chinese travellers to the Far West during these two centuries were very rare, the most widely cited reason was because travelling abroad was banned by Chinese law, but there were also two other key factors as strong internal constraints. One was the Confucian's teaching about "one ought not to travel far (even within his own country) while his parents are alive". In ancient China, to attend one's parents with filial piety was considered the number one virtue to be held above everything else. For this reason, banishment to the frontier was a major penalty. The second reason was due to the sense of cultural superiority; there was a lack of inner drive among China's educated class to undertake the risky and treacherous journey to explore foreign cultures and ideas. These two reasons are often overlooked, but perhaps more important, as there would always be breakaways from law if there were strong inner urges, like the smuggling of tea and opium; but when it goes with social conventions and people's mindsets, it helps explain the rareness of Chinese travellers and the restrictive laws explains why these few Chinese visitors left little to none records in China despite making history by being the first in their own ways, and interacting with some eminent figures in the Great Britain who also made history in their own ways. However, the

DOI: 10.4324/9781003156383-4

rareness did transform their encounters into cross-cultural advocacy, and magnified the impact each visitor had produced and the legacies they left behind.

This chapter narrates the four earliest Chinese travellers to the British Empire, analysing the important roles they played as the first-generation cultural ambassadors, though none of them were sent by the Qing court. It examines how their encounters with the British society contributed to the production and dissemination of knowledge about China. Their stories remain little known in China today largely because of the common belief that imperial China was essentially closed off from the Western world. Therefore, it is all the more important to trace their cultural footprints that had helped create a precious Yin-Yang flow between China and the West that only existed in this period of time, which will be shown in this chapter by pairing each visitor with the Britons they interacted with.

Before I start with their stories, I wish to emphasise that they are the first known travellers with names in written records in Britain and even with portraits in existence, while the very first Chinese person travelled to the British Isles could well be dated back to between the second and fourth centuries AD according to the archaeology discovery made in September 2016. Rebecca Redfern, curator of human osteology at the Museum of London, said the two skeletons, which were found close to the south end of London Bridge during excavations of a Roman cemetery, clearly showed ties between Britain and Asia stretch much farther back than people had previously imagined. Of course, they can only be identified as people with Asian ancestry and "possibly being of Chinese origin".[1] There were also Chinese sailors who came to England when the British-run Taiwan Factory from 1670–1685 was allowed to replace dying sailors with natives, meaning that there must have been more interactions between the two empires of the time than what was recorded.

3.1 Shen Fuzong and Thomas Hyde: The first exchanges of a learned nature

Michael Shen Fuzong (沈福宗) was brought to Europe as a Chinese convert to Catholicism by the Belgian Jesuit Philippe Couplet (known as Bai Yingli in China, 柏应理), when he returned to Europe in 1682 after spending 25 years in the Qing China. Couplet was also a noted scholar of Confucian philosophy, often known as the translator of *Chinese Philosopher Confucius* (*Confucius Sinarum Pholosophus*), although it was a collective work and a cumulative effort dating from the time of Matteo Ricci and even Michele Ruggieri who arrived before him in 1579.[2] This magnum opus represented a culmination of the public dissemination of Jesuit scholarship in China in the seventeenth century. Following its first publication in Paris in 1687, its translation into English in 1691 pushed the English discussions of China and anything Chinese to a new height.

It was against this background that we can well imagine how the rare presence of a Chinese person became an "exotic" attraction and captivated the attention of Europeans. Shen was well-regarded by foreign monarchs and scholars throughout his time in Europe (1682–1691). For example, according to Foss (1990), Shen appeared before Louis XIV in a green silk tunic and a deep blue brocade vest with figures of Chinese dragons, performed the reverential kowtow bows and even taught him how to use chopsticks. He also showed him how calligraphy works was produced with ink and brush by giving him a demonstration, using the set of "four treasures of the study" (brush, ink, inkstone and paper) he brought along. The French King was so impressed with Shen and Couplet and the gifts they brought him that he had all the fountains at Versailles switched on, an honour usually reserved for royal visitors and ambassadors. The King also agreed to sponsor a French Jesuit mission of scientists and mathematicians to set off for China under the auspices of the Academie. Shen also caused a sensation in Rome in 1685. He was received by the Father General of the Society of Jesus, prominent Roman aristocrat families, and met Queen Christina of Sweden, who was particularly curious about Chinese tea-drinking habits (Melo, 2018). Pope Innocent XI was deeply impressed by Shen and the Chinese library that Couplet gifted, which is still kept at the Bibliotheca Apostolica Vaticana today.

As in Paris and Rome, Shen became a celebrity when he arrived in London in March 1685, a time when fascination with Chinese culture and scholarship was well fostered in England. The Bodleian Library at Oxford already accumulated 70 printed Chinese books by 1674, with 1604 marking its first datable accession. An original 1667 copy of Athanasius Kircher's *China Illustrata* was gifted to the Library by the aristocratic natural philosopher and chemist Robert Boyle. When the English version came out in 1669, it stimulated greater interest in China and inspired more English Sinophiles. For example, John Webbs' work *An Historical Essay Endeavouring a Probability that the Language of the Empire of China is the Primitive Language* (1669) argued rather fanatically that China had preserved the most primitive form of language since the biblical deluge. He also proposed the Chinese system of meritocracy as a model for the British to change its aristocracy system. Issac Vossius, a fellow of the fledgling Royal Society in London, published a Latin essay in 1685, arguing that all the arts and sciences were Chinese in origin, and that Chinese culture was the greatest and the oldest the world had ever known. Another member of the Royal Society, Robert Hooke, not only lectured on the Chinese abacus in 1685 but also built one by himself and a module of a wheelbarrow, even experimenting with Chinese moxibustion and acupuncture (Poole, 2010).

All these meant Shen visited England at a propitious time, it was into this period of Oriental curiosity that he was granted an audience with

King James II shortly after his arrival in 1687. The King was so fascinated by him that he instructed Sir Godfrey Kneller to paint Shen's life-size portrait. It subsequently hung in the king's drawing room next to the bed chamber. The painting (see Figure 3.1), named the *Chinese Convert*, has long been recognised as a key image in the growing fascination with China in the West. It is currently on display in Windsor Castle.

Apart from this impressive portrait that Kneller considered one of his best works, more significant and lasting legacies left by Shen were the

Figure 3.1 Michael Alphonsus Shen Fuzong by Sir Godfrey Kneller, 1687. Oil on canvas, 212 × 147 cm. Courtesy of the Royal Collection Trust.

Chinese books he helped catalogue and the letters exchanged between him and Thomas Hyde, the foremost Orientalist in the country at the time, working as Bodleian's librarian. After hearing Shen's arrival in London, Hyde invited him to Oxford where he spent the summer of 1687 and helped catalogue and annotate the Library's collection of Chinese materials, including the late Ming Selden Map of China. With his knowledge of both classical Chinese and Latin, Shen was able to offer translations by scribing on their title pages or fly-leaves in three vertical lines of a Chinese description of the book, a romanisation, and then a Latin gloss on the title. These can still be seen today, carefully preserved in the new facility of the Oxford Weston Library. Shen also showed Hyde the correct way to hold a Chinese book, so that the titles and contents of the mysterious Chinese works were made accessible to a British scholar for the first time. Melo's account (2018) recorded the King's visit following Shen's work at Oxford on 5 September 1687. The University offered a banquet in honour of him, but the king seemed to have been less impressed by the pantagruelian menu of 111 hot and cold dishes than the Bodleian catalogue. He asked if the library had a book translated by a Jesuit, referring to the *Confucius Sinarum Philosophus*, perhaps motivated by his recent encounter with Shen.

After cataloguing the Bodleian Chinese books, Hyde developed his interest in China. Shen helped him with various projects relating to Chinese weights and measurement and calendrical practices and discussed a wide range of subjects of mutual interests. For example, in one of the earliest letters from Shen to Hyde, written in May 1687 before they had met, Shen explained the two characters of 车 (*ju*, currus) and 马 (*ma*, equus) to answer Hyde's question about the names of chess pieces. Hyde referred to Shen in several of his subsequent oriental works, including *De ludis orientalibus libri duo* (1694). In one of the chapters, *De Shahiludio Chinensium*, he described various Chinese games including Coan ki (樽棋), and also gave the first full Latin description of *Weiqi* (围棋). During Shen's visit in Oxford, they played the game together. Hyde also became the first Englishman to receive lessons in both written and spoken Chinese. The notes used by Shen in these lessons show a range of topics covered from talking about food and drink, to expressions for the new year and new moon, as well as the twelve animals as zodiac signs. Figure 3.2 is one of such sheets on which were written the words for morning, midday and evening meals, as well as snacks, feast and wine. There was also a box of loose working papers on which Shen drew characters and added Romanised vocalisation, with Hyde annotating character meanings in Latin. This "treasure box" is now kept in the Sloane MSS at the British Museum.

Shen's time in Oxford was considered to be a seminal moment for setting the foundations for what would later become the academic discipline of Sinology. The letters exchanged between him and Hyde in Latin as the common language, six in existence that are now kept in the British

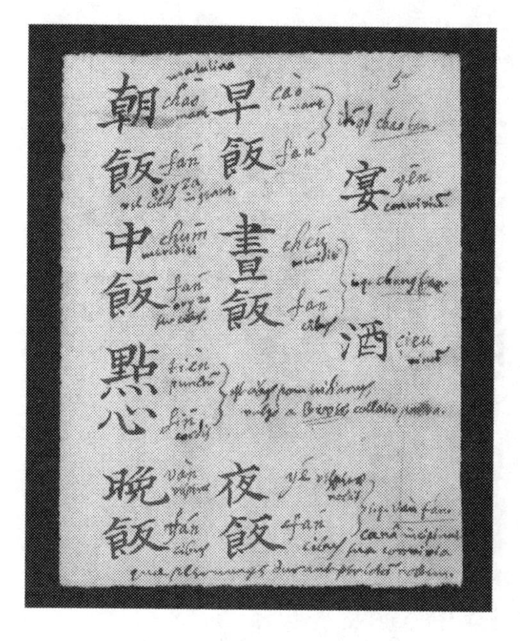

Figure 3.2 A scrap of paper used by Shen to teach Hyde Chinese, Sloane MS 853a f005r. Courtesy of the British Library.

Library, were the earliest surviving examples of correspondence of a learned nature in the Anglo-Chinese context. They represent effective communications of a Chinese person with an English scholar, whose sustained fascination with China flowed through these exchanges and shaped the collection at the Bodleian. As a testimony to Shen's influence, when Hyde resigned as Bodley's librarian in 1701, he decided that in his official portrait he should be depicted holding a scroll with Chinese characters (see Figure 3.3).

When Shen left Oxford, Hyde wrote him a reference letter to Boyle:

> SIR, THE bearer hereof, the Chinese, hath been with us at Oxford, to make a Catalogue of our Chinese books, and to inform us about the subjects of them. We have some of Confucius's books; but most of what we have is physick [...] His Latin is a little imperfect; but it is well he hath any Latin; for before him there was never but one (who is dead) that understood any Latin. [...] You may make a shift to understand him, though he speaks but imperfectly.
>
> (cited in Poole, 2010: 8)

Though this letter showed that Shen was not the first Chinese person to reach Oxford, none of those before him left any names, let alone any

Figure 3.3 Thomas Hyde's portrait. Courtesy of the Bodleian Library.

records of interactions with the local society. Shen became the first recorded Chinese visitor described by Hyde in another letter to Thomas Bowrey as "a Scholar in all the Learning of their country, read all their books readily, and was of great honesty and sincerity, and fit to be relied upon in everything; for indeed he was very knowing and Excellent man, very Studious and Laborious in all things" (cited in Poole, 2021: 6). In 2018, an exhibition about Shen Fuzong was hosted in the St Hugh's College by the Oxford China Centre. According to the exhibition's publicity material: "During the six weeks Shen spent in Oxford with Thomas Hyde, Bodley's Librarian, they inspected together the Library's collection of more than seventy Chinese books, purchased as curiosities over the previous 100 years, which were now with his help being read and understood for the first time".[3] Then in October 2019, a plaque in honour of Shen Fuzong was unveiled at Oxford, with inscriptions describing his contributions as being the "first Chinese scholar to visit Oxford. Collaborated with the Bodleian Librarian and Thomas Hyde, and created the library's first catalogue of its Chinese-language material". As Poole put it (2010), the intellectual collaboration between Hyde and Shen offers a rare glimpse of one of the most remarkable cross-cultural encounters of the entire early-modern period.

Shen stayed for over a year in Britain, allowing his contributions to continue after finishing his work in Oxford. Shen returned to London where he had regular contacts with Robert Hooke, whose mind ranged over a vast field apart from being one of the greatest experimental physicists in history. They met multiple times between London and Oxford and engaged in long conversations with topics from Chinese language, literature, history, philosophy to science. These personal contacts with a native Chinese who possessed practical knowledge and could decipher Chinese-language materials informed Hooke's writing of "Some observations and conjectures concerning the characters and language of the Chinese" published in January 1687, which contributed to a longstanding debate over the philosophical and historical significance of the Chinese language. The paper also described the advanced Chinese method of printing that "one man alone will print off 1500 sheets in one day" along with "other arts of pottery, staining and furnishing", and a detailed description of Chinese abacus in comparison with the Roman abacus (Hooke, 1687: 66).

Although no direct acknowledgement was made to Shen in this paper, Hooke (1687: 68) did mention that "upon perusing all the accounts I could meet with in books, I found very little satisfaction as to what I principally *inquired* after which was first concerning the method of the Character, whether it consisted of a certain number of marks methodically …… and secondly concerning the number of these Characters? To which I found as little satisfaction, for, by some relations, I found that there were 120000, by others 80000 and by others 60000". This indeed was a question that is hard to provide a very definitive answer as it depends on the level of learning, but 120,000 is definitely an exaggeration.[4] From the annex to the book (see Figure 3.4), we can almost be sure that Hooke had made the inquiry to Shen, based on the following three points.

Firstly, The Chinese characters on the right side included numbers from one to ten thousand, and some basic vocabulary such as year, month, day, person, big, heaven, etc. The actual example of a date given read "13 May 1686", written all in Chinese characters – this happens to be the time when Shen was in London and frequented the learned society.

Secondly and probably the biggest clue comes from the three characters included in the last line as examples of more compound characters: 汤若望 (Tang Ruo Wang), which is actually the Chinese name for Joahann Adam Schall von Bell, a German Jesuit and astronomer who spent most of his life as a missionary in China from 1619 to 1666. He came to Beijing in 1630 and became the first Jesuit to take on official duties as *Qintianjian* (钦天监), the Director of the Imperial Observatory and the Tribunal of

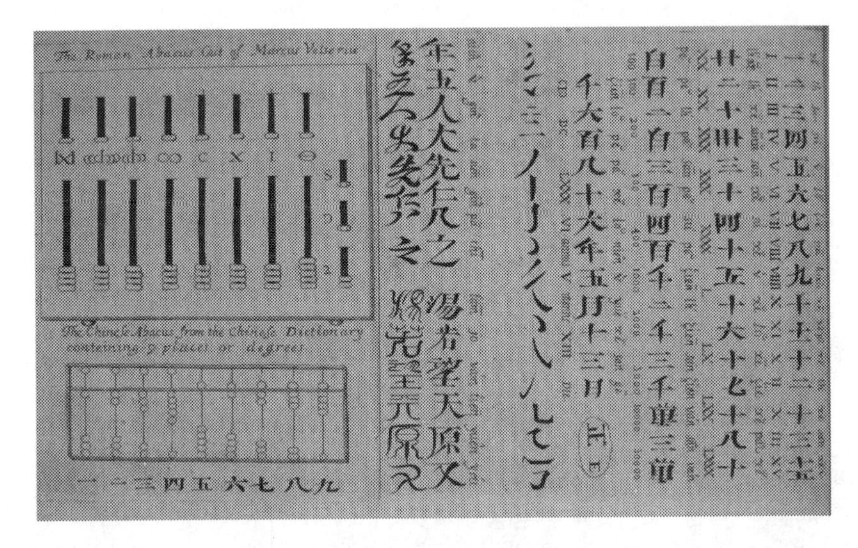

Figure 3.4 Some observations and conjectures concerning the characters and language of the Chinese by Robert Hooke (1687). Courtesy of the Royal Society.

Mathematics (the section of the Chinese bureaucracy charged with preparation of the state calendar and keeping an official record of celestial events). Philippe Couplet came to China in 1656 and met with him in Beijing in 1660. We can well imagine, the only reason 汤若望 was included in this very brief character list was the multiple contexts in Hooke's conversation with Shen: Chinese language and characters, its numeration and calendar system, which was modified by Joahann Adam Schall von Bell to provide more accurate predictions of eclipses of the sun and the moon.

Thirdly, Hooke (1687: 71) mentioned the vertical way of Chinese writing. Obviously, this cannot be self-explained by a mere "observation" of a Chinese book. It was recorded as demonstrating to Hyde by Shen the right way of holding a Chinese book. Curiously, this could possibly be another reason for Hooke's dissatisfaction with the answer he received as he seemed to strongly believe that this was "not the primitive and first way of writing or reading" as "it must be very inconvenient for writing". This statement was repeatedly made in this paper – from "I conceive" on page 67 to "I suppose" on page 71, to further elaborations on page 75:

> For the way of writing and reading it, I conceive might it first be exactly the same with that of the Greece, Romans, English, and all other European Nations. That is, they began at the top of the page towards the left hand, and so proceeded towards the right in the *Horizontal* line to the end of it, and then began at the left end of

> the next line under the first and proceeded with that in the same manner ……. It came to make the *present* form of their book, which being laid as we generally place our books before us, they seem to begin at the top of the page on the right-hand, and to proceed to the bottom, and then at the top of the next line towards the left hand, and descend as in the former; proceeding in this order with all the rest, which way must be very inconvenient for writing, however they may use their pencil differing from our pen.

The last part gave his reason but also revealed his ignorance: the Chinese writing was done with brushes at the time, and it had always been written vertically since the earliest writing on oracle bones, though both ways were acceptable at that time. By the bronze time, it had been written from right to left because of the materials it is inscribed on – bamboo slips and ancient bronze objects before paper was invented. Unlike the variant length of spelling of the European languages, each Chinese character, in disregard of the number of strokes, can fit into the same size of writing space. It was only changed to the Western horizontal way of writing in the 1950s. This may serve as an example of what Mugello named "proto-sinologists", characterised by "curious" investigation and inadequate knowledge of China.

Shen's last letter to Hyde provided a best example highlighting the "academic exchange" nature between China and England, in which he asked politely for a return of favour: some mathematical instruments or telescopes for him to carry back to China: "If however you would be pleased to send curious glasses such as microscopes or optic tubes, and the like, things most pleasing to the Chinese and to me, they would be an eternal monument to your benevolence. Farewell to you, mindful of me, most learned master: of whom shall I too always live mindful, even in China" (cited in Poole, 2010: n.p.). Unfortunately, Shen never made it back to China. He left London for Lisbon in April 1688 amid the political turmoil that led to the overthrow of James II. In 1691, Shen departed for China, but he died of an epidemic during the journey on September 2, 1691, two days before reaching Mozambique. We can only imagine what an "eternal monument" this could have been if those instruments representing modern Western technology could be brought back to China by someone who experienced Europe during the Age of Enlightenment.

The interactions between Shen and the learned class during his time in England was a fascinating chapter in the history of scientific, cultural and philosophical encounters between the two empires. The enduring friendship based on equality in partnership served as a model of fruitful collaborations between European and Chinese civilisations. I would argue it represents a precious Yin-Yang equilibrium between China and the West that only existed in this period of time. By Yin and Yang, I mean they are not a mutually exclusive dichotomy but a benign cultural relativism that allows Self and Other to enrich each other in their encounters and interactions. One is never meant to override the other, let alone replace it. More importantly, the centre is exactly where Yin and Yang meet each other. In other words, when China-centric civilisation meets Euro-centric civilisation, they create a centreless fusion in this Yin-Yang nexus. Another important feature of this duality that is distinguished from the Us-Other polarity is that they are opposite yet equal to each other, inspiring and complementing each other while containing a dot of each other and must depend on each other to form an organic whole. The beauty of their interaction is that each side remains as Yin and Yang, which never tries to convert or homogenise the other. Being centreless and symbiotic is what creates an organic and harmonious whole rather than division. Imagine drinking Chinese tea in a Wedgewood chinaware made in England, or strolling through an English garden with a Chinese pagoda built by the British – the stories in the next sections would help demonstrate how a Yin-Yang harmony is reached.

3.2 Loum Kiqua and William Hickey: The first taste of Chinese music and Chinese food

In 1757, Canton was made the only trading port between China and the West until the end of the Opium War in 1842, thus becoming a prime site where most of the direct contacts between the two empires took place. It was not only a place of global trade and exchange, but also a site of cross-cultural encounter and knowledge production. Meanwhile in Britain, Samuel Johnson made the famous remark in 1777 that "When a man is tired of London, he is tired of life; for there is in London all that life can afford". The stories in this section are about a Cantonese man in England and a Londoner in Canton, who never met each other, yet they both travelled on EIC ships, reaching the other's hometown at a similar period of time, and giving the British their first taste of Chinese food and music.

It was in the same year of 1757 that a musical notation under the heading of "A Chinese Air" was published in the prominent British journal, the *Gentlemen's Magazine*. This was not a purely textual exercise of transcribing a piece of music that had been previously written in Chinese notation but by ear from an actual performance given by a Chinese person in London. According to the transcriber and the author of a brief accompanying note, the music was played by a "Chinese merchant lately arrived in this city from Canton". The author "accidentally fell in company with the Chinese visitor a few days ago" (Clarke, 2017: 547), and since the note was dated 16 December 1756, we can conjecture the meeting and the performance transcribed might date to the second week of December 1756. Not much information was given in the Magazine about the performer, except that "he understands very little of our language", thus "to make up the want of conversation, he played several Chinese tunes upon a musical instrument something resembling a guitar" (ibid: 547). However, given the rarity of Chinese visitors to London during the time, Clarke (2017) made a reasonable inference that he was the same person as in the portrait (see Figure 3.5) now being kept at the British Museum.

Figure 3.5 Portrait of Loum Kiqua (Lin Qi Guan). Courtesy of the British Museum. This was an engraving by Thomas Burford (c. 1710–1776) after the original painting by Dominic Serres (c. 1719–1793), which has been lost.

This portrait shows a man in full Chinese gown and hat, with a long-stemmed smoking pipe in his left hand, and a lighter in his right, standing in front of an open view to a landscape that includes a pagoda, and the junks sailing along its rivers signifying the lucrative trade that Canton is known for. The Latin inscription of the print stated some important information, including that the original painted portrait was made from life, and the man's name was Loum Kiqua, with perfectly legible Chinese characters showing 林奇 (Lin Qi) followed by 官 (Guan, literally means official), an honorific title commonly appended to names of prominent Chinese, similar to the use of "Esquire" in English. This was an important clue as *Guan* was used to address merchants who work for the Thirteen Factories[5] or Hongs in Canton, considered as representing the Qing court in the eyes of foreign merchants. The inscription also claimed the year of his arrival in London in 1756 from Lisbon after escaped with life from the earthquake, and noted the "honour" he received in London, distinguishing Britain from its Portuguese trade rivals as a nation with more decency:

> After many hardships & ill treatments from the Portuguese, he [Loum] came over to England, where he met with different usage, having had the Honour to be seen by his Majesty, and the rest of the Royal-Family: most of the Nobility &c. by whom he was much caress'd, [and] having made application to the Honble. the East India Company for his passage home, he was kindly received and generously accomodated [sic] on Board one of their Ships to carry him to Canton.

This information pieced together a highly probable identification of Loum Kiqua as a "Chinese merchant", and the coincidental year of his arrival with the music performance captured in *the Gentleman's Magazine* gave Clark his purported assumption that they are the same person. Williams (2014:5) simply presented it as a fact that "Loum also gave the first public performance in Europe of a "Chinese air", published in musical notation in *The Gentleman's Magazine*". In disregard of how likely it was Loum Kiqua who performed those Chinese tunes, what we can be certain was that Chinese music was performed in London at least as early as 1756. The first British performance in China happened much later in 1793 during the Macartney Embassy to China, which brought along a German band "to ensure the embassy was conducted in an appropriately impressive style" (Hibbert, 1970: 7). The band gave a concert at Yuanming Yuan every morning. "Indeed, so struck was the mandarin in charge of the Emperor's orchestra with both the music and the instruments that, having attended every concert, he asked permission to send some artists to make exact drawings of the clarinets, bassoons, French horns and flutes, so that he could have similar instruments manufactured in China" (Cranmer-Byng, 1962: 104). It was a pity that there was not much comment on the Chinese music style in the Magazine. As mentioned in Chapter 2, music was one of the few aspects of China that Ricci considered inferior to the West. During the Amherst Embassy to China in 1816, Ellis had commented on his distaste of Chinese instrumental music: "from its resemblance to the bag-pipes might have been tolerated by Scotchmen, to others it was detestable" (Hibbert, 1970: 66).

Loum's visit offered London's elites a more personal form of encounter with China than the exotic images on the sides of their Chinoiserie vases. A striking difference between Loum Kiqua and Shen Fuzong is that he came as an individual traveller with no Jesuit companion and no communicative language ability. However, he was still received as the representative of a sophisticated empire, granted audiences with the king and aristocrats, and had a portrait made by an established artist. This may be another example showing that anything associated with the remote civilisation of China was considered culturally significant. The cultural impact he produced can be traced in a number of British publications on China over the following decade, including Oliver Goldsmith's widely read work *The Citizen of the World* (1760–1761), which was inspired by Loum's visit according to Williams (2014: 5). Indeed, the protagonist's name was Lien Chi (the Mandarin pronunciation of Loum Kiqua). It was written in the form of letters exchanged between him as a Mandarin from Canton, a visitor to London and an Oriental observer to the English society, and his mentor Fum Hoam, the first President of the Ceremonial Academy at Beijing. Goldsmith used the conceit of a Chinese traveller in England to develop the idea of a shared standard of civility connecting the two empires. As set out in the Preface: "the truth is, the Chinese and we are pretty much alike. Different degrees of refinement, and not of distance, mark the distinctions among mankind" (Goldsmith, 1762: iv–v). In presenting England "as a geographical convergence with the standards of imperial China" (Williams, 2014: 5), "rather than imaginatively dividing the world into opposing cultural and geographical poles of East and West" (Ballaster, 2005: 14), it expounded the idea that these two geographically distant but equally "polite" empires might share common standards of civility. This echoed Kant's argument that the parallel development of different cultures will lead not just to improved communication between nations but to a perfect civil union of the human species through converging standards of politeness. Most notably and still highly relevant today was what Lien Chi called for "connecting" the two empires was not by expanded trade, but through broader cultural and scientific exchanges.

A few years later in 1769, the cultural sophistication of the Canton trading world where Loum Kiqua came from and returned to, was described by a British lawyer and adventurer William Hickey (1749–1830), who was initially expected to join the EIC army as an officer cadet when he arrived in India, but he was put off by the unimpressive payment level.

He got back on board an East Indiaman on his return journey to England, but the ship travelled on first to China. Hickey gave an extraordinarily vivid account of life in Canton at that time with insightful reflections and comparisons with London in the *Voyage to China* as part of his famous *Memoirs of William* (Hickey, 1913, vol. 1: 199):

> The view of the city as you approach it is strikingly grand, and at the same time picturesque. The magnitude and novelty of the architecture must always surprise strangers. The scene upon the water is as busy a one as the Thames below London Bridge, with this difference, that instead of our square rigged vessels of different dimensions, you there have junks, which, in the middle of the fair weather season they navigate all along the coast of China, and even to the Straits of Malacca, yet never go out of sight of land, and for this plain reason they are wholly ignorant of navigation and all its advantages. A junk is so constructed that one would be led to suppose inventor's principal object had been to deter mankind from venturing upon salt water.

Hickey also described the social strata of foreigners in China at that time (ibid: 202): "they stood in the following order: First, the Dutch, then, the French, the English, the Swedes, and last the Danes. …. the English being far more numerous than any other nation trading with China, their range of buildings is much the most extensive". However, due to the strict restrictions of the Canton System,[6] foreign merchants were only allowed to trade for a fixed period of time and "no Europeans were ever allowed to pass the gates of the city" (ibid: 209), therefore, despite the largest presence of British supercargoes (12 in total) and the use of "residents" to describe them, in a strict sense, no British had resided in China on a long-term basis before the Macartney Embassy, as there was no English missionaries in the country until much later.

A particularly fascinating part in Hickey's Memoir was the descriptions he gave about the Hong merchants' life, especially of Pankeequa (Pan Qi Guan, 潘啟官, 1714–1788), once the richest among the Hong merchants. His Chinese name is Pan Zhencheng (潘振承),[7] and the character *Guan* was a honorific title in Chinese as explained before. When Lord Macartney visited in 1793, it was recorded in his report to the EIC and his own Journal that he also engaged with Pan Qiguan as one of the "principal Hong merchants" (Cranmer-Byng, 1962: 207), but this was actually the second generation, the son of Pan Zhencheng who inherited his position and title after Pan Zhengcheng died in 1788. Pan's firm, Tongwen Hang, beginning trading in the 1730s, thrived for 100 years until the 1830s when the Canton System eventually declined. According to Sun (2013: 42), Pan was the first one who accepted money order from London as means of payment when silvery was the currency at the time.

He proposed the re-establishment of the Cohong and was appointed the first Chief of the Thirteen Factories by the Qing Court in 1760. This position played the intermediator role between foreign traders and the Qing Court as the strategy was to "use official to check merchants and use merchants to check foreigners". This meant the only Chinese person foreign merchants could come into contact with at the time were those from the Thirteen Factories. Pan was able to communicate with the foreign traders in basic Spanish, Portuguese and English, and Hickey was lucky enough to be invited to a sumptuous two-day banquet during his short stay in Canton. The performance after dinner in the appropriate cultural style for this cross-cultural audience was the most amazing thing. Clarke (2017: 503) commented that "clearly this pair of evenings was a self-conscious performance of cross-cultural knowledge on the host's part, displaying his understanding of Western culture in order to enhance his personal prestige and thus consolidate his position as one of the leading merchants in the city's international trade". Therefore, Hickey's detailed description of this culturally enriched gala banquet is worth quoting in full:

> These fetes were given on the 1st and 2nd of October, the first of them being a dinner, dressed and served a la mode Anglaise, the Chinamen on that occasion using, and awkwardly enough, knives and forks, and in every respect conforming to the European fashion. The best wines of all sorts were amply supplied. In the evening a play was performed, the subject warlike, where most capital fighting was exhibited, with better dancing and music than I could have expected. In one of the scenes an English naval officer, in full uniform and fierce cocked hat, was introduced, who strutted across the stage, saying "Maskee can do! God damn!" whereon a loud and universal laugh ensued, the Chinese quite in an ecstasy, crying out "Truly have muchee like Englishman".
>
> The second day, on the contrary, everything was Chinese, all the European guests eating, or endeavouring to eat, with chopsticks, no knives or forks being at table. The entertainment was splendid, the victuals supremely good, the Chinese loving high dishes and keeping the best of cooks. At night brilliant fireworks (in which they also excel) were let off in a garden magnificently lighted by coloured lamps, which we viewed from a temporary building erected for the occasion and where in there was exhibited sleight of hand tricks, tight and slack rope dancing, followed by one of the cleverest pantomimes I ever saw. This continued until a late hour, when we returned in company with several of the supercargoes to our factory, much gratified with the liberality and taste displayed by our Chinese host.
>
> (Hickey, 1913, vol. 1: pp. 223–224)

Another interesting Chinese character Hickey described in his *Memoirs* (1913: 227–228) was his visit to a portrait modeler's studio in Canton in 1769: "there was a China man who took excellent likeness in clay, which he afterward coloured, and they were altogether well executed". Hickey also mentioned that he himself even "sat and had good likeness taken". This Chinese portrait modeler known as Tan-Che-Qua travelled to London on another East Indianman in the same year of 1769 and stayed until around 1772. Like Shen Fuzong and Loum Kiqua, he also met various important figures of the age, including King George III, Prince Augusta, William Chambers, Josiah Wedgewood and his business partner Thomas Bentley. But much more important than being a social celebrity was his respected status as an artist, who not only became the first Chinese artist whose work was shown in a public art exhibition in the West, but also had works on display in the Museum of London today. This legendary figure is our next protagonist.

3.3 Tan Che-Qua and William Chambers: The first Chinese artistic legacy that can still be seen in the UK today

Tan Che-Qua, also appears as Tan Chet-qua or Chitqua in different sources, travelled to London in 1769. He had already gained certain fame before coming to London, as evidenced in a letter from Bentley to Wedgewood[8] on 4 November 1769: "A Chinese portrait modeller, lately arrived from Canton; one of those artists who made the mandarin figure that are brought to England, a pair of which you may remember to have seen at Mr. Walley's shop" (Jewitt, 1865: 209–210). This was further endorsed by a letter from Richard Gough, an active member of the Society of Antiquaries of London, in 1770: "He came over with Captain Jameson, last year, from Canton, some say on a motive of curiosity, others to avoid creditors. This man is so well known by our people who have been at Canton, where he keeps a shop for making figures, that there is not the least room to suspect this statement" (Shih, 2015: 83). This gave him a ladder to reach his career's peak quickly. Only one year after his arrival, he was invited to exhibit his portrait figure in the second Royal Academy Exhibition in the Great Room of the academy's building on 24 April 1770. It was listed as number 245, "Mr. Chitqua, Arundell-Street; A portrait of a gentlemen, a model".[9] This was the first record that a named Chinese artist was included in any public art exhibition in Europe, or indeed anywhere in the world. Based on this early written record showing his professional recognition, I will stick to Chitqua as his reference in the rest of this section except in direct quotations, although Tan Chet-Qua was printed as his name in Chamber's book, and another written record dated December 1770 kept at the British Museum reads "Che Qua, a Chinese modeler, who was in England in 1769, have read and explained the characters in this book, which he said were in the Mandarin language"

(Clarke, 2017: 508). This handwritten note was incorporated within the album of paintings produced in China dated to around 1735, after his visit to the British Museum to examine its collection of Chinese books.

In addition to this symbolic inclusion in the British artistic community, at least two pieces of Chitqua's artwork are still on display today: one is a seated clayed figure of Dr. Anthony Askew, now in the collection of the Royal College of Physicians in London; another is a clay figurine of Thomas Todd, a leading British entrepreneur as a tea merchant (see Figure 3.6). It was made a central exhibit at the Museum of London in 2011 after the museum purchased the piece from one of Todd's descendants.

By 1771, Chitqua was reported by *The Gentleman's Magazine* (XLI, February, 1771: 93) as "the celebrated Chinese Artist" who "had the honour to have his portrait introduced by Mr. Zoffani, into a capital picture of the members of that noble institution". This "capital picture" was the oil painting by Johann Zoffany, *the Academicians of the Royal Academy* (see Figure 3.7), attributed to King George III. A miniature painter, Jeremiah Meyer was depicted as turning to Chitqua (in the left corner) in conversation in the painting, showing that he is part of "us",

Figure 3.6 Thomas Todd by Chitqua, c.1770, clay statuette. Courtesy of the Museum of London.

Figure 3.7 Chitqua appeared in the same oil painting with William Chambers in *the academicians of the royal academy*, by Johann Zoffany (1733–1810). Courtesy of the Royal Collection Trust, The Queen's Gallery.

and not an outsider. William Chambers, the other protagonist in this story, was also in the painting (in front of the mantlepiece, wearing a red and gold waistcoat with one of his legs stepping on the wooden box). He had travelled on three trading voyages with the Swedish EIC in the 1740s, two of them were to Canton (1743–1745 and 1748–1749), returning with copious notes, drawings and first-hand impressions of a country that Englishmen would not visit in large numbers for another hundred years. According to Min (2018: 230), Chambers "seemed to have spoken enough Chinese to discuss with a visiting artist known as Chitqua", and from Chitqua's social and professional life as someone running his modelling portraiture business in London, we assume that he should also be able to converse in English. This made it possible for him to engage with a much wider spectrum of British society and people from different circles. For example, it was confirmed in Bentley's 1769 letter to Wedgwood that "I have paid him three visits and had a good deal of conversation with him, for he speaks some English" (Jewitt, 1865: 210). He was also invited to some high-profile social events, including a grand dinner held by the Royal Academy in April 1770, among other dignitaries including the statesman and philosopher Edmund Burke, and the writer and politician Horace Walpole (Clarke, 2017; Shih, 2015).

Chambers seemed to have developed a much more intimate relationship with Chitqua when he described that he "had three wives, two of whom he caressed very much; the third but seldom for she was a virago, and hard large feet. He dressed well, often in thick sattin; wore nine whiskers and four long nails, with silk boots, calico breeches, and every other ornament that mandarins are wont to wear" (Honour, 1961: 158). Richard Gough, a prominent and influential antiquarian who served as Director of the Society of Antiquaries of London from 1771 to 1791, also gave an interesting account of Chitqua that not only described his striking feature as "on his head no hair except the long lock braided into a tail almost a yard long", but also disclosed that "I always understood that it was a capital offence to quit the country, but am since told it can be compounded for £10" (Price, 2019: 15). From this we can see how Chitqua as a run-away from the Middle Kingdom was made a rare cultural representation of the "exotic" China: his hair and dress style, the Chinese traditions of polygamy and women's bound feet. This also made him a desirable model to pose among his peer English artists: two drawings produced by Charles Grignion now reside in the collection of the Ashmolean Museum in Oxford, and one oil painting by John Hamilton Mortimer is in the collection of the Hunterian Museum of the Royal College of Surgeons of England in London. All these images show him in Chinese clothes, retaining a distinctive cultural identity.

Chamber's first book, *Designs of Chinese Buildings, Furniture, Dresses, Machines and Utensils, Engraved by the best hands, from the originals drawn in China,* was a fanciful elaboration of Chinese architecture and naturalistic style of gardening and had a significant influence on the British contemporary taste. Published in 1757 in London, it brought together his experience in China in the 1740s and later architectural education received in Paris in 1749 and Rome in 1750, putting him in a privileged position to be considered the first European to study both Chinese and Western architecture systematically.[10] More importantly, Chambers tried to demonstrate equal values of antique Greco-Roman and ancient Chinese styles by identifying classical Greek analogues to various features of Chinese temple architecture. He considered China as "great, or wise, only in comparison with the nations that surround them; and have no intention to place them in competition either with the ancients, or with the moderns of this part of the world" (Honour, 1961: 155).

However, this idea was not very well received at the time. There were already complaints from authors of *The Connoisseur* in June 1755 that "Chinese taste, which has already taken possession of our gardens, our buildings and our furniture, will also find a way into our churches; and how elegant must a monument appear, which is erected in the Chinese taste, and embellished with dragons, bells, pagodas and mandarins?" (cited in Liu, 2005: 87). From Chamber's writing below (1773: 115) we can see the suspicion and resistance he had experienced in introducing the Chinese elements to Western landscape, which mirrors the similar difficulty in introducing Western ideas of trade and diplomacy to the Qing Empire:

> Every new system naturally meets with opposition; when the monster Novelty appears, all parties, alarmed at the danger, unite to raise a clamour: each cavils at what it doth not like, or doth not comprehend, till the whole project is pulled to pieces, and the projector stands plumed of every feather; not only robbed of the praise due to his labour and good intentions, but, like a common enemy, branded with scorn and abuse .... biased by interests and prejudices, the angry champions of the old, rarely show mercy to the new; which is almost always invidiously considered, and too often unjustly condemned.

This background preluded one of the most extraordinary cultural encounters between him and Chitqua. Chambers first published *Dissertation on Oriental Gardening* in 1772. Its second edition was published in 1773 with an annex of "*An Explanatory Discourse* by Tan Chet-Qua, of Quang-Chew-Fu, Gent." as shown on the front cover. There was also a Preface and Introduction to this Annex written by Chambers. The paragraph below from Chitqua's *Discourse* showcased how deep going their minds must have connected that perhaps "soulmates" would be the best word to describe their relationship:

> It is true, that dissentions in opinion, however well meant, will often bear an invidious aspect, and always must offend some interested individuals; yet, to the community, they are generally advantageous, and should always be favourably received, as they give birth to new discoveries, and ultimately point out the highest perfection: had no man ever ventured to dissent from his neighbour, our age would be as dark as were those of Fo-hii, Shing tong, or Whoang-tii.[11]
>
> (Chambers, 1773: 123)

In the Introduction, Chambers (1773: 115–116) complimented that "all the world knew Chet-qua ...... a pretty general scholar and a complete gentleman", while giving a vivid description of his character: he composed love letters at pleasure, recited verses either in Manchurian or Chinese and sang love songs in many languages. Most importantly, he was "always vastly pleasant, and very communicative. Among his favourite topics were painting, music, architecture and gardening". Interestingly enough, he said Chitqua took one line from the Qianlong Emperor's famous poem *Ode to Tea*(《三清茶》) as his motto: 毡庐适禅悦(*zhan lu shi chan yue*), meaning "tasting the pleasure of Zen in tea in a tent". This shows Chitqua must have explained the Chinese philosophical concept of Zen to Chambers, even though in the same poem, another line says 可悟不可说 (*ke wu bu ke shuo*), meaning that "this can only be understood in mind but not described in words". The emperor described in the poem how, sitting in his tent on a military campaign, tea can soothe the mind and allow meditative reflection on the activities of the day, and this particular kind of tea mixture of plum flower, fingered citron and pine nut (as depicted on the tea saucer in Figure 3.8) was created by the

Figure 3.8 Teacup with the Qianlong Emperor's poem and tea saucer with the three ingredients of the Sanqing tea. Courtesy of the National Palace Museum in Taipei.

Qianlong Emperor himself. The way it was prepared, brewed, drank, and appreciated were all captured in this poem, often inscribed on the porcelain teacups during Qianlong's reign (see Figure 3.8),[12] perfectly blending the quintessential elements of Chineseness: poetry, tea and porcelain, all elevated to a higher degree of curiousness when they were from such an eminent figure as the Qianlong Emperor. The translation of the poem was first published on 14 July 1770 in a London newspaper the *Public Advertiser* under the title of "A Prose-Translation of an Ode on Tea. Composed by Kien-Long, the present Emperor of China and Tartary in the Year 1746",[13] but Chambers also included a substantially enriched verse translation in his own book in 1773 (pp. 120–121).[14] We can only imagine the "vastly pleasant" discussions Chambers must have had with Chitqua, and the idea that cultivated landscape gardens as a physical expression of philosophical thoughts of "harmony with nature" can only be shared and understood by such spiritual level of communications.

Another legacy left by Chambers was when he served as George III's Surveyor General, he influenced the Regent's choice to install a Chinese drawing room in his Carlton House residence in 1790. In 1814, the Regent sponsored a lavish Chinese pageant in St. James Park to celebrate the recent victory over Napoleon. A temporary decorative Chinese style bridge and a seven-story pagoda, the two most distinctive symbols of Chinese architecture, were erected over the canal for the firework display, "situating China at the very heart of an event crucial in the formation of British national identity" (Kitson, 2013: 223). Although the bridge and pagoda were destroyed by fireworks on the night, its image was captured in the painting below that is kept at the British Museum (see Figure 3.9). A rather interesting mirror image was that in 1751, when the Qianlong Emperor was celebrating his mother's 60th birthday, temporary Western style architectures were also erected on both sides of the street from the Summer Palace to the Forbidden City: Figure 3.10 is part of a long scroll depicting the scene of processions, now kept at the Palace Museum in Beijing. They served as an important endorsement to the very precious period of Yin-Yang echo between China and the West, just like the black and white dot in the Yin-Yang symbol embedded in the other and became part of the other.

Out of the numerous building projects Chambers designed for the royal family, about 20 were ornamental garden buildings for the royal botanical garden at Kew, "a strangely heterogeneous scene in which ancient, modern and exotic elements were juxtaposed. The garden represented the height of mid-eighteenth design" (Talbot, forthcoming: 39). Here still stand today is the most significant legacy of Chamber's study of Chinese architecture: the Chinese Pagoda built for Princess Augusta (mother of King George III) in 1761. As his most well-known surviving building, the Chinese pagoda was considered the first recognised reproduction which

Figure 3.9 Chinese Pagoda and Bridge in St. James's Park, London, 1814, Courtesy of the British Museum.

Figure 3.10 Birthday Celebrations for the Empress Dowager Chongqing, 1751. Courtesy of the Palace Museum, Beijing.

successfully kept the oriental style. As Porter noted (2000: 182), "in the first half of the eighteenth century, an increasing tide of Chinese imports contributed to a popular vogue that filled drawing rooms with the fanciful porcelain productions of chinoiserie and gardens from Potsdam to Kew with temples and pagodas 'after the Chinese taste'". However, the limited access to first-hand experiences of Chinese cultures and the restricted circulation contributed to the mystification and misrepresentation of the Chinese taste in exaggerated motifs of an oriental exoticism, to the extent that they do not look like anything remotely Chinese with authentic characters in Chinese eyes. Thanks to Chambers' first-hand experiences in China, Kew's pagoda became an epitome of Chinese architecture and gardens, being acclaimed as the "most scholarly pagoda to be seen in Europe" (Honour, 1961: 155). As described by the architect himself, "all the angles of the Roofs are adorned with large Dragons,[15] being Eighty in Number, covered with a kind of thin Glass in various Colours, which produces a most dazzling Reflection; and the whole ornament at Top is doubly Gilt" (cited in Mayor, 1941: 113).

Although Chambers had never visited the Chinese emperor's imperial garden at Beijing, Kew in many ways is a mirror image of the Yuanming Yuan in Beijing. Chambers relied on a letter written by Jean Denis Attiret, a French Jesuit, in 1745, which was translated into English in 1752. As the first European person to provide a detailed written record of the famed garden Yuanming Yuan, Attiret praised profusely the infinitely varied valleys, rivers, and ornamental buildings of the Chinese emperor's pleasure ground, in what he called "a beautiful Disorder and a wandering as far as possible from all the Rules of Art" (cited in Liu, 2005: 92). Such descriptions may belong to the "imaginary land of Cathay" as Macartney found with his own eyes in 1793: "From everything I can learn, it falls very short of the fanciful descriptions which father Attiret and Sir William Chambers have intruded upon us as realities" (cited in Barrow, 1817: 133). However, Macartney showed real enthusiasm at the gardens and the grounds of the imperial summer retreat at Rehe, praising it as "one of the finest forest-scenes in the world" (cited in Barrow, 1804: 134). In 1796, after the failed embassy, Macartney wrote to George Staunton, imagining an idyllic scene in which "our King at Kew & the Emperor of China at Jehol solace themselves under the shade of many of the same trees & admire the elegance of many of the same flowers in their respective gardens" (cited in Kitson, 2013: 139). In this imagination, the universal language of botany united these monarchs in their enjoyment of their mirrored royal gardens. Macartney had also commented in his Journal that "Had China been accessible to Mr. Brown or to Mr. Hamilton, I should have sworn they had drawn their happiest ideas from the rich sources which I have tasted this day"

(Cranmer-Byng, 1962: 126). Chambers had indeed drew happy ideas from Chinese gardens and contributed to shaping a distinctive English garden style often referred to as "Le Jardin Anglo-Chinois". His communication with Chitqua played a role in this cross-fertilisation of inspirations from China and the West that put the naturalistic Chinese garden style of *Sharawadgi* into practice, in which a more sinuous form of nature took precedence over an imposed structure. This will be looked at in more details in the next chapter when we compare Chinoiserie with Euroiserie.

Chitqua returned to China in 1772, like his predecessors, he seemed to have faded into the background with little retraceable records. An interesting anecdote is that the Macartney Embassy's draughtsman, Alexander, may have visited Chitqua (a Chinese face sculptor who claimed to "sa-vy Mis-sa Banks velley well") during their time in Canton. Presumably, this was Chitqua who was reported to have died three years later in 1796 (Kitson, 2013: 225). However, at least one young man was inspired by this returning run-away and decided to follow his footsteps. His name is Huang Yadong (黄亚东), or Whang At Tong and Wang Y-Tong, who continued the trail of rare Chinese visitors to Britain during the eighteenth century, interacted with the local intellectual community and left with more legacies.

3.4 Huang Yadong and William Jones: The first English letter exchanged between the two peoples

Huang Yadong arrived in England in August 1774 in his early twenties. This was recorded in a letter dated 18 February 1775 attributed to Sir Joshua Reynolds, founder and first president of the Royal Academy of Arts:

> I have lately met in company Whang-At-Ting, the Chinese, who is now in London [...] He is a young man of twenty-two, and an inhabitant of Canton, where having received from Chit-qua, the Chinese figure maker, a favourable account of his reception in England, two or three years ago, he determined to make the voyage likewise, partly from curiosity, and a desire of improving himself in science, and partly with a view of procuring some advantages in trade, in which he and his elder brother are engaged. He arrived here in August, and already pronounces and understands our language very tolerably, but he writes it in a very excellent hand, which he acquired with ease by using the copy books recommended by Mr Locke [...] He has a great thirst after knowledge, and seems to conceive readily what is communicated to him [...].[16]

This was still a time when the Chinese imperial administration discouraged its subjects from travelling abroad. What made this venture possible was perhaps a combination of "push" and "pull" factors: on the one hand, we can see from the letter that Huang seemed to be both intelligent and adventurous, travelling to Europe for reasons very similar to those that drove enterprising Europeans to venture in the opposite direction: curiosity, thirst for knowledge and even gaining advantages in trade. On the other hand, if we remembered what happened to his few predecessors, we might see the motivation for John Bradby Blake (1745–1773), who was a resident Supercargo for the EIC in Canton, to take him to England as an embodiment of Oriental fascination. Besides, Blake himself had a keen interest in naturalism while Huang is knowledgeable about the use of Chinese plants. Unfortunately, Blake fell ill and died just before Huang arrived in England. So he was passed into the care of Blake's friend John Frederick Sackville, Duke of Dorset, and became a page boy at Knole. Like those who came before him, Huang also became a minor celebrity in intellectual circles, meeting aristocrats, writers, antiquarians and artists during his service at Knole, where his portrait painted by Reynolds is still hanging today (see Figure 3.11),[17] bringing a touch of Oriental exoticism to Knole. He appeared in traditional Chinese hat and clothes, wearing red shoes and holding a fan in his hand, perched cross-legged on a Chinoiserie settee. Bruijn (2011: 10) described it as "an enigmatic image, at once respectfully realistic and deliberately exotic".

Coming as a relatively young man, Huang Yadong became the first international student at the Sevenoaks School (then Queen Elizabeth's Grammar School), as well as being the first Chinese person who studied in England, gaining him a mixed education background and a privileged position in bridging the knowledge gap. For this reason, he is arguably to

Figure 3.11 Huang Yadong, by Joshua Reynolds in 1776. Courtesy by the National Trust.

have made more "knowledge transfer" than his predecessors due to his language ability. For example, apart from helping identify Chinese books in a library at St. John's College in Oxford in June 1775, he also visited the Royal Society in London and met with Josiah Wedgewood, who started to make the unglazed jasperware in contrasting colours. Huang's help with information about "the Chinese method of manufacturing their chinaware" was recorded in Wedgewood's commonplace book, which noted particularly that "Mr. Whang at Tong says that the blue Nankin china is always painted before it is put in the kiln, which is the reason the blues never wash off, which the red, gold, etc, does – for the gold, red, etc, is added afterwards, and then burnt or baked again" (Mozley, 1936: 4).[18] The so-called "Wedgewood blue and white" had reached an industrial scale by 1792 and the best pieces were selected as gifts for the Chinese emperor by Lord Macartney.

A different area of knowledge Huang helped disseminate was acupuncture when he explained the Chinese "drawing or print representing a naked man, with straight lines drawn to different parts of the body" (Clarke, 2017: 518) to Andrew Duncan, who went to China as a surgeon on an EIC Ship in 1768 and later became the president of the Royal College of Physicians of Edinburgh. Yet the greatest example of cultural exchange can be seen in his interactions with Sir William Jones, who was a member of the famous Literary Club founded by Sir Joshua Reynolds. According to Hevia (1995: 65), the membership of the Club, which included Lord Macartney, was regarded as an "intellectual aristocracy in Georgian England" devoted to the ideas of rationality, morality and the exchange of ideas, which framed knowledge about China. Indeed, Reynolds himself acted like a hub of connections: Jones and Huang met at a dinner held by him. Apart from painting the portrait for Huang, Reynolds also painted the portrait for Macartney, and his portraits of King George and Queen Charlotte were brought to Beijing by Macartney in 1792 as presents to the emperor.

Jones taught himself Chinese with the aid of books in the Bodleian Library, and at some stage he also acquired a manuscript of Chinese and Latin dictionary. His treaties *On the Second Classical Book of the Chinese* and *Seventh Anniversary Discourse* were important contributions to the emerging discipline of sinology in Britain. In his *Seventh Anniversary Discourse* (1807, vol. 3: 138), Jones referred to China as "a celebrated and imperial land, …… a pre-eminence among Eastern kingdoms analogous to that of Britain among the nations of the west". For this, Kitson (2013: 58). added that he was "willing to accept Confucian philosophy and Chinese literature on exactly equal terms with that of Socrates, Plato and Aristotle". Jones was particularly fascinated by the Chinese *Book of Songs* (*Shijing,* 《诗经》), he commented that "in spite of its brevity, it has a wonderful stateliness: each line has only four words in it. It follows that the diction is very often elliptical, which gives sublimity and obscurity at the same time" (cited in Kitson, 2013: 47). He compared one ode in the Chinese manuscript with Couplet's version and produced two versions of the ode, one a literal translation and the other a poetic one, which was published in 1774 entitled "Ode Sinicae Antiquissima". As the English were often bewildered by conflicting accounts of China by French writers at the time, it was William Jones who created "direct cultural contact" (Fan, 1998: 325). However, Jones' knowledge of Chinese never got beyond the stage of deciphering characters, so he sought out Huang's help to translate the whole book in 1784. He re-established contact with Huang via John Henry Cox, son and agent of James Cox, famous manufacturer of lavishly ornamented articles for the "sing-song" trade with China.[19] Unfortunately, Huang already went back to Canton by this time while Jones was in India, Huang's reply to Jones became a significant legacy as it was the very first English letter written by a Chinese person, in which Huang wrote "I shall always remember the kindness of my friends in England". However, he declined politely Jones's request while sending him two copies of the books: "The Chinese book, Shi King, that contains three hundred poems with remarks thereon, and the work of Con-fu-tsu, I beg you will accept; but to translate the work into English will require a great deal of time; perhaps three or four years; and I am so much engaged in business, that I hope you will excuse my not undertaking it" (cited in Clarke, 2017: 518). Although the academic collaboration that Jones was very keen on creating as part of his new research network between Canton and Calcutta did not work out, this attempt represented a first step to grow a sophisticated network of exchanging knowledge about China involving the flows of people, ideas, commerce and commodities between London and Canton.

From the four stories we can see that all these early Chinese travellers to the British Empire were acclaimed by English society, gained an audience with royalty, or met with elite members, and had portraits painted by the most celebrated artists, leaving legacies that can still be seen in museums today. To a certain extent, this fact may reflect the different power distance both between the two empires at the time, and between the monarch and "foreigners" compared with Lord Macartney's visit to the Forbidden City – the first British granted an audience with the Chinese emperor only happened in 1793, over a century later than Shen Fuzong's meeting with the British King in 1687. However, the first British visited China much earlier than the other way round, and from Peter Mundy to William Jones, the British had clearly gained and spread more knowledge about China from the seventeenth to the nineteenth century than the other way round. Jones wrote in 1792 that "give us time ..... for our investigations, and we will transfer to Europe all the sciences, arts and literature of Asia" (Cannon, 1975: 224). No wonder Clarke (2017: 520) would lament in comparison:

> Without a Canton equivalent to Joseph Banks or William Jones, with their unquenchable thirst for encyclopaedic knowledge of distant cultures, or a Chinese equivalent to Josiah Wedgewood attempting to put such knowledge to practical use in industrial production, none of these three visitors to England was to play a role within their own home cultural environment comparable to that which John Bradby Blake played in British intellectual life through his gathering of information about Chinese botany and other matters while in Canton.

In contrast, how does the fact that no Chinese record of those early travellers to the Far West reflect the Chinese view of the West? After the three latter travellers managed to return to China, they seemed to disappear into almost complete darkness. As stated by Clarke (ibid: 520), they "emerged into a spotlight of temporary celebrity during their time in England, playing significant roles in the expansion of British knowledge about China", however, "while we are able to track some of their roles as cultural ambassadors in the West, it seems their extraordinary overseas experience and connections did not enable them to play a similar role of bridging cultures when back in China", where they enjoyed no social prominence and failed to appear in any historical records, or left any written accounts of their time spent in Europe. To my knowledge, there only existed one Chinese travel account to Europe before the nineteenth century, which did not include Britain; and the first one including Britain only appeared in 1820, but it is worth including a brief section about these two early Chinese travel accounts to Europe and to Britain before we close this chapter.

3.5 The first Chinese travellers who wrote about Europe and Britain

The two Chinese persons who made history by being the "first" in recording their travels to the Far West were not household names, their accounts were only circulated in a limited circle and produced little impact on Chinese society at the time, and still remain largely unknown today. The first one was actually sent by the Kangxi Emperor in 1708. He was also a convert like Shen Fuzong but managed to return to China after a decade-stay in Europe, thus becoming the first known Chinese person to travel to Europe, return and write an account of his travels. His name was Fan Shouyi, or Louis Fan (樊守义). In 1708, the Kangxi Emperor ordered a mission to Europe in response to the decree received from Pope Clement XI in January 1707, forbidding Catholic converts in China from participating in Chinese rituals, causing the controversy over the legitimacy of Confucian and ancestral veneration. The mission was thus sent to change the Pope's mind on the subject. Fan accompanied three Jesuits on board the Portuguese ship and left Macau in January 1708 and arrived in Lisbon in

September 1708. After over a decade of stay mainly in Portugal, Spain and Italy, Provana and Fan were sent back to China by Pope Clement XI on 19 May 1719. Provana died during the voyage, and Fan returned to China alone. He travelled north to Beijing for an audience with the Kangxi Emperor that was held on 11 October 1720. In the following year, Fan produced a written report of his experiences in Europe and named it *Shen Jian Lu* (*First-Hand Account,* 《身见录》), which offered a rare glimpse of first-hand observations of all aspects of eighteenth-century Europe. However, such a rare opportunity to study the West was dismissed by the Qing as the emperor was only interested in the novelty of Western technical craftsmanship, not in learning more about the Christian civilisation, let alone learn *from* the West.

An interesting description in the book was when Fan attended the birthday celebration of King João V of Portugal, he observed that the ritual of reception was only three bows and a kiss of the hand of the King, who did not appear as unapproachable as the Chinese emperor. From this we know that the information on European ritual ceremony was made known to the Qing emperor by its own subject in 1721. However, this account was only circulated inside the imperial court and never went into print. The original manuscript somehow found its way back to Italy and was left hidden and forgotten in the Vatican Library until 1936, when it was discovered by a visiting scholar from China, Wang Chongmin, who mentioned it in a publication on *Book Quarterly* in Beijing. This sparked research interest of another Chinese scholar, Yan Zonglin, who made the book known more widely as the very first Chinese travelogue about Europe.

In comparison, the second author played a more critical role of enhancing Chinese knowledge of the British Empire as this traveller was among the first to leave a first-hand record of England in his book, which was later studied and cited by other eminent figures such as Wei Yuan and Lin Zexu, who were widely acclaimed as being the first persons "opening their eyes to see the world" in modern Chinese history. His name was Xie Qinggao (谢清高), a merchant who suffered from a shipwreck en route to Southeast Asia in 1782 when he was only 18 years old. He was rescued by a Portuguese captain and escorted all the way to Lisbon, Portugal. He decided to stay and spent 10 years travelling throughout western Europe from 1783 to 1793 though much of the time was probably spent onboard Portuguese ships. When he eventually returned to China and settled down in Macau in 1793, he lost his eyesight and became blind. He asked a scholar Yang Bingnan to record his oral account of his remarkable travel story and published it in 1820 under the title of *Hailu*(《海录》), meaning *Records of the Sea.* In the Preface written by Yang, the book was written to "perpetuate his knowledge" (Po, 2015: 355).

As a keen maritime observer and the first Chinese writer to report on world geography, history and cultural customs based on his personal experience, Xie's book provided a detailed account of over 90 countries and regions in the world, including European seaborne powers such as Portugal, Dutch and England. He described countries from the "Great Western Ocean" (*Daxiyang*, 大西洋) as culturally exotic, and technologically advanced because they had gained eminence in "harnessing guns and cannons". Their sailing ships were equipped with new weapons, as well as accurate, scientific techniques in navigation and cartography, which enabled them to reach almost every corner of the globe and extend their influences around the world. Most importantly, in his writing, maritime countries previously described as inferior tributary states now appeared as industrialised civilisations. For example, he was impressed by the running water system and high-rise buildings in London. Perhaps due to his own merchant background, Xie particularly admired the British global commercial expansion. His description of England captured the national character and power status rather accurately:

> Maritime commerce is one of the chief occupations of the English, and wherever there is a region in which profits could be reaped by trading, these peoples strive for them, with the result that their commercial vessels are to be seen on the sea. Commercial traders are to be found all over the country. A large foreign mercenary army is also maintained. As a consequence, although the country is small, it has such a large military force that foreign nations are filled with fear.[20]
>
> (cited in Po, 2015: 358)

Although the Middle Kingdom needed not fear the British, Xie commented on the European threat to Southeast Asia, and alerted the encroaching of the seagoing European nations in the region that had tributary connections with China. For example, he included specific information that Bangladesh and Bombay were colonised by the British and the Indonesian port Palembang was more awed by the British than Qing China. As such, Xie sent messages that the Qing government shall not remain oblivious to changes in the East Asian geopolitical sphere, and even suggested the Qing court to imitate the Western way of using trade links more effectively to counteract their influence in these regions.

Although Xie was the first Chinese that ever told his countrymen what the outside world looked like, his story did not appeal to many contemporary literati, and his endeavour to redefine these West Ocean powers also failed to evoke serious responses from officials in the Qing court. They were still clinging to the vision that the maritime world could not compete with the Confucian classics, and contacts with foreigners would contaminate Chinese culture unless it were strictly regulated, but it did influence some renowned scholars such as Wei Yuan and Commissioner Lin Zexu. Wei studied *Records of Sea* and cited it in his own work *Haiguo tuzhi (Illustrated Treatise the Sea Kingdoms,* 《海国图志》), while Lin commended the book in one of his memorials to the throne in 1839,[21] also citing

Xie's description of England. This was at the eve of the First Opium War, when eminent figures such as Wei and Lin had begun to shift their worldviews from a Sino-centric to a global perspective, urging the Qing court to prepare to deal with the fierce ambitions of various imperialistic powers.

In 1867, a Qing scholar named Wang Tao, who worked with James Legge in translating the *Four Books and Five Classics*, a corpus of ancient Chinese philosophy, travelled to Europe at the invitation of Legge. He wrote a travelogue *Manyou Suilu*(《漫游随录》), or *Jottings from Carefree Travel* (1890) about his over two years travelling in Europe, in which he claimed to be a pioneer in travelling to the Far West. This indirectly showed the limited audience Xie's book had reached. Wang's status as a scholar and the age of "Westernization Movement" (from 1860s to 1890s) did make his book widely read, hence became known as the first travel book about Europe by a Chinese scholar, although his travelling happened over 80 years behind Xie. Wang did become the first Chinese scholar who gave a speech at the Oxford University in 1867.

With Xie's story we are concluding this chapter, and the era of interpersonal cultural encounters between the two empires. In the following chapters, we will shift our focus onto the next era of Sino-British relations with commercial interactions, diplomatic missions and eventually, military conflicts. The two timeline coordinates sketched out in Xie's story will take us to the next two key events in the encounters between the two empires: 1793, when Xie returned to China while the first British Embassy also arrived in China, hoping to knock the door of the Middle Kingdom open with letters and gifts; then in 1839, when Xie's description of England was cited in Lin's memorial to the Qing court, gunboat diplomacy was already being conceived to force open the door. But in the next chapter, let us first construct a better understanding of the background to Lord Macartney's embassy by revealing the mutual reflections of material culture through Chinoiserie and Euroiserie at the time, as well as the mutual perception gaps between imagination and reality.

Notes

1 Source: https://archaeologynewsnetwork.blogspot.com/2016/09/two-ancient-chinese-skeletons-found-in.html#dtuTfpUd5Yu6Vj88.97

2 Couplet worked together with Lgnace da Costa and P. Prosper Intercetta in translating the first five chapters of the Confucian classics *Da Xue* (*the Great Learning*) and *Lun Yu* (*The Analects*) into Latin, named Sapientia Sinica. Intercetta also translated *Zhong Yong* (*The Doctrine of the Mean*) and the Biography of Confucius, which includes eight pages of bibliography of Confucianism. At least seventeen known European Jesuits were listed in the opening pages, but when the book was published in Paris, only four missionaries' names were printed. Philippe Couplet's contribution was the greatest, he wrote a long preface and brought the draft back to Europe to have it published.

3 Available at: https://www.st-hughs.ox.ac.uk/exhibition-shen-fuzong-the-first-chinese-visitor-to-oxford/

4 The *Kangxi Dictionary* (Kangxi Zidian, 《康熙字典》) completed in 1716 included 47,035 characters. The most widely used *Great Compendium of Chinese Characters* (Hanyu Da Zidian, 《汉语大字典》) (2010 edition) contained 60,370 characters, while *the Most Comprehensive Dictionary of Chinese Characters* (Zhōnghuá Zì Hǎi, 《中华字海》) (1994 edition) had a total entry of 85,568 characters.

5 The "factories" here were not workshops or manufacturing centres but refer to offices, trading posts, and warehouses of foreign traders.

6 The so-called "Canton System" means that Canton was the only port where international trade can be carried out between October and March or May (changes over time) and in the European factories, after which foreign traders had to leave for Macau. All trade at Canton had to be conducted through the Hong merchants, the only Chinese officially sanctioned to deal with foreigners, who were not allowed any direct communication with officialdom in Peking . In 1720, the Hong merchants formed a guild known as the Co-hong, which collected customs duties and other sundry fees on behalf of the government. But it was dismantled the next year and only resumed in 1760. This system was intended to enable the Qing to consolidate coastal defence as well as to monopolise commercial profits and control the interaction with Europeans.

7 His portrait is now kept at the Museum of Gothenburg in Sweden.

8 There were some documents which seemed to suggest that Chitqua also made Wedgwood his first portrait in 1770 (Clarke, 2017), unfortunately, this story of the "long-lost" Chitqua portrait of Wedgwood was disproved by the Wedgewood Museum in 2013 (Shih, 2015: 86).

9 The Exhibition of the Royal Academy MDCCLXX, p. 22. Available at: https://www.royalacademy.org.uk/art-artists/exhibition-catalogue/ra-sec-vol2–1770

10 Although books such as William and John Halfpenny's *New Designs for Chinese Temples, Triumphal Arches, Garden Seats, Palings etc.* and Paul Decker's *Chinese Architecture Civil and Ornamental* were published earlier in the 1750s.

11 The original footnotes read: "some of the first emperors of China; who invented the eight qua's, together with the kay-tse, and created colsus" (p.164). The modern spellings are Fuxi, Shennong and Huangdi, they are the three legendary sovereigns of the third millennium B.C. in China, not real emperors.

12 The poem was first discovered in France "stamped upon Sets of Tea Cups of a particular Kind of Porcelain" owned by Henri Léonard Bertin, the Sinophile secretary of state who had once administered the French EIC (Ellis et al., 2015). Barrow (1804: 187) also recorded that "the late emperor Kien-Long was considered among the best poets of modern times, and the most celebrated of his compositions is an ode in praise of tea, which has been painted on all the teapots in the empire".

13 The English translation appeared in the London press was probably translated from the French translation made by the Jesuit missionary Jean Joseph Marie Amiot (1718–1793). Another English translation was published two years later in 1772 in the same newspaper, perhaps also from Amiot's French version. John Barrow also included an English translation of the poem in his *Trave to China* (1804). Peter Pindar John Wolcot even composed a poem for Qianlong in 1792, *Odes to Kien Long,* calling him the "Prince of Poets".

14 The colours of the Mei-hoa are neve brilliant, yet is the flower always pleasing; in fragrance or neatness the fo-cheou has no equal; the fruit of the pine is aromatic, its odour inviting. In gratifying at once the fight, the smell and the taste, nothing exceeds these three things; and if, at the same time, you put,

upon a gentle fire, an old pot, with three legs, grown black and battered with length of service, after having first filled it with the limpid water of melted snow; and if, when the water is heated to a degree that will boil a fish, or redden a lobster, you pour it directly into a cup made of the earth of yue, upon the tender leaves of superfine tea; and if you let it rest there, till the vapours which rises at first in great abundance, forming thick clouds, dissipate by degrees, and at last appear merely as a flight mist upon the surface; and if then you gently sip this delicious beverage, it is labouring effectually to remove the five causes of discontent which usually disturb our quiet; you may feel, you may taste, but it is impossible to describe the sweet tranquillity which a liquor, thus prepared, procures.

Retired, for some space of time, from the tumults of business, I sit alone in my tent, at liberty to enjoy myself unmolested; in one hand holding a fo-cheou, which I bring nearer to my nose, or put it farther off, at pleasure; in the other hand holding my dish of tea, upon which some pretty curling vapours still appear; I taste, by intervals the liquor, by intervals, I consider the mei-hoa – I give a fillip to my imagination, and my thoughts are naturally turned towards the sages of antiquity – I figure to myself the famous Ou-tsuen, whose only nourishment was the fruit of the pine; he enjoyed himself in quiet, amidst this rigid frugality! I envy, and wish to imitate him – I put a few of the kernels into my mouth; I find them delicious.

Sometimes, methinks, I see the virtuous Lin-fou, bending into form, with his own hands, the branches of the mei-hoa-chou. It was thus, say I to myself, that he relieved his mind, after the fatigues of profound meditation, on the most interesting subjects. Then I take a look at my shrub, and it seems as if I were assisting Lin-fout, in bending its branches into a new form – I skip from Lin-fou to Tchao-tcheon, or to Yu-tchouan; and see the first in the middle of a vast many tea-cups, filled with all kinds of tea, of which he sometimes tastes one, sometimes another; thus varying incessantly his potation; while the second drinks, with the profoundest indifference, the best tea, and scarcely distinguishes it from the vilest stuff – My taste is not their's; why should I attempt to imitate them?

But I hear the sound of the evening bell; the freshness of the night is augmented; already the rays of the moon strike through the windows of my tent, and with their lustre brighten the few moveables with which it is adorned. I find myself neither uneasy nor fatigued; my stomach is empty, and I may, without fear, go to rest – It is thus that, with my poor abilities, I have made these verses, in the little spring of the tenth moon of the year Ping-yn, of my reign Kien-long.

15 The original pagoda dragons were removed in 1784 and have since disappeared. The dragons on the pagoda today were recreated in 2018 as part of Historic Royal Palaces' restoration of this iconic building.

16 Quoted in an anonymous article entitled "Hints Respecting the Chinese Language", in The Bee, XI, 12 September 1792, pp. 50–52. The letter is also mentioned (but not quoted fully) in William W. Appleton, *A Cycle of Cathay: The Chinese Vogue in England during the Seventeenth and Eighteenth Centuries*, New York, Columbia University Press, 1951, pp. 134–136.

17 The National Trust information at Knole shows his name as Wang-y-Tong (about 1753–84), and Sackville "acquired this portrait of him from Reynolds for 50 guineas in 1776, took him into service at Knole, where the English servants called him Warnoton, and had him educated at the gramma school in Sevenoaks". There was another drawn profile portrait by George Dance that was thought to be him by many sources (Bruijn, 2011; Clarke, 2017), but

according to information published by the British Museum, where the portrait is kept, a man named Daniel Sieh pointed out in 2019 that since the man in that drawing wears his hair in a Western style, "this might be Mr. John Anthony, a Chinese serving as a translator for the British EIC in London. Interestingly, he applied for and was granted British citizenship in 1799. Manchu queues were a distinctive style required by law in China, and to get rid of it was tantamount to treason. Since John Anthony became a naturalized British citizen, he had nothing to lose by getting rid of his Manchu queue". I think this is a reasoned argument, particularly because Huang had always planned to go back to China after this adventure, and the two men in both realistic portraits do not share many resemblances. https://www.britishmuseum.org/collection/object/P_1967-1014–67. John Anthony also made history by being the first Chinese person to become a British national. The request was unprecedented, and the Act of Parliament naturalised him as a subject of the King.

18 This was also mentioned in the National Trust information at Knole.

19 One of the automatons they made, in the form of a chariot pushed by a Chinese attendant, was also included in the gifts to the Qianlong Emperor by the Macartney Embassy.

20 Xie, Qinggao (1820), *Hailu*, p. 251. The text is translated by Jeanette Mirsky. Also see her "The Great Chinese Travellers", in Mark A. Kishlansky, ed., *Sources of World History* (1995), New York: Harper Collins College Publishers.

21 This can be found in *Memorials to the Throne*, volume of Lin Zexu, (1956), Beijing: Zhonghua Shuju, p. 680.

References

Ballaster, R. (2005) *Fabulous Orients: Fictions of the East in England, 1662–1785*. Oxford: Oxford University Press.

Barrow, J. (1804) *Travels in China: Containing Descriptions, Observations, and Comparisons, Made and Collected in the Course of a Short Residence at the Imperial Palace of Yuen-min-yuen, and on a Subsequent Journey Through the Country from Pekin to Canton*. London: T. Cadell and W. Davies, in the Strand.

Barrow, J. (1817) *Embassy to China. Chinese Travel, Life and Customs. A Review with Textual Excerpts*. Published by Quarterly Review. London: John Murray.

Bruijn, E. (2011) 'An 18th-century ornamental adventurer: The enigmatic and ambiguous portrait of Huang Ya Dong at Knole, National Trust Arts, Buildings and Collections Bulletin', *ABC Bulletin*. Available at: https://www.academia.edu/9404479/An_18th-Century_Ornamental_Adventurer_the_Enigmatic_and_Ambiguous_Portrait_of_Huang_Ya_Dong_at_Knole

Cannon, G. (1975) 'Sir William Jones, Sir Joseph Banks, and the Royal Society'. *Notes and Records of the Royal Society of London*, 29(2) (Mar), pp. 205–230.

Chambers, W. (1773) *Dissertation on Oriental Gardening*. London: W. Griffin. Available at: https://archive.org/stream/dissertationonor00cham?ref=ol#page/n9/mode/2up

Clarke, D. (2017) 'Chinese visitors to 18th century Britain and their contribution to its cultural and intellectual life', *Curtis's Botanical Magazine*, 34(4), pp. 498–521.

Cranmer-Byng, J.L. (1962) *An Embassy to China, Being the Journal Kept by Lord Macartney during His Embassy to the Emperor Ch'ien-lung 1793–1794*. London: Longmans.

Ellis, M., Coulton, R., and Mauger, M. (2015) *Empire of Tea: The Asian Leaf that Conquered the World*. London: Reaktion Books Ltd.

Fan, C. (1998) 'Sir William Jones's Chinese studies', in Hsia, A. (ed.) *The Vision of China in the English Literature of the Seventeenth and Eighteenth Centuries*. Hong Kong: The Chinese University Press, pp. 325–337.

Foss, T.N. (1990) 'The European sojourn of Philippe Couplet and Michael Shen Fuzong 1683–1692', in Heyndrickx, J. (ed.) *Philippe Couplet S.J. (1623–1693): The Man Who Brought China to Europe*. New York: Routledge.

Goldsmith, O. (1762) *Citizen of the World (1760–61)*. Dublin: Printed for George and Alex, Ewing.

Hevia, J. (1995) *Cherishing Men from Afar, Qing Guest Ritual and the Macartney Embassy of 1793*. Durham and London: Duke University Press.

Hibbert, C. (1970) *The Dragon Wakes, China and the West, 1793–1911*. London: Longman.

Hickey, W. (1913) *Memoirs of William Hickey: 1749–1809*, 4 Volumes, edited by Alfred. London: Hurst & Blackett Ltd. Vol. 1 (1749–1775), Chapter XV. Available at: https://archive.org/stream/memoirsofwilliam015028mbp/memoirsofwilliam015028mbp_djvu.txt

Honour, H. (1961) *Chinoiserie, The Vision of Cathay*. London: John Murray.

Hooke, R. (1687) 'Some observations and conjectures concerning the characters and language of the Chinese', *Philosophical Transactionsof the Royal Society* (London), 16(35), pp. 63–78. Available at: https://royalsocietypublishing.org/doi/pdf/10.1098/rstl.1686.0011

Jewitt, L.F.W. (1865) *The Wedgwoods: Being a Life of Josiah Wedgwood, with notices of his works and their productions, Memoirs of the Wedgwoods and Other Families and a History of the Early Potteries of Staffordshire*. London: Virtue Brothers and Co.

Jones, W. (1807) 'Seventh anniversary discourse, on the Chinese, delivered 25th February 1790'. *The Works of Sir William Jones*, 13 vols, vol. 3, pp. 137–161. London: Stockdale.

Kircher, A. (1667) *China Illustrata*. Translated by Van Tuyl, C.D. in 1986. Available at: https://htext.stanford.edu/content/kircher/china/kircher.pdf

Kitson, P. (2013) *Forging Romantic China, Sino-British Cultural Exchange 1760–1840*. Cambridge: Cambridge University Press.

Liu, Y. (2005) 'The inspiration for a different Eden: Chinese gardening ideas in England in the early modern period'. *Comparative Civilisations Review*, 53(53), Fall, Article 6. Available at: https://scholarsarchive.byu.edu/ccr/vol53/iss53/6

Mayor, H. (1941) 'Chinoiserie', *The Metropolitan Museum of Art Bulletin*, 36(5) (May), pp. 111–114.

Melo, J.V. (2018) 'The Chinese Convert'. *Travel, Transculturality and Identity in England, c. 1550–1700*, An ERC-funded project. Available at: http://www.tideproject.uk/2018/02/16/the-chinese-convert/

Min, E.K. (2018) *China and the Writing of English Literary Modernity 1690–1770*. Cambridge: Cambridge University Press.

Mozley, G. (1936) 'Captain Blake's Chinese Boy'. *Notes and Queries*, 170, 4.

Po, R.C. (2015) 'Writing the waves: Chinese maritime writings in the long eighteenth century', *American Journal of Chinese Studies*, 22(2) (Oct), pp. 343–362.

Poole, W. (2010) 'The Chinaman and the Librarian, The meeting of Shen Fuzong and Thomas Hyde in 1687'. A Lecture for the Oxford Bibliographical Society, 1 March 2010. Transcripts available at: https://ora4-prd.bodleian.ox.ac.uk/objects/uuid:6ce9489d-9858-4543-a31d-69b2962b05ba/download_file?file_format=pdf&safe_filename=Visit%2Bof%2BShen%2Bto%2BHyde%2B%2528lecture%2Btext%2529.pdf&type_of_work=Record

Poole, W. (2021) *Epistola de Mensuris et Ponderibus Serum seu Sinensium (1688), A Forgotten Chapter in the History of Sinology*, edited with a translation. Editiones Pariores No. 1. New College, Oxford.

Porter, D. (2000) 'A peculiar but uninteresting nation: China and the discourse of commerce in eighteenth-century England', *Eighteenth-Century Studies*, 33(2), Winter, pp. 181–199.

Porter, D. (2010) *The Chinese Taste in Eighteenth-century England.* Cambridge: Cambridge University Press.

Price, B. (2019) *The Chinese in Britain, A History of Visitors and Settlers.* Gloucestershire: Amberley Publishing.

Shih, Y. (2015) 'Chitqua: A Chinese modeller and his portraiture business in eighteenth-century London'. *Meishu Yanjiu* (*Fine Arts Journal*), Issue 1, Dec. National Kaohsiung Normal University, pp. 71–106.

Sun, J. (2013) 'The 'Thirteen Hongs' and the rise and decline of foreign trade in Late Qing Dynasty', *Memories and Archives*, 9(2013), pp. 40–43.

Talbot, A. (forthcoming) 'The Influence of Chinese Gardens in Early Modern England'. Available at: https://www.academia.edu/42721019/The_Influence_of_Chinese_Gardens_in_Early

Williams, L. (2014) 'Anglo-Chinese caresses: Civility, friendship and trade in English representations of China, 1760–1800', *Journal for Eighteenth-Century Studies*, 38(2), pp. 277–296. 10.1111/1754-0208.12208

4 Chinoiserie vs. Euroiserie: Mutual reflections of material culture and perception gaps

> We need to "historicise cross-cultural encounters by situating individual stories within the larger political, cultural and intellectual currents".
>
> – Hevia (1995: 229)

Along with the expanded trade between China and Europe, there was growing fascinations with Chinese culture and taste in Europe. The attraction of Oriental otherness was almost the inverse of Said's version of Orientalism when the popularity of Chinoiseries peaked in the eighteenth century, a term describing fantastical European artistic responses to China in its domestication of an alien aesthetic as they represented a combination of novelty and antiquity. China was viewed as highly civilised in having exquisitely finished art, therefore, owning a Chinoiserie piece represents social status and intellectual engagements with China. However, employing a bifocal lens reveals that the fashion for Chinoiserie in the West also had an echo of Chinese interest in European goods known as Euroiserie, when "imperial enthusiasm for European and other imports – a preoccupation that mirrored the eighteen-century European craze for Chinoiseries – was intense and spearheaded a widespread passion for things European among the elite in China" (Waley-Cohen, 2000: 6). According to Wang (2017: 42), the term "Europerie"[1] was first used by Kisch in 1937 in talking about the interaction between Chinoiserie and stimulation of European exotica in Chinese art creation: "through emulation, adaptation, and re-creation, Chinese art and visual culture in the late seventeenth and eighteenth centuries emerged and created a whole new visual language derived from European origins". Porter's statement (2010: 23) put Chinese art as representing "a competing aesthetic standard worthy of comparison to classical and Renaissance norms", with its paintings and architecture regularly compared with distinguished "counterpoints" from the Western tradition. As a matter of fact, the words "Orient" and "Occident" derive from the Latin for rising and falling, orior and occido, alluding to the sun's movement across the day and night, just like the relationship between the Chinese concepts of Yin and Yang that originally mean shade and light,

DOI: 10.4324/9781003156383-5

alluding to the moon and the sun. In this sense, Chinoiserie and Euroiserie can be understood as the black and white "dots" embedded in each other in a symbiotic way.

Employing this bifocal lens allows us to see that this relationship as living contemporary is completely different from a separation of East and West, and the ensued binaries between the "colonial self" and "colonised other" that was developed following the two British embassies, when "open Enlightenment Orientalism" was succeeded by an Orientalism informed by increasing "romantic nationalism and xenophobia" (Aravamudan, 2012). It also allows me to carry out a two-pronged analysis that concerns material culture on the one hand, even though "Chinoiseries had passed the zenith of its popularity by about 1760 in England, but it lingered on fitfully for another half-century and even survived into the opening years of Queen Victoria's regin" (Honour, 1961: 183–184); and at the intellectual level on the other hand, there was a changing attitudes towards China after 1750s, with more and more disillusioned criticisms against the Chinese system. The year 1757 marked a divergence when the Canton System was imposed in China to tighten control over foreign trade, while the Battle of Plassey in the same year gained the British a foothold in Bengal, starting an era of robust expansion, with emerging political system of constitutional monarchy at home, and industrial and commercial revolution that stimulated foreign trade phenomenally. China's splendid cultural past was considered equal to Europe, but its debased nepotism present rendered it inferior. As Hung (2003: 263) put it, "Chinese antiquity, previously regarded as a virtue, suddenly became a vice" when progress was the new currency. Yang (2011) used embracement and rejection to describe the contradictory British reception of Chineseness at the material and intellectual levels. China was much more than a geographical location for many Britons; it was also a way of seeing and being seen that could be either embraced as creative inspiration or rejected as contagious influence. This love-hate complex will be unfolded in this chapter.

4.1 The seemingly Yin-Yang flow between the two empires in material culture

According to Mayor (1941: 112), one of the earliest recorded uses of oriental art for interior decoration in England appeared in 1682, when "the landscapes on the screens represent the manner of living and country of the Chinese". By the 1730s, when being exotic and aesthetic were joined together to become a fashion statement, a Chinese room, decorated with imported paper and screens, porcelain vases on the mantlepiece, blue and white plate lining the walls, was a class distinction and symbol of a sophisticated taste, wealth and status. If you are what you collected, Chinoiserie has the capacity "not only to reflect – but also to shape – taste, identity, and political opinion" (Slobada, 2014: 3). This made Chinese goods more than a new fashion statement; when luxuries of tea and porcelain were used by British consumers to define the self, these same objects also defined the other. As Jenkins (2013: 3) put it, they were used to place "the English self in a mutually defining relationship with things Chinese". The growing vogue for all things Oriental peaked in the 1740s to 1780s in Britain, spreading from the luxurious niche market catering to social elites to a middle-and upper-class homes, driven by the new merchant classes' contagious ambitions. In the space of little more than a century, the "curious emblems of otherness" was transformed into "paradigmatic emblems of Englishness" (Porter's, 2010: 4), to the extent that "it was impossible to conceive of English identity without attendant notions of Chineseness", and "writing China into English selfhood was one way of asserting England's global relevance as a cosmopolitan nation" (Jenkins, 2013: 1, 4).

This was also the time when the English were importing and consuming tea in ever-increasing quantities. Since tea-wares were essential accessories to the newly fashionable beverage, porcelain cabinets or china closets were made popular by Queen Mary II in the late seventeenth century. Porcelain retained its particular enchantment for European consumers out of all the export commodities from China. They were fascinated by this marvellous material that appealed to sight, sound and touch, which was further enhanced by its origins in an ancient, distant and splendid empire. In contrast to European earthenware, china porcelains were wonderfully smooth, thin and decorated with vibrant, lustrous coloured glazes unequalled in European ceramic production. It even had a distinctive sound, ringing when struck. The secret of its creation had eluded the Europeans for centuries since Marco Polo's time, who had described the Chinese manufacture of porcelain in amazed admiration: clay for these porcelain vessels was "stacked in huge mounds and then left for thirty or forty years exposed to wind, rain, and sun", such that "when a man makes a mound of this earth he does so for his children", and this peculiar science of making porcelain will "only pass on to their kin" (Harmondsworth, 1958: 238). In this type of language of marvel, words like "astounding" and "ingenious" conjure up images of both creators and their creations: people who made this extraordinary material culture can be nothing but extraordinary themselves – such requirements of patience, skill and foresight also indicated the superiority of the Chinese civilisation. Besides, as Ricci reported, it could "bear the heat of hot foods without cracking and, what is more to be wondered at, if it is broken and sewed with a brass wire it will hold liquids without any leakage" (Gallagher, 1953: 14–15). It thus represented a technological disparity between the two empires at the end of the century.

It was not until Semedo et al's account[2] (1655: 12) that the veil of magic began to lift, revealing similarities between Chinese porcelain making and European earthenware: "there are not those mysteries that are reported of it here, neither in the matter, the form, nor the manner of working; they are made in the same time, and the same manner, as our earthen vessels, only they make them with more diligence and accurateness". On his first visit to Ming China, Semedo spent time in Nanjing (the old capital of the Ming) to gain competence in the Chinese language, then he went to Canton and left there in 1620 for Hangzhou and Jingdezhen.[3] He did not return to Europe until 1637, and then embarked on a second trip in 1644 to what had become the Qing Empire, he eventually died in Canton in 1658. He concluded in the book that Chinese "inventions in many things" made them appear "in no way below us, but in many superior". Then in 1712, a detailed description of porcelain manufacture was introduced to Europe by French Jesuit priest Père Francois Xavier d'Entrecolles who lived seven years in Jingdezhen, which had become the primary porcelain manufacturing centre that produced Western-style patterns destined for European markets. But until as late as 1720, John Bell (1763: 160) was still investigating "the truth of the opinion which the Europeans entertain, 'that the clay must lay a century, to digest, before it is fit for use'" when he visited China.

According to Berg (2003: 14), "English imitations of Chinese and European porcelains generated two new products attuned to much wider markets: the bone china recipe and the creamware body". In 1748, a consortium of London merchants established a factory to exploit an innovative recipe for a soft-paste porcelain that led to the development of fine "bone china". Cream ware, a regional technological achievement, which was built on cumulative and interactive innovation among large numbers of small firms concentrated in a small area of Staffordshire, "became a British version of oriental exportware" (ibid: 14). Works were established at a place they named "New Canton" in imitation of the EIC factory in China, later perfected by other potteries in the later eighteenth century, especially by Josiah Spode and Josiah Wedgwood in Derby and Stoke. During the process of imitation, they were inspired to seek innovative techniques and methods to invent and design products of their own features that can be distinguished from the imports. Wedgwood's biography entry in the Britannica reads as: "English pottery designer and manufacturer, outstanding in his scientific approach to pottery making and known for his exhaustive researches into materials, logical deployment of labour, and sense of business organization".[4] The few key words of "scientific approach", "researches" and "business organisation" summarised the English character and explained his recipe to success. Wedgwood was elected a fellow to the Royal Society in 1783, primarily for inventing the pyrometer to measure oven temperatures.

Staffordshire ware, like Chinese blue and white, quickly established itself as a global product made in England: modern, fashionable and high quality. This was considered "a creative, technological and scientific response to the disruptive influence of Chinese porcelain in commercial and social life" (Ellis et al., 2015: 157). Wedgwood was recorded to say in 1767 that "don't you think we shall have some Chinese missionaries come here soon to learn the art of making Creamcolor?" (cited in Berg, 2007: 81). That was why it was so significant when the Macartney Embassy proudly presented to the Chinese emperor a collection of British-made porcelain. It showed that clay can be processed to a better standard "by the improved mills of England, than by the very imperfect machinery of the Chinese" (Staunton 2: 341–342), while the "precarious" nature of Chinese porcelain manufacture could surely be controlled by European science: "Mr. Wedgwood's thermometer, founded on the quality, ... of clay contracting in proportion to the degree of fire to which it is exposed, might certainly be of use to a Chinese potter" (Staunton, 3: 300–301). This British perception that their own technology had now matched, and even surpassed, that of China found no better expressions than porcelain making. It was quickly commercialised that UK-made Chinese style porcelains entered widely into ordinary British families by the early eighteenth century. Once exotic and magical, it had now been de-mystified, and the British fascination with both China and china shifted.

Before the English porcelain factories reached a steady output of blue-and-white wares decorated with Chinoiseries, Chinese export-ware with a "fusion" style was produced by local artists that played to the Western fantasies of the "exotic Orient". Indeed, as defined by Slobada (2014), Chinoiserie was the Chinese-inspired aesthetic style and objects fashioned in the Chinese taste, that were made *in Europe or China*. They were made in China to cater to this aesthetic intentionally. Its style of combining Chinese and Western techniques and mixing conventions of pictorial motif "re-presented distorted mirrors of the self, emblems of false representation and vanity" to some eighteenth-century critics (Batchelor, 2012: 284), however, its popularity gripped Western consumers who jostled to obtain imported hand-painted porcelain, wallpaper and lacquered cabinets. Since such commodities were made to order according to European designs, it started a strange process of making Chinoiseries a product of local production with alien exoticism: Chinese craftsmen were striving to outdo one another in their renderings of cliched Western preconceptions of Chinese art, or even in imitation of Western Chinoiseries with designs copied from European prints, such as Figure 4.1. This most popular "willow pattern" design was originally engraved by Thomas Minton in about 1793[5] when he established his own pottery factory and subsequently employed by many factories. Incorporating several Chinese motifs, this pattern resembled the ideal of an Anglo-Chinese garden. Even a romantic story was invented to explain the significance of the pagoda, houses, the three little figures hurrying over the bridge and the two birds hovering over them. Eventually, it was exported to the East to be copied on export ware by Chinese painters. In these instances, the process of design and manufacture can be

Figure 4.1 Early Willow Pattern dish in Dovania shape by Spode, c. 1800. Courtesy of Spode Museum Trust.

understood as a point of Sino-European cultural contacts to create a synergy between imitation and innovation.

As an illustration of eighteenth-century Chinese interest in the West, Euroiserie offers a parallel to rebalance this vogue of Chinoiserie. Fascinated by the skills and exquisite quality of European products such as glassworks, clockmaking and enamel painting that constantly flowed into the imperial court as tributes and gifts to please the emperor, all kinds of workshops were founded by the Kangxi Emperor for the domestic production. For example, he established the first imperial glass workshop in 1696 next to a Catholic church near the Forbidden City, supervised by the missionary Kilian Stumpf. Under his guidance, Chinese craftsmen soon mastered the techniques of making translucent and opaque glassware in all kinds of colours, including rare colours like ruby-red or dark blue with gold spangles, identical to glassware made in Italy. The Kangxi Emperor was very proud of the production from his own workshops and gave pieces as diplomatic gifts to European kings and the Pope (Wang, 2017: 47). During the Yongzheng Emperor's reign, a second imperial glass workshop was set up in Yuanming Yuan to satisfy the demand for high quality glassware in the court. It was further expanded by the Qianlong Emperor from Beijing to a much larger network predominantly centred in the south. Clock-making had also reached its peak during the reign of Qianlong when there were more than 100 staff working inside the Imperial Palace workshop. These objects can be considered porcelain's counterparts in China, however, they were mostly made to please the emperor and the ruling class. Qianlong had had such a large collection and expert connoisseurship of clocks that those brought by Macartney failed to impress him.

The making of painted enamelware is another example. The importation of such objects from Europe spurred the development of painted enamels at the Qing court during the late Kangxi era. An enamel workshop was set up in the court and European missionaries skilful in oil painting, such as Matteo Ripa and Giuseppe Castiglione, participated in painting the enamelware. Like glassware, the emperor was not content to merely imitate European works, but wanted to surpass them; he even guided production personally. Through numerous experiments with new raw materials and technologies, the workshop managed to create a distinctive category of imperial painted enamelware and applied it to at least four distinct media: copper, glass, porcelain and Yixing stoneware. This could have been a perfect parallel of British porcelain making in surpassing the original technique, but for the Chinese emperor, the mastering of the production of painted enamelware was a culture race between himself and the European rulers (ibid: 47). This marked the biggest difference between commercialisation of Chinese technology for mass production in the UK and utilisation of western craftsmanship for exclusive status in China. When painted enamel vases were included as return gifts from the Qianlong Emperor to the British King, as the example below showing two gentlemen and a servant in European dress wander in a Chinese landscape (see Figure 4.2), almost a perfect combination of the Chinoiserie and Euroiserie motifs popular at both empires at the time, they were also meant to prove to the West that they had now mastered and exceeded the Western technique.

The range of eighteenth-century Chinese Euroiserie is vast, encompassing various combinations of styles, subjects, materials, formats, techniques and technologies. Sometimes, glass paintings that copied subjects from European copperplate engravings were put into a purple sandalwood frame carved with traditional Chinese-style auspicious cloud and dragon patterns, blending the familiar and the exotic and enabling the Chinese elements to highlight the Westerm auras. This dual nature joined European Chinoiserie with Chinese Euroiserie. After 1757, when all foreign trade was restricted to Canton, Chinese artists there engaged directly with Western drawings, copperplate engravings and other sources as models for both export objects and domestic Euroiserie (Shang, 1986), demonstrating that foreign origin was not as important as indications of foreignness in the works themselves (Kleutghen, 2014: 131). Euroiserie works became more broadly distributed and widely available than just rarities exclusive to the court, offering an object-based window onto how China engaged the West in a trading-inspired cultural exchange.

Figure 4.2 Gifts from the Qinalong Emperor to the Macartney Embassy. Courtesy of the Royal Collection Trust.

Another dimension of Euroiserie is the incorporation of 50 scientific instruments, many of which were from the West or made by Western missionaries, in the book *Illustrated Regulations for Ceremonial Paraphernalia of the Imperial Qing Dynasty*. This unprecedented change to the ritual system is significant, not just in expanding the scope of ritual paraphernalia but more in China's recognition of Western technology and the exchange. However, the impact of the West remained on a superficial level. As put by Wang (2017: 54), "the European art and scientific knowledge that was introduced by the missionaries, from their first appearance until the end of the eighteenth century, was seen as *exotic or wonderful* rather than, perhaps, *important* and *useful*", and the Euroiserie objects reached far greater numbers of Chinese than did Western ideas. This is actually a shared feature between Chinoiserie and Euroiserie in that they both represented a kind of superficial exoticism and a fashion that eventually faded away. Therefore, the echoing between Chinoiserie and Euroiserie only showcased a short-lived period of Yin-Yang flow between China and the West in appearance, but not in essence, as they were used to compete with each other to establish or assume superiority of one over the other, thus not in conformity to the Yin-Yang nexus that stresses on a duality *in relation to*, but also *equal to each* other. This mutual reflection also found its embodiments in architecture and garden styles as the next section will present.

4.2 China's Yuanming Yuan and Britain's Kew Garden and Brighton Palace

I am not the first one to see Yuanming Yuan and Kew Garden as mirror images. Honour (1961: 50) had commented that the Kew Garden was "no more and no less alien and exotic than the Qianlong Emperor's Xiyang Lou". As the most brilliant and classic western-style architecture in Beijing, the Xiyang Lou (The Hall of Western Ocean Pleasure, 西洋楼) was built at a similar period of time, from 1747–1783, to Kew Garden that was opened in 1759 with its Chinese Pagoda completed in 1761. It was a masterpiece located inside Yuanming Yuan, Garden of Perfect Brightness (圆明园), where Chinese emperors had built a huge complex of palaces and other fine buildings since 1707,[6] as a vast and sumptuous repository of the greatest productions and treasures from all over the world. This cultural embodiment of imperial prestige was designed by the most influential Jesuit and court painter Joseph Castiglione who lived in China for 51 years throughout the three prosperous reigns of Kangxi, Yongzheng and Qianlong. Xiyang Lou was an ensemble of art, architecture and landscape, consisting of more than 10 European buildings and courtyards adorned with European facades and interior decoration. It represented a creative attempt at combining European-style architecture, fountains and topiary with garden and landscape in the Chinese taste, merging both European and Chinese aesthetics. The blending of Chinese and Western elements was everywhere. For example, the most famous water clock in front of the Grand Hall were made in the design of the 12 zodiac animals, as replacements of nude sculptures in Western architecture; inside the maze that itself was a borrowed idea from a typical European garden was a miniature of the Middle Kingdom worldview with the central pavilion surrounded by eight circles representing the four corners of the world from eight directions. Figure 4.3 was plate 15 from a set of 20 engravings, depicting the prime view of the Great Fountain: next to the ornamentally clipped tall trees were two 13-story fountains in the shape of Chinese pagodas with lotus flower-shaped spouts.

By Qianlong's reign, this impressive complex was known as the "Chinese Versailles". Ringmar's (2013: 37) description of the Audience Hall well captured the bi-focal image: "The throne was carved in rosewood and decorated with dragons …. Below it and along the opposing wall were side tables with books and yellow silk covers, porcelain bowls, a celestial and terrestrial globe, and a musical clock made by George Clarke, Leadenhall Street, London". In a way, we can see clocks decorate the rooms as porcelain vases; singsong boxes are like lacquerware; Western painting are like Chinese wallpaper and enamel ceramics often

Figure 4.3 "Dashuifa zhengmian (The Great Fountain main façade)" from "*Xiyang Shuifa Tu* (*Pictures of the Western-style Buildings and Waterworks*)", ca. 1783–1786, copperplate engraving printed on paper, 507 × 877 mm. In public domain: https://zh.wikipedia.org/wiki/%E5%A4%A7%E6%B0%B4%E6%B3%95#/media/File:Yuanmingyuan_dashuifa.jpg

feature Western ladies and architecture. Fanciful, intricate, imaginative and delicate became commonly shared descriptive words to portray both the Chinoiserie and Euroiserie. However, when it was also considered the Qianlong Emperor's "cabinet of curiosities" (Wong, 2016), it indicated that this first imitated European park in China was intended to show "everything under the heaven" as a display of the emperor's extended knowledge and power. The large collection of European scientific instruments and decorative arts, paintings, European-style furniture and tapestries, as well as magnificent pier glasses gifted by Louis XV in 1767 that particularly fascinated the emperor, were all put under the gaze of Chinese dragons. As mentioned earlier, the emperors' fascinations with these exotic objects and novel products from Europe also inspired their enthusiasm to emulate and create their own versions in the imperial workshops, supervised by Jesuit missionaries. Many decorations in Xiyang Lou were made by such imperial workshops, including the fountains that fascinated the Qianlong Emperor the most. However, the main reason to have the waterworks built inside the Yuanming Yuan was to show off that China was majestic to have all wonders. They were made prime sites to entertain and impress foreign embassies, including the Macartney Embassy in 1793, again showing that Euroiserie was merely a way to define China's own superiority. In fact, the Xiyang Lou quarter only accounted for about 2% of the whole Yuanming Yuan, and was located in its northern corner, signifying its position in the *Hua-Yi* atlas.

On the other side of the globe, the Chinoiserie obsession gripped England and reached its zenith between the 1750s and 1760s when countless Confucian temples and Chinese bridges had sprung up in landscape gardens across England. This gained Yuanming Yuan, the Chinese Emperor's imperial garden, the prestige of being the ultimate example of a visual representation and cultural statement of the so-called "fantastic Sharawadgi". The exotic term *Sharawadgi* was first coined by William Temple in his essay *Upon the Garden of Epicurus* (1685), in which he contrasted the principles of European and Chinese garden design. He claimed it unequivocally as the Chinese word to describe the idea of a pleasing natural beauty without order in garden design, in contrast to the straight lines, geometrical shapes, regularity, and symmetries then popular in European gardens. However, this claim subsequently became controversial, as no Chinese origin of *Sharawadgi* had ever been corroborated, though there were some attempts, or rather guessworks, made by Chinese scholars. For example, Chang (1930: 223) translated the word as meaning "beautiful disorder", "anti-symmetry" or "unorderly grace", and as a Chinese way to govern the garden layout and design in his essay "*A Note on Sharawadgi*", but no Chinese original expression was given. It elaborated how the art of putting irregularity together to form an "admirable variety", which gave visitors a delightful and enchanting feeling. Another famous scholar Qian Zhongshu also devoted a lengthy discussion to William Temple in his Master thesis completed at Oxford between 1935–1937, titled "*China in the English Literature of the Seventeenth and the Eighteenth Centuries*". In discussing where Temples got the word *Sharawadgi* from, Qian (1945) argued that "shara" might come from "*san lan*" (*scattered,* 散乱) or "*su lo*" (*sparsely dotted,* 疏落), while "wadgi" may come from "*wai chi*'" (*location,* 位置). Combined together, the meaning of *Sharawadgi* refers to space tastefully enlivened by disorder. However, it was not very convincing especially because the key to this concept is not "location" but anti "man-made regularity". There are also other scholars who suggested that the word may derive from a Japanese word "Sorowaji" (Shimada, 1997; Shih, 2015: 75), which means to leave things as they are or not to touch.

In disregard of the actual origin of the word, Temple's essay led to a drastic transformation of English taste in landscaping, being "the first suggestion ever of a possible beauty fundamentally different from the formal, a beauty of irregularity and fancy" (Talbot, forthcoming: 8). It started a new aesthetic current, which was further popularised by Addison's extensive essay written for the *Spectator* in 1712, "*The Pleasures of the Imagination*", in which he cited Chinese gardens as an example of a new principle of beauty that could be applied to all forms of art. While Temple was a little cautious about the new asymmetric and natural look, Addison embraced it wholeheartedly. It was his essay that brought the word *Sharawadgi* to a much wider audience and established it as the term to describe the aesthetics of Chinese gardens (ibid: 18). Yet, the most peculiar parallel was the symmetric European topiary in the foreground at Xiyang Lou as shown in Figure 4.3, just like the dots of Yin and Yang in the Chinese and European gardens.

The concept of *Sharawadgi* may seem very Chinese in reflecting the philosophy of being harmoniously ordered with the nature, however, since neither Temple nor Addison had ever been to China, the concept was very much shaped with their own imaginations that the Chinese gardens were created with free-style varieties. This made me think that perhaps the word *Sharawadgi* itself is the best embodiment of Chinoiserie: it had a self-claimed origin from China, but not immediately recognisable by any Chinese person, yet it was taken as the representation of Chineseness. Just like the porcelain we looked at in the section above, it was those made in China for the European market following European designs, that were extraordinarily popular.

The Brighton Pavilion was another example of Europeanised form of Chinoiserie that was often considered another mirror of the European-styled Xiyang Lou in England. Like the Qianlong Emperor, the Prince Regent also had orientalist fantasy and large collections of exotic items. In 1802 the Prince Regent was given some beautiful Chinese wallpaper and decided to make a Chinese gallery for it in the Pavilion he was then building at Brighton. As the building went on year after year, the interior became extravagantly Chinese while the exterior was Hindu, a representation of exoticism and Chinoiserie. Mayor (1941: 114) described that "there was a corridor like an immense Chinese lantern with walls and ceiling of stained glass of an oriental character, and exhibiting the peculiar insects, fruits, flowers, etc. of China". On one wall of the Banqueting Room was "a vast dragon, finely carved and most brilliantly coloured, the wings and scales being redolent of metallic green and silver", which was well captured in the caricature below (see Figure 4.4). It also showed a Chinese pagoda hanging from the ceiling, with the self-indulgent image of the Regent at the central position, presenting a letter to the ambassador dressed in a Chinese robe and hat to take to China. When the Amherst Embassy was sent to China from this Palace, the instructions included getting "fresh patterns of Chinese deformities to finish the decorations of ye Pavilion". As we would find out in Chapter 6, Amherst came back with a disillusioned image of China, and by the time when the Pavilion was finally completed in 1822, the tide of China's popularity was also on the wane, the refinement that Chinoiserie used to represent was now read as excessiveness, evoking "a China of imperial extravagance and self-indulgence" (Kitson, 2013: 225).

Today, both the Chinese pagoda at the Kew Garden and the Brighton Palace still stand imposingly for people to admire their magnificence, but the Yuanming Yuan in Beijing was looted and burnt down in 1860 by the French and British forces during the Second Opium War.[7] It left a deep,

Figure 4.4 The Court at Brighton a la Chinese! Courtesy of The Lewis Walpole Library. Courtesy of Yale University.

unhealed historical wound in the British relations with China. Some of the items, including the "throne of the Emperor of China" was taken back and presented to Queen Victoria, on display at the Victoria and Albert Museum today. "They wanted to transfer the political and cultural prestige attached to the emperor's belongings to their own sovereigns" (Thomas, 2008: 12). A cannon of European manufacture was found inside Yuanming Yuan and identified as a gift from King George III to the Qianlong emperor brought by the Macartney Embassy, which was also taken back and placed at the Royal Arsenal at Woolwich where it had been manufactured. Liu (2006: 217) believed that both the "taking possession" of the chair and "repossession and repatriation" of the cannon amounted to "settling an old score". To the British, this was both a most delightful dreamland where "the variety of the picturesque was endless, and charming in the extreme; indeed, all that is most lovely in Chinese scenery" (Swinhoe, 1861: 301),[8] and a place "in which the ambassador of an English king had been insulted with impunity" (Wolseley, 1862: 226), while for the Chinese emperor, it was a retreat that Qianlong believed "every emperor and ruler must, upon retiring from his official duties and audiences, have a garden in which to stroll, to look round and find rest for his heart" (Singer, 1992: 40). For the Chinese people today however, it was a site of ruins that became an "patriotic education base" that tell the story of “a century of humiliations”. As all school children in China are taught, it was once the most beautiful collection of architecture and art in the country and the world.

As the epitome of superiority between the two civilisations, the fate of Yuanming Yuan became a symbolic witness of the evolving relationship between the two empires: first as a pleasure ground for the Chinese emperor to enjoy a life of poetry and graciousness, drinking tea in a waterside pavilion beneath a weeping willow; then a wonderland of a most sophisticated Chinese garden with enchanting architectures and landscapes that inspired European art form; when the Macartney Embassy came, it was the showcase space where the British gifts were displayed with mutual admirations, though not openly expressed by the Chinese; but then turned into a humiliating venue where the second embassy of Lord Amherst was rejected; and finally it became a theatre that staged the most tragic cultural destruction in human history. Victor Hugo compared it to the Parthenon of Greece, the Pyramids of Egypt and the Coliseum of Rome that took generations of work to create, but “this wonder is no more …... We Europeans are civilised, and to us the Chinese are barbarians. Here is what civilisation has done to barbarism!” (cited in Peyrefitte, 1992: 530). To this Lord Elgin and General Montauban claimed that “only through acts of barbarism could civilisation be spread” (Ringmar, 2011: 293). Ringmar (2013) called the destruction an act of “liberal barbarism”, “it was only by first defining, and then defeating, the wonders of the East that the Europeans could come to take their place” (Ringmar, 2011: 294). The marvels of the palace served to glorify their victory, with which the British had finally emerged as the uncontested rulers of the world. “The destruction of the emperor’s palace”, said Wolseley (1862: 281), “was the strongest proof of our superior strength; it served to undeceive all Chinamen in their absurd conviction of their monarch’s universal sovereignty”. The relationship of power had shifted. England was the first Western Ocean country trying to change China’s century-old Tributary System, while China was the last major non-European country to openly defy the British supremacy.

A comparison of the three accounts of Yuanming Yuan written over a century apart shows how dramatic these transformations have been. “Everything there is grand and truly beautiful which I could never express”, the Jesuit missionary Jean Denis Attiret assured his European correspondent in 1745, “and I am all the more struck by it, since I never have seen anything like it” (cited in Ringmar, 2011: 274). Yet in 1793, the palaces’ style was considered too heavily decorated and “not only destitute of elegance but in a wretched state of repair” by members of the Macartney Embassy (Anderson, 1795: 111). John Barrow, who spent five weeks inside the palace, “saw none of those extravagant beauties and picturesque embellishments” that had made Yuanming Yuan famous throughout Europe. “Of those parts contiguous to the palace, which may be supposed the most carefully cultivated, and the numerous pavilions and ornamental buildings in the best order, I can say nothing in praise; no care whatever appeared to be taken of any, nor regard had to cleanliness" (Barrow, 1804: 85–86). Then in 1860, in refusing to marvel, the British commanders emphasised the powerlessness of the Chinese in the face of European imperialism. "In this way the language of wonder provides us with a way of characterizing the relationship between Europe and China, and its transformation over time" (Ringmar, 2011: 275): "the frisson of wonder was no longer caused by an unknown Oriental other, but by a new, previously unknown self" (ibid: 294).

These changing accounts of Yuanming Yuan correlate with the changing fortunes of Chinoiserie. By the 1790s, Chinoiserie, which had been a symbol of China's exquisite beauty and a display of sophisticated taste, thus become integral to "Englishness", was reduced to fragile, breakable objects whose style was often regarded as vulgar, at least among men of neoclassical tastes as they became disillusioned with the partly imagined China they had once so admired. By the time of the Macartney Embassy to Beijing in 1793, the commodities imported into England from China – porcelain, silk, tea, fans, screens and so on – had become markers of a culturally feminised Chinoiserie, a "lynchpin for changing aesthetic attitudes and changing perceptions of social, gender, and national identity" (Markley, 2014: 518). Orientalism, whose discourse established the East as antithetical to the West as argued by Said, came to redefine the cultured British self by rejecting the appreciation of, and desire for, Chinese commodities as a standard of cultural sophistication (Jenkins, 2013). This shift can be clearly seen in the changing perceptions of China at the intellectual level when the first embassy was proposed.

4.3 The British perception of Qing China and the perception gap to the real Qing

What was shown in the first two sections of this chapter is China's role in offering the British luxury material goods, and its changing status as the inspiration of aesthetics; this section will show the more significant role China played as an imagination of civilisation, as well as Britain's changing perceptions of this role, to contextualise the general knowledge level and the perception gap held by the British when the first embassy was conceived. Before the Macartney Embassy, the British and Chinese rarely visited "the other" empire, information about each other came from second-hand sources: hearsay, missionary writings and translations of foreign accounts. As explained in previous chapters, early European travellers wrote immensely popular accounts about China, impressed and sometimes awestruck by its wealth beyond measure, its intricate bureaucracy regulating an expansive territory, its documented history and enviable cultural achievements. After the Age of Exploration, knowledge of China derived more from reports made by Jesuits with residential experiences, many lived in China for years or even decades, allowing them to gain new deeper insights into the Chinese empire and its culture. When they returned to Europe, they wrote books about China and mingled with celebrities and scholars at the time, such as Gottfried Wilhelm Leibniz, Baron de Montesquieu and Voltaire, who believed that "If, as a philosopher, one wishes to instruct oneself about what has taken place on the globe, one must first of all turn one's eyes towards the East, the cradle of all arts to which the West owes everything" (cited in Reichwein, 1925: 90). As a central theme of intellectual dialogues and debates during the Enlightenment and Romantic periods, China as an empire ruled by a wise despot, in consultation with a rational civil service, abstaining from pointless wars and religious persecution, played a crucial role in the transformation of European ideas of civilisation, enlightenment and aesthetics. Therefore, albeit with different motivations, missionary writings continued to contribute to the construction of "Chineseness" in the European imaginations and inspired many more writings on China by those who had never been to China themselves, further nourishing decades-long English interest in China.

Images and texts, even maps, were all carriers of knowledge on China, which was used by people who did not have first-hand experience to justify their knowledge claims. For example, the book acclaimed by Voltaire to provide the "fullest" and "best" description and comprehensive knowledge about China in the world was *Geographical, Historical, Chronological, Political and Physical Description of the Empire of China and Chinese Tartary* compiled by Du Halde, who himself had never left Paris and read no Chinese characters. It was drawn from the Jesuit reports he collected, first published in four volumes in French in 1735, then translated into English as *The General History of China* in 1736. In a way, the book was the mental map he drew about this distant land whose encounter with the West was more in the forms of traded goods than exchanged ideas at the time. Samuel Johnson (1846, vol 2: 590) complimented it as "the most copious and accurate account yet published, of that remote and celebrated people, whose antiquity, magnificence, power, wisdom, peculiar customs and excellent constitution, undoubtedly deserve the attention of the public". These works had definitely captured attention of the intellectuals and elites from England. For example, a catalogue of Macartney's library, dated 1786, included writings of Du Halde, Libnitz, Samuel Johnson, Locke, Voltaire and Hume. Adam Smith also had a copy of Du Halde's book in his library when he was writing the *Wealth of Nations* in 1776.

As Williams (2014: 3) observed, "the decades between Loum's visit to London and the Macartney Embassy mark a period in which, although opportunities for contact between the two sides were increasing, British impressions of Chinese merchants and court officials still remained structured by idealising fantasy rather than revised (frequently in negative ways) by closer acquaintance". Indeed, the arrival of merchants changed the way China knowledge was predominately produced by missionaries, the fresh first-hand accounts provided by such "closer acquaintance" added a different layer to the image of China. The biggest difference between these two groups of visitors is that the missionaries were willing to adapt to the Chinese way, while the merchants found the Chinese way of conducting trade hard to accept. The other difference was that the main contacts of these new visitors to China were no longer the upper or middle classes of Chinese society but the Chinese merchants and seamen who belonged to the lower stratum and who were much more disposed to take advantage of foreign merchants engaged in commerce with them. These first-hand accounts led to a changing image of China and anti-Chinese writings kept emerging, showing a divided image of China between "extremes of unreserved contempt and uncritical admiration" (Hung, 2003: 255). In a way, the knowledge and perception of eighteenth-century China was like a collage of philosophical ideas, missionaries' accounts, travellers' narratives and merchants' reports. As Yang (2011:18) summarised, for eighteenth-century readers, China embodied "contradictions like civilisation and barbarism, enlightenment and despotism". These contradictory images tangled up one another in "a contemporary ambivalence in Britain towards the much-vaunted achievements of Chinese civilisation as well as a common reluctance to grant too much credit to a potential rival on the world stage" (Porter, 2010: 41).

Macartney packed away a good representation of such a collage in his voyage as it took about nine months to complete. He "stocked the Lion's library with nearly every book on China published over the past century" (Peyrefitte, 1992: 25). As Macartney declared in the Appendix to his China Journal, "[b]efore I set out upon my Embassy to China, I perused all the books that had been written about the country in all the languages I could understand. With everybody from whom I had hopes of information I endeavoured to converse, and where that could not be done, I corresponded with them by letter" (Cranmer-Byng, 1962: 278). Such sources of information include the Royal Society that Macartney was a fellow of. Its then president, Sir Joseph Banks, held a genuine admiration for the Chinese civilisation and viewed China not as a stagnant polity in need of Western civilisation but as one from which the British had much to learn from. As a matter of fact, he was the mastermind behind both embassies to China. Macartney was also a member of "The Literary Club" mentioned in Chapter 3. Other members such as William Jones, Adam Smith and Thomas Percy shared the interest in the Orient.

For example, Adam Smith, although never travelled to China, had pinpointed some striking features of China in the *Wealth of Nations*. After describing China as "has been long one of the richest, that is, one of the most fertile, best cultivated, most industrious, and most populous countries in the world" (Smith, 1776: 88), he pointed that "the poverty of the lower ranks of people in China far surpasses that of the most beggarly nations in Europe" (ibid: 56). His description of peasants also remained true even in today's rural China: "if by digging the ground a whole day he can get what will purchase a small quantity of rice in the evening, he is contented". But "the Chinese have little respect for foreign trade" (Smith, 1776: 88), actually rejecting international commerce as a primary driver of national prosperity. This was in direct opposition to the laissez-faire trade practice that he promoted in the modern conceptual framework. So he treated the paradox of China's prosperity as a "singular case". He exemplified the Chinese economy as an example of a "natural" economic path that focused on labour-intensive forms of development and on improving its domestic economy, while Britain was an example of "unnatural" path of intensive capital development fuelled by extensive foreign trade. Overall, Smith believed China had long been stationary. "Marco Polo, who visited it more than five hundred years ago, describes its cultivation, industry, and populousness, almost in the same terms they are described by travellers in the present times" (ibid: 88). Hume also saw little or no progress in the Chinese sciences since the time of Confucius and attributed this absence to an inability to break with the past, while Percy blamed on the rote learning of the Chinese, which in many ways a preface to Joseph Needham's Grant Question[9] later in the twentieth century.

If Smith's analysis was more into Britain's expansive capitalism vs. China's feudal political order and economic model, Percy's *Pleasing History,* the first English translation (in abbreviated form) of a Chinese novel, was more about China's national characters, manners and customs. In the index to the book that was published in 1761, under the heading of "CHINESE (the)", he listed 14 entries of "the dark side of their character" such as affected, crafty, corrupt, and cowardly, and 12 entries of "the bright side of their character", such as complaisant, decent, dextrous, dutiful to their parents (cited in Porter 2010: 161). These two sides may represent Percy's own conflicting attitude to China, with the scale slightly tilted to the negative side. He defined the Chinese in opposition to English in that "The English embrace political and by extension imaginative freedom; the Chinese know only servile submission, they are the most politically restrained people in the world", and "the Chinese are the most ceremonious and complaisant people in the world" (ibid: 168–169). Porter (2010: 163) believed that "no other major eighteen-century writer in England ventured so far as Percy in asserting commensurability between the great ancient civilisations of East and West". This commensurability echoes the Yin-Yang flow I described earlier. China exhibited some qualities that can serve as a model of inspiration is some aspects, as the notion of European superiority was not yet fully established at this time. As Anderson put in the Preface to his *Narrative of the British Embassy to China* (1795: 1): the embassy was from "our enlightened country, to the only civilised nation in the world", and the purpose was to achieve "an important national object" of "a commercial alliance between the Courts of London and Pekin".

By this time, there were also a few travelogues available written by British people[10]: *A Voyage round the World by George* Anson (1748), *A Voyage to the East Indies in 1747 and 1748* by Charles Frederick Noble (1762), and John Bell's *Travels from St Petersburg in Russia to Divers Parts of Asia* (1763),[11] offering diverse perspectives. Anson was a British naval officer who later became First Lord of the Admiralty, Noble was a former EIC trader who had lived in Canton from 1747–1748, and Bell was a Scottish physician and traveller in the suite of a Russian embassy sent by Peter the Great to the Kangxi Emperor. Noble (1762: iii) stated in his Preface that the travel genre should strike a balance between giving information on "the laws, manners, and customs of foreign nations, [which] enable us to consider society in a more philosophic and comprehensive view", and promoting "a spirit of enterprise" in its readers. He presented his experience of Canton that blended philosophical enquiry with commercial pragmatism as "a narrative of deepening cultural insight", permitted by intimacy with a local Chinese merchant, "a man endowed with a degree of knowledge and sagacity greatly beyond what is commonly possessed by people of that class". For this reason, Williams (2014: 10) thinks Noble's book reworks Goldsmith's *The Citizen of the World* (1760–61), in a similar philosophical and comparative perspective, and his experiences in the city offered a stark contrast to Anson's five years earlier.

Before we look at what was written in these travel accounts, we need to keep two things in mind: First, memory is always a selective thing, thus accounts based on memories are also selective, and reference to them only became more selective to suit different purposes. As well-said by Porter (2010: 39), "the cognitive dissonance may be experienced at the moment of encounter as surprise, self-alienation, perplexity, or aesthetic delight, but it seems safe to assume that its effects colour enduring memories of this seminal moment and leave their traces upon its subsequent representation", and "their representations of the foreign must always arise from distinct subject positions whose historical and social particularities lend themselves to certain limited and limiting ways of seeing the world".

Second, as Hargrave (2016: 518) pointed out, the problem with travel narratives is that "rather than engaging in intellectual research into Chinese history and culture", they "assumed a predominantly comparative method of describing China, a method that, to ventriloquize Edward W. Said, tells us more about England than China". Since all writers are more or less conditioned by their immediate society, their accounts are the cultural products of the encounter, where images of "the other" tend to reflect the contrasting relationship with "self" and the collective ideology of the home society. For example, Marco Polo was impressed by the prosperous and benevolent ruling of the Chinese emperor with reference to Italy back then, while Anson's account revealed the image of China in a naval commander's eyes 500 years later. Hung (2003: 263) called this changing perception "grounded on the specific intercivilisation balance of power", and "the thrust of capitalist growth and colonialism titled the balance of power between East and West". Yet, when we compare Anson and Bell's descriptions of China, it is most interesting to see how differently the "other" may be depicted by people of the same country, from a similar period of time, but in different identities and under different circumstances when their encounters with China took place.

Anson's squadron reached Macau and Canton in late 1742 and early 1743. However, the book treated Canton as an epitome of China as a whole, and based its evaluation of China and Chinese people on what they had seen or experienced in Canton. This treatment alone shows the limitation of Anson's knowledge level of China, whose territory size is close to the whole continent of Europe with an even bigger size of population and large regional disparities. It is almost as fallacious as using England to represent the whole of Europe. The visit was not a planned one either but a forced stay to seek help: the squadron was originally sent round Cape Horn of South America to damage Spanish interests in the Pacific as the Great Britain was at war with Spain at the time. After a voyage of many disasters that all but the flagship *Centurion* was lost, they touched the Chinese coast for repairs and supplies of fresh food. Due to a number of bad communications with the local Chinese officers and being cheated by some of the local merchants, Anson had a bitter experience and his story of Chinese dishonesty and cupidity was published in his travelogue *A Voyage round the World by George Anson,* finished by Richard Walter, the chaplain of the *Centurion.* His biting narration painted a China acting in contrary to the spirit of the age that a vessel requiring aid should not be treated as an intruder. However, *Centurion* was not the first warship that had arrived at the Chinese coast in distress. An entry in the Qing court archive dated 17 November 1700 showed "China Gives Aid to the Ship-wrecked English":

> The viceroy of Fukien and Chekiang, Kuo Shih-lung, memorialized that one warship of the Kingdom of the Red-haired Barbarians, Ying-kuei-li (England) was driven ashore by a storm. The Imperial edict stated: The ship of Ying-kuei-li (the English) has been blown ashore by the storm: indeed it is pitiful. Let the local magistrates take good care of her crew, give them sufficient clothes and food, and then dispatch them back in due time, conforming to our ideas of treating foreigners with hospitality.
>
> (Fu, 1966: 111)

Again, Anson used his individual unfortunate experience to represent China's resistance to the progress of the modern world. Besides, according to Coates's narration (1966: 50), the "refitting and replenishment" was completed and "Anson left the coast in April 1743", but "three months later he re-entered the river towing the Spanish treasure ship for the 1743 season, master of several hundred Spanish prisoners and a booty of £400,000, one of the richest prizes ever taken in war". This made the Chinese view the British as being "more dangerous than any barbarian seen in China within living memory, a pirate on a terrifying scale" (ibid: 51). As a matter of fact, in the *Documentary Chronicle of Sino-Western Relations (1644–1820),* the entry regarding Anson's visit was dated 21 September 1743 under the heading of "The First British Warship Enters the China Sea" (Fu, 1966: 175), which was consistent with Coates's narration (1966: 51–52) that Anson first sailed as far as Tiger Island and asked for provisions as on his previous visit, then "in September, still without provisions, Anson went up to Canton by barge".

Most travelogue authors reflect on the differences between the land and people they visited in comparison and contrast with their own home cultures. In Anson's book, ruthless comparisons were made using British culture and military strength as a yardstick to judge China. As expected, Anson as a naval commander from the sovereign of the sea, despised China, whose poor military force was "extremely defective" in his eyes (Anson, 1748: 512). He claimed that "the *Centurion* alone was capable of destroying the whole navigation of the port of Canton, or of any other port in China, without running the least risk from all the force the Chinese could collect". He even suggested that the British crew had behaved with great "modesty and reserve" not to attack the "defenceless" Chinese (ibid: 479–480). He gave many examples to discredit the Chinese and complained that China, in comparison to England, was an autocratic and stagnant country. All the complimentary descriptions of Chinese people by Marco Polo were almost replaced by their antonyms: the Chinese were arrogant, greedy, hypocritical, selfish, timid, backward, unhygienic and unintelligent. In comparison, England was an efficient, powerful, progressive, warlike, wealthy and well-governed country, and the British were brave, civilised, disciplined, dutiful, honest, humane, hygienic, industrious, ingenious, intelligent, righteous, talented and unselfish. The whole book's perspective is confined to this comparative frame, with no effort made at understanding, even the Chinese language was seen to reflect "obstinacy and absurdity", and that "the history and inventions of past ages, recorded by these perplexed symbols, must frequently prove unintelligible; and consequently the learning and boasted antiquity of the Nation must, in numerous instances, be extremely problematical" (ibid: 543). His resentful sentiment in these lines was apparent, but after he returned to England, he built a Chinese House in his garden at Shugborough in 1747 and ordered 114 armorial plates from Jingdezhen, showing the prevailing influence of Chinoiserie at the time. One thing he could not have imagined was how his own visit would go down in Chinese records as an example of "boasted absurdity": in the Mandarin's report sent to Beijing, the emperor was informed that "a dangerous red barbarians in a heavily armed ship had threateningly attempted to enter the Pearl River, but terrified by the might of Chinese arms he had been driven away" (cited in Coates, 1966: 53). Of course, Chinese language would be wrongly blamed for such absurdity, but the system of autocracy, which means the emperor was often hoodwinked as all the Mandarins cared was to please him so as to protect their own positions, not to protect the national interests. We have seen this in their glossing over the casualties in the military skirmish with Weddell in Chapter 2, we will see a more dramatic example in their dealings with the Amherst Embassy in Chapter 6. Similarly, when the Chinese emperor turned the page of this incident with no particular attention paid, he could never have imagined what happened to this commander during his very brief stay at only one port of China would be shaping the British perception of China for decades to come, as his book became a best-seller instantly and was reprinted in full or abridged forms in numerous editions.

In sharp contrast to Anson's book, John Bell's account of his overland journey to China made in 1719–1722, across the ancient caravan trails known as the Silk Road, gave a very balanced evaluation of China in both advantages and disadvantages. Compared with British merchant adventurers, who were confined to a trading compound at Canton with denied access to China's interior, Bell was the first British writer to visit the capital of China in person,[12] had an audience with the Chinese emperor and had written about him based upon his own first-hand observations. The Russian embassy sent by Peter the Great entered the Chinese territories on 22 September in 1720 and left China on 6 April 1721. During his stay in China, mostly in Beijing, Bell kept numerous notes that became the raw materials for his book published decades later. The content of these notes covered a wide range of aspects of Chinese life, such as the imperial ceremony of receiving foreign delegates, the hunting sport of the Kangxi Emperor, the royal banquets, the duties of foreign missionaries at the Chinese imperial court, the structure and size of the Great Wall, the natural resources of China, the history of military conflicts between the Tartars and the Chinese, the main religions of the Chinese, the Chinese New Year festivals, as well as the diplomatic relationships between China and its neighbouring states. Bell seldom reflected morally or philosophically on the differences between Britain and China, he positioned himself more as an observer, recording his impressions accurately by separating fact from fiction, and hearsay from what he witnessed at first-hand.

In Bell's writing, the Chinese were a civilised and hospitable people; complaisant to strangers, and to one another; very regular in their manners and behaviour, and respectful to their superiors; but, above all, their regard for their parents, and decent treatment of their women of all ranks, ought to be imitated, and deserve great praise (Bell, 1763: 182). In addition to the good qualities listed above, Bell further attributed many positive characteristics to the Chinese, such as decency in manners, honesty in conducting business, parsimoniousness in workmanship, patience in finishing works, ingeniousness and sobriety and peace-loving in handling international affairs (ibid:184). While complimenting Chinese skills at porcelain making and paper-making, he also pointed that "their workmanship in metals is but clumsy; except only founding, at which they are very expert. The arts of statuary, sculpture, and painting, have made but small progress among them .... The making of clocks and watches was lately introduced, under the protection of the present Emperor" (ibid: 182). On the whole, Bell found the Chinese to be highly civilised and enjoyed his time there greatly. Nash (2015: 106) commented that Bell's narrative "pictures an empire that has flourished because it values civility, liberty and the rule of law under a benevolent monarchy solicitous of its subjects' welfare".

Bell's description of the reception with the Chinese emperor offered a rare glimpse of the imperial palace to the British eyes. The emperor was praised as a man of humanity, good nature, affability, self-discipline, generous disposition and more than once referred as a philosopher. Bell clearly distinguished the ruling Tartars from the subjected Chinese in his writing. He also explained why the Kangxi Emperor kept the habit of going out to hunt with his sons and the Tartar nobles at such an advanced age: it was because the Tartar monarch wished to prevent his nomadic army from falling into idleness and effeminacy among the Chinese (Bell, 1763: 138, 150, 155, 162–163, 169–172 and 179). However, there was none of that splendour Bell expected to see from reading the pages of Marco Polo, whose account kept giving rise to disillusions to latecomers. But contrary to the national pride deeply held by Anson after Britain became the greatest maritime power in Europe, Bell, as a member of the Russian Embassy, illustrated "Britain's relative inconsequence compared with the importance of imperial Russia to the mighty Chinese empire" (ibid: 106). For example, according to his account, the Russian Ambassador not only had multiple audiences with the Emperor during their six-week stay in Beijing, he was also invited to the Palace for Chinse New Year celebration and Lantern Festival celebrations, and even a hunting trip with the emperor. The last audience of leave took place at the Emperor's bed-chamber. Most importantly is the negotiation regarding the ceremony of the Ambassador's introduction to the Emperor, which finally agreed on the terms that "the Ambassador should comply with the established customs of the court of China; and when the Emperor sent a minister to Russia, he should have instructions to conform himself, in every respect, to the ceremonies in use at that court" (Bell, 1763, Vol 2: 4). A spirit of reciprocity can be seen in these negotiations.

As Nash (2015: 92) described, Bell's account

> opened the gate into the splendours of the Imperial Palace at Peking, which for more than a century had been seen refracted mainly through Jesuit accounts. He is received hospitably by the Jesuits and witnesses the honours lavished upon a fully credentialled Russian ambassador, a reception unknown to the British after six decades of desultory efforts to expand trade and establish diplomatic relations, and one that would elude Lord Macartney when, more than half a century later, he led Britain's first embassy to China in 1793.

Therefore, Macartney should find his accounts particularly informative. Bell also acknowledged that the Chinese presents were more of symbolic value as he found "the presents, consisting of a complete Chinese dress, some pieces of damasks, and other stuffs, were, indeed, of no great value" (ibid: 137), but he suggested that huge profits might be made by importing Chinese tea and chinaware into Europe.

Bell's observation of China's relationship with Russia and England was in conformity with Fu's (1966) *Documentary Chronicle of Sino-Western Relations (1644–1820)*. Among all states having contacts with China during the Kangxi, YongZheng and Qianlong's reigns, Russia dominated the Sino-Western Relations. Both were extensive and expansive land-based empires, on signing the Treaty of Nipchu[13] in I689, China recognised the Tsar as a foreign monarch and demarcated a border line between the two empires, an area fraught with dangers and numerous invasions. The negotiation did not begin with the presentation of tribute gifts; instead, delegations presented their credentials to each other, and they faced each other in equal status, each observing their own customs: the Russians on chairs, the Qing on cushions on the ground (Perdue, 2010: 348). For these reasons, Perdue (ibid: 341) argued that "the Nerchinsk Treaty stands out in world history as a remarkable victory for diplomatic cross-cultural interchange" as "China and Russia have accepted roughly the same principles of equality". Relations between the two empires remained remarkably non-confrontational after the treaty was signed, which also guaranteed "mutual commerce" by establishing set trade routes and for the next decade, Russian caravans came to Beijing every year (and about every two years after that). The 1721 embassy[14] was even granted permission to install a representative in Beijing who would oversee all Russian commerce and, when problems arose, spoke for the Russian Empire and its various policies. Although it only lasted for about two years, it showed Western-style diplomacy might be allowed to function in China at certain times and under certain circumstances, as a strategy to maintain peace and balance of power.

In 1729, a Chinese delegation was dispatched by the Yongzheng Emperor with lavish gifts to congratulate the new tsar Peter II, who suddenly died before they arrived and tsarina Anna Ivanovna was on the throne, so a new delegation was dispatched. "Each of the two embassies was granted an initial audience and most unusual of all, several narrators have informed us that the Manchu ambassadors did not hesitate to kowtow before the Russian throne when presenting their messages from the emperor, an unprecedented sign that Russia was not being considered as a tribute nation" (Muller, 1732–1764, 1: 47–48, 52, 61, 68). Little wonder that these ceremonies captured the imagination of numerous eyewitnesses, and in addition to archival documents in Russian, a detailed record of each audience was published in German in 1732 (Muller, 1732–1764, 1: 34–74). A French text of the first one was also forwarded to London by the secretary to the British consul-general at St. Petersburg, who rightly remarked that "this is the first embassy from the Chinese court to any prince in Europe" (Diplomaticheskaya, 1889, 281–282, 283–870, cited in Keevak, 2017: 155). As Keevak (2017, 155–156) summarised, in so many ways these two legations seem indistinguishable from those that the West had been sending to China: they were diplomatic operations initiated by Beijing, making a series of requests to a foreign government couched in a mission of congratulations. More importantly, "they attempted to convince the other side of their sincerity through elaborate gifts and by observing all necessary protocols; and they operated under the premise that both sides should be able to negotiate as equal partners". All these were what the British wanted, but this recognition of mutual obligation and national sovereignty based on equal status was never achieved by Britain, which was considered a small island nation beyond the seas by Qing China, in no comparison to the Russian Empire.

The reasons why Anson and Bell's accounts reached such wildly different conclusions of China are multiple. The most important one is China being a giant empire with huge divergence and complexity. The distance from Canton to Peking is six times greater than between London and Paris, and the size of Qing China is over 160 times bigger than that of Britain. Therefore, the picture one got depends on which region they visited and who they came into dealings with – merchants in south China for Anson and court officials in Beijing for Bell. They belonged to different social classes in the very hierarchical society of China. If we compare the imperial garden to Du Halde's description of Chinese "kitchen gardens", we will see the point I try to make here: the Emperor's garden may project a picture of a dreamland, while ordinary people "seldom make use of their land for superfluous things, such as making fine gardens, cultivating flowers, or making Alleys, believing it more for the public Good, and what is still nearer, their private Benefit, that every Place should be sown in order to produce useful things" (Honour, 1961: 147). Both the imperial garden that impressed Bell and the kitchen garden described by Du Halde were true reflections of Chinese gardening, except that they belonged to vastly different social classes, and the differences were not just in the level of grandeur, but more in their functions to serve different purposes.

It also depends on the traveller's identity and the purpose of the journey – to convert, trade, establish official contacts or simply to travel and learn. Between Anson and Noble's accounts that were both based in Canton, Noble's experience of living there as an EIC trader gained him some insider perspective and regular communication channel, while Anson's unplanned arrival in China in a warship painted his own identity as an outsider. Compared with Bell's identity as a member of the Russian Embassy, no wonder they saw a completely different China. Therefore, despite that both accounts were based on first-hand knowledge, it does not equal to painting a "truthful picture" of China as they each employed a different lens, and different perspectives of the narrator leads to different tones of the travelogue, just as we can find from the eight different accounts offered by the members of the same Macartney Embassy in the next chapter. As the composition of the embassy itself "constituted a microcosm of the British class system, each of whom read China according to his specific perspective" (Chen, 2004: 194), and each can be selective in the use of evidence to support his own theses, to the point that when the Sinophobe and Sinophile readers were crossing fire at each other, they could draw ammunitions from accounts about the same mission. Like today, when people visit a distant land for the first time, they may come with some preconceived images of the land and people they are about to visit, they may be there subconsciously to find evidence to confirm what they believed, and China is simply big enough to offer all kinds of evidence one is looking for, and the problem is, most authors did not realise that their accounts only presented a partial view of the giant empire. It is almost like the Chinese story of "blind men feeling the elephant": One blind man gropes the tail and says that the elephant is like a rope; someone else fumbles its ear and says that the elephant is like a fan. China is like the giant elephant, since they are writing about different aspects of China and are generalizing from their own observations of those aspects, it is hardly surprising that these accounts sometimes contradict each other: some depicted an enchanting picture of a mighty and wealthy kingdom, a politically sophisticated model state, while others regarded it as an insulated and static empire incurious about new technology, and governed by arrogant, ignorant autocrats. The fact that they did not realise that these contradictions defined the very complexity of China shows the knowledge gap. In both accounts, China was just as much an imaginary place as a real one, devoid of any deep regional, ethnic or class distinctions.

These mixed writings with both awe and frustrations represented a shift in European views of China from admiration and idealisation to disillusion and degradation by the time of the Macartney Embassy. The British dominance over other European countries only increased their scepticisms over the superiority of Chinese civilisation. However, until this time, there were only sporadic cultural exchanges and limited trade links between the two empires, with no permanent residence or missionaries from Britain. On the flip side of the coin, the Chinese knowledge about Britain was even more limited and lagged behind. Just like there was no fine distinctions drawn between China, Japan and India in England by the seventeenth century – they were all considered parts of the Orient; by the eighteenth century, no clear distinctions were made between Spain, Dutch and England in China – they were all considered red-haired barbarians at the far end of the world in the eyes of the Middle Kingdom. The next section will look at the Chinese perception of the British Empire at the time and the perception gap to the real British.

4.4 The Chinese perception of the British Empire and the perception gap to the real British

> *England consists merely of three islands, simply a handful of stones in the Western Ocean. Her area is estimated to be about the same as Taiwan and Hainan island …. Even if the soil is all fertile, how much can be produced locally?*
>
> (*cited in* Mann, 1986*: n.p.*)

The above text was from a nineteenth Century Chinese geography text, showing just how difficult for the two countries to grasp the mere geographical sense of each other from self-centered perspectives: one looks out into the ocean, while the other looks down at the soil. A country's political weight was considered "in proportion only to its size" (Gao, 2020: 39) by the ministers of China at the time, that is why Russia managed to get the negotiations done with the Qing on a roughly equal footing in 1689, and the exchange of embassy took place in the 1720s. It showed the pragmatic flexibility of the Qing court in working out a solution to maintain security of China's northern border. When the Office of Foreign Affairs (Lifan Yuan, 理藩院) was set up as an innovation in Qing, it was only to handle Qing relations with its frontier Inner Asia regions, including Russia. They trained linguistic and cultural experts, created dictionaries and researched on the geography, history and the genealogies of important personages of Inner Asia, whether Mongol or Turkic, Buddhist or Islamic. While in comparison, much smaller in size and beyond the seas with no perceived imminent threat, European countries were regularly lumped together as "Western Ocean countries" in Qing court records and became objects of Chinese "Occidentalism". Since Britain was mostly eclipsed by the Dutch in trading activities in China for the period of the seventeenth century, and resembled them in physical appearnce in Chinese eyes, they were considered the same species of "red-haired barbarians" (*Hongmao fan* or *Hongmao yi*). Although *Yingguili* was mentioned separately in a treatise entitled *Haiguo Wenjian Lu* (*Records of Information about Overseas*

Figure 4.5 *Huangqing Zhigong Tu* (Fu, 1751: 46–47). The book adopted the European practice of using one male and one female figure to represent each nation or ethnicity. In public domain. Available at: https://ctext.org/wiki.pl?if=gb&chapter=472128&remap=gb

Countries, 《海国闻见录》) written by Chen Lunjiong in 1730, it was mistaken as a vassal state of Holland even after Britain superseded the Dutch in controlling the trade routes and factories in the China Seas from the eighteenth century onward, as shown in the *Huangqing Zhigong Tu* above (*The August Qing's Illustrated Accounts of Tribute-bearing Domains,* 《皇清职贡图》)[15] published in 1751 (see Figure 4.5). In 1843, a separate study on England, *Hongmao Fan Yingjili Kaolue* (*A Study of the Red-haired Foreigners Called English,* 《红毛番英吉利考略》),[16] was completed by Wang Wentai to clarify some previous misinformation about England. Although it partially corrected its status into a "*former* vassal state of Holland" as it was alleged to have "later invaded Holland" (to refer to its prevailing over the formerly stronger Holland), it continued to use *Hongmao fan* to refer to this European state who had now vanquished the Qing army in the Opium War.

A short annotation is provided in *Huangqing Zhigong Tu* to introduce some general customs of the British people:

> English [England] is also a vassal state of Holland.[17] The clothes of these English people are similar to those of the Dutch. This state is very rich. The men usually wear clothes made with beautiful velvet

> and like to drink alcohol. The women like to girdle their waists and make them look slender before they get married. Besides, they usually wear their hair long and let it fall on their shoulders. Their upper outer garments are short and their skirts multi-layered. When these English people go out, they put on overcoats and bring with them snuffboxes rimmed with gold threads.
>
> (Fu, vol. 1: 47. cited in Chen, 2007: 91)

As we can see from above, except for the mistake of classifying Britain as a vassal state of Holland, which might be caused by the fact that only the Dutch had sent embassies to China when the text was published, there was nothing negative in this description. Similarly neutral but more detailed accounts can be found in other books published by the imperial Qing government, such as *Qingchao Wenxian Tongkao* (*A General Investigation into the Documents of Qing Dynasty, 1747* 《清朝文献通考》) and *Qingchao Tongdian* (*A Cyclopaedia of Qing Dynasty, 1785–86* 《清朝通典》). However, the misinformation regarding Britain's sovereign state implied that until decades before Lord Macartney's embassy, the Chinese ruling class had paid little attention to Britain as a strong European power, although it had defeated its major rival France in the Seven Years' War of 1756–1763, and through its foothold in Bengal, setting the framework for its dominance over other Western traders in the South and East Asian seas. It was still considered one of the red-barbarians until after the first Opium War.

Apart from those books, a key source I draw heavily on is Fu's (1966) *Documentary Chronicle of Sino-Western Relations (1644–1820)*, which provides detailed accounts of Qing's interactions with England from its first founding emperor untill Qianlong and Jiaqing's reign when the two British embassies visited. The very first entry documenting England was titled "The English Initiate Trade at Amoy" in the year of 1675: "England (Ying-kuei-li-wan), Siam, and Annam all brought their native products to Amoy and thus soon restored the prosperity and commerce to the returning population" (Fu, 1966: 49). The second entry was about the English shipwreck in 1700 quoted earlier during Kangxi's reign (1662–1722). Two important points we can gather from these is that first of all, England was known to the Qing court as a kingdom among the "red-haired barbarians", which are "the slyest, most treacherous and most unpredictable. Among them are Ying-kuei-li (England), Kan-ssu-la (Castile, i.e. Spain), Ho-lan-hsi (France), Ho-lan (Holland), and Greater and Lesser Western Ocean countries, and so on. Although their names are different, their blood stock is the same" (ibid: 126).[18] Secondly, although they were considered "sly and treacherous", the principle of "cherishing the man from afar" was emphasised as seen from the second entry of giving aid to the shipwreck, and another one in 1755 regarding "Sick English Sailors Hospitalized at Yang-chiang".

There was only one entry during Yongzheng's short reign (1723–1735) dated 5 September 1725 under the title of "Six out of Ten Foreign Ships Come to Canton from Great Britain" (ibid: 141), with some details given on the commodities the mercantile ships were laden with: barbarian coins, woollen goods, lead, pepper, sandalwood and other commodities. Though there was only one entry, it did indicate the expanded scale of trade with the British, with the name of the country changing from Ying-kuei-li to the Great Britain.

Then it swelled to over 20 entries during the Qianlong Emperor's reign (1736–1796), with 18 prior to the Macartney Embassy, reflecting the growing awareness and knowledge about the British, which can be seen from a glance at the list of their titles and dates below (Fu, 1966: 175–331), starting with "The First Warship Enters the China Sea":

1. 21 Sep. 1743: Commodore Anson Comes to China;
2. 4 Sep. 1745: British Privateers Chase French Ships Outside the China Sea;
3. 10 Dec. 1755: Sick English Sailors Hospitalized at Yang-chiang; British Ships Sail for Ning-Po;
4. 4 Aug. 1756: One British Ship Arrives at Ning-po; Again British Ships Sail for Ning-Po;
5. 20 Sep. 1757: English Ship Again Sails for Ning-po in Spite of the Heavier Duties;
6. 10 Dec. 1757: China Still Hopes the British Will Return to Kwangtung (Canton); The Episode of James Flint;
7. 21 Jul. 1759: The Natives of Chekiang Are Ordered not to Trade with the English;
8. 5 Sep. 1759: Another Plea of the English Merchants Is Presented in Fukien and Chekiang;
9. 13 Oct. 1759: An English Ship Again Sails for Chekiang;
10. 7 Nov. 1759: The English Merchants Must Trade at Canton;
11. 22 Nov. 1759: Flint Is Confined for Three Years Whereas the Chinese Who Wrote His Petition Is Beheaded;
12. 12 Dec. 1761: England Petitions for the Release of Flint;
13. 4 Jun. 1762: English Merchants Petition to Be Allowed to Export Silk;
14. Mar. 1780: The English Demand Payment of Debts Owed Their Merchants;
15. 23 Dec. 1784: Two Chinese Killed by an English Gunner;
16. 3 Dec. 1792: China Approves an English Embassy;
17. 1 Mar. 1793: Russia Reports that an English Ambassor Will Come;
18. 18 Apr. 1793: British in India Advise the Ghorkhas to Surrender to China;

We can almost see a list of "troubles" the British had been creating for the Qing authority since the very first entry about Anson's incident: they chased French ships; sailed for Ning-po again and again in spite of the heavier duties, to the point that the government had to order the Natives of Chekiang not to trade with the English specifically, which led to the impose of the Canton System in 1757, yet the British still sailed for Ning-po when everyone must trade at Canton; and then there were legal consequences when James Flint (known as 洪任辉 in Chinese)[19] was imprisoned for filing a direct petition to the emperor and the Chinese who wrote the petition for him beheaded; the last entry before the news of the English embassy was two Chinese people were killed by an English Gunner ...... This list helps us contextualise Macartney's embassy that came to China near the end of Qianlong's reign. The EIC itself admitted in its instructions to Lord Macartney that English sailors at Canton were "dissolute and riotous" (Hevia, 1995: 76), but I wonder how much they let their home country know the Canton System was a direct response from the Qing government to control the recalcitrant British. Besides, it is important to clarify that there was another embassy dispatched to China in 1787 headed by Charles Allan Cathcart, with the same goal and loaded with gifts carefully prepared for the Qianlong Emperor, but he unfortunately died en route on 10 June 1788, so the Macartney Embassy should be more accurately understood as the first embassy that reached the destination and delivered the King's letter and gifts. In preparation for the Cathcart's embassy, the EIC official at Canton already warned that "the Chinese government looks with contempt on all foreign nations. Its ignorance of other force gives it confidence in its own strength. It does not look on Embassies in any other light than acknowledgement of inferiority" (Gelber, 2008: 160).

Then during the much shorter Jiaqing's reign (1796–1820), a total of 28 entries addressed interactions with the British, documenting events from the "Emperor's Gift to the King of England Delivered at Canton" in 1796 to "Three English Warships Arrive at Canton" in 1799; from "The British Must Go!" in 1808 to the last entry on 12 December 1820 regarding "An Englishman Kills One Chinese and Wounds Three". This was also the last entry for Fu's chronical itself, he decided to conclude it here "because it was in the reign of Tao-kuang that the Celestial Empire ceased to be a model for the West" (Fu, 1966: 417). This list seems to suggest that a turning point of Chinese perception of the British from neutral to negative was when the British troops intruded into Macau in September 1808,[20] which made the Chinese government see the aggressive nature of British colonialism. Gong (1998: 248–249) also said since 1808, the Chinese emperors and officials often applied negative adjectives like arrogant, avaricious and deceitful, brutal, crafty, disrespectful, cunning and unpredictable to describe the British. These negative descriptions were repeated more and more and eventually became a group of cliche to depict the characteristics of the British. Besides, increasing commercial disputes arose from opium-smuggling and debts also made the Chinese more and more alert to the British. This again helps us contextualise the second embassy's visit in 1814.

If the above revealed the official portrait of the British, Macartney himself observed that the Chinese people were "full of prejudices against strangers, of whom cunning and ferocity a thousand ridiculous tales had been propagated, and perhaps industriously encouraged by the government, whose political system seems to be to endeavour to persuade the people that they are themselves already perfect and can therefore learn nothing from others" (Cranmer-Byng, 1962: 226). An example of such tale was that the Chinese boy appointed to wait upon young George Staunton would not sleep in the same house with other European servants, "being afraid that they would eat him". Lord Macartney himself was aware that "it must be confessed, that the impressions hitherto made upon their minds, in consequence of the irregularities committed by Englishmen at Canton, are unfavourable even to the degree of considering them (British) as the worst among Europeans" (ibid: 226).

Then the rumoured gift list brought by Macartney to the Chinese emperor showed that perhaps Europe was even more exotic in Chinese people's imagination than the blue-and-white porcelains in British eyes. The following items were listed in a local gazette: several dwarfs or little men not twelve inches high, but in form and intellect as perfect as grenadiers; an elephant not larger than a cat, and a horse the size of a mouse; a singing-bird as big as a hen, that feeds upon charcoal, and devours usually fifty pounds per day; and lastly, an enchanted pillow on which whoever lays his head immediately falls asleep, and if he dreams of any distant place, such as Canton, Formosa, or Europe, is instantly transported thither without the fatigue of travelling. Macartney decided to keep "this little anecdote, however ridiculous" in his Journal (Cranmer-Byng, 1962: 114). True, however ridiculous this may sound to a British and Chinese person today, Britain seemed to be both infinitely remote and infinitely bizarre (ruled by a young woman) to the Chinese at that time.

It is only fair to say that China indeed knew little of the British Empire when the British learned something of the Qing Empire. A clear asymmetry of knowledge played a key role in the wider perception gap for the Chinese towards the British. Until the late part of the eighteenth century, direct British contacts with the Chinese were limited to the few interactions detailed in Chapters 3 and 4 so far. The geographic, cultural, institutional, and linguistic barriers that separated the two empires were formidable, with mutual knowledge based more on third-hand stories than first-hand experiences. Unlike the French, Portuguese and Italian, who had missionaries at the Qing court, wearing Chinese robes, speaking fluent Mandarin, conversant with court politics and the etiquette, and favourably impressed Chinese emperors with their advanced scientific knowledge, there was no such British "insiders" in Beijing before the Macartney Embassy, leaving their knowledge of China not only second-hand but also outdated.

This had a direct toll on the success of the embassy. For example, they spent a great sum on scientific gifts to the emperor, without knowing that European priests and envoys had been bringing them to Beijing ever since Ricci's day, so the Forbidden City was full of scientific marvels. Nor did they know a foreign envoy was expected to offer the emperor a personal gift during the reception. Macartney came completely unprepared, with all gifts marked and listed as from the King to the Emperor. He had to turn to members of the embassy to purchase objects they have brought along to sell: some watches of very fine workmanship as his gifts to the emperor and two elegant air guns as Staunton's gift (Cranmer-Byng, 1962). For the two magnificent carriages (for summer and winter), they chose yellow as the imperial colour but did not realise that the design was considered most inappropriate as the coachman's position was even higher than the emperor's seat. Such faux pas would definitely be avoidable if there were British missionaries inside the palace as advisors.

The other factor contributing to the failure of the embassy was that they were not able to find even one eligible interpreter between the two languages at the time.[21] The only "tolerable" interpreter they found in Italy left China at a young age of 13, so he was not familiar with the style of court language, nor about court politics. It was with this kind of knowledge level and entourage that Macartney set sail for his mission to China. In an ironical way, the reason why the British placed so much expectations on this embassy was because they knew so little of China. The Qianlong Emperor's edict best summarised this mutual knowledge gap that doomed the mission:

> I do not forget the lonely remoteness of your island, cut off from the world by intervening wastes of sea, nor do I overlook your excusable ignorance of the usages of our Celestial Empire. But the demands presented by your embassy are not only a contravention of dynastic tradition but would be utterly unproductive of good result to yourself, besides being quite impracticable (Appendix 5).

Now, let the story tell itself in the next chapter.

Notes

1 Other scholars tend to use the term Euroiserie or Occidenterie to discuss the same phenomenon.

2 Semedo's work was originally published in Portuguese as *Relação da propagação da fé no reyno da China e outros adjacentes* (Madrid, 1641). The text was revised in 1642, and subsequently rendered into English as *The History of that Great and Renowned Monarchy of China: Wherein All the Particular Provinces Are Accurately Described, as also the Dispositions, Manners, Learning, Lawes, Militia, Government, and Religion of the People, Together with the Traffick and Commodities of that Countrey* (John Crook, 1655: London). It covered the

"Politicks, Oeconomicks, Sciences, Mechanicks, Riches, Merchandise Etc." of China.

3 Hangzhou is famous for producing green tea while Jingdezhen is known as China's porcelain capital.
4 Available at: https://www.britannica.com/biography/Josiah-Wedgwood#ref241910
5 Honour (1961: 195) put the year 1780 as the time when Thomas Minton engraved the pattern. But according to G.A. Godden, "The Willow Pattern", *The Antique Collector* June 1972, pp. 148–150, he had worked on Chinoiserie landscape patterns including willows at that time for Caughley Pottery Works in Shropshire, but it was not the standard willow pattern that included the bridge and the fence in the foreground, which was only produced after he left Caughley in 1793.
6 Many sources put the year of its starting construction at 1709. It was corrected to 1707 by the Yuanming Yuan Museum based on more accurate historical document. Since Xiyang Lou was mainly stone built while the traditional Chinese architecture were wooden built, only the Xiyang Lou ruins can be seen today, leading to some commonly held misperceptions that the whole Yuanming Yuan was Western style.
7 The picture of the ruins was often used as evidence to show how Yuanming Yuan was burnt down in 1860, but some historical pictures taken in 1870s and 1880s showed that many architecture were not destroyed then, but were left to dereliction over the years.
8 Robert Swinhoe was a British interpreter who gave a most widely quoted account of the expedition in 1860.
9 In his own words, the "Needham's Grand Question" is: "Why did modern science, the mathematization of hypotheses about Nature, with all its implications for advanced technology, take its meteoric rise only in the West at the time of Galileo?", and why it "had not developed in Chinese civilisation" which in the previous many centuries "was much more efficient than occidental" in applying natural knowledge to practical needs?
10 The memoirs produced by William Hickey who visited Canton in 1769 were only composed in 1808–1810 and published between 1913 and 1925, so Macartney would not have benefitted from reading his account before departing for China in 1792.
11 Since Macartney was appointed envoy extraordinary to Russia in 1764, it is mostly likely that he would have read Bell's account carefully. He succeeded in negotiating with Catherine II an alliance between Great Britain and Russia, which was one of the reasons why he was appointed to be the first ambassador to China.
12 Thomas Garvan visited the capital of China five years earlier than Bell. Garvan also used to work for the Russian Czar before he was invited by the Kangxi Emperor to work at his court in Beijing. Nevertheless, Garvan did not leave any written records about his life in China. This consequently made Bell the first British writer who ever visited the capital of China and wrote about his life there.
13 The treaty was known as Treaty of Nipchu in China and Treaty of Nerchinsk in Russia.
14 It is noteworthy that when the 1721 Russian embassy visited China, it was during Kangxi's reign, the widely considered ablest, wisest and longest ruling emperor (61 years) that China has known for several centuries. It took the Qing to the zenith. Although the empire still looked imposing by many measures during his grandson Qianlong's reign, Qianlong was more arrogant, and had

become more close-minded with his world view as a very old emperor (83 years old) when the Macartney Embassy visited. Westad (2013: 8) described Kangxi and Qianlong as two remarkable emperors: "Kangxi was mercurial and dynamic, curious about the outside world but fiercely protective of his power and that of the Manchus. Qianlong was cultured and hard-working, but he was not as intelligent as his grandfather and was therefore more doctrinaire on civil and political matters. Both were knowledgeable about the people they ruled and about the world that surrounded them, and adept at the diplomatic and military tools needed to navigate a complex region".

15 According to Tang's research (2001), the texts and images of "red barbarian countries" and "West ocean countries" in the book *Sancai Tuhui* (《三才图会》) published in 1607 was not fact-based but created with imaginations and based on hearsays. However, a less well-known book compiled by Cai Ruxian and published much earlier in 1586 was actually the earliest pictorial depictions of Europeans produced by Chinese. This is a book called *Images of Barbarians* (《东夷图像》), in which twenty-four accounts of foreign countries were recorded, among them, twenty were accompanied with illustrations of their people. Both the images of the Portuguese and the Spanish show appropriate facial features and apparel of the time with curious hats. This was when Queen Elizabeth I tried to establish contact with Ming empire, so no illustration of the British was included yet in the book.

16 There is no set date of its publication which exists in two versions. The handwritten copy included a Preface dated 1843, though the content in Wang's compilation ended with the Battle of Bogue in 1841; and the printed version included a postscript written by his student Cheng Hongzhao dated 1844. Both copies are available at the National Library of China in Beijing.

17 Hevia (1995: 52)'s reference to it is inaccurate: "The August Qing's Illustrated Accounts of Tribute-bearing Domains, for instance, lists England separately, but also says that it, like Sweden, is another name for Holland". It is not "another name", but a vassal state of Holland.

18 The fact that Portugal was not listed among the "red-haired barbarians" showed its special status as being the first one to reach an agreement with the Chinese authority in 1557, to have Macau established as an enclave with permanent buildings erected there.

19 James Flint was a fluent Mandarin speaker, he was EIC's very first Chinese interpreter. For the crime of creating a petition directly to the emperor that violated the Tributary System protocol, and for attempting to overthrow the single port trade system, he was imprisoned in Macau for three years. Thereafter he was deported from China and banished from the country forever.

20 With the invasion of Portugal during the Napoleonic War in 1807, the French navy stepped up its activities in the Far East. In 1808, in order to take advantage of the chaotic situation as well as to secure its trade with China, the British Viceroy to India argued that if the strong French army launched an attack against Macau from land and sea at the same time, the Portuguese would be unable to resist. The Portuguese Viceroy to India was forced to allow the British to occupy and "defend" Macau. The British dispatched the HMS Russel. As documented in letters between Rear-Admiral Drury (HMS Russel), the Governor of Macau and Mandarins of the Qing court, the British desisted from occupying Macau's Forte de Monte with troops, in the face of Chinese opposition.

21 Since James Flint, as the only English man who could speak fluent Chinese at the time, was not appointable for being banished from China, George Stanton, the deputy ambassador went to procure Chinese interpreters from the Naples

College of the Propaganda in the spring of 1792, and he took his son George Staunton Junior with him on this journey. Staunton put in his *Memoirs* (1856: 11) that "it was at Naples that I first saw any of the natives of China; and it was in the course of the journey home from thence to England, and the outward-bound voyage to China, which soon followed, that my ears were first familiarised to the sounds of a language in which, during the next five-and-twenty years of my life, I had so much exercise". It was only after the Macartney Embassy that permission was given for Chinese language teaching to the EIC's employees at Canton.

References

Addison, J. (1712) 'The pleasures of the imagination', *The Spectator*, June 21, No. 411. Available at: https://www.sas.upenn.edu/~cavitch/pdf-library/AddisonJ_Spectator411-21.pdf

Anderson, A. (1795) *A Narrative of the British Embassy to China, in the Years 1792, 1793 and 1794*. London: J. Debrett.

Anson, G. (1748) *A Voyage Round the World in the Years MDCCXL, I, II, III, IV by George Anson*. Walter, R. (comp.). London: W. Bowyer and J. Nichols, W. Stahan, J. F. and C. Rivington.

Aravamudan, S. (2012) *Enlightenment Orientalism: Resisting the Rise of the Novel*. Chicago: University of Chicago Press.

Barrow, J. (1804) *Travels in China: Containing Descriptions, Observations, and Comparisons, Made and Collected in the Course of a Short Residence at the Imperial Palace of Yuen-min-yuen, and on a Subsequent Journey Through the Country from Pekin to Canton*. London: T. Cadell and W. Davies, in the Strand.

Batchelor, R. (2012) 'A taste for the interstitial (間): Translating space from Beijing to London in the 1720s', in Sabean, D.W. and Stefanovska, M. (eds.) *Space and Self in Early Modern European Cultures*. Toronto: University of Toronto Press.

Bell, J. (1763) *A Journey from St. Petersburg in Russia, to Pekin in China, with an Embassy from His Imperial Majesty, Peter the first, to Kamhi Emperor of China, in the Year MDCCXIX*. Published as part of *Travels from St. Petersburg in Russia, to Diverse Parts of Asia* (1763), and republished as J.L. Stevenson (ed.) (1965). *A Journey from St Petersburg to Pekin, 1719–1722*. Edinburgh: Edinburgh University Press.

Berg, M. (2003) 'Asian luxuries and the making of the European Consumer Revolution', in Berg M. and Eger E. (eds.) *Luxury in the Eighteenth Century*. London: Palgrave Macmillan.

Berg, M. (2007) *Luxury and Pleasure in Eighteenth-Century*. Oxford: Oxford University Press.

Chang, Y.Z. (1930) 'A note on Sharawadgi'. *Modern Language Notes*, 45, Apr., pp. 223–224.

Chen, C.H. (2007) 'Images of the other, images of the self: Reciprocal representations of the British and the Chinese from the 1750s to the 1840s'. PhD thesis, unpublished. Available at: http://webcat.warwick.ac.uk/record=b2241443~S1

Chen, J.G.S. (2004) 'The British view of Chinese civilisation and the emergence of class consciousness'. *The Eighteenth Century: Theory and Interpretation*, 45, pp. 193–205.

Coates, A. (1966). *Macao and the British, 1637–1842: Prelude to Hong Kong*. Hong Kong: HKU Press.

Cranmer-Byng, J.L. (1962) *An Embassy to China, Being the Journal Kept by Lord Macartney During His Embassy to the Emperor Ch'ien-lung 1793–1794*. London: Longmans.

Ellis, M., Coulton, R. and Mauger, M. (2015) *Empire of Tea: The Asian Leaf that Conquered the World*. London: Reaktion Books Ltd.

Fu, H. (1751)《皇清職貢圖》[*August Qing's llustrated Account of ribute-bearing Domains*]. Available at: https://ctext.org/wiki.pl?if=gb&chapter=472128&remap=gbI

Fu, L.S. (1966) *A Documentary Chronicle of Sino-Western Relations (1644–1820)*. Tucson: The University of Arizona Press.

Gallagher, L.J. (trans.) (1953) *China in the Sixteenth Century: The Journals of Matthew Ricci: 1583–1610*. New York: Random House.

Gao, H. (2020). *Creating the Opium War, British Imperial Attitudes Towards China, 1792–1840*. Manchester: Manchester University Press.

Gelber, H. (2008) *The Dragon and the Foreign Devils: China and the World, 1100 B.C. to the Present*. London: Bloomsbury.

Gong, Y. (1998)《鸦片战争前中国人对英国的认识》[*Chinese people's knowledge about Britain before the Opium War*], in Huang, S. (ed.) *Dongxi Jiaoliu Luntan (Forum of East-West Exchange)*. Shanghai: Shanghai Wenyi Publishing House.

Hargrave, J. (2016) 'Marco Polo and the emergence of British sinology', *SEL Studies in English Literature 1500–1900*, 56(3), Summer, pp. 515–537.

Harmondsworth, R.L. (trans.) (1958) *The Travels of Marco Polo*. London: Penguin Books.

Hevia, J. (1995) *Cherishing Men from Afar, Qing Guest Ritual and the Macartney Embassy of 1793*. Durham and London: Duke University Press.

Honour, H. (1961) *Chinoiserie, The Vision of Cathay*. London: John Murray.

Hung, H.F. (2003) 'Orientalist knowledge and social theories: China and the European conceptions of East-West differences from 1600 to 1900'. *Sociological Theory*, 21(3), Sep., pp. 254–280.

Jenkins, E.Z. (2013) *A Taste for China: English Subjectivity and the Prehistory of Orientalism*. New York: Oxford University Press.

Johnson, S. (1846) *The Works of Samuel Johnson's LL.D.*, in two volumes. New York: Alexander V. Blake Publisher.

Keevak, M. (2017) *Embassies to China: Diplomacy and Cultural Encounters before the Opium Wars*. Singapore: Palgrave Macmillan.

Kitson, P. (2013) *Forging Romantic China, Sino-British Cultural Exchange 1760–1840*. Cambridge: Cambridge University Press.

Kleutghen, K. (2014) 'Chinese Occidenterie: The diversity of 'Western' objects in eighteenth-century China'. *Eighteenth-Century Studies*, 47(2), Winter, pp. 117–135.

Liu, L.H. (2006) *The Clash of Empires, the Invention of China in Modern World Making*. Cambridge, MA and London, England: Harvard University Press.

Mann, J. (1986) 'British monarch eagerly awaited: Queen's visit to China: A dramatic turn in history'. *Los Angeles Times*, Oct. 7. Available at: https://www.latimes.com/archives/la-xpm-1986-10-07-mn-5021-story.html

Markley, R. (2014) 'China and the English enlightenment: Literature, aesthetics, and commerce'. *Literature Compass*, 11(8), August, pp. 517–527.

Mayor, A. Hyatt (1941) 'Chinoiserie', *The Metropolitan Museum of Art Bulletin*, 36(5) (May), pp. 111–114.

Muller, G.F.V. (1732–1764) *Sammlung Russischer Geschichte*, 9 vols. St. Petersburg: Kayserliche Academic der Wissenschaften.

Nash, P. (2015) 'A scotsman on the road to Cathay: John Bell's journey to China (1719–1722)'. *Studies in Travel Writing*, 19(2), pp. 91–108.

Noble, C.F. (1762) *Voyage to the East Indies in 1747 and 1748*. London: M, DCC, LXV.

Percy, T. (1761) *Hau Kiou Choaan: Or Pleasing History*. London: R. and J. Dodsley.

Perdue, P. (2010) 'Boundaries and trade in the early modern world: Negotiations at Nerchinsk and Beijing'. *Eighteenth-Century Studies*, 43(3), China and the making of global modernity (Spring), pp. 341–356.

Peyrefitte, A. (1992) *The Immobile Empire*. Translated by Rothschild, J. New York: Alfred Knopf.

Porter, D. (2010) *The Chinese Taste in Eighteenth-century England*. Cambridge: Cambridge University Press.

Qian, Z. (1945) *China in the English Literature of the Seventeenth and Eighteenth Centuries: Three Essays*. Publisher unidentified, https://books.google.co.uk/books/about/China_in_the_English_Literature_of_the_S.html?id=8d27YgEACAAJ&redir_esc=y

Reichwein A. (1925) *China and Europe: Intellectual and Artistic Contacts in the Eighteenth Century*. New York: Barnes and Noble.

Ringmar, E. (2011) 'Malice in Wonderland: Dreams of the orient and the destruction of the Palace of the Emperor of China', *Journal of World History*, 22(2), June, pp. 273–298.

Ringmar, E. (2013) *Liberal Barbarism and the European Destruction of the Palace of the Emperor of China*. New York: Palgrave Macmillan.

Semedo, A., de Faria e Sousa, M. and Martini, M. (1655) *The History of that Great and Renowned Monarchy of China: Wherein All the Particular Provinces Are Accurately Described, as also the Dispositions, Manners, Learning, Lawes, Militia, Government, and Religion of the People, Together with the Traffick and Commodities of that Countrey*. London: John Crook.

Shang, Z. (1986)《清代宫中的广东钟表》[*Cantonese clocks of the Qing Dynasty in the palace*]. *Gugong Bowuyuan Yuankan*, 3, pp. 10–12.

Shih, Y. (2015) 'Chitqua: A Chinese modeller and his portraiture business in eighteenth-century London'. *Meishu Yanjiu* (*Fine Arts Journal*), Issue 1, Dec. 2015. National Kaohsiung Normal University, pp. 71–106.

Shimada, T. (1997) Is 'Sharawadgi' derived from the Japanese Word 'Sorowaji'?' *The Review of English Studies*, 48(191) (August), pp. 350–352.

Singer, A. (1992) *The Lion and the Dragon, The Story of the First British Embassy to the Court of the Emperor Qianlong in Peking, 1792–94*. London: Barrie & Jenkins.

Slobada, S. (2014) *Chinoiserie: Commerce and Critical Ornament in Eighteenth-century Britain*. Manchester: Manchester University Press.

Smith, A. (1776) *Inquiry into the Nature and Causes of the Wealth of Nations*. London: W. Strahan and T. Cadell. Available at: https://www.gutenberg.org/ebooks/3300

Staunton, G. (1856) *Memoirs of the Chief Incidents of the Public Life of Sir George Thomas Staunton*, printed for private circulation. London: L. Booth, 307 Regent Street.

Swinhoe, R. (1861) *Narrative of the North China Campaign of 1860: Containing Personal Experiences of Chinese Character, and of the Moral and Social Condition of the Country; Together with a Description of the Interior of Pekin*. London: Smith, Elder and Company.

Talbot, A. (forthcoming) The influence of Chinese Gardens in Early Modern England. Available at: https://www.academia.edu/42721019/The_Influence_of_Chinese_Gardens_in_Early

Tang, K. (2001)《中国现存最早的欧洲人形象资料——东夷图像》[*The Earliest European Pictorial Profiles in China – East Yi Images*], *Palace Museum Journal*, 2001(1), pp. 22–28.

Temple, W. (1685) *Upon the Garden of Epicurus*. Available at: http://sublime.nancyholt.com/Temple/index.html

Thomas, G.M. (2008) 'The Looting of Yuanming and the translation of Chinese art in Europe'. *Nineteen Century Art Worldwide*, 7(2). Available at: http://www.19thc-artworldwide.org/autumn08/93-the-looting-of-yuanming-and-the-translation-of-chinese-art-in-europe (no page number).

Waley-Cohen, J. (2000) *Sextants of Beijing, Global Currents in Chinese History*. New York: Norton.

Wang, C.L. (2017) 'Chinoiserie in reflection, European objects and their impact on Chinese art in the late seventeenth and eighteenth centuries'. *Exchange Gazes, Between China and Europe, 1669–1907*, pp. 42–55. Michael Imhof Verlag GmbH & Co. KG.

Wang, W. (1843)《红毛番英吉利考略》[*A Study of the Red-haired Foreigners Called English*], printed in Beijing by Huang Pengnian, editor of the Imperial Academy.

Westad, O.A. (2013) *Restless Empire, China and the World since 1750*. London: Vintage Books.

Williams, L. (2014) 'Anglo-Chinese caresses: Civility, friendship and trade in English representations of China, 1760–1800'. *Journal for Eighteenth-Century Studies*, 38(2) Available at: 10.1111/1754-0208.12208

Wolseley, G. (1862) *Narrative of the War with China in 1860; to Which Is Added the Account of a Short Residence with the Tai-Ping Rebels at Nankin and a Voyage from Thence to Hankow*. London: Longman, Green, Longman, and Roberts. Wilmington, Del., Scholarly Resources [1972].

Wong, Y.T. (2016) *A Paradise Lost, The Imperial Garden Yuanming Yuan*. Springer, jointly published with Foreign Language Teaching and Research Publishing Co. Ltd.

Yang, C.M. (2011) *Performing China: Virtue, Commerce, and Orientalism in Eighteenth-Century England, 1660–1760*. Baltimore: Johns Hopkins University Press.

5 When the lion meets the dragon: Lost in translation or beyond translation?

> Who controls the past controls the future. Who controls the present controls the past.
>
> – George Orwell (1949)

As explained in Chapters 2 to 4, Britain was a latecomer in trading with China, and it was the British traders (the Flint incident) that had directly led to the establishment of the Canton System in 1757, which restricted all foreign trade to the only port of Canton and through the Thirteen Factories. Since merchants were put at a low stratum in the traditional Chinese social structure and foreigners were considered barbarians and dangerous, the Chinese government itself had little direct contact with foreign merchants but adopted a strategy of "using official to check merchants and using merchants to check foreigners". For many years this system had been acceptable to both the Europeans and the Chinese, but it was the British again who wished to change the system when it overtook its European neighbours to become the most important Western influence in the East. In 1773, in the wake of overseas expansion that followed Britain's victory in the Seven Years' War, Lord Macartney made the famous remark that Britain was now a "vast empire on which the sun never sets, and whose bounds nature has not yet ascertained". This victory confirmed British primacy in Europe and command at sea. Then, following the Industrial Revolution, driven by a combination of rapidly increasing demands for imports of tea from China and a bigger market to export their manufactured goods to, the British sought to expand their trade opportunities in China and establish Western-style diplomatic relations with the Chinese. So, when Macartney set sail for China, Britain was not just the greatest sea power, but considered itself the bearer of international notions of reciprocity and modernity.

The Qing China under Qianlong's reign, on the other hand, believed that it had eliminated all significant challenges after defeating its major rivals in northwest Eurasia including the Zunghar Mongols and the

DOI: 10.4324/9781003156383-6

conquest of Xinjiang in the 1760s, winning the Qianlong Emperor a laudatory title of an "old man with ten feats". Therefore, China continued to assume a haughty self-conception that placed themselves at the centre of the world where all foreigners were expected to gravitate toward the superiority of Chinese civilisation by becoming his symbolic vassal – via carefully worded letters, meticulous ceremonies, and presentation of best native produce as tributes.

As the de facto first mission to China, both prior to and decades after the Macartney Embassy, it was discussed in the press, presented in caricatures, narrated by various members of the embassy, debated in scholarly works, mentioned in private diaries and letters, even described in novels such as the *Mansfield Park* and inspired a number of satires. A wealth of literature has also been made available throughout the past two centuries, including a new surge of writings in 1992 on its two centennial anniversaries when more Chinese sources were made available. Therefore, I would not repeat the whole story as has been well told by books such as *The Crucial Years of Anglo-Chinese Relations, 1750–1800* (Pritchard, 1970); *The Immobile Empire,* (Peyrefitte, 1992); the *Lion and Dragon* (Singer, 1992); and *Cherishing Men from Afar, Qing Guest Ritual and the Macartney Embassy of 1793* (Hevia, 1995). What I would contribute is a new narrative of the old tale, as much has been written about the failure of the mission, which was mostly treated as an inevitable consequence of a cultural divide made manifest by the issue of the kowtow. I will argue it as a system conflict from a broader international context in this chapter: it is the incompatible Tributary System and Westphalian System that made the embassy a mission impossible.

The Qing Dynasty was established in 1644, only a few years before the end of Europe's Thirty Years' War with the signing of the Treaty of Westphalis in 1648. The rest of the chapter will employ this new lens in analysing this system divide reflected in gift and letter exchanges, it will also shed more light on the unresolved mystery of whether Macartney performed the kowtow or not by piecing together all the clues offered by different sources so far. It will also explore the role language and translation played in this communication failure, which is beyond the linguistic level. Finally, it will highlight the value of the embassy in representing the beginning of the end of the second-hand fanciful views of China prevalent in England throughout the eighteenth century. It was the first time that English officials had been in a position to gain insight to China by first-hand observations, which laid the basis of British knowledge about China for the next three decades. The end of his mission started a new era in the Anglo-Chinese encounters with a new set of mutual perceptions and a paradox: the more mutual knowledge was gained, the more mutual deprecation generated, and less mutual affinity left.

5.1 Tributary System Vs. Westphalian System: Mission impossible for the Macartney Embassy to China

The mission had produced at least eight books, including Lord Macartney's own journal, which only came out in 1962. The official account produced by his deputy, Sir George Staunton, *An Authentic Account of an Embassy from the King of Great Britain to the Emperors of China* was published in 1797 with Figure 5.1 as the frontispiece. Williams (2014: 12) offered a fascinating interpretation of the scene as it "shows the British delegation standing before a doorway, through which a prospect view of China's riches can be seen: trade (represented as a European female) pulls aside the curtain, the English are courteously invited over the threshold by a Chinese dressed in the pearls and robes of the imperial court". He carried on to say that the encounter that unfolded "is perhaps best understood not as a 'collision' between incompatible imperial systems but as a more subtle engagement between two overlapping systems of civility". I would challenge this interpretation as it was the two world views that were incompatible and irreconcilable, which caused the collision that could not be rescued by the two "overlapping systems of civility".

As explained in Chapter 2, the Tributary System, through which China had traditionally tried to manipulate foreign traders and envoys into

Figure 5.1 Frontispiece of *An Authentic Account of an Embassy from the King of Great Britain to the Emperors of China*, 1797.

expressing allegiance, was an antithesis to the Westphalian System established in 1648 whose fundamental principle was that all sovereign nation states, regardless of size or power, were to be treated equally under international law. Westphalian diplomacy also had its own set of ritual and law, which involved three forms of action according to Hampton (2009): negotiation, mediation and representation. These directly run counter to the Chinese control of trade, border and society.

Obviously, the two empires did not share a common language, here I do not mean linguistically, but that they did not share the same connotations of the same vocabulary, thus breeding some wrong assumptions on the British side:

1 Everyone would agree that we live in the same "world", or at least the same "globe". But China did not talk about "the world" politically or "the globe" geographically, they talked about *Tianxia* ideologically. Under these notions, "China forms a world of its own, rather than a part of the world" (Mao, 2014: 8), thus the Chinese emperor was the "lord of the world".
2 Trade is a mutually beneficial thing that will result in mutual improvement and progress. This was a deeply embedded belief in the British mind as seen from Queen Elizabeth I's letters, and still held as a doctrine much later, as Lord Palmerston told the Parliament in 1839: "The great object of the Government in every quarter of the world was to extend the commerce of the country" (cited in Darwin, 2009: 36). Therefore, even if we may have different trading powers, negotiations can be done on that basis. While trade was more than a "want", but an "essential need" for the British, for the Chinese emperor however, exchanging goods was a grace or benefaction bestowed upon the tributary states, or "men from afar", it would be treated with caution if it may disturb China's own "essential needs" for security and stability.
3 "Counterparts" exist even though each country may have a different governing structure. That was why Macartney proposed to have an "equivalent official" from the Qing court to perform the same ceremony in front of King George III's portrait. However, the post of ambassador was categorically distinct in the Westphalian System, with no equivalent in imperial China. For the British, ambassador stood for the sovereign they represented when visiting another country. An ambassador was invested further with political authority to speak on behalf of their sovereign at another court where the status of both sovereigns, in theory, was equal (Hampton, 2009: 10). While for the Chinese, the role and status of an ambassador was beyond their hieratical system – who can represent the monarch? An ambassador was considered a mere messenger sent to deliver their sovereign's letter and bear their tributes to the emperor. As Mancall (1970: 65) explained, "an ambassador's credentials and the letters he

carried from his master were valued more highly, and treated with greater reverence, than the person of the ambassador himself". So the ambassador's status was considered inferior to the Qing officials and court eunuchs, who had to prostrate themselves in front of the emperor as a daily ritual to maintain internal political order, thus they saw no ground for Macartney to negotiate an exemption of the protocol. As the embassy later learned that "the ministers of the empire, who, more than the Emperor himself, adhered to this antiquated claim of superiority over other nations" (Staunton, 1797: 308). At least when the welcome banquet was given in Tianjin in the name of the emperor, Qinalong had specified in one of his edicts that "if the tributary envoys would perform the kowtow to receive the imperial honour, we would certainly not decline it; but if they do not, we could also allow them to follow their own customs, no need to compel them" (倘伊等不行此礼, 亦只可顺其国俗, 不必加之勉强. Shanghai Publishing House, 2010: 630). A similar "mistake" was made when Macartney regarded the "First Minister" Heshen as a counterpart of the British Prime Minister. Though sounded close enough in title, a minister in the Qing court would call himself a "minion" or "lackey" (*nucai,* 奴才) to the emperor, a self-deprecating address used in the Qing Dynasty. The servile submission conditioned by the powerful court hierarchy was something that the British never fully appreciated throughout the interactions.

The above three assumptions were ingrained in the British minds as "common sense" that they never cast any doubts on, or made to doubt, based on their previous dealings with other European countries, but of course, China was no other country. Basing their requests on the wrong assumptions made the mission doomed to fail. The embassy had two main goals: the first was to request the relaxation of restrictions on the Canton System, as following the Industrial Revolution, "where Europe's 100 million had once been China's new market, now it was time to seek out markets for British goods among China's 300 million" (Berg, 2003: 24). The second goal was to seek permission to establish a permanent British embassy in Beijing that would enable direct communication with the emperor instead of through the Hong merchants and officials in Canton, presumably making it easier to protect British interests in China.

Such requests seemed illogical to the Qing government as they did not see the need for any change: if the Canton System was working well, why change it? And why was it necessary to have an ambassador in Peking, at such a great distance from their fellow countrymen trading in Canton? Most importantly, the Chinese authorities saw no reason for the British to be treated differently from others who had made similar requests before but were rejected, the Chinese government must be consistent and fair. It also applied to the issue of kowtow as none of the other European powers had any difficulty complying with the established Chinese ceremonial forms, why the British deserve special treatment that required changing the antiquity system handed down by ancestors? However, to perform kowtow to the Chinese emperor also seemed an illogical request in the minds of the British, again showing the incompatibility between the two systems. Under the Tributary System, there was no such concept of "trade partners", but only tributaries who had to perform kowtow before any exchange of goods can take place. Since compliance with correct ritual behaviour was essential for the Tributary System's operation, "the impasse of protocol masked a confrontation of two different worlds" (Peyrefitte, 1992: 89), built on two different systems and buttressed by conflicting assumptions.

Of course, we can argue that the whole Tributary System was also built upon wrong assumptions made by the Chinese. As Waley-Cohen (2000) pointed, a fundamental paradox flawed the system as it can only function properly when others acquiesced in it or at least agreed not to openly dispute the Chinese version, and such acquiescence was only possible when China was strong enough to compel compliance. Many of the preconditions of China's assumed superiority simply withered away over time, when Enlightenment developed the European cultural brilliance as well as economic, technical and political clout, and the Industrial Revolution put the British in a league of its own. The arrival of the first British embassy came at such a junction in time. Over two centuries later, I will try to recount this failed mission by deciphering the different assumptions held by the two empires about how trade and diplomatic relations should be carried out.

5.2 Gift or tribute: Two words, two worlds

Gift giving follows a shared principle across both cultures that "it is the thought that counts", but it was exactly the different thoughts nurtured by the two systems that made gift-giving a cause of conflict. To the British, gift giving was a tool to show respect and goodwill and serve the purpose of enhancing mutual understanding while demonstrating the need of exchanging goods. Since gift exchange was a prelude to the forming of diplomatic relations, they also viewed the gifts returned by the Chinese emperor as a symbol of goodwill, at least in principle, they represented an equal exchange between reciprocally respectful nations. China, on the other hand, was willing to allow trade without diplomatic relations but would only allow diplomatic relations within the traditional Tributary System, under which the embassy's mission was accomplished when the tributes (*Gong*) were delivered as a symbolic gesture to recognise the status of China being the centre and supremacy. *Gong* is the same word used by Chinese local officials in bringing presents to please the emperor, indicating that the Tributary System was an extension of the hierarchical order inside China.

Until the 1818 edition of the *Collected Statutes* (*Ta-Ching Hui-tien,* 《大清会典》), England was listed as a tributary state together with Portugal under the category of "Western Ocean". Its "frequency of mission" was marked as "tribute at no fixed periods" and "route" showed "via Macau" (Fairbank, 1970: 11). It is interesting to observe the change of terminology in these year-by-year records, for example, "tributary objects" were used until 1886 and "imperial gifts" were used after 1887. This small change of word reflected a fundamental change of the world order. However, when the Macartney Embassy arrived in Beijing in September 1793, it was still a time when foreigners were only allowed to visit the capital on tributary missions, at least nominally, so they were treated based on this assumption, and there was a whole genre of official writing in Chinese. For example, when the gift list from the Embassy was placed in front of the Qianlong Emperor on 6 August, he immediately pointed out the wrong terminology used in the Chinese translation and issued an edict to correct the mode of address from *qinchai* (imperial legate, 钦差) to *Gongshi* (tributary envoy, 贡差). He questioned:

> How could a tribute-bearing envoy be called *qinchai*? This must be the act of their *tongshi* (interpreter/translator, 通事) seeking to elevate the envoy by imitating official titles in the Celestial Empire. Excusable as the folly may be on their part, there is the danger of our officials charged with their reception, out of ignorance and insensitivity to the importance [of language], also calling the envoy *qinchai*, which would be grossly unacceptable. They should therefore be notified by Zheng Rui (Qianlong's Legate) that the British envoy and his deputy are both to be addressed as *Gongshi* in accordance with the established usage.
>
> (FHAC, 1996: 120)[1]

It is worth noting though, in 1718, when an ambassador was sent by "the Western Ocean King of Cultivation" (*xiyang jiaohuawang*, 西洋教化王), that is, the pope, its arrival was reported as a "western ocean mandarin" (*xiyang daren,* 西洋大人). Another ambassador sent by the pope in 1725, recorded by the Qing to be a tribute, but was called the "western ocean ambassador" (*xiyang shichen*, 西洋使臣), indicating that an equivalent for ambassor did exist in Chinese language, but a trade mission was considered lower in status and esteem than a religious representative.

Following the edict, all changes were made to assure the emperor: "ever since the said tributary envoy sailed into our harbour, inland officials and people have, without exception, referred to him as "red-haired tributary envoy" rather than *qinchai.* The copies made of the tributary gift list are all duly corrected, and no copy has leaked outside" (FHAC, 1996: 368). So, when the embassy arrived in North China in a warship with a total entourage of over 800 people and 600 packages of magnificent presents[2] that required 90 wagons, 40 barrows, 200 horses, and 3,000 porters to carry them to Peking, they were immediately labelled as "tributes". When they were brought to the old Summer Palace and called "tributes" by the Qing officials, it was corrected and emphasised by the embassy interpreter as being "gifts", starting a battle of words and translations that was actually fought between the two systems rather than two languages. In Staunton's (1797, 1: 49) descriptions, the gifts were "specimens of the best British manufactures, and all the late inventions for adding to the conveniences and comforts of social life, might answer the double purpose of gratifying those to whom they were to be presented, and of exciting a more general demand for the purchase of similar articles". However, using "specimens" as gifts was as offensive to the Chinese emperor as calling them "tributes" to the British, as "specimen" indicates a utilitarian exchange to establish a business relationship between trading partners, while "tribute" clearly defines the unequal relationship between the two. Therefore, although the specimens were literally "an industrial and scientific exhibition, a showcase of Britain's industrial enlightenment" (Berg, 2010), they failed to achieve neither of the two purposes stated by Staunton.

First of all, the emperor was not impressed. The scene of gift presenting was captured in a silk tapestry that was gifted back by Qianlong and is now kept at the Royal Museums of Greenwich (see Figure 5.2). The

Figure 5.2 Tapestry depicting the Macartney Embassy. Courtesy of Royal Museums Greenwich.

centre piece was a huge astronomical instrument, though not in the least like the planetarium that was actually presented according to Singer (1992: 93), the objects were drawn from published illustrations of items given to the emperor by the Jesuits earlier in the century. What mattered here was the "exotic foreign people" who brought the characteristic products of their country to the emperor as tributes. Very much like the elephant or other exotic animals presented from other traditional tributary states of southeast Asia, this picture depicted England as a new tributary state by using the same motif, only that their "native produce" were scientific instruments and artilleries.

Most interestingly, a poem composed by the emperor himself in 1793 to record the embassy was embroidered in the top right-hand corner[3]:

> Formerly Portugal presented tribute;
> Now England is paying homage.
> They have out-travelled Shu Hai and Heng-zhang;
> My ancestors' merit and virtue must have reached their distant shores.
> Though their tribute is commonplace, my heart approves sincerely.
> Curio and the boasted ingenuity of their devices I prize not,
> Though what they bring is meagre, yet,
> In my kindness to men from afar I make generous return,
> Wanting to preserve my good health and power.
>
> (cited in Singer, 1992: 85)

From this we can clearly see the Qing attitude to the British embassy. England was not recognised as the new game changer but merely a new addition to the old world order. There was no hope to achieve the second purpose of expanding trade by stimulating Chinese demand for British goods as they were considered as "commonplace, boasted, and meagre". Is this evidence of the emperor's arrogance and ignorance as commonly believed? Perhaps not, at least not for the first two modifiers.

Let us see why they were considered "commonplace" in the eyes of the emperor. Macartney himself was exasperated that "neither Qianlong himself nor those about him appeared to have any curiosity" with regard to the inventions, and he concluded that it was "the policy of the present Government to discourage all novelties, and to prevent their subjects as much as possible from entertaining a higher opinion of foreigners than of themselves" (Cranmer-Byng, 1962: 234). It seems it never crossed the British minds that this was because their gifts were *not* "novelties" at all. According to Staunton (1797), they vetoed the suggestions from the two interpreters hired for the mission of sending mechanical devices such as sing-songs, considering that the emperor and high class had already accumulated a collection of such exotic curiosities and given the emperor's senior age, they decided to focus on British craftsmanship and manufactures that can demonstrate the scientific development, technological superiority and military power held by the British. However, they did not realise that such products were just like the sing-songs, considered as nothing novelty as the emperor had been entertained by many and varied versions of the same devices since the age of Enlightenment from other West Ocean countries, and also internal tributes from the officials in charge of the trade in Canton. As if to make him see the point, Macartney was taken to view the imperial palace at Rehe and stopped to visit 50 pavilions filled with intricate European clocks and mechanical devices. This was noted in Macartney's own account: they "are all furnished …… with every kind of European toys and sing-songs, with spheres, orreries, clocks, and musical automatons of such exquisite workmanship, and in such profusion, that our presents must shrink from the comparison and hide their diminished heads". He was also told that the fine things they had seen were "far exceeded by" others kept at Yuanming Yuan (Cranmer-Byng, 1962: 125).

Many of the extra efforts did not pay off either: the centre piece of Planetarium represented "the utmost effort of astronomical science and mechanic art combined together, that was ever made in Europe" (Staunton, 1797: 126), but it was manufactured by the German Philipp Matthaus Hahn, thus not considered appropriate tribute as it did not represent the product of the giving nation. It was also ostentatiously embellished with gilt and enamel to make it more appealing to the emperor based on the assumptions they made from the popular Chinoiserie style in the West, but again they did not realise that there was already a similar Celestial Globe that was literally made in China 120 years ago, designed by the Belgian Jesuit Ferdinandus Verbiest in 1673,[4] which still stands at the Beijing Ancient Observatory today.

This naturally brings us to see why the British gifts were considered "boasted ingenuity" as these gifts were not only less grand than the court already possessed but also not as unique and extraordinary as claimed by the British themselves. For example, "two camera obscuras were returned, foolishly enough, as more suited to the amusement of children, than the information of mean of science" (Wood, 2019: 218). Such cameras were very similar to the peep-boxes showing European scenes that were already popular in China at the time. More importantly, it was the pompous style of describing its own gifts, the opposite of Chinese modesty in downplaying the significance of one's own presents to show respect to the recipient, that proved to be counterproductive. Although in the Chinese translation, the description was already "toned down a good bit" (Hevia, 1995: 148), the reduced version was still considered as being exaggerating and pretentious in Qianlong's comments, treating it as a reflection of the conventionally boastful barbarian character (FHAC, 1996: 120). For example, the original descriptions of the British gifts carefully selected to demonstrate "any art, science, or observation, either of use or curiosity, with which the industry, ingenuity and experience of Europeans may have enabled them to acquire" (Morse, 1926: 246) was reduced to one phrase of "*caineng qiaowu*" (talents and ingenious articles, 才能巧物), a term held in apparent disdain in the Qing imperial discourse. Therefore, as Hevia argued (1995: 188), "what was being objected, was not trade with Great Britain, nor British manufactures, and not the gifts at hand, but Macartney's claims about the gifts, claims which had been elicited in the ritual process and identified as excessive". It also contributed to the Chinese impression of the British Embassy as being arrogant, an interesting mirror image of the British view of the Chinese, both due to their self-perceived superiority and a lack of knowledge of the other. The most quoted lines in Qianlong's reply to King George III was about the gifts: "Our dynasty's majestic virtue has penetrated unto every country under Heaven, and Kings of all nations have offered their costly tribute by land and sea. As your Ambassador can see for himself, we possess all things. I set no value on objects strange or ingenious, and have no use for your country's manufactures" (Appendix 5).

This hurt the British deeply, as even the emphasised utilitarian value was not delivered. But it perhaps also showed a lack of cultural knowledge on the British side. For example, another important reason to explain Qianlong's reaction was the Chinese etiquette of not displaying enthusiasm on the value of the item when receiving gifts; it was considered a lack of upbringing and bad manner in paying more attention to the material value than the symbolic gesture of gifts. This cultural difference is still a common lesson today to explain to Westerners why Chinese people do not open gift boxes until after the guests leave.[5] The Chinese cultural norms of modesty, both in downplaying one's own gifts to others, and in refraining from showing delight in the gift value from others were not appreciated by the British, who interpreted it as the emperor's arrogance or ignorance in science.

On the other hand, there were also good reasons for the British to use "ignorance and stubborn" to describe the Chinese reaction, particularly to Fraser's globes as recorded by Anderson (1795). As explained in Chapter 2, Ricci had allegedly accommodated the map of the world to please the Ming Emperor, so the Qing officials showed suspicion that China had been deliberately reduced in size by the English with an ideological goal to decentre China and Chinese culture, and questioned why was China so small on the terrestrial globe? Was it deliberately made small by the English? They also refused to believe that in Europe firearms had long since superseded bows and arrows. To this, Barrow's (1804: 605) interpretation was that "we've overestimated the Chinese knowledge and understanding of modern science. They don't value things they do not understand as that courts jealousy and hurt their sense of pride". Ye (2008) offered a similar reading of Qianlong's mind. From his poem we can see the principle of *bo lai hou wang* (bountiful bestowal, 薄来厚往) in "generous return to meagre tributes" as a way to cherish the men from afar and show benevolence of the Celestial Court, but the "bountiful tributes" from the British took away his sense of superiority and stung his pride.

So the last word used by Qianlong to describe the British gifts, "meagre", can be interpreted differently. The British gift list was later used as a benchmark to compare with other embassies, for example, the Dutch embassy's tributes a year later was held in contempt as it was in no comparison to the value and amount of the British gifts. All the major British gifts were allocated a permanent place of display in January 1795 (Guo, 2019: 136). Careful considerations were put into site selections, for example, the weaponry was kept at the Military Achievement Temple, which showcased items of historical significance to commemorate Qing's territory expansion. Keeping the British guns and cannons there showed Qianlong's wariness and vigilance of their military strength. If only the British had missionaries stationed in Beijing or inside the Forbidden City, they would have known what happened to their gifts after they left, and the genuine perception of these gifts. Therefore, rather than taking Qianlong's open despise to the British gifts as showing concomitant resistance to progress, a number of scholars have argued it as showing his "prudent statecraft" (Kitson, 2013: 130). The Qing denied their very real interest in European science, military and naval technology for political reasons (Waley-Cohen, 2000: 128), as the emperor was clearly aware that "among the Western Ocean states, England ranks foremost in strength" (Liu, 2006: 58). The Qing archives had records about recent British expansions in Asia, particularly in neighbouring India, and that the British had plundered other West Ocean ships on the high seas. However, openly admitting an interest in foreign goods was "susceptible of unfavourable interpretation as an intimation of inferiority" in Chinese minds, so "China's self-sufficiency was consciously declared to a foreign state with potential menace against Chinese national security" (Waley-Cohen, 2000: 125). The realisation that China may no longer be the sole possessor of an admirable civilisation, or "the bamboo curtain of Chinese exclusiveness" being penetrated in Cranmer-Byng's words (1962: 22), simply added to the emperor's sense of insecurity and defensiveness.

This could explain the single gift that most intrigued the emperor was the 110-gun model of the warship HMS *Royal Sovereign*, which was particularly selected to show that Britain was "acknowledged by the rest of Europe to be the first maritime power, and is truly sovereign of the seas" (Staunton, 1797: 130). The Ambassador had to come in vessels of a "less considerable size, on account of the shallows and sands of the Yellow Sea", but even so, as recorded by Staunton (ibid: 118), the two officials who came to welcome the ambassador "have never seen a ship of the *Lion*'s construction, bulk or loftiness. They were at a loss how to ascend her sides". Qianlong however, had a long-standing interest in European military technology, and impressed the British with the "technical knowledge his many questions revealed" (Waley Cohen, 2000: 124). The warship might remind the emperor of the George Anson incident in 1742, which was recorded in the Qing archives as detailed in Chapter 4 (Fu, 1966: 175). After the embassy left, over 20 edicts were issued by Qianlong to strengthen sea front defence (Guo, 2019: 144). A Court letter was also sent to the Viceroy of Canton before the edict was issued to Macartney, outlining the emperor's intention to refuse his requests and warning that the English might ferment trouble in the merchant communities of Canton and Macau. He also instructed Chang Lin to reach Canton ahead of the embassy on their return journey to inform the entire foreign business community there that the emperor had not granted special privileges to the English, anticipating that the English might try to use the opportunity to monopolise trade in Canton by coercing or intimidating other West Ocean nations who had maintained stable trade relations with China for centuries. These suggested that the Qing court was entirely aware of the imperial ambitions of the British and intended to contain their influence and curb their colonial ambitions when India and the countries of Southeast Asia succumbed to its colonial rule (Liu, 2006: 58). In this sense, Qianlong's reception of the embassy had managed to ward off the British penetration of China by changing the terms of trade to their favour. Therefore, I would like to interpret the emperor's attitude towards British gifts as being externally still but internally stirred; publicly contempt but privately contemplate.

According to FHAC (1996: 96–106), the Qing court started preparing the return gifts to the Macartney Embassy as early as June 1793, in strict adherence to the principle of giving back more than what was received. Harrison (2018) compared the gifts to the British embassy with those given to the Portuguese and commented that far more was given to the British than to other embassies, and the scale of the emperor's generosity was also emphasised by the number of different occasions: the first and largest number of gifts were sent to reciprocate those of the British king, but significant further sets were given at the audience for the emperor's birthday; when Macartney was invited to attend a feast; when he was given a tour of the imperial gardens; when the embassy left Beijing; on several occasions during the journey south; and on the embassy's arrival in Canton, where the British gifts were presented in one go. Barrow (1804: 605–608) included in his account of the embassy a comparison between the sums that the Chinese spent on hosting the embassy and the total cost of the British gifts: the embassy cost the Chinese 519,000 taels or approximately £173,000, not including the gifts provided from the palace storehouses. By comparison, the total cost to the British, including the gifts but not the cost to the navy of providing the ship, was £80,000.[6] The Qianlong Emperor gave back gifts of over 3000 pieces, mainly silk and various examples of traditional Chinese arts and crafts, including jade ware and porcelain.

If the British emphasise of use value over symbolic value was not well-received by the Chinese, conversely, the British did not appreciate the symbolic value of the main return gifts given by the Chinese emperor either, to both the British King and the ambassor as well as the vice ambassador on the day, the jade sceptre (*ruyi*) (Figure 1.7 in Chapter 1). Macartney candidly described it as "to me it does not appear in itself to be of any great value" though he understood it as "the symbol of peace and prosperity" (Cranmer-Byng, 1962: 122). What he did not know was that jade not only had an ancient history in China but was also a characteristic product of the new territory of Xinjiang, the furthest extent of the emperor's domains as the result of a recent military victory over the Zunghars. Similarly, the gifts also included boxes of Tibetan sugar, representing the Qing control in the area. The symbolic meanings carried by the origins of these gifts were completely lost to the British.

The other important gift was an old box delivered from the emperor's own hand into that of the ambassador to show the high regard and esteem for the King of Great Britain, with its special value explained:

> Deliver this casket to the King, your master, with your own hand, and tell him, though the present may appear to be small, it is, in my estimation, the most valuable that I can give, or my empire can furnish: for it has been transmitted to me through a long line of my predecessors, and is the last token of affection which I had reserved to bequeath to my son and successor, as a tablet of the virtues of his ancestors, which he only to peruse, as I should hope, to inspire him with the noble resolution to follow such bright examples.
>
> (Wood, 2019: 195)

However, it was only briefly mentioned in Macartney's *Journal* as a small box "written and painted by his (emperor's) own hand" to be presented to the King "as a token of his friendship, saying that the old box had been eight hundred years in his family" (Cranmer-Byng, 1962: 137). This meant to give a clear hint to the British that they should follow China as a bright example of superior civilisation, and by giving something reserved for the emperor's son to the British King, it implied a relationship between suzerainty and tributary states rather than a "brother monarch". Such a hidden message certainly went lost again. Gifts like "large parcels of the best tea of the country" were appreciated much more, in sight, smell and taste, as recorded by Anderson: "made up in solid cakes, in the size and form of a Dutch chesses. It is thus baked together, by which means it will never be affected by air or climate, or ever lose its flavour, though kept without any covering whatever" (Wood, 2019: 190).

So the Chinese could not appreciate the value of Britain's modernity, just as the British could not understand the meaning of China's antiquity. In the aftermath of the embassy, the British blamed their failure on the inability of the Chinese to understand their gifts, but they never realised their own inability to understand the Chinese gifts and why their own gifts may have played a counterproductive role. As summarised by Harrison (2018: 96), "neither side attempted to understand the gifts in the terms that the giver intended, instead, both aimed to use the gifts to display their own wealth and power". If gifts exchange failed to create a dialogue between the two, the next section shows how "neither British nor Chinese correctly read the symbolism of each other's rituals" (Kitson, 2013: 152).

5.3 To kowtow or not to kowtow, that is the question

In Macartney's own account, the subject of kowtow was strenuously negotiated with British firmness and rectitude as this ritual was regarded as the symbol of despotism, thus considered humiliating and incompatible with the Westphalian System whose basic building blocks were sovereignty and equality of nations. In his introduction to the Chinese emperor, Macartney presented the embassy as a "compliment … by the first Sovereign of the Western world to the Sovereign of the East" (Cranmer-Byng, 1962: 76). In the negotiations, he "dwelt upon the propriety of something to distinguish between the homage of tributary Princes and the ceremony used on the part of a great and independent sovereign" (ibid: 119). For China, this was the first time in its 2000 years of imperial history that it was confronted by a modern state demanding equal treatment as "brother monarchs". This was "whole novel in ideas, in power, in technology, in arms and in political demands, and not assimilable by China and its ways" (Gelber, 2008: 182). In hindsight, we can recognise that this was the first formal encounter between the two most powerful and wealthy empires in the world at the time. However, the Chinese emperor did not have the foresight to see the British claim of an equal sovereign, as China had only known one type of relationship with others, who came to learn, to admire and to pay tribute, but not to negotiate, least of all as equals. This was therefore a whole new experience for the Chinese tradition of dealing with foreigners.

Meanwhile, Macartney was fully aware of what ceremony reflected in the Chinese culture. He noted in his "Observations of China" that the Chinese considered their ceremonies of demeanour "as the highest perfection of good breeding and deportment, and look upon most other nations, who are not expert in this polite discipline, as little better than barbarians" (Cranmer-Byng, 1962: 222). He also witnessed the Chinese performance of kowtow in front of the Emperor's portrait hung in the ship *Lion* on 30 June 1793: "A Chinese pilot came on board with some of his people, who seemed never to have seen such a ship as the Lion before. They examined everything with great curiosity, and observing the Emperor of China's picture in the cabin, immediately fell flat on their faces before it, and kissed the ground several times with great devotion" (ibid: 65). What is telling is the contrast here, between the "great curiosity" Chinese people showed in front of something they had never seen before, and the "great devotion" they showed to a picture of their monarch by throwing themselves to the floor.

If "to kowtow, or not to kowtow" was the question faced by Macartney at the time, whether or not he performed the kowtow has become the question that had haunted the second embassy and even "obsessed the British imagination for nearly two centuries" (Liu, 2006: 57). The crux of this mystery is that there were numerous occasions[7] with the ritual involved throughout the embassy's stay in Rehe, Beijing and Canton; and there were three components in the full ceremony of kowtow, or the so-called *Sangui Jiukou* (three kneelings and nine head-knockings, 三跪九叩). This was explained with no ambiguities at the start of the negotiations on 14 August 1793, which was consistently recorded in detail in both the Qing Archive (Fu, 1966: 325) and Macartney's own *Journal* (Cranmer-Byng, 1962: 85): "in China the form was to kneel down upon both knees, and make nine prostrations or inclinations of the heads to the ground, and that it never had been, and never could be, dispensed with". However, for the first component of kneeling, the Chinese word *gui* only means bending the knee to the ground but not distinguishing on one or two knees, plus it would be hard to see clearly if Macartney has knelt down on one or both knees in his loose and voluminous robe; the second component is to knock the head. This is the literal meaning of the Chinese word *kowtow*, but also used as a shorthand for the full ceremony of *Sangui Jiukou*. So strictly speaking, if one only knelt down without knocking the head, he could claim that he *did not kowtow*. Besides, from a distance, it would be hard to see if one's head had touched the ground or just bowed deeply *to* the ground. What can be easily observed is the third element, which is the number of times this should be repeated. Even from a distance, it can be seen clearly as this was done to a loud chanting of the ceremony that would draw one into a collective move along with other court princes, mandarins and envoys from other vassal states. Since the first two components left some room for different interpretations, it also left room for a compromised version through negotiations. Macartney's account had smartly avoided mentioning how many times it was performed, while for the Chinese side, "kneeling nine times to the ground" could pass for a kowtow.

In fact, this was the exact wording to describe the ceremony according to one unpublished account written by Winder, one of Macartney's secretaries in 1793, now kept at the National Library in Dublin. Winder wrote "as he passed we were led from our tent and drawn up in a line, opposite to a row of mandarins and Tartar princes. We paid our respect *in the usual form of the country, by kneeling nine times to the ground* (emphasis added)" (cited in Peyrefitte, 1992: 224). Although he descried it as the "usual form of the country", it is insufficient to be taken as meaning the full ceremony for the ambiguity just explained. A Chinese rendition by Chen Kangqi used no ambiguous language but had no credibility as an eyewitness: "once in the presence of the Qianlong Emperor, the British ambassador fell on both knees and prostrated (*shuanggui fufu*, 双跪俯伏) (Pritchard, 1943: 175–179). Another account using the accurate expression was given by the Russian interpreter Vladykin who was in Peking at the time and stated that the "British ambassador did perform the three kneeling and nine head-knockings" (Rockhill, 1897: 632–633[8]; Liu, 2017: 87), but there was no record for him to be present at the reception either. Rather, there seems to be enough reasons to doubt this (Pritchard, 1943: 175). The young Staunton's diary (1793)[9] was quoted in many books (Peyrefitte, 1992; Hevia, 1995) in which he wrote "as he passed we went upon one knee and bowed our heads down to the ground", except that the entry had the words "to the ground" crossed out (Hevia, 1995: 168). Another witness account that had been largely overlooked was by Johann Christian Hüttner, the young Staunton's German tutor and the embassy's Latin interpreter, who was present on the day and published a German account in 1797. It corroborated that the whole retinue performed the ceremony in the way "auf ein Knie nieder" (down on one knee) when the emperor passed by, and then "beugten bloss ein Knie" (only bent one knee) again in front of the emperor (cited in Huang, 2007: 53). Pritchard's (1934) research also concluded that the evidence contained in the missionary letters supported that Macartney did not perform the Chinese style of kowtow.

According to the embassy's own account, the negotiation lasted for some ten days before the Chinese finally agreed to "adopt the English ceremony", which was to "kneel upon one knee only on those occasions when it was usual for the Chinese to prostrate themselves" (Barrow, 1807: 119). Macartney presented his refusal to kowtow as a success in safeguarding both the British pride and the accepted norms of the Westphalian System. Barrow also described the negotiation as a true test of the British character: the Qing court was presented as proud, haughty, and insolent, until confronted by a determined British embassy who had "broken through some of their laws that were declared unalterable" (ibid: 153–154). Therefore, this historic reception was not humiliating at all in Macartney's own *Journal*, as he described this reception as "very gracious and satisfactory", and "a true representation of the highest pitch of human greatness and felicity (Cranmer-Byng, 1962: 122, 124). He even added a touch of comparison that "the commanding feature of the ceremony was that calm dignity, that sober pomp of Asiatic greatness, which European refinement have not yet attained". Therefore, there was no trace of humiliation but only admiration felt on this historic audience in his own words. Staunton (1797: 306) also used the words of "distinction and even splendour" to report that the embassy was received "with the utmost politeness, treated with the utmost hospitality, watched with the utmost vigilance and dismissed with the utmost civility". In Macartney's self-evaluation, he also wrote: "If when the dispute happened in the year 1759,[10] a royal ambassador had been sent to the Court of Pekin, I am inclined to think the affair would have taken a very different turn. They would certainly have received the Embassy with respect, possibly indeed with less honours and distinctions than mine" (Cranmer-Byng 1962: 213).

In Macartney's official report to Dudas, it was stated that he "delivered the box and letter into his Imperial Majesty's own hands and *with one knee bent, as had been settled* (emphasis added), made the most reverential obeisance" (cited in Pritchard, 1934: 23). However, in his 2.5-page long entry of the day in his own *Journal*, he only mentioned that "as he (the Emperor) passed we paid him our compliments by kneeling on one knee, whilst all the Chinese made their usual prostrations" (Cranmer-Byng, 1962: 122). Inside the tent, he only described the letter delivery "into the emperor's own hands", followed by detailed descriptions of the exchange of presents and the banquet (Cranmer-Byng, 1962: 122–123) and briefly mentioned Staunton's "kneeling upon one knee in the same manner which I had done" when he was introduced to the emperor as the vice ambassador. Such a long-rehearsed ceremony was brushed off in such a manner begged the question of "why not mentioned" after such a strenuous negotiation over the issue, and "why not mentioned" if it was such a victory?

Staunton (1797, 3: 38–39) also highlighted the victory as being "particularly honourable and distinguished" as "Ambassadors being seldom received by the emperor on his throne, or their credentials delivered into his own hands, but into that of one of his courtiers. These distinctions, so little material in themselves, were however understood by this refined people as significant of a change of opinions of their government in respect to the English: and made favourable impression upon their minds". This narration had clearly tried to elevate the British treatment to a privileged position to please the domestic audience who were not aware that there were actually a number of precedents, from the Russian embassy recorded in Bell's account, to the Portuguese embassy in 1727 and 1753, the ambassadors were all allowed to deliver a communication directly into the hands of the emperor. The British themselves might not realise that an important reason to put them on a par with the Russian and Portuguese was actually its distance from China, being the farthest away from the sea-based periphery. It was specified in one of the Qianlong's edicts that "originally, I planned to receive them as per the precedent of the 1753 embassy, and even more gracious to the British due to their longer journey on the sea" (并因其航海来朝道路较远, 欲比上次更加恩视, Shanghai Publishing House, 2010: 657). One of the most famous sayings of Confucius goes like: What a delight to greet a friend from afar! We can also see this repeated in Qianlong's poem, calling them "man from afar", who "have out-travelled Shu Hai and Heng-zhang" to prove that China's virtue "must have reached their distant shores". As an emperor who had expanded Qing to its largest territory size in history,

Qianlong was proud and pleased to have Britain as a representation to his expanded sway influence, almost an addition to his honour as being the "old man with ten feats". In the Qing archive dated 17 June 1793, we can see the Emperor had emphasised that England was not to be compared with other regular vassal states such as Myanmar and Vietnam, this was their first mission that came from afar and must be well looked after, "the reception cannot not perfunctory that did not impress them" (Shanghai Publishing House, 2010: 623) This factor was also explained to Macartney in giving concessions to the kowtow arrangement (Cranmer-Byng, 1962: 120), but was not fully appreciated by the ambassador.

Another occasion for this specific message to put across was through a traditional opera staged on the second day of the emperor's birthday celebration. Macartney referred to it as the "grand pantomime" with a plot of "the marriage of the Ocean and the Earth" "as far as I could comprehend it" (ibid: 137). According to Ye (2008: 99), this opera was specially scripted for Macartney's visit and was also the only occasion that the Qing court ever put up a show bespoke to a visiting embassy. Such a real privilege that could have elevated the British status was completely unrecognised. The emperor himself had penned comments on the script and wrote: "Here comes England with tributes, who was drawn to our land by admiration. This country is miles and miles further away than Vietnam, they have to travel in months and months to arrive in China ...... such an unprecedented grand event should go down in history".[11] Most interestingly, Macartney's understanding of the plot as "the marriage of the Ocean and the Earth" revealed the British vision of regarding the mission as bringing the two empires, or even the two civilisations together, while the Chinese name of the play *Sihai Shengping* (《四海升平》) means "Peace within the Four Seas". Since "four seas" is a Chinese literary expression for "the whole world", this can be translated as "Pax Sinica", or a vision for a Sino-centric world. The Qing Dynasty was about 150 years old at the time, focusing on keeping stability, while in Europe it was a time of change and revolution. The British and Chinese understandings of the mission was as poles apart as their world views. As the opera embodied, this first embassy failed to start a dialogue between the two empires, or rather, the dialogue was like between a blind man and a deaf man, unable to hear each other or see the same picture.

To the Chinese, having a tributary state from such a great distance was unprecedented, while to the British, they wanted to gain some unprecedented treatments from China. But the concessions made in kowtow ceremony was not unprecedented. As recorded in Bell's account introduced in Chapter 4, after agreeing that the ambassador should comply with the established customs of China, on the Lantern Festival celebration, when the Chinese made their kowtows at the appearance of the emperor, Bell (1763: 60) wrote that "but we were permitted to make our compliments in our own fashion". He also commented that "it seemed somewhat strange to a Briton, to see some thousands of people upon their knees, and bowing their heads to the ground, in most humble posture, to a mortal like themselves". The Russian experience was recorded in Staunton's account (1797: 304) as being "the only minister that had hitherto gained any point in negotiations with the Chinese court". So, they might use the Russian precedent in negotiating with the emperor and reached a similar compromise: mixed forms of ceremony were performed for different occasions throughout the mission.

This compromise itself was the seed of future disputes. What kind of adapted ceremony was adopted? And for which occasion? There were large discrepancies between the Chinese and British accounts regarding these. First about the occasion. As the Deputy Director of the First Historical Archives of China (FHAC), Qin was the major contributor to the edited volume of the *Compiled Historical Records of Lord Macartney's Visit to China*, with an introduction on "A Look at the Historical Facts of Lord Macartney's visit to China from the Qing Archives" (1996, pp. 10–22). In the book he co-authored with Gao, *The Qianlong Emperor and Lord Macartney, An Account of the First Embassy to China* (1998), they presented multiple sources of Chinese records to show that after many rounds of negotiations, a compromise was finally reached: "during the banquet in the Garden of the Ten Thousand Trees, the British ambassador would perform the ritual according to the British fashion. But at the official audience in the Place of the Absence of Desire and Sincere Deference, the three prostrations and nine kowtows would be performed"[12] (Qin and Gao, 1998: 6). The sources include the *Imperial Edict Archive during Qianlong's Reign*; *The Whole Story of England Paying Tribute to Qianlong in 1793*, an account given by Su Ning'a, the General Officer in Tianjin where the Macartney Embassy landed; archives during Jiaqing and Tongzhi's reign; and *The Draft History of Qing,* a draft manuscript of the official history of the Qing Dynasty compiled by a team of over 100 historians in 15 years and published in 1928. Su's book also included the full version of the memorial prepared by the Grand Councillor He Shen and marked with Qianlong's comments. Most importantly, according to Qin and Gao (1998: 85), the first reception held at the Garden of the Ten Thousand Trees (Wanshu Yuan, 万树园) on 14 September 1793 inside the round tent was just an informal meeting meant to be a rehearsal for the big day. The formal reception took place on Qianlong's birthday on 17 September in the Place of the Absence of Desire and Sincere Deference (Danbo Jingcheng Dian, 淡泊敬诚殿), where the letter of credence was presented with the full kowtow ceremony. This procedure and venue surely made more sense in terms of the ritual ceremony, however, the British accounts gave a very elaborate report of the Wanshu Yuan reception with illustrations (see Figure 5.3), as that was where and when the letter and gifts were presented, and a very brief report on the actual day of the emperor's birthday celebration.

Figure 5.3 The Approach of the Emperor of China to receive the British Ambassador, Lord Macartney. By William Alexander, 1799. Courtesy of the Royal Asiatic Society of Great Britain and Ireland.

The painting above by the embassy's draughtsman William Alexander captured the grandiose outfit Macartney was in as part of the effort to make a great impression as the first ambassador: "a suit of spotted mulberry velvet with a diamond star, and his ribbon; over which he wore the full habit of the order of the Bath, with the hat, and plume of feathers, which form a part of it" (Anderson, 1795: 146). This painting is of great significance as it depicted the first occasion of the ceremony but framed the moment just *before* the ritual was due to be performed: when the emperor arrived and passed them outside the tent, they must perform the ceremony, in whatever the agreed form. Then, in another illustration by Alexander that depicted the scene inside the tent, Lord Macartney was kneeling down on one knee to present the King's letter of credence to the emperor, it also captured the whole retinue of 12 members with a full list of their names provided on the top right corner.[13] This number was consistent with the Chinese archive kept at the FHAC: apart from Lord Macartney, the vice ambassador Staunton and his son, and the interpreter Mr. Li, there were also "eight other gentlemen" who participated in the reception.[14]

Yet, a more famous and most powerful representation of this reception is the caricature by James Gillray (see Figure 5.4), which instead of

Figure 5.4 The Reception of the Diplomatique (Macartney) and his Suite, at the Court of Pekin. Courtesy of the British Library.

showing it as a "success" as claimed by Macartney and Staunton, rendered the first official encounter between the two empires into a traumatic scene by bringing the failure of gift giving into it.

The most amazing thing is the time when this caricature was created: on the bottom right corner was pencilled the date of publication as 14 September 1792, a few days before Macartney even set on his journey to China and exactly one year before the actual reception took place on 14 September 1793. All the details depicted in this busy scene made Gillray a genius prophet. For example, it not only captured all the 12 gentlemen in the reception, but the one-knee-down ritual performed by Lord Macartney, which was the result of a strenuous negotiation after they arrived in China. I cannot help wondering how could he predict this one year earlier? What is more intriguing is the six gentlemen behind him were actually performing the kowtow. This was again a possible scenario as a way of concessions made during the negotiations: only the ambassador himself was allowed to adopt the compromised version. Also, it captured the most peculiar gifts, such as the porcelain tea set, the model warship, the yellow-coloured carriage, and the hot air balloon.[15] Other major gifts that were supposedly samples of cutting-edge British technology were presented as children's toys. This is again incredible as discussed in the section above, even the "best brains" who put up the gift selection together did not see this coming, how could Gillary foresee the Chinese emperor's reaction to British gifts?

The Chinese admission of the Europeanised ceremony was disclosed when the second embassy wanted to negotiate on the ceremony again. Amherst was informed that "the Qianlong Emperor was most unhappy with Macartney's European homage and had been adamant that it should not become a precedent for future occasions" (Stevenson, 2021:177). However, the Qing officials specified that "Macartney had bowed before the Qianlong emperor on his first audience, but thereafter had kowtowed during the second audience at the time of the celebrations of the emperor's birthday" (ibid: 188). The Amherst Embassy's own account also mentioned that an extract from the imperial records was shown to Amherst, affirming that Lord Macartney had kowtowed to Qianlong and that the Jiaqing Emperor remembered this (Fu, 1966, vol. 1: 404; Ellis, 1817: 154). Amherst had subsequently reported this to George Canning in February 1817 that "I have since been given to understand that on an occasion subsequently to his first audience, Lord Macartney multiplied his bow nine times in conformity to the usual number of prostrations made by the Chinese" (Amherst to Cannning, February 12, 1817, PRO FO 17/3/59, cited in Platt, 2018: 161), but the wording here changed kowtow into "bow" and only confirmed "nine times".

So, what was the subsequent occasion that Macartney kowtowed as claimed by the Chinese? Was it the emperor's birthday (17 September) as recorded in those documents in Qin and Gao's research? According to Macartney, "we saw nothing of him the whole day", as the emperor "remained concealed behind a screen" on the actual day of his birthday. All eyes were turned towards the "place where he was imagined to be enthroned" inside the Danbo Jingcheng Palace. When the music played with chanting of "Bow down your heads, all ye dwellers upon earth, bow down your heads before the great Ch'ien-lung, the great Chi'ien lung", "all the dwellers upon China earth there present,[16] *except ourselves* (emphasis added), bowed down their heads and prostrated themselves upon the ground at every renewal of the chorus. Indeed, in no religion either ancient or modern, has the Divinity ever been addressed, I believe, with stronger exterior marks of worship and adoration than were this morning paid to the phantom of his Chinese Majesty" (Cranmer-Byng, 1962: 131). Staunton (1797: 303) also recorded that "it is difficult to imagine an exterior mark of more profound humility and submission, or which implies a more intimate consciousness of the omnipotence of that being towards whom it is made". The entry for the day in Fu's (1966: 326) compilation recorded it as "the ambassadors of Burma and England performed the ceremonies of congratulation", but did mention that "the princes" (including the future Jiaqing Emperor) were present on both the first day of the audience and the birthday celebrations that "all were feasted and entertained daily until the fifteenth day". Most importantly, the title of the entry read "The English Embassy Honoured for Three Days".

This pointed to another potential occasion, when on the second day of the birthday celebration, Macartney was invited to watch the Chinese opera and other shows with the emperor that lasted the whole morning from eight to noon. It was recorded in Macartney's *Journal* that "soon after we came in, the Emperor sent for me and Sir George Staunton to attend him", a subsequent conversation took place. Since the show time was so long, Macartney even "endeavoured" to "lead him towards the subject of my Embassy, but he seemed not disposed to enter into it farther than by delivering me a little box of old Japan" (Cranmer-Byng, 1962: 137). As explained earlier, this gift *was* the emperor's answer to the British requests, but the hidden message was not picked up by the British. The point here is, on such occasions of face-to-face conversation and gift-giving (not just the box with the emperor's own writing and painting as a gift to the British King, there were also some personal gifts presented to Macartney and Staunton), it was not possible to take place without any due ceremonies performed, yet nothing was mentioned in the *Journal*. However, Macartney did include another brief meeting with the Emperor on the second day after the Wanshuyuan reception: they met the Emperor again in the morning when he "entered into conversation with us" (ibid: 124) before going to the pagoda to pay his morning devotions, and the following day (16 September), Macartney's *Journal* started with the line "Having now twice paid our obeisance to the Emperor" (ibid: 129), indicating that a certain form of "obeisance" had been performed.

Another possible occasion was in Canton, where the shadow of the kowtow followed them after they left Beijing. According to Staunton's *Diary 1792–1793*, the Mandarins made nine bows and three genuflections before a throne representing the emperor where the British "followed their example" (cited in Stevenson, 2021: 176). During the Amherst Embassy, the Mandarins claimed that Macartney had kowtowed, not only in the presence of the emperor but at other times as well, whenever the occasion demanded (Staunton, 1824: 46; Ellis, 1817: 92). One official even appealed to Staunton to vouch that Macartney performed the kowtow at Canton, as he remembered that the young Stanton was present as well. But Staunton was evasive, saying that the embassy was so long ago, and he had been so young, that he could not remember which ceremony had been performed, but he was certain that it was not the kowtow (Staunton, 1824: 47).

Peyrefitte's book (1992: 206) referred to the "Essays on the History of the Qing Dynasty" which stated that "an imperial edict consequently permitted the use of the Western ceremony", but no one seemed to be able to locate this edict,[17] except the edict issued by the Jiaqing Emperor to the British King during the Amherst Embassy, which confirmed that "your former Ambassador, in the fifty-eighth year of Ch'ien Lung (Qianlong), did duly perform the whole prescribed ceremony, including the genuflexion and kotow. How, then, could any deviation from this course be permitted on the present occasion?" (Backhouse and Bland, 1914: 382; Hevia, 1995: 227). The full version can be found in Appendix 7. With multiple documentary evidence and accounts that can be gathered from both sides so far, it seems that only one thing can be corroborated: that Macartney did not kowtow to the Emperor when he delivered the letter of credential in Wanshuyuan, but we are not able to ascertain on which occasion Macartney may have performed the kowtow, nor can we use the Chinese claims to establish a firm conclusion that he did perform the full kowtow ceremony at some point, as the British records avoided mentioning them on purpose, while the Chinese claims lacked trustworthy written records to clarify the specific ritual on each occasion. This "intentional ambiguity" on both sides is a sign of mutual compromise, as a way to leave some room so that each side can document the ceremony to fit their own claims of victory in front of its own people by highlighting the parts they wanted to highlight. In this sense, if we look at the kowtow mystery as an outcome of complex negotiations, it did represent a creative result that managed to meet each other halfway and get the best out of the worst scenario. It could be called a "success" as mutual concessions were made after finding the bottom lines of each side, and mutual victories claimed when both expressed wishes for further exchange of visits: Emperor Qianlong expressed his wish for the British King to send a representative to participate in his abdication ceremony and Macartney recommended Staunton to come back as the ambassador in 1796, but he fell ill and was not able to make the trip.

Therefore, my answer to Macartney's kowtow mystery is Yes and No, as it is an intentional man-made mystery. This answer seems to be the most tenable explanation for why there were multiple versions in different accounts, and also why it became problematic when referred to as a precedent during the Amherst Embassy, as each side clung to their own handed-down versions. The most likely scenario is the embassy was allowed to adopt a reduced or hybrid form of *Sangui Jiukou*, which was like a repertoire, from which different elements were chosen to adapt to different occasions. Even on the first reception day, they may have followed different ritual performances – when they welcomed the emperor's arrival outside the tent, and when Macartney handed over the credential inside the tent, where other members of no diplomatic status might have performed the full kowtow (as shown in Figure 5.4), as Macartney's own *Journal* only confirmed Staunton had performed the ritual in the same way while Winder's account said "kneeling nine times to the ground". Further adaptations may be made in other occasions, depending on how public the occasion was and if there were other foreign envoys at present, as it was all about "face", which is a "commonality between the British and Chinese: both can be proud and vain" (Hevia, 1995: 207). For example, some occasions may only have Macartney, the two Stauntons, and the Chinese interpreter present. If Macartney had kowtowed, it would most likely be kept a secret among this tightly inclusive group to keep to the "official" British story, so as to save face and claim a kind of "victory". Even its own member such as Anderson (1795: 29–30), who was not present at the audience, held such suspicions: "various conjectures occurred, but no man, except Sir George Staunton, was likely to know what had passed. The incident and its circumstances, whatever they might be, were hushed up, and nothing said, as if nothing particular had happened". In 1818, a 31-page pamphlet entitled *A Delicate Inquiry Into the Embassies to China* and *a Legitimate Conclusion from the Premises* was published after the second Amhurst Embassy, as an attempt to inquire into how the result of the first missions could justify the second. It blamed Macartney for hiding the truth which resulted in the failure of the Amherst embassy, and exposed that although George Staunton had done his utmost best to disguise the truth, "it failed completely, and that the failure was accompanied with many circumstances of humiliation to the ambassador, and of slight and disgrace to the Sovereign he represented" (Ellis, 1817: 437).

This answer might also explain why Lord Macartney did not wish to have his *Journal* published until after his death, for fear of the book getting back to China. But the interesting fate of his *Journal* was that its Chinese translation was first published in China in 1916,[18] while the full version of the English *Journal* was only published in 1962.[19] The English accounts by other embassy members published earlier played an important role in shifting the Chinese narrative regarding the matter.[20] Liu (2017) traced the changing Chinese accounts of the Macartney Embassy throughout the Qing Dynasty and revealed a rather interesting evolvement: during the Qianlong's reign, there were only detailed records of the negotiation process with full versions of the memorials prepared by the Grand Councillor and marked with the emperor's comments but no record with clear descriptions of the actual ceremony performed on the day of the receptions. By the Jiaqing's reign, the dispute with Amherst Embassy led to clarified and confirmed discourse to dispel the ambiguities from early records. Jiaqing Emperor's own witness account was used to reconstruct the official narrative, which was subsequently widely and consistently stuck to in various documents. In 1873, this dispute still haunted the negotiation with the British Minister Thomas Wade, the then Zhili Governor-General Li Hongzhang claimed to have checked court records on the two British embassies as well as the Dutch embassy of 1795: "The records indicated that Macartney and the Dutch ambassor had both performed kowtow, but that when Amherst refused, he was not granted an audience" (cited in Hevia, 1995: 228).

However, by 1890 when China received overseas reports sent by Xue Fucheng who was appointed the ambassador to the four European countries of Britain, France, Italy and Belgium, the narrative of Macartney performed the Europeanised ceremony started to gain currency. More detailed information was included in Xue's diary that drew on the British accounts to support this argument (Liu, 2017: 90–91). However, his reference to the Treaty of Tianjin that scraped the kowtow ceremony in diplomatic relations revealed the most important reason for this new narrative to prevail: the Qing government was under great pressure at the time to find a way out of the predicament caused by Western countries' requests to adopt modern ceremony that symbolise equality. Macartney's case can serve as an ancestral precedent to provide political legitimacy for the Qing court and save them face from the unsustainable Tributary System that had been shattered by the two Opium Wars. Therefore, behind the shifting of the Chinese narratives was the power shift between the two empires and the two systems. This was a perfect example for Harrison's (2017: 682) point that archives were often released and used to serve a political purpose, "particularly in the aftermath of major political transitions which demand that the past should be reconstituted to justify the present". Perhaps no one said it better than George Orwell (1949: 34): "Who controls the past controls the future. Who controls the present controls the past".

While there is no way for us to restore historical truth in full details, it is more important to understand why the truth was shielded and why historical reality is so elusive. It reminds us that all accounts need to be read with caution as they could be coloured with any shade, magnified to any extent or simply have entries removed. The official accounts of the British embassy could be just as self-interested as those earlier missionary writings, as well as Chinese entries in the archives as a court artifice. Between fact and fiction, there is often only a fine line. As Cook (2009) had boldly pointed out, archivists could play the role of "co-creator" of history in the choices they make about what to keep and what to exclude from the archive. This taught us that even if we hold two similar accounts, it would be dangerous to assume that "they confirm one another, therefore they are true". Even today, when pictures and videos are used for news reports, selected exposure is still a commonly used tactic to "present fact as truth" – the selected fact being presented is not fabricated but presenting one frame as the whole picture or using one quote out of context is a way to manipulate and distort the whole truth. In a way, this is what this book tries to achieve, to add more missing frames to the pictures that have already been shown, so that we can piece together a more comprehensive continuum of causes and effects in history.

Another missing piece to the embassy's experience was its sudden dismissal from Beijing, perhaps the most humiliating part according to their own accounts, even Macartney's valet Anderson found "the manner in which the Ambassador was dismissed from Pekin was ungraceful and mortifying in the extreme …… It is wholly irreconcilable to the common rules of political decorum and civility, as well as the principles of justice and humanity, that an ambassador, of so much consequence as Lord Macartney, should be dismissed, under his peculiar circumstances, without the least ceremony" (Wood, 2019: 222–223). How could a planned reception "more gracious" than the previous embassies end with such a lack of civility? According to the *Imperial Edict Archive during Qianlong's Reign* (1991: 410), not only a farewell banquet was originally planned in the Hall of Justice and Honour of Yuanming Yuan but a wide range of other activities were arranged back in June,[21] including a show to watch and a tour of various halls inside the magnificent Forbidden City, a dragon boat ferry in the Summer Place and a full display of the fountains in Yuanming Yuan, which would have been a significant gesture to copy a Western ritual to receive an ambassador. But they were later all cancelled by the emperor. The first cancellation of the show and tour in Beijing was made on the first day when the embassy arrived in Rehe, after Macartney was said to have "malingered" (qianyan zhuangbing, 迁延装病) from meeting the first Minister. This "malinger" was recorded in Macartney's own *Journal* dated 8 September, the day when they arrived at Rehe after making "a very splendid show" for his public entry (Cranmer-Byng, 1962: 115): "It being very hot weather, and the servants greatly hurried and fatigued with the operations of the day, and our baggage, etc. not being yet unpacked or put into order, I excused myself with a civil compliment". But he sent the vice ambassador Staunton to the Minster's house to meet him, as "the first Minister had received a hurt in his knee, which rendered it inconvenient and painful to him to move much about". Macartney was also told that "as there would not be sufficient room in my apartment for all the first Minister's suite, he, the first Minister, hoped I would excuse him from coming to me in person, and that it would be the same thing if I would be so good as to come to him" (ibid:118). Obviously, Macartney did not recognise this was a "test" for him, nor was he aware of the consequences of not attending the meeting in person, which directly led to the reduction of bestowals and prestige. The decision was explained by Qianlong as the "art of dealing with barbarians: If they are sincere and submissive, then we would cherish them and grace them; if they show arrogance, then they do not deserve our benevolence, we would reduce the bestowal to show them propriety" (外夷入觐, 如果诚信恭顺必加以恩待, 以示怀柔, 若稍涉骄矜, 则是伊无福承受恩典, 亦即减其接待之礼, 以示体制, 此驾驭外藩之道宜然. Shanghai Publishing House, 2010: 657). Then, a few days after the ceremonies at Rehe, an edict was dispatched, specifying the cancellation of the banquet at Yuanming Yuan (ibid: 663). This could serve as a circumstantial evidence that the ceremony performed by Macartney at Rehe was not considered as being "sincere and submissive", thus not deserve the emperor's benevolence. Anderson's final word became widely quoted and circulated: "In short, we entered Pekin like paupers, we remained in it like prisoners, and we quitted it like vagrants" (ibid: 224), which was also included in the advertisement page for William Winterbotham's book, *An Historical, Geographical, and Philosophical View of the Chinese Empire,* published in 1795.

Looking back, the intriguing thing is that although the kowtow allegedly did not happen and even claimed as a "success" of the negotiations, nor was it mentioned as an issue in both the embassy accounts and the Qianlong emperor's edicts or letters, it became the most humiliating public memory of this embassy, even planting seeds in future generations' minds to be used as justifications to settle old scores with China when the gunboat diplomacy was conceived. John Quincy Adams, the sixth president of the United States, had boldly claimed that the Opium War was not caused by opium, but the kowtow, "the arrogant and insupportable pretensions of China that she will hold commercial intercourse with the rest of mankind not upon terms of equal reciprocity, but upon the insulting and degrading forms of the relations between lord and vassal" (cited in Gelber, 2008: 188). As a matter of fact, the word "kowtow" became the first Chinese word entering English language that remains a term of derision, repeatedly in use today as an embedded rhetoric in criticising the government's soft stance of developing closer relations with China. This linguistic legacy shows that the kowtow issue has been fermented into something intoxicating over time.

However, kowtow was not the single element defining suzerain-vassal relationship, rather, as a ritual tradition, it can be defended as both following the principle of "when in China, do as the Chinese do", and the precedents set by other European countries. Pritchard (1943: 197–199) argued that "after having conformed to all other parts of the suzerain-vassal relationship", to refuse to kowtow was "in reality pointless". Compared with kowtow as a ceremonial form, gifts labelled as tributes and left on permanent display, and letters written in or translated into tributary vocabulary and kept in archives, are carriers in a more lasting physical form to legitimise the relationship. Therefore in my view, "to kowtow, or not to kowtow", that is *NOT* the key question and would not change the result of the mission, the humiliations were as much, if not more deeply etched into the discourse of the letters exchanged.

5.4 Letters, letters

Over two centuries after the first undelivered letter from the British Empire, King George III's letter as from the monarch of "the most powerful nation of the globe" to the ruler of "the only civilisation under heaven", was successfully delivered to the hand of the Qianlong Emperor on 14 September 1793. The letter (Appendix 4) defined the embassy not as a "purpose of conquest", nor for "acquiring wealth, or even of favouring the commerce of Our Subjects", but "for the sake of increasing

Our knowledge" of the part of the world "where they were hitherto little known" with the help of "the most wise and learned of our own people", claiming the encounter arose from a common interest in "extending the peaceful arts to the entire human race". It set out the assumptions of an enlightened English king who "directed his people to discover new regions of the globe", "to extend knowledge of the world and to find the various productions of the earth" and to communicate "the arts and comforts of life to those parts of the world where it appeared they had been wanting". This section will trace the shifts in the tone and rhetorical emphasis between Queen Elizabeth I's letters and King George III's, between the British monarch's and the Chinese emperor's, and between the original letters and their translations.

The letter began with introducing the British King in the pompous and pretentious title of "His Most Sacred Majesty George the Third, by the Grace of God King of Great Britain, France and Ireland, Sovereign of the Seas, Defender of the Faith and so forth", who has "obtained victories over [his] enemies in the four quarters of the world", yet mercifully granted them "the blessing of peace upon the most equitable conditions". After portraying himself as the most powerful monarch who had the well-being of all humanity in mind, George III went on to compliment China for having "carried its prosperity to such a height as to be the admiration of all surrounding nations", expressing the wish for "unreserved and amicable intercourse, between such great and civilised nations as China and Great Britain". Compared with Queen Elizabeth I's letter addressed to the "great, mighty, and invincible" Emperor of Cathay, this letter only addressed Qianlong as the "Supreme Emperor of China Kien-long worthy to live tens of thousands and tens of thousands thousand years". This astounding shift reflected the changing power status of the two empires during the two centuries in between, or more specifically, the changing position of the British Empire in its own eyes as the most powerful nation globally, while China as a respectable civilisation with its sway reaching "surrounding nations", was only a regional power. It was this perceived power shifts, together with the notion of sovereign equality developed in the Westphalian System and the Christian notion of universal brotherhood that prompted George III to adopt discourse of "brotherly affection" to the Qianlong Emperor as "brethren in sovereignty".

However, the glowing terms used in the letter showed that China was still considered an advanced civilisation by the British. In the King's private instruction to Macartney, George III described the Chinese as "a people, perhaps the most singular upon the globe, among whom civilisation had existed, and the arts been cultivated, through a long series of ages, with fewer interruptions than elsewhere" (Staunton, 1797: 47–48). Another element that remained unchanged from the Queen Elizabeth I's time was the enduring national character of the British – the English curiosity about the world, the desire to learn about other land and people, the voyages sponsored by the king to gather knowledge of distant and unknown region, and the interest in developing benevolent ties with a great empire like China, although all these were seen by Qianlong as "earnestly inclining your heart towards civilisation" (Appendix 5). Of course, trade remained the core theme of the letter, which can be seen from George III's reference to the benefits nations derive from the "interchange of commodities" and the "general obligation upon Nations to promote mutual commerce with one another". Although these notions in the Westphalian System had become universalised in the Western world for about one and a half centuries, China had never thought of itself as a "nation", it was an empire and a civilisation that did not have the word "trade partner" in its dictionary. Instead, they had a rigid set of discourse used in the correspondence under the tributary relationship, which still set the terms of Sino-Western trade by this time.

The incompatibility between the two systems was thus reflected in the untranslatability of the letter of credence, which found no equivalent in register or genre in Chinese. For example, all letters from foreign rulers to the Chinese emperor fell squarely into the genre of *Biao* (tributary memorial, 表), a term which relegated the addressers to an inferior position and ruled out the possibility of communication on an equal basis in the same way as *Gong* did (tribute).

It may be possible to decipher the language, but impossible to translate the cultural contexts and incompatible world views, as "translations are not ideologically neutral but are shaped by the background and outlook of the translator"(Clarke, 2003: 185), who then proceeded to relocate them within their own frames of discourse. Wang (2020: 12) explained the dilemma of the translator when "confronted with the competing claims of two distinct discourses, the first decision to be made is wherein their discursive loyalty should lie". For those in China, the choice was clear-cut as otherwise you would be risking your life.[22] Since the two interpreters hired by the embassy were not familiar with the court style, there were two different Chinese versions produced, one by them with a copy kept at the British Foreign Office archives, one was "corrected" by the missionaries serving at the Qing court to fit in the right and rigid frame and kept in the Chinese archives (FHAC). Although it was a common practice to do "re-translation" of non-submissive memorials, such as those from earlier European (Portuguese and Dutch) embassies to the Qing court during Kangxi's reign (Wills, 1984: 178), an important difference for the British was that they did not have their own missionaries in Beijing at the time, so the letter had to be re-translated by European missionaries from the Latin translation of the original letter as they did not understand English, nor would they defend the British interests.

In the Chinese version kept at FHAC, to start with, the King's lengthy self-introduction became "King of the English *Dahongmao* (big red hairs, 大红毛), France and Ireland, Sovereign of the Seas", who had "longing for some material rewards" and been "aspiring to your highly civilised empire" by "respectfully sending an embassy bearing a *Biao* and *Gong*" (进献表贡, 向化输诚, FHAC, 1996: 165). The original purpose of the embassy was completely distorted to fit into the *Biao,* and the overblown rhetoric used in George III's original style was translated into humble and respectful "equivalents". Similarly, the "Ambassador Extraordinary and Plenipotentiary" "truly worthy of representing Us" was translated into "*tributary envoy*" (Gongshi, 贡使). Here, what mattered was the genre and diction to fit in the fixed discourse of *Biao*, not "style" as put by Wang (2020: 10), "the style expected is discursive obedience rather than linguistic elegance". In other words, it was not about high or low in register, but right or wrong in diction; not about how sophisticated the language is, but almost on the contrary, in how straightforward it is. However, this can hardly be called a "translation" if compared with the "back translations" of the Chinese version into English.

On the other hand, a faithful translation of Qianlong's reply to the British King would sound more intolerable and inappropriate in Western genre of diplomatic correspondence. This most frequently quoted flamboyant letter (Appendix 5), full of patronising vocabulary and ideological expressions in explaining in great length the reasons for his refusal to grant the requests of the embassy, is a classical exposition of the relationship between "China and the rest" in the eyes of the Chinese emperor; a "stagnant East and a progressive West" in the Western eyes; and the conflicting world views bred by the two systems to modern readers. As Hevia (1995: 239) put it, "The letter came to stand for China's traditional culturalism, isolationism and sense of self-sufficiency nicely and conveniently compacted into one text". There were also two translated versions into English, both were published over a 100 years later after Macartney brought it back. As Cranmer-Byng (1962: 336) explained, the "Jesuit fathers who were charged with translating this edict from Chinese into Latin deliberately modified expressions here and there which they thought would offend the English". The first full text translation was done by E. H. Parker in 1896 but a more widely circulated version was done by Backhouse and Bland in 1914. However, since it was "more in the nature of a paraphrase than a close translation, so that Chinese ideas are sometimes made to fit into English conceptions and phrases", Cranmer-Byng decided to attempt a literal translation to "bring out the full flavour of the haughty and condescending tone", which "must have been extremely satisfying to the emperor and his officials", but were "lost on the western barbarians in their English translation" (ibid: 336–341). Both versions are included in Appendix 5.

Cranmer-Byng's (1962: 341) translation read like a reprimand of Britain's insolent request to establish direct diplomatic and trade relations with China: China is the centre of the world and the prototype of civilisation. Any barbarian country may send a special envoy to the capital to present tribute and so partake briefly in the benefits of a super civilisation. As regards to trade, this is a privilege which is granted to foreigners and must be kept under close supervision; it is not necessary to the Celestial Empire. It is permitted out of compassion to the barbarians who need tea and silks and porcelain with which to make their lives bearable. As for the idea of a regular ambassador residing at Peking, it is unheard of. How can barbarian states have permanent intercourse with the Celestial Empire itself? "The Celestial Empire produces all things in abundance" and "there is really no need for goods from outer *Yi* (barbarians) to balance supply and demand". They do not know the correct etiquette, their only task is to remain at peace, and from time to time to show their submission and loyalty by presenting tribute to the imperial throne.

Another important point made in this letter was China's conceptualisation of trade as being more than a commercial activity of exchanging goods but with social and political implications. Because of the interest involved, trade activities have the potential of producing conflict among people, as well as greed and avarice in individuals. As explained in Chapter 2, merchants were considered as a low class in social stratum in Confucian society. With such people "no relations, except that of suzerain and vassal, made sense" (Singer, 1992: 177–178). This put the British appeals in two prongs: while they wanted equality with China by rejecting being treated as a tributary state, they also wanted to secure their status as the leading nation in their trades with China. In other words, what they wanted was a privilege that can distinguish them from other European rivals. As for China, they did not want to set up such a precedent and saw no need to change the centuries-old precedent just to please one country. As reiterated in the Emperor's letter, the Canton System was already well established for all West Ocean people to trade, and the Qing court wished to treat them all with "equal benevolence" and compassion (yi shi tong ren, 一视同仁), i.e. equality among the inferiors. It is interesting to see that both sides used equality to reason, however, it did not lead to any agreement but only discrepancy under the two systems and conflict of interests between the two empires.

Following the return of embassy, a number of letters and gifts were further dispatched in 1795 in an endeavour to consolidate the gains from the mission. Five letters in all were sent, each of which was addressed from one British official to his presumed counterpart, including a second letter from George III to the Chinese emperor dated 20 June 1795. It is important to note that despite bearing the King's signature and seal, these letters were written by then British Secretary of State Henry Dundas or his secretary (Hevia, 1995: 60). Similarly, the two edicts from Qianlong were drafted by secretaries in his Grand Council (Barrow, 1807: 325).[23] All these letters were therefore more discursive than personal in nature. The King's second letter was again accompanied by a Latin and a

Chinese version, but it was "full of linguistic and grammatical errors and hardly intelligible", that the viceroy of Canton had to order "a *tongshi* (interpreter) conversant with that country's language to check the Chinese *Biao* against the accompanying copy in *Yi* language (referring to the English original) and produced a new translation" (FHAC, 1996, 234). Wang (2020) and Wong (2013) did a thorough study of the two King's letters and their four Chinese versions, and found that the British had clearly learned the style in using the special vocabulary in the second letter, also the *Biao* format of visually putting the British king in an inferior position: references to Qianlong, either as the Emperor or the Great Emperor, stood two characters above the general head margin, while those to the English King are raised by only one character. But they had stuck to the use of *qinchai* (imperial legate) in the second letter, which was again duly corrected in the Chinese version produced by the unnamed translator at Canton. The tone was again translated into the humble submissiveness befitting a lesser lord. The King thanked the Emperor for "graciously accepting the tributary gifts", and "bow[s] respectfully in receiving the Great Emperor's imperial bestowals". He also looked forward to another chance of sending a "tributary envoy" to "kowtow to the Great Emperor and express the sincerity of distant *Yi*" (FHAC, 1996: 232–233). The British also learned to put letters to the emperor in a small yellow silken bag while those for the Viceroy in a bag of green silk. The gifts were also divided into two groups accordingly and graded on the basis of quality and rank, in a manner reminiscent of the emperor's gifts to the British embassy (Hevia, 1995: 219). Unfortunately, when the letter and gifts arrived in Canton addressed to the Viceroy that Macartney had cultivated friendly relationship during the mission, he was no longer there and his successor refused to accept letters and presents meant for his predecessor.

Two days before Emperor Qianlong's abdication[24] in 1796, he addressed the last letter to King George III (Appendix 6). From the wording used in this letter, such as referring to the letter and gifts as "memorial with tribute", conveyed by "barbarian vessels"; the Macartney's embassy as a "tribute mission", and the whole act as "reverent submission", not much change can be observed from the Qing side, still seeing the world in a dichotomy of barbarism and civilisation. Macartney himself never saw the letter in its original form, as the missionaries who translated the letter into Latin had again already altered the tone and removed the offensive phrases, but they were still considered too inappropriate to be made public. Macartney and Staunton deleted anything that might hurt the British pride, and an abridgement of the letter was only released long after they both had died. As well put by Hevia (2003: 228), "'the other' was reconstructed, internalised and imagined, at the moments of both production and reception of a given text. The translation hides more than it reveals". Yet ironically, it was through translation that radical discursive change in China was eventually realised. In the second half of the nineteenth century, Chinese "equivalents" were increasingly created for Westphalian terms, and China's claim of universal sovereignty gradually yielded in its own language to the penetrating discourse of sovereign "equality". Like the kowtow, the Qing Court's rigorous control and manipulation of translation was retaliated by the British when the reversal of "otherness" took place by the time of the Opium War. This will be looked at in Chapter 7.

5.5 Change of the mutual perceptions between the two empires

As argued from the first section in this chapter, the Macartney Embassy stood no chance of success from the very beginning as what he must break through was "the intellectual and bureaucratic barriers of the Tributary System" (Hevia, 1995: 11). There was simply no common ground of understanding between the two empires to build any trading and diplomatic relations in the modern sense. It was also overambitious, trying to accomplish multiple goals through the first official delegation sent under the name of celebrating the emperor's birthday. Actually, this "excuse" as its proclaimed purpose of the visit may doom the mission from the start, as it would be the occasion with most peculiar attentions paid to the ceremony, especially when many representatives from other vassal states would be present as well, a new embassy from the furthest corner of the world would be used to show the extended glory to the emperor's *Tianxia.* So it would be the most inopportune time to negotiate on not complying with the ceremony. Peyrefitte (1992: blurb) described the encounter of 1793 as a clash of two planets, a "mutual discovery of two refined yet incompatible cultures, one celestial and lunary, the other quite down-to-earth: mercantile, scientific, and industrial". When I first read this powerful statement, I had to use a dictionary to confirm the meaning of "lunary", which is so elusive that I tried to understand it from the context – being used together with "celestial" and in contrast with "down-to-earth". To me, this carefully chosen word to describe Chinese culture is most interesting, it seems only such an obscure word can describe the indescribable Chinese culture, which can only be made sense of as the opposite to those straightforward modifiers to describe "us". This made the so-called journey of "mutual discovery" only reach an Orientalised understanding of "the other".

Although the mission failed to achieve its primary goals, it did gain plenty of other expected and unexpected results according to the agenda set for it to "obtain all the information possible about China, not only economic and political, but also military, intellectual, cultural and social as well as information about China's relations with Russia and other countries", and to "find out what new articles might profitably be exported from

China to England" (Cranmer-Byng, 1962: 30–31). In the returning journey departing from Beijing, the embassy became the first Europeans to navigate the northern coastline of China, and the British curiosity allowed them to acquire new information about Chinese waters, as well as mulberry trees and silkworm cocoons. They were even allowed to remove several premium tea plants and to ship them to Bengal for cultivation. There were also artists, naturalists, medical experts, and botanical gardeners included in the embassy that "transformed what might have been a narrower diplomatic mission into a voyage of Enlightenment comparative anthropology" (Kitson, 2013: 142). This enabled the mission to return with taxonomical records of the natural landscape and ethnographical information, and hundreds of illustrations of Chinese peoples, society, customs and costumes by the embassy's draughtsman William Alexander,[25] including drawings produced with exact measurement, such as the Rehe Potala Palace. Most importantly, it brought back information on China's government apparatus, its official views, and court characters for the first time for the British. It saw the xenophobia that lay under the surface of official politeness and the Chinese contempt for anything new or foreign, and indeed the whole non-Chinese world. More importantly, the range of accounts produced by different members of the embassy started a paradigm shift in British perceptions by challenging old Western assumptions, and substituting the biased Jesuit-inspired writing and Chinoiserie fantasy with first-hand accounts of real events that happened in real China.

Many would thus assume the mission served to unveil the real China in its true colour. However, as Varisco (2007: 501) commented, "re-presentation from an outsider's perspective, is never going to be an exact duplication". While removing the imaginary veil of a Utopian China, these accounts continued to paint China with their brushes, from their perspectives. It is important to remember the context that "Macartney and Staunton had to gloss over or withhold certain aspects of the embassy, while at the same time, to exaggerate the good relationship they had allegedly built up with the Qing court" to glorify the embassy's achievements (Gao, 2020: 46). Also because of their own background as a member of learned society and the exposure to missionary writing that emphasised the great traditions of elite Chinese society, Staunton and Macartney's accounts of China were generally more positive. Williams (2014: 2) commented that Macartney had developed a "more 'genteel' mode of travel-writing on China, focused less on the projection of exoticism and inferiority than on the representation of Chinese hospitality and civility". His *Journal*, along with the detailed and insightful observations made about thirteen aspects, i.e. *Manners and Character; Religion; Government; Justice; Property; Population; Revenue; Civil and Military Ranks and Establishments; Trade and Commerce; Arts and Sciences' Hydraulics; Navigation; and Chinese Language*, functioned as a substantial first-hand report that made a valuable contribution to the new

European knowledge of China at the time. The Chinese translator (Liu, 1916: 1) of his *Journal* put in the Preface that "although the embassy seemed to go home empty-handed with only the gifts received from the Chinese emperor, the value of this *Journal* is worth ten thousand times more than the gifts they received, and hundred times more important than the original requests they came to seek from China".

If Staunton's official account had left bits and pieces of China's legendary image intact, other accounts written by lower classes who held no official posts and therefore felt no compulsion to tread any particular line, "painted a picture of backward, degenerate country unworthy of its reputation for high civilisation" (Peyrefitte, 1992: 491). For example, two widely quoted accounts include the one given by Aeneas Anderson, Macartney's valet de chambre, that became the first to be published in 1795; and John Barrow's *Travels in China* that was published in 1804. They exemplified a shift "from identifying standards of civilisation with elite culture to concentrating on the common practices in ordinary life as a measure of social, cultural, and economic standing. Such a shift contributed, perhaps more than any other factor, to the fading of Chinese high civilisation in the British mindset" (Chen, 2004: 194). Since they were all prepared to be impressed by a civilisation that had reached high standards of civic life, court culture, and social organisation from previous readings, when China was judged by how "it performed at the *present* time in terms of military power, effective government, scientific knowledge, technological skill and the living standards of the mass of the population" (Gao, 2020: 12), a stagnant and backward image began to take shape. The evolving perception was not only bound to reflect the time the accounts were written, but also the different angles it was observed by the diverse writers' own social backgrounds. They are like various threads woven into the fabric of the image of China to make its portrait become three-dimensional. Looking back, they represented "a moment of historical watershed or transformational change in which competing views of China begin the uneven process of hardening and homogenising" (Kitson, 2013: 15).

For example, George Staunton (1797, 1: 23) used his three-volume *Authentic Account* to claim that, although the Chinese court was admittedly "guided by maxims peculiar to itself" and suspicious of outsiders, a "firm foundation" had been laid for future success. However, Barrow's account (1804: 11) portrayed court rituals as obfuscation intended to conceal military weakness, and dismissed any hope for future diplomacy: "what advantages can reasonably be expected to accrue from a servile and unconditional compliance with the submissions required by this haughty government?"[26] However, he agreed with the official account in achieving the other goal set by the government: to reshape the Chinese view of the British national character. As Staunton (1797: 1:15) recorded, the Qing court's contact with Englishmen had been limited to "vulgar and uninstructed" British seamen and "other persons of inferior station", such as the audacious moves of John Weddell and James Flint discussed earlier. Therefore, the negative British image was mainly shaped by sailors and merchants before the first embassy, but also its recent military interventions in Tibet, which came to be associated with a national representation of the British as being especially troublesome among the West Ocean barbarians, warlike and dangerous. The instructions Lord Macartney received was to create a favourable impression of thc British character, both by a good conduct of his suite and also by demonstrating England's scientific knowledge and technical achievement. To this Barrow (1804: 621–622) acclaimed that "the late Embassy, by shewing the character and dignity of the British nation in a new and splendid light, to a court and people in a great measure ignorant of them before … has laid an excellent foundation for great future advantages". In his reports to London, Macartney proudly claimed that

> It is no small advantage arising from the Embassy that so many Englishmen have been seen at Pekin, from whose brilliant appearance and prudent demeanour a most favourable idea has been formed of the country which had sent them. Nor is it any strain of vanity to say that the principal persons of rank who, from their intercourse with us, had opportunities of observing our manners, tempers and discipline very soon dismissed the prejudices they had conceived against us, and by a generous transition grew to admire and respect us as a nation and to love us as individuals.
>
> (cited in Hevia, 1995: 213–214)

Claiming such a complete turnover of the national image is obviously over-optimistic, not just because they blew their own trumpets, but simply because it would take a long time to reverse any prejudice, especially when it was perceived as a menace to national security. It also showed their unrealistic expectations on the influence one diplomatic mission may exert.

Meanwhile, some of the old stereotypes about Chinese people was also corrected by the embassy. For example, Chinese was believed to have "a very limited knowledge of mathematics and astronomy" (Cranmer-Byng, 1962: 264), which was disputed by James Dinwiddie, the Scottish physicist and astronomer who joined the embassy and recorded an incident happened on the day when they arrived in Beijing. There was an eclipse forecasted, Dinwiddie initially "suspected that precision was not within the capabilities of the Chinese, and that the necessary calculations had been acquired from the Jesuit mathematicians in their employ", but he "found to his surprise" that the Chinese predictions was accurate (Singer, 1992: 42). The other incident that surprised him was when one of the spherical segments for the Ptolemaic system of the Planetarium was broken, it was not the English who repaired it, but "a Chinaman managed the business with the use of a red hot iron" (ibid: 70). Although he was particularly hurt by the Chinese limited ability to appreciate British technology and blamed the inappropriate selection of gifts as a principal cause of the embassy's failure, he also attributed the failure to a simple fact that "we could not speak to the people": "what information could we derive respecting the arts and sciences in a county where we could not converse with the inhabitants?" (ibid: 179). This is telling, as it showed that the new "knowledge" of China produced by the embassy accounts were no more than subjective projections and constructed interpretations of China from their own social and political backgrounds, not true understandings of China in its own context. However, even if an interpreter could help bridge the language barrier, they would not be able to bridge the deep gulf of different world views which are beyond translation. This will soon be revealed from the fate of the Amherst Embassy, which despite being staffed with the top team of linguistic experts available at the time, still failed miserably.

When Macartney observed "the extraordinary ignorance of the Chinese in the art of navigation", what surprised him most was "although about two hundred and fifty years are elapsed since they have been acquainted with Europeans, and although they see and admire our ships and our seamanship yet they have never in the slightest point imitated our build or manoeuvres, but obstinately and invariably adhere to the ancient customs and clumsy practice of their ignorant ancestors" (Cranmer-Byng, 1962: 81). Looking back, these contrasts between a progressive "we" and a stagnant "they" contoured the first reversal between China and the West, from the previous "Us. vs. an exotic and sophisticated Other" to later "Western power" vs. its "Eastern equal", then further to "modern" against the "old". Although I agree with Peyrefitte's (1992: 489) evaluation of the embassy in stimulating "a refashioning of China's image in the West" into "a stationary, non-progressive polity, devoid of historical change and that rejects European science and technologies" (Porter, 2010: 152), I do not think it "brought a century of diplomatic and commercial initiatives to a close" (Peyrefitte, 1992: 489), as we can see from the next chapter, it surely continued with the Amherst Embassy. Actually, the timeline of the development of Orientalism, from the last two decades of the eighteenth century to the first two decades of the nineteenth century, roughly corresponded with the two British embassies to China. Therefore, I would like to describe the Macartney Embassy as a precursor to the Orientalism when the "new" against the "old" gradually evolved into the "superior" against the "inferior". I use "precursor" because the evolvement brought by the Macartney Embassy was mainly between modernity, marked with industrial power and scientific progress as well as political liberty brought by the Enlightenment; and antiquity, carrying a shell of stagnating polity with ossified ceremonialism and restrictive trading system. Yet it was not a straightforward binary between superiority and inferiority between the two civilisations. For example, when Macartney was proud of how far advanced the British navigation was over China, he was also deeply impressed by the Chinese postal system on land. The encounter worked like a mirror, it showed the flaws and merits that one did not normally realise without comparing. In this sense, I think Macartney's attitude towards China is better described with contemplation rather than contempt.

I also disagree with Peyrefitte's (1992: 545) summary that "Macartney's retinue approached China in the certainty that they were superior to all other Europeans. They returned with a new certainty: that they were also far superior to the Chinese. They found that the empire whose wonders had been hailed since Marco Polo's day was actually quite backward". The statement is oversimplified in treating the whole "retinue" as one voice and one view of the "new certainty". Second and more importantly, since the embassy saw both advanced civilisations and primitive conditions, it substantially enriched and complicated the British understanding of China. I think the biggest contribution the embassy made to generating new knowledge of China was to realise the old projections was not only divided, but also polarised, which was very misleading and lopsided in presenting a country as vast and diverse as China, be it idealised or demonised. Rather than confirming which side was correct, what the Macartney Embassy found pointed to a need of a more complex understanding of this sophisticated civilisation. For this reason, a most important conclusion reached by Macartney was to stop using a Eurocentric perspective to look at China. As written on the front page of his own *Journal*, "nothing could be more fallacious than to judge of China by any European standard". Ironically, if that was the lesson he learned, what was spread after the embassy was not this admonition but the very judgement of China by the European standards of international diplomacy, national sovereignty and commerce. While the embassy narrowed the gap between the polarised British perceptions towards China, it also exposed how deep the gulf was between the two, and marked a shift of the power balance that determined whose rules prevail.

Although with the wisdom of retrospect, it seems easy to see why the Macartney Embassy failed its mission, the outcome was a bitter disappointment at the time. Not initiating a dialogue between the two empires, it did start a debate within the British Empire. When the news of its failure reached England in the summer of 1794, it received divided receptions and a series of alternative interpretations that challenged the one-sided narratives about the embassy presented by the British elites. By 1795, we can sense the public distrust in the official accounts when Plowden (1795: 187) argued, despite efforts by the government "to fascinate the people into a persuasion, that the enormous expenses of Lord

Macartney's embassy to China had procured the greatest commercial and other advantages to this country, whilst the total and disgraceful failure in the objects of that embassy is a matter of melancholy notoriety". In analysing the cause of the failure, some believed it "might lie in the assumptions, conduct, and national character of British elites" (Williams, 2013: 89). They believed the embassy revealed Macartney's numerous misrepresentations and delusions about his own country and its economic focus on frivolous consumer goods and Chinoiserie trinkets; and some viewed Macartney's haggling over the ceremony as an act of pride which had needlessly damaged diplomatic prospects. For example, the *European Magazine* (April 1798, 33: 258,) denounced Macartney's "singularity" in refusing to kowtow as "nonsensical scrupulousness". Barrow (1804: 7) however, argued this was "a very mistaken notion" that an unconditional compliance of Lord Macartney with all the humiliating ceremonies would have been productive of results more favourable to the embassy. He blamed it all on China's failure to interact with the wider world, which had brought a lack of both social and commercial progress. He diagnosed China as a country worn out by "old age and disease" (1804: 258), and that the Chinese civilisation had grown stagnant and lifeless. True, over the past centuries, the Tributary System had influenced the Chinese eye in seeing all other countries as inferior, and now the rising of post-Industrial Revolution British Empire was on course to collide with it.

One commentator in 1803 presented Macartney's failure as a historical crux still balanced between two opposing points of view: "the failure of [the embassy] has been ascribed by some authors to the narrow and jealous spirit of Chinese policy, while others have affected to discover in it a superior degree of wisdom and prudence in the government of China" (cited in Williams, 2013: 104). The entry on "China" in the 1807 volume of Abraham Rees's *Cyclopaedia* (1802–1820) claimed that the Chinese "have wisely prevented the European nations, who have overthrown all the other eastern governments, from obtaining a footing in China" (ibid: 104). Williams (2013: 106) put the encounter into the historic context: "for the majority of Britons in the 1790s, five decades before the first Opium War, China could be understood as a limit point for British global ambitions". He then concluded that:

> This debate can be seen to determine the place China would occupy in the nineteenth-century geopolitical imagination. If British officials had begun the decade with fantasies of a union between two equal global empires, the Sovereign of the Seas meeting the emperor of the Middle Kingdom, they had by its end moved closer to Macartney's metaphors of China as a rotting tree or anchorless ship, ready for British intervention and direction.
>
> (Williams, 2013: 106)

After reading and seeing China and comparing what he saw and heard on the spot, with what he had read in books or been told in Europe, Macartney's insightful observation had depicted the changing trajectory of the two empires during the past two centuries. He recognised that China during Ming was "very civilised in comparison of their Tartar conquerors, and their European contemporaries, but not having improved and advanced forward, or having rather gone back, at least for these one hundred and fifty years past, since the last conquest by the northern of Manchu Tartars; while we have been every day rising in arts and sciences, they are actually become a semi-barbarous people in comparison with the present nations of Europe" (Cranmer-Byng, 1962: 222). "A nation that does not advance must retrograde, and finally fall back to barbarism and misery" (ibid: 226). A famous legacy in Macartney's description of China is the three metaphors he used, which are worth quoting in full. The first was:

> The Empire of China is an old, crazy First rate man-of-war, which a fortunate succession of able and vigilant officials have contrived to keep afloat for these one hundred and fifty years past, and to overawe their neighbours merely by her bulk and appearance, but whenever an insufficient man happens to have the command upon deck, adieu to the discipline and safety of the ship. She may, perhaps, not sink outright, she may drift some time as a wreck and will then be dashed to pieces on the shore; but she can never be rebuilt on the old bottom.
> (Cranmer-Byng, 1962: 212–213)

The second metaphor was "I often perceived the ground to be hallow under a vast superstructure, and in trees of the most stately and flourishing appearance I discovered symptoms of speedy decay"(ibid: 239), and finally, "It is possible, notwithstanding, that the momentum impressed on the machine by the vigour and wisdom of the present Emperor may keep it steady and entire in its orbit for a considerable time longer, but I should not be surprised if its dislocation or dismemberment were to take place before my own dissolution".[27] In retrospect, we can see that Qing China managed to stay at its zenith created by the Kangxi Emperor until the Qianlong's reign. Without significant modification of policies and indeed, a systematic change, no progress can result from change of dynasties, let alone change of emperors as we can see from what happened to the second British embassy in the next chapter.

If the British had learned so much about China and about themselves from this embassy, what did China gain from this first encounter? Not much. The embassy was often regarded as a missed opportunity for China to modernise itself, on equal terms with the West. There was so much they could have learnt from each other as the two empires' strengths are quite mutually complementary: one civilisation was bred on the sea and the other on the land. There was a potential Yin-Yang symbiosis relationship between the two, inspiring each other in a positive and mutually enhancing way. However, China turned her back on advances in science and technology and missed the opportunity to get to know this global empire and its industrialised products, and most importantly, what the world was like beyond the Celestial Empire, and how it would develop. They did start to see the Western Ocean countries as diverse, and the emperor sensed the British threat, realising that it had different ambitions to other European states and tried to curb it by balancing the interests among them. But the Qing lacked the ability to reflect on itself, let alone the needs to "turn its back on the past and to take lessons from the West" (Blue and Brook, 1999: 4). As Peyrefitte (1992: 35) pointed out, although the Qianlong Emperor "had widened China's borders, he had not opened them" to new ideas and progress. I would like to add that although the Great Wall was not used to defend China's borders militarily during the Qing, it had closed China off from the rest of the world and built walls around people's minds, while the British were busy building factories to export their goods and ideas all over the world. It was this idea of scientific progress as well as the new passion for political liberty that set European nations to be superior. In a way, the debate inspired by the Macartney Embassy continued in today's academia: Although China today became the one that is busy building factories, the fact that it also built a great fire wall and never fully embraced the idea of political liberty only strengthened the West's long-lasting and persistent habit of imagining China as its own polar opposite of the progressivist ideology.

Greater mutual understanding is normally the first step towards reducing prejudices and conflicts, but the first British embassy turned out to be a paradox. They came with the huge perception gap discussed in Chapter 4; when a better understanding of the real China proved their old perceptions "fallacious", the more intimate acquaintance with China only increased the psychological distance. In Barrow's (1817: 82) words, there was a "woeful change of sentiments". The two empires were indeed as different as the land and ocean: one is ancestor-dictated, order-oriented, boundary-restricted, and self-contained; the other is rule-based, interest-driven, knowledge-seeking, and outward-looking. By boundary-restricted I mean an enclosed and entrenched structure coexisting between the hierarchical governance rule from top to bottom, and a lateral social structure that features insider and outsider, applying to both Chinese perception of its own empire and foreign countries, and Chinese people inside and outside their own social circles. It is a very compartmentalised structure that no country and no subject can escape from their assigned places in the established pyramid. The fact that the emperor and his court treated the embassy gifts as tributes and ingenious "toys" added to the sense of contrast between the superiority of an ancient civilisation with a glorious past and the inferiority in its present proficiency in science and technology. What then came out was a paradoxical mirror effect of "us and other": apart from both seeing each other as being "arrogant" as explained before, they also saw each other as "barbarians". The only difference was that China was happy to stay in peace with the "barbarians" as long as they pledged tribute to acknowledge China's superiority and suzerainty over them, while the British deemed that barbarianism "should be overthrown" (Tsiang 1934: 783–827). That is why they attempted to force open the door of imperial China after failing the knock with letters and gifts.

Peyrefitte (1992: 489) saw the first embassy as "a kind of hinge in the history of relations between the West and the Far East, simultaneously a point of culmination and of departure". This can be seen in the next chapter where the second Amherst Embassy marked the first step in this departure: though still a diplomatic effort, it demonstrated the collision between the appeasing and the hard-line attitudes in Britain's approach to China. As Cranmer-Byng (1962: 38) summarised, "Macartney's embassy failed to obtain better conditions for trade, but on the Chinese side the failure was more fundamental: it was a failure of perception, a failure to respond to challenge". In the emotional and historical context, we can see the British failure may be remembered as an "embassy of humiliations", but the Chinese failure gave them a "century of humiliations", inflicted on this once proud civilisation starting from the First Opium War.

Notes

1 FHAC is the acronym of First Historical Archives of China, this reference refers to their edited volume of the *Collection of Archival Materials on the Macartney Embassy to China* published in 1996.
2 The gift list has been well documented in a number of narrative accounts that I will not duplicate here. A full list can be found on p.185 in Wood, Frances (2019) (ed.), *Aeneas Anderson in China, A Narrative of the Ill-fated Macartney Embassy 1792-94*, Hong Kong: Earnshaw Books Ltd.
3 The original poem was kept in 清高宗实录第一千四百三十四卷记,《红毛英吉利国王差使臣马嘎尔尼奉表贡至，诗以志事》: 博都雅昔修职贡, 英吉利今效荩诚。竖亥横章输近步, 祖功宗德逮远瀛。视如常却心嘉焉, 不贵异听物翊精。怀远薄来而厚, 衷深保泰以持盈。Qianlong was famous for being prolific in poem writing. He composed over 40,000 poems in his life, including six composed during the Macartney Embassy alone (Qin and Gao, 1998: 49).
4 As mentioned in Chapter 4, Jesuits not only introduced European technologies to China, but were used to supervise imperial workshops to produce them in China. For the Observatory in particular, European Jesuits had been appointed as imperial astronomers since the Ming Dynasty, such as Johann Adam Schall von Bell, who also helped the Ming court make Fusiform Culverins Cannon.
5 The younger generation today tend to open gifts in front of the gift-givers as a result of westernised influence. It also depends on the relationship between the giver and recipient.

6 Previous studies of the embassy's gifts have tended to imply that the most important gifts were scientific instruments. However, when the procurements were made in London, the most expensive gifts were actually textiles, mainly high-quality woollen broadcloths, which cost £2,020 to purchase. This proved to be an unworthy investment as it was considered cheap textile in China. The next most costly item was a pair of summer and winter carriages for the emperor (£1,656). It has also gone to waste as it was unacceptable by the Chinese protocol for the coachman's seat to be in an elevated position to the emperor. Third in terms of cost was the planetarium, which was a combined clock, globe and orrery (£1,384). Other costly gifts were a pair of globes (£971), a pair of chandeliers (£949), and various guns and pistols (£939) (Harrison, 2018: 69).

7 At least five occasions involving meeting the emperor as per Macartney's *Journal*, four times in Rehe and once in Yuanming Yuan; and multiple other occasions of receiving banquet and edicts from the emperor that also required a ritual ceremony performed in front of the empty chair representing the emperor.

8 Rockhill (1854–1914) is not an ordinary scholar but an American diplomat best known for drafting the US's Open Door Policy for China and then served as the US Minister to China from 1905 to 1909. He was one of the West's leading experts on the modern political history of China.

9 Unpublished diary from 10 August 1793 to 1 February 1794, kept at Duke University in Durham, North Carolina.

10 Referring to the James Flint incident that was discussed in Chapter 4. "22 Nov. 1759: Flint Is Confined for Three Years Whereas the Chinese Who Wrote His Petition Is Beheaded" (Fu, 1966: 222).

11 The line in original Chinese was: "故有英吉利国，仰慕皇仁，专心朝贡。其国较之越裳(指越南)，远隔数倍。或行数载，难抵中华……载之史册，诚为亘古未有之盛事也" (Ye, 2008: 99).

12 The Table of Contents and Preface of the book is provided in both Chinese and English translations. This direct quote is the original English translation printed in the book. A picture of the Palace of the Absence of Desire and Sincere Deference was made the book cover.

13 The picture is now kept at the British Library with shelf mark of WD 961 f.57. The 12 people listed are: 1. Colonel Benson; 2. Mr Crewe; 3. Lord Macartney; 4. Dominus Ly – a Chinese; 5. Lieutenant Parish; 6. Captain Mackintosh; 7. Sir George Staunton; 8. Doctor Gillan; 9. Mr Baring; 10. Mr Winder; 11. Mr Staunton; 12. Mr Hutner.

14 Since only the first four were introduced to the emperor, some accounts inaccurately recorded that only the four of them were admitted in.

15 The planned flight was dismissed by the ministers. It took China another century to see the first experiment of hot air balloon in 1890.

16 Actually, not just those "there present". On Qianlong's birthday, mandarins who were in Yuanming Yuan also performed the kowtow ceremony before the emperor's empty throne there.

17 Hevia (1995: 168) acknowledged that no original Palace archives had been found to prove this, after research by himself and other contemporary scholars.

18 The Chinese book title was《乾隆英使觐见记》, translated by Bannong Liu (刘半侬) and published by Chung Hwa Book Co. Ltd. (中华书局) in 1916. Available at the National Library of China in Bejing.

19 In the Preface to Cranmer-Byng's (1962: xi) edited volume of *An Embassy to China, being the journal kept by Lord Macartney during his embassy to the Emperor Ch'ien-lung, 1793–1794,* it was explained that "the three manuscript volumes of the Journal were sold by the descendants of Lord Macartney in

1854, but remained in a private library in England until 1913 when they were sold to a private collector in Peking. Finally in 1917 they were again sold, and this time were taken to Tokyo where they eventually became part of a large Public Library".

20 All the six major accounts have now been translated into Chinese, including Macartney's *Journal*, Staunton's *Authentic Account*, Barrow's *Travel to China*, young Staunton's *Memoirs,* Anderson's *Narrative*, and Alexander's *Journal of Voyage to Pekin in China.*

21 The original dates in the Chinese Archive were based on the lunar calendar, while those in the English accounts were based on the Gregorian calendar. For example, the entry of 14 June here of the lunar calendar is 21 July in the Gregorian calendar.

22 For this reason, the young Staunton had to copy several letters in Chinese for Macartney when the embassy's interpreters dreaded to be associated with their contents.

23 Another interesting fact worth noting is that the draft of the edict was prepared even before Macartney stepped ashore in China. Macartney expressed his surprise at the supposition made in the Emperor's letter that he was desirous of introducing the English religion into China, this may be due to the assumption that the British were just like the other Europeans, who had always been active in propagating their faith. This also showed that the Qing was not prepared to regard Britain as a new game changer. The final version was approved by the emperor nine days after he had received Macartney in audience.

24 It was not a normal practice for Chinese emperors to abdicate, nor did Qianlong do it for health reasons, but out of respect to his grandfather Kangxi, whose reign lasted for 60 years. Qianlong lived up to his ambition to emulate but not exceed the reign of his grandfather, so he relinquished the throne to his son Jiaqing in 1796, but continued to "instruct" Jiaqing until his death in February 1799, an extra three years as the retired supreme emperor.

25 Alexander's illustrations were used in George Staunton's official account published in 1797, and later in John Barrow's book in 1804. Alexander himself also published these images separately in 12 books from 1797 to 1804, which were compiled into one book in 1805 under the title *The Costume of China*, including forty-eight engravings. The book was very popular and went through several editions later. A new print in 2007 was included in the References of this chapter.

26 However, according to Stevenson (2021: 64), the call for another embassy to China in 1815 was exclusively Barrow's initiative. This will be looked at in the next chapter.

27 Macartney died in 1806, 10 years before the Amherst Embassy.

References

A Delicate Inquiry into the Embassies to China, and a Legitimate Conclusion from the Premises (no author) (1818). London: Printed for Thomas and George Underwood, and J.M. Richardson Cornhill, Available at: https://play.google.com/books/reader?id=Yd8Kak5p_jwC&hl=zh_CN&pg=GBS.PA1

Alexander, W. (2007) *Journal of Voyage to Pekin in China on Board the Hindostan EIM, Which Accompanied Lord Macartney on His Embassy to the Emperor, Kept by William Alexander, Draughtsman to the Embassy 1792–1794*. London: Adam Matthew Digital.

Anderson, A. (1795) *A Narrative of the British Embassy in China*. London: printed for J. Debrett.

Backhouse, E. and Bland, J.O.P. (1914) *Annals and Memoirs of the Court of Peking*. Boston: Houghton Mifflin.

Barrow, J. (1804) *Travels in China: Containing Descriptions, Observations, and Comparisons, Made and Collected in the Course of a Short Residence at the Imperial Palace of Yuen-min-yuen, and on a Subsequent Journey Through the Country from Pekin to Canton*. London: T. Cadell and W. Davies, in the Strand.

Barrow, J. (1807) *Some Account of the Public Life, and a Selection from the Unpublished Writings, of the Earl of Macartney*. Cambridge: Cambridge University Press.

Barrow, J. (1817) *Embassy to China. Chinese Travel, Life and Customs. A Review with Textual Excerpts*. Published by Quarterly Review. (An historically interesting & important article, extracted from an original issue of this uncommon journal. Disbound. 46 pages.). London: John Murray.

Bell, J. (1763) *Travels from St. Petersburg in Russia, to Diverse Parts of Asia*, Vol. 2. Glasgow: Printed for the author by R. and A. Foulis. Reprinted by Forgotten Books: London.

Berg, M. (2003) 'Asian luxuries and the making of the European consumer revolution', in Berg, M., Eger, E. (eds.) *Luxury in the Eighteenth Century*. London: Palgrave Macmillan.

Berg, M. (2010) 'Britain's Asian century: Porcelain and global history in the long eighteenth century', in Cruz, L. and Mokyr, J. (eds.) *The Birth of Modern Europe, Culture and Economy, 1400–1800*. Leiden: Brill, pp. 133–156.

Blue, G. and Brook, T. (1999) 'Introduction', in Brook, T. and Blue, G. (eds.) *China and Historical Capitalism: Genealogies of Sinological Knowledge*. Cambridge: Cambridge University Press.

Chen, J.G.S. (2004) 'The British view of Chinese civilisation and the emergence of class consciousness', *The Eighteenth Century: Theory and Interpretation* 45 (2004), pp. 193–205.

Clarke, J.J. (2003) *Oriental Enlightenment: The Encounter Between Asian and Western Thought*. London: Routledge.

Cook, T. (2009) 'The archives is a foreign country: Historians, archivists, and the changing archival landscape', *Canadian Historical Review*, 90(3) (2009), pp. 497–534.

Cranmer-Byng, J.L. (1962) *An Embassy to China, Being the Journal Kept by Lord Macartney During His Embassy to the Emperor Ch'ien-lung 1793–1794*. London: Longmans.

Darwin, J. (2009) *The Empire Project, The Rise and Fall of the British World-System 1830–1970*. Cambridge: Cambridge University Press.

Ellis, H. (1817) *Journal of the Proceedings of Lord Amherst's Embassy to China*. London: John Murray.

Fairbank, J. (ed.) (1970) *The Chinese World Order*, Cambridge. Massachusetts: Harvard University Press.

FHAC《中国第一历史档案馆》[*First Historical Archives of China*], (ed.) (1991).《乾隆朝上谕档》[*Imperial Edict Archive during Qianlong's Reign*]. Beijing: Dangan Chubanshe.

FHAC《中国第一历史档案馆》[*First Historical Archives of China*], (ed.) (1996)《英使马戛尔尼访华档案史料汇编》[*Collection of Archival Materials on the Macartney Embassy to China*]. Beijing: Guoji Wenhua Chuban Gongsi.

Fu, L.-S. (1966). *A Documentary Chronicle of Sino-Western Relations (1644–1820)*. Tucson: The University of Arizona Press.

Gao, H. (2020) *Creating the Opium War, British Imperial Attitudes Towards China, 1792–1840*. Manchester: Manchester University Press.

Gelber, H. (2008) *The Dragon and the Foreign Devils: China and the World, 1100 B.C. to the Present*. London: Bloomsbury.

Guo, F. (2019) 'A Study of the Gifts Presented by the Macartney Embassy to the Qianlong Emperor'. *Modern History and Cultural Relics Studies* (2), No. 187, pp. 130–145.

Hampton, T. (2009) *Fictions of Embassy*. Ithaca, NY: Cornell University Press.

Harrison, H. (2017) 'The Qianlong Emperor's Letter to George III and the Early-Twentieth-Century Origins of Ideas about Traditional China's Foreign Relations'. *American Historical Review*, 122(3), June, pp. 680–701.

Harrison, H. (2018), 'Chinese and British diplomatic gifts in the Macartney Embassy of 1793', *The English Historical Review*, CXXXIII(560), February, pp. 65–97.

Hevia, J. (1995) *Cherishing Men from Afar, Qing Guest Ritual and the Macartney Embassy of 1793*. Durham and London: Duke University Press Books.

Hevia, J. (2003) *English Lessons: The Pedagogy of Imperialism in Nineteenth-century China*. Durham and London: Duke University Press.

Hevia, J. (2009), 'The ultimate gesture of deference and debasement: Kowtowing in China'. *Past & Present*, 203(4), pp. 212–234.

Huang, Y.L. (2007) 'Impression Vs. reality, A study on the guest ritual controversy between Qing China and Britain', *Bulletin of Institute of History and Philology, Academia Sinica*, 78(1), pp. 35–106.

Kitson, P. (2013) *Forging Romantic China, Sino-British Cultural Exchange 1760–1840*. Cambridge: Cambridge University Press.

Liu, B. (trans) (1916) 《乾隆英使觐见记》, [*Journal of the British Ambassador on His Mission to Meet the Qinglong Emperor*]. Beijing: Chung Hwa Book Co. Ltd. (中华书局).

Liu, L.H. (2006) *The Clash of Empires, The Invention of China in Modern World Making*. Cambridge, MA, London: Harvard University Press.

Liu, Y. (2017) 《论清代有关乾隆朝英史觐见礼的记述变化》 [*Charting the changing records of Macartney's reception with the Qianlong emperor during the Qing Dynasty*]. *The Palace Museum Journal,* 3, (191), pp. 85–93.

Macartney, G. (1773) 'An account of Ireland in 1773 by a Late Chief Secretary of that Kingdom. p. 55', in Kenny, K. (2006). *Ireland and the British Empire*. Oxford University Press. p. 72, *fn. 22.*

Mancall, M. (1970), 'The Ching Tributary system: An interpretive essay', in Fairbank, J., (ed.) *The Chinese World Order*. Cambridge, MA: Harvard University Press.

Mao, H. (2014) 《天朝的崩溃》 [*The Collapse of the Heavenly Dynasty: A Restudy of Opium War*]. Beijing: Sanlian Publishing House.

Morse, H.B. (1926) *The Chronicles of the East India Company Trading to China*, 1635–1834. London: Oxford University Press. Digitalised version available at: https://www.univie.ac.at/Geschichte/China-Bibliographie/blog/2018/05/20/morse-the-chronicles-of-the-east-india-company-trading-to-china-1635-1834/

Orwell, G. (1949). *Nineteen Eighty Four*. London: Secker & Warburg.

Peyrefitte, A. (1992) *The Immobile Empire*, translated by Rothschild, J. New York: Alfred Knopf.

Platt, S.R. (2018) *Imperial Twilight: The Opium War and the End of China's Last Golden Age*. London: Atlantic Books.

Plowden, F. (1795) *A Short History of the British Empire During the Year 1794*. London: Printed for G.G. and J. Robinson.

Porter, D. (2010) *The Chinese Taste in Eighteenth-century England*. Cambridge: Cambridge University Press.

Pritchard, E.H. (1934) 'Letters from missionaries at Peking relating to the Macartney Embassy (1793–1803)', *T'oung Pao*, 31(1), pp. 1–57. doi: 10.1163/156853235X00011

Pritchard, E.H. (1943) 'The Kotow in the Macartney embassy to China in 1793', *Far Eastern Quarterly*, II(2), pp. 163–203.

Pritchard, E.H. (1970) *The Crucial Years of Anglo-Chinese Relations, 1750–1800*. New York: Octagon Books.

Qin, G. and Gao, H. (1998)《乾隆皇帝与马戛尔尼, 英国首次遣使访华实录》[*The Qianlong Emperor and Lord Macartney, An Account of the First Embassy to China*]. Beijing: Forbidden City Publishing House.

Rees, A. (ed.) (1807) *The Cyclopaedia: Or, Universal Dictionary of Arts, Sciences, and Literature*, vol. 7. London: Printed for Longman, Hurst, Rees, Orme and Brown.

Rockhill, W.W. (1897) 'Diplomatic missions to the Court of China: The Kotow Question II'. *The American Historical Review*, 2(4) (Jul.), pp. 627–643. Published by: Oxford University Press on behalf of the American Historical Association Stable. https://www.jstor.org/stable/1833980

Shanghai Publishing House (2010)《英史马嘎尔尼来聘案》[*Yingshi Magaerni Laipin An*],《清代档案史料选编》[*Selected Archives in the Qing Dynasty*], Vol. 3, pp. 613–675. Shanghai: Shanghai Publishing House.

Singer, A. (1992) *The Lion and the Dragon: The Story of the First British Embassy to the Court of the Emperor Qianlong in Peking 1792–94*. London: Barrie & Jenkins.

Staunton, G.T. (1793) *Diary 1792–1793: Journey to China, 1792–1793*. London, England: Adam Matthew Microform Publications. Retrieved from China Trade, Politics & Culture, 1793–1980 database at: www.china.amdigital.co.uk

Staunton, G. (1797) *An Authentic Account of an Embassy form the King of Great Britain to the Emperor of China*, 3 vols. London: G. Nicol.

Staunton, G.T. (1824) *Notes of Proceedings and Occurrences During the British Embassy to Pekin in 1816*. London: Henry Skelton (for private circulation only).

Stevenson, C.M. (2021). *Britain's Second Embassy to China, Lord Amherst's Special Mission to the Jiaqing Emperor in 1816*. Acton: Australian National University Press.

Tsiang, T. (1934) 'The great changes of China and the modern world', *Journal of Tsinghua University*, 4, pp. 783–827.

Varisco, D.M. (2007) *Reading Orientalism: Said and the Unsaid*. Seattle: University of Washington Press.

Waley-Cohen, J. (2000) *Sextants of Beijing, Global Currents in Chinese History*. New York: Norton.

Wang, H. (2020) 'Translation between two imperial discourses: Metamorphosis of King George III's letters to the Qianlong emperor', *Translation Studies*, 13(3), pp. 318–332. doi: 10.1080/14781700.2020.1714474.

Williams, L. (2013) 'British Government under the Qianlong Emperor's Gaze: Satire, Imperialism, and the Macartney Embassy to China, 1792–1804', *Lumen*, 32, 2013, pp. 85–107. Selected Proceedings from the Canadian Society for Eighteenth-Century Studies. Available at: https://www.erudit.org/fr/revues/lumen/1900-v1-n1-lumen0563/1015486ar/'

Williams, L. (2014) 'Anglo-Chinese caresses: Civility, friendship and trade in English representations of China, 1760–1800'. *Journal for Eighteenth-Century Studies*, 38(2), pp. 277–296. doi: 10.1111/1754-0208.12208

Wills, J.E. (1984) 'Embassies and illusions: Dutch and Portuguese envoys to K'ang-hsi, 1666–1687'. *Council on East Asian Studies.* Cambridge: Harvard University.

Winterbotham, W. (1795) *An Historical, Geographical, and Philosophical View of the Chinese Empire*. London: J. Ridgway & W. Button.

Wong, L.W.C. (2013) 'Dahongmaoguo de laixin: Majiaerni shituan guoshu zhongyi dejige wenti《大红毛国的来信：马戛尔尼使团国书中译的几个问题》[*Letters from the Redhaired Barbarians: On the translation of the Letter of Credence of the Macartney Embassy*]', in Wang-Chi, W. L. (ed.) *Fanyishi Yanjiu*《翻译史研究》2013 [*Studies in Translation History 2013*]. Shanghai: Fudan University Press, pp. 1–37.

Wood, F. (ed.) (2019) *Aeneas Anderson in China, A Narrative of the Ill-fated Macartney Embassy 1792–94*. Hong Kong: Earnshaw Books Ltd.

Ye, X. (2008) '*Peace across the four seas*: A tributary play created for the Macartney Embassy by Qianlong'. *The Twenty-first Century*, 105(Feb.), pp. 98–106.

6 The Amherst Embassy to China, an insurmountable generation gap between the two empires

> The head of state in China is a despot, and he leads a systematically constructed government with a numerous hierarchy of subordinate members … the individual has no moral selfhood.
>
> – Hegel, 1822[1]

In the space of one generation, the seeds sown by the Macartney Embassy bore fruits by way of the second embassy led by Lord Amherst: it was dispatched by the Prince Regent, son of King George III in 1816 to meet the Jiaqing Emperor, son of the Qianlong Emperor. The vice ambassador, George Thomas Staunton, was also the son of Macartney's vice ambassador, George Leonard Staunton. More interestingly, both Staunton and the Jiaqing Emperor were the only eyewitness from each side but provided conflicting testimonies to what happened to their fathers' encounter in 1793, which indicated the negative assets inherited from the first embassy that contributed to the second failure. But most importantly, the generation gap between the two embassies must be looked at through the lens of global power recalibration, as this significant event in the Anglo-Chinese encounter was also a milestone marker of Britain's own imperialist history.

Looking back, we can see that Qianlong's reign represented the zenith of the Qing expansion and glory but left Jiaqing's reign starting with a treasury almost depleted by his father, which was further exhausted by the continuous outbreak of river flooding and various rebellions. By the time when the Amherst Embassy arrived, the worrying signs of a declining Qing included its greatly deteriorated military strength, serious internal insurrections and pirate problem on the southern coast. For the British, its defeating of Napoleon at Waterloo in 1815 marked the Britain's emergence as the most powerful maritime force in the world, ushering in a century of the Pax Britannica as the heyday of the British Empire with its economic prowess and ideological influence starting to spread all over the world. This encouraged a more open flaunting of British superiority with the growth of nationalism and a patriotic identity

DOI: 10.4324/9781003156383-7

in representing a most modern civilisation. Meanwhile, "after 1815 the pace of industrial expansion was even more remarkable. In the period from 1815 to 1860, Britain was responsible for 60 per cent of the total growth of world manufacturing" (McDonough, 1994: 20), prompting them to look for new markets. As summarised by Platt (2018: 155), "a deeper sense of entitlement" with the "post-Napoleonic surge of British national pride, the confidence of being the preeminent military and commercial power on earth" surrounded the second British mission to China in 1816. However, when the British very proudly informed the Qing government that they had defeated the French Empire, thus became the most powerful nation in the West, the news seemed to fall on deaf ears as shown by the emperor's reply to the British: "Your Majesty's kingdom is at a remote distance beyond the seas, but is observant of its duties and obedient to our law, beholding from afar the glory of our Empire and respectfully admiring the perfection of our Government" (cited in Soothill, 2009: 97). Therefore, this generation gap was widened by the contrast of a "changing" Britain to a relatively "changeless" China, whose civilisation has begun the downward spiral, during the period wherein Britain thrived through the Enlightenment and the Industrial Revolution.

We can clearly see "the Great Divergence" of the two empires discussed by Pomeranz (2000) in the context of global history. In this work, Pomeranz traced the point at which the West's Industrial Revolution resulted in their economic, political and military superiority over the Chinese Empire. As the metaphor used by McLeod (1817: 158), the Chinese "have had for some thousand years a dawn of civilisation" but "from the operation of the most narrow-minded principles", it "has never brightened into day". At the core of this narrow-minded autocracy system was the emperor, whose individual vision and ability to rule was considered the largest bearing on the fate of the country. Macartney's famous remarks about China's prosperity was credited to the "vigour and wisdom of the present Emperor", and that it may sink "whenever an insufficient man happens to have the command upon deck", only confirmed the view that the decline of the Qing was due to a less competent emperor at the helm, which also made many blame the failure of the second British embassy on the Jiaqing Emperor. However, I see it merely the symptom, while the root cause of the "great divergence" lies at the two different governing systems. The autocracy system meant the emperor's decision-making was often based on highly infiltrated information to please him, controlled by the ministers and court officials, whose roles were largely missing from the analysis so far. This chapter will use the Amherst Embassy to explore questions including: How big is this missing part? And how critical is this missing part? What part did the first embassy play in the failure of the second embassy? And what new knowledge was produced from this failure?

The Amherst Embassy produced around 15 accounts by its members, the most significant ones include: The *Journal of the Proceedings of the Late Embassy to China* by Henry Ellis the third commissioner, which became the de facto official account of the embassy published in 1817; George Staunton's *Notes of Proceedings and Occurrences during the British Embassy to Pekin in 1824,* and his *Miscellaneous Notices Relating to China, and our Commercial Intercourse with that Country*; Robert Morrison's *A Memoir of the Principal Occurrences during an Embassy from the British Government to the Court of China in the year 1816*; Clarke Abel's *Narrative of a Journey in the Interior of China in the Years 1816–1817* published in 1818; and John Davis's *The Chinese: A General Description of the Empire of China and Its Inhabitants* published in 1836 and *Sketches of China* published in 1841.

Among the few scholars who have researched and written about this embassy, Stevenson's book (2021: 2) presented the first comprehensive and detailed account of the Amherst Embassy from its conception to its conclusion and reassessed its historical importance for Anglo–Chinese relations and the changing British perceptions of China. From the published accounts of the embassy, it is hard to imagine the First Opium War would break out in just over 20 years' time. Cooperation and negotiation between the two empires still seemed viable options in the minds of most Britons; however, if the Macartney Embassy never stood the slightest chance of success from the very beginning, the burden of this precedent made the curse more applicable to the Amherst Embassy. In Tuck's view (2000: xxi), even the appointment of Staunton as the vice ambassador may have "doomed the Embassy from the start".

6.1 The negative assets from the Macartney Embassy

From its conception, it was hostage to the legacy of the Macartney Embassy. The false picture of the positive impact they had made on the Qing court, which suggested that any future British mission would be treated outside the framework of the Tributary System, turned out to be a myth, rendering the second embassy not just being remembered and recorded as a failure but "a hudibrastic fiasco".

Like Macartney, Amherst also did diligent research about China to prepare himself for the mission. He drew on three main sources of information as seen from his notes. The first consisted of the published accounts of previous Western embassies to the Qing court. Of course, his chief reference was Macartney's Journal, as well as other extracts published in the second volume of Barrow's (1807) biography of Macartney. This direct legacy of the Macartney Embassy had a significant impact on the Amherst Embassy's reading of China. Barrow's book, *Travels in China,* was especially influential in shaping and influencing the views of China held by the senior members of the Amherst Embassy. All of them had read

Barrow's book and several carried copies with them to China, especially Ellis, whose first published account of the embassy was accepted as the official record, made no secret of his indebtedness to Barrow. Staunton (1824: 205) complained in his private account that Barrow and others of the Macartney Embassy had left him with little new to report on China: "The comparative success of the former mission, and the interest and novelty of first discovery, are wanting on the present occasion".

But they did have a new source of knowledge that was not available to the first embassy, the new generation of Britons residing in China and dealing with the Canton authorities including British missionaries, traders, EIC employees and scholars such as Staunton, Morrison and Davis, whose scholarship, knowledge of Chinese language and practical experience represented a fundamental shift in the depth of British understanding about China. Hargrave (2016: 516) named it "Empirical Sinology" that was produced by their experiential knowledge of China and first-hand observations with text-based analyses of Chinese culture, religious doctrines, novels and legislation. They also sent back reports containing intelligence from Canton. They provided a substantial body of new knowledge about China from the perspective of an established commercial presence and their increasing involvement with the empire.

His third and final source of information were the letters and reports written by foreign missionaries at Peking containing their views on the failure of the Macartney Embassy and advice on what might be required for a successful mission. For example, De Poirot had thought that the Macartney Embassy's omission of presents for the mandarins at the court had contributed to the embassy's failure. Accordingly, the Amherst Embassy carried an extra range of gifts including crystal chandeliers and glassware, porcelains, fine linens, clocks and watches, perfumes and snuffs. With these rich resources available to Amherst, although not having the language and cultural knowledge or in-country experience of Staunton, he may be judged as having an open mind to practical strategies and approaches to dealing with China (Stevenson, 2021: 91). Another key reason identified for the failure of the first embassy was lacking their own interpreters and local expertise on the inner workings of the Qing bureaucracy, thus the Amherst Embassy was composed of the most accomplished Chinese experts of the day, not just in linguistic proficiency but also their knowledge and experience of handling China. However, the appointment of Staunton and Morrison, who were both highly talented men and certainly had the required knowledge and skills, turned out to be the wrong remedy. How so?

Because their inside knowledge of China as an outsider was viewed with deep suspicion by the Qing court and the emperor. George Thomas Staunton was the only one who had participated in the Macartney Embassy. He returned to China in 1799 to become a writer in the EIC at Canton, then its interpreter in 1801. Staunton drew up his first plan for another embassy to the Qing court in 1800. When another mission was planned in 1809, he was to be the King's ambassador to Beijing according to his *Memoir* (1856: 43–44). This did not happen because "upon further consideration, it was thought most advisable not to include in it any person who was actually in the service of the EIC", and then the mission plan was abandoned altogether, until 1816. He was already the President of the Select Committee of the EIC when he was appointed to be the vice ambassador. While Macartney's mission was ostensibly sent to celebrate the Qianlong Emperor's birthday, Amherst was visiting the Qing court uninvited and at a less auspicious time. As a matter of fact, when Staunton raised the proposal to the Viceroy in Canton, it was firmly dismissed as "There is no occasion for you to send another Embassy to Pekin. The Emperor knows it is a long way, and does not wish you to trouble yourselves. Besides the Climate does not agree with you; you may catch infectious Distempers. No! Your Nation must not send an Embassy. I will not allow it. It is out of the Question and you must not think of it" (Morse, 1926, vol. 3:173). However, in Staunton's eagerness to make the embassy happen, he did not report it back. The possibility of another embassy to the Qing court and the prospect of playing a leading role in such a major diplomatic initiative had long sustained Staunton's ambitions for recognition and fame beyond the accumulation of wealth as a EIC employee in Canton. Staunton argued that the British now had a person "never as yet afforded of conversing unreservedly and without the aid of interpreters, with those who influence the emperor's councils", a person who was familiar with "the modes of acting and thinking peculiar to the Chinese" and would enable a British ambassador to "enter into confidential communications on subjects of mutual interests of both empires … it will not be too much to expect the most important and beneficial results from his negotiations" (Stevenson, 2021: 49). Staunton also translated the *Ta Tsing Leu Lee* (*LAWS AND STATUTES OF THE DYNASTY OF TSING,* 《大清律例》) in 1810, his knowledge about how the legal and trading systems worked in China, combined with his literacy in Chinese language along with his direct experience in the first embassy stood him out as the most suitable candidate. His appointment was vigorously endorsed by Barrow as "an advantage which we never before possessed", when "communications are to be held with the jealous and corrupt government through the interventions of Catholic missionaries" (Barrow to Buckinghamshire, 14 February 1815, in BL IOR G/12/196 (Reel 1) F 2–6). Barrow was now second secretary to the Admiralty and had direct access to Cabinet ministers, politicians and members of government boards. His reputation as the foremost British-based expert on China ensured his views carried weight at the highest level decision-making.

However, this turned out to be the first wrong decision made. Although Staunton's view of China was on the whole very positive at the time, and he depicted the Jiaqing Emperor as "a sober and talented ruler", a decisive monarch who displayed a "political courage and sagacity which are requisite in the character of a monarch of a great and powerful empire" (Staunton, 1810: 493), the Jiaqing Emperor ordered an investigation into Staunton in January 1815 for his tough stance during the course of several disputes with the local authorities at Canton. Jiaqing described him in an edict that

> There is an English foreigner named Staunton (si-dang-dong), who once came to the capital along with his country's tribute mission. He was youthful and cunning then, and on the way home he made careful maps of the terrain of our mountains and rivers. After getting to Canton, he did not return to his home country[2], but instead stayed on in Macau. He has been there for twenty years now and is thoroughly proficient in Chinese. By regulations, foreigners who live in Macau cannot enter the provincial capital of Canton, but Staunton has now been there for so long that when new foreigners come, most of them look to him for guidance. I fear that before long he will cause trouble.
>
> (cited in Platt, 2018: 152)

Amherst was then informed of the emperor's disapproval of Staunton in a private letter from Thomas Metcalfe, the second member of the EIC Select Committee, who however, also told him that Staunton's inclusion in the embassy was ordered by the British sovereign and could not be disobeyed (Morse, 1926, vol. 3: 259). They did not know that the worst was yet to come: since Staunton and the Jiaqing Emperor were the only two present at the Macartney's ceremony, when Jiaqing said he had personally witnessed Macartney kowtowing to his father, Staunton's refusal to vouch this had caused the Emperor great rage. Jiaqing issued a special edict following the departure of the embassy to ban Staunton from entering China again, calling him "flagitiously equivocate, and full of lies" (支吾可恶，所言甚属欺诳).

The other interpreter Morrison was also a subject of concern. Morrison started to learn Chinese in 1805, two years before he set to leave for China to be the first British missionary in 1807. His first Chinese teacher was a young man called Yong Sam-tak (容三德), who came to England to study English for commercial purposes under the protection of the East Indian captain, Henry Wilson. They lived together and Morrison was able to make daily progress with his Chinese. After Morrison went to Canton in 1807, Rong also returned to Canton in 1808, they met again and Rong taught Morrison Cantonese and acted as his advisor. Morrison translated a number of Chinese classics into English, including *The Three-Character Classic* (《三字经》), *the Great Learning* (《大学》) and *Account of the Sect TAO-SZU* (《太上老君》). However, like the Chinese people described in Chapter 3 that helped the first generation of British sinologists to become historical figures for their outstanding contributions to British understandings of China, Rong's name was hardly known in any of the Chinese records. He was described as "bright, educated with strong opinions and a fiery temper" and as his temperament was quite different from Morrison, they did not get on well. Their relationship came to an end when Young became upset at Morrison's attempts to convert him (Price, 2019: 69). In a way, the personal relationship between these two individuals reflects the relationship between the two empires at that time: each of them was deeply entrenched in their own beliefs and wanted to change the other. Rong wanted Morrison to embrace the Chinese ways along with learning the language, to accept the Chinese cultural superiority and teacher authority that he held dearly to, while Morrison was fully devoted to his missionary duties and believed in an equal relationship between teacher and student, especially as adults. Morrison came to the attention of Chinese authorities for illegally teaching Mandarin and compiling a Chinese-English dictionary sponsored by the EIC, illegally setting up a Chinese printing press at Macau, and illegally translating and publishing the Bible from English into Chinese, all of which were strictly forbidden under the Canton System. The authorities thus conducted a raid on his office, destroying his printing press and arresting a Chinese employee (Staunton, 1856: 37). Therefore, both Morrison and Staunton, who played major roles in the Amherst Embassy, were actually "persona-non-grata" to the Chinese government, who viewed them as potential threats to the fabric of Chinese society and a source of political instability.

Also appointed to Amherst's staff was John Francis Davis, the eldest son of the EIC Director who was appointed an EIC writer in Canton in 1813 and learned Chinese from Robert Morrison. He was a smart student who mastered the language fairly quickly and produced an essay on the writing of Chinese characters and vocabulary list for merchants in Canton. He later became a member of the Royal Asiatic Society, founded by George Thomas Staunton in 1823. He established himself as the major British expert on China after Robert Morrison's death and Staunton's retirement. He later became the second Superintendent of British Trade in China alongside Lord Napier in 1833, and the Chief Superintendent following Napier's death in 1834. His book published in 1836, *The Chinese: A General Description of the Empire of China and Its Inhabitants,* which drew extensively on his observations during his residence of over two decades in China, and *Sketches of China* (1841) as a recount of his travel and experiences in the interior China during the Amherst Embassy, became standard works on China. With a strong literary interest in Chinese literature, drama and poetry, Davis also became the first translator of two Yuan dramas and made them well-known plays in Europe. However, like Staunton, their Company status were viewed by the imperial court and mandarins as mere traders and not worthy of inclusion in a mission sent in the name of the British monarch (Morrison, 1820: 52).

Therefore, the perceived benefits of using their own interpreters with local knowledge were completely outweighed by the Qing court's distrust or contempt of them. This unexpected effect itself shows inadequate British understanding of China.

The embassy composition also indicated a shift in the aim of the mission. The Macartney Embassy included scientists, mathematicians and other representatives of the sciences and technology, as part of the goals was to impress and to learn, while the Amherst mission was primarily driven by the EIC's anxiety about the preservations of its China trade, as this mission was "the only remedy that was likely to be effectual in order to place the [trade and] intercourse upon a satisfactory and stable footing" (Stevenson, 2021: 118). According to Berg (2010: 11), by the first decade of the nineteenth century, goods from Canton accounted for 67 per cent of all Company sale income earned in London. Therefore, the mission was "concerned primarily with pragmatic and material interests founded on commerce, signifying Britain's ascendency in manufacturing and trade" (Stevenson, 2021: 31). However, as argued by Min (2004), these overriding commercial aims of the Amherst Embassy forced it into a curious position to further a commercial agenda that was at odds with Qing standards of social class, national identity and diplomatic status.

As explained in Chapter 5, the goals of the first embassy rested on three wrong assumptions. Despite various self-examining reflections following its failure, no one seemed to realise the root cause by examining the Chinese system. Instead, more wrong assumptions were made from Macartney's report, such as the belief that compromise could be reached from negotiations and a new British embassy could be handled outside the Tributary System. This view was repeated by Barrow and Staunton to protect Macartney's legacy and their own involvement in the embassy, and in Staunton's case, the need to also guard his father's legacy (Stevenson, 2021: 309). This led to the erroneous belief that it would be possible for Amherst to enter into negotiations with the Qing court on British trade requests, and he noted in his pre-departure research that the Treaty of Nerchinsk signed with Russia in 1689 served at least as an example of negotiation if mutual interests were involved. However, they did not have any bargaining power in the eyes of the Qing as compared with Russia for the reasons explained earlier: What the British can offer was not what the Qing needed, and what the British needed can already be achieved through the Canton System. The point that the British had become the strongest power in Europe now, militarily, economically and politically, may have played a counterproductive role in being perceived as a threat by the Qing and turn them down for a different reason, and most importantly, the Tributary System remained unchanged in the Middle Kingdom. This was made clear in Jiaqing's edict to George III on 7 December 1805: "if you can lead all your subjects to present tribute and serve Us as our vassals, then you will fulfil Our sublime principle of loving strangers and extending our benevolence to them" (Fu, 1966, vol. 1: 361).

Like what happened to the Macartney Embassy, the Chinese translation of letters from the embassy was again adapted to fit in the tributary discourse, that the ambassador was referred to as the "tributary envoy" and the gifts were changed to "tributes". Wong's research (2010: 12–13) showed that Morrison had actually added a note of 220 words to explain that it was the Qing Court that wished to impose these references. Morrison (1820: 15) also added that when they talked to the Chinese, they would normally follow the British way to call them "ambassador" and "gifts", but it was out of their control how the Chinese would put them into writing. The copy of the Prince Regent's letter was also returned as his address to the emperor headed "Sir, My Brother" was considered "inadmissible" and had to be changed (Staunton, 1824: 53). According to Morrison (1820: 35), they did not agree to this request, which was confirmed by Staunton, but the Chinese record said the British agreed to delete the term (Morse, 1926: pp. 278–279).

Therefore, Davis was not surprised to notice that the flags on the boats bore the Chinese characters for *Gongshi* or "tribute envoys" but, being unauthorised to speak on the subject, he made no comment (Ellis, 1817: 75). However, as explained in Chapter 5, gift as *Gong*, letter as *Biao* and kowtow as a ceremony came as a package, once accepted the status of being a "tribute envoy", negotiations would be out of question as Chinese never negotiate with tributary states. Besides, all the embassy emphasised in the negotiation was to follow the Macartney precedent which itself was open to disputes as explained earlier: The mandarins asserted with most obstinate perverseness that Macartney had kowtowed when the Jiaqing Emperor was present, and at other times as well, whenever the occasion demanded. Ellis (1817: 154) admitted, "with this imperial assertion before us, however false or erroneous, it will be difficult, in the event of a renewed discussion, to press the precedent of Macartney".

Another negative asset from the Macartney Embassy was the growing mutually negative perceptions between the two empires. As argued in Chapter 5, the Macartney Embassy had largely changed China's image in a disillusioned manner, its reports also portrayed China as a "difficult and monotonous destination", "a curious country on the far side of the world". None of Amherst's friends and relatives, who were representatives of the privileged upper class of British society, "viewed China with any enthusiasm as a destination, nor thought about its importance to Britain" (Stevenson, 2021: 90). Chinese people were regarded as heathens and pagans by the British, while the British was still treated as barbarians by the Chinese. The British reputation of being the most troublesome of all Westerners with a voracious appetite for trade and warlike character was not reversed by the Macartney Embassy as it claimed, rather, there was a hardening of the Qing attitude and more suspicions towards the British by Jiaqing's reign (Gao, 2014: 58). He was keenly aware of Britain's naval ambitions in the China Seas, particularly when the British made two attempts to occupy Macau in 1802 and 1808,[3] gaining them the reputation of being "the most harsh and cruel barbarians" who "lived by plunder" (ibid: 65). In 1802, when the reports of the British invasion of Macau reached the Jiaqing Emperor in Beijing, he issued an edict to the governor-general in Canton that "such a brutal eruption at Macau indicates an effrontery without limit", completely dismissing the British claim that their force was merely trying to protect Macau from the French: "to invoke such a pretext is to freely insult the Chinese empire", Jiaqing wrote in a stern tone. "It is important in any case to raise considerable troops, attack the foreigners, and exterminate them. In this way, they will understand that the seas of China are forbidden to them" (*Da Qing Renzong Rui (Jiaqing) Huangdi Shilu*, 《大清仁宗睿嘉庆皇帝实录》 1964, juan 202, pp. 29b–30a). In his instructions to the authorities in Canton, he described the British as "proud, tyrannical and generally obnoxious" and "always unreasonable and dishonest" (Fu, 1966: 371). He also blamed the governor-general for being too compromising with the British and removed him from office. The British backed down for fear that "it would exclude the English forever, from the most advantageous monopoly it possesses in the Universe", which was agreed by London that "they would rather see France in possession of Macau than suffer the risk of a rupture with the Chinese government" (Platt, 2018: 92–93).

Then in 1805, after learning that the British were sending gunships to protect their merchant vessels against pirate raids as they sailed up to Canton, while ordering the governor-general to strengthen the region's costal defences, the Jiaqing Emperor referred to a recent letter from King George in his edict: "apparently he has heard of occasional instances of robbery on the ocean and thinks we might need his military power to join with our own. Do we now have to borrow help from vassal states to eliminate pirates?!" (cited in Platt, 2018: 112). Clearly, the Jiaqing Emperor regarded the British and their motives with a high degree of mistrust. Wang (2014: 248) argued that these attempts raised serious alarm about Britain's imperial ambitions and expanding naval power. Even Staunton (1824: 238) himself admitted later that "the Chinese had … seen our troops more than once landed on their shores; and our naval forces had, during successive years, hovered about their coasts, with no hostile intention it is true, but in a way, which even the most unsuspicious nation might have considered in some degree questionable".

Even the lesson learned from the Macartney Embassy regarding preparing gifts did not pay off. The Amherst Embassy decided to "impress the court not with grandstanding spectacular scientific gifts" as they "prefer articles of intrinsic value, to those of mere show or curiosity" (Cranmer-Byng, 1962: 226). More importantly, they had to be "manufactures of this Country, and exquisite specimens of the high degree of refinement to which the useful and elegant arts are advanced here" (Kitson, 2016: 74–75). The total cost of all the presents was £22,005 (equivalent to over £2 million in today's values), of which the box containing the letter of the Regent to the emperor, a very handsome large-chased gold box enriched in the centre of the cover with a fine enamel of the Prince Regent, was valued at £1500 alone. However, when it was shown to the legates, "they expressed little or no admiration at the sight of it. Infinitely greater was the extreme veneration with which they regarded a yellow silk purse, which had been given by the late emperor, Qianlong, to the second commissioner Staunton, and which he produced to them on this occasion"[4] (Davis, 1841: 86) (See Figure 1.7 in Chapter 1).

What is worth special mentioning is again the inclusion of British porcelain under this new selection criteria of being magnificent both in value and workmanship to rival the Chinese porcelain. According to Stevenson (2021: 152), during the first social encounter with the mandarins, "they were astonished to learn that these were made in England and not in Canton; even greater disbelief was expressed by the mandarins when being told that finer specimens of china were available in England". Unfortunately, the gifts were never formally presented to the emperor – because Amherst refused to perform the kowtow and therefore rejected by the emperor according to the majority of analyses, but is it really so?

6.2 To kowtow or not to kowtow, was this still the question?

As mentioned in Chapter 4, Amherst received his instructions from the Regent at the Chinoiserie styled Royal Pavilion in Brighton, including specific instructions to follow the procedures of ceremony at the emperor's court and conform "to all the ceremonies of that Court, which may not commit the honour of your Sovereign or lessen your own dignity, so as to endanger the success of your mission" (Castlereagh to Amherst, Foreign Office, 1 January 1816, in BL IOR MSS EUR F 140/43 (a)). He also received two important and specific instructions from the Foreign Secretary before departure. One informed him to follow the procedures of ceremony at the emperor's court, and the second gave him authority to "consider yourself at liberty to act upon your own responsibility, in case of any difference of Opinion between you and the other Commissioners" (ibid, cited in Stevenson, 2021: 118). Amherst's readings of Macartney's Journal contributed to his awareness of the importance of ceremony in Qing diplomatic encounters, but the notes he penciled below also showed that he still persisted in viewing his upcoming mission within the terms of Westphalian diplomatic principles of equality between nations: "Negotiation should be conducted in the spirit of cordiality and with the feeling of equality. Firmness, dignity, and patience essential requisites" (Amherst, pencil notes on "The objects of the Embassy" in BL IOR MSS EUR F 140/36; cited in Stevenson, 2021: 104). This revealed his lack of awareness of the practicalities of dealing with the Qing court where there was no scope for dialogue of any kind and no channel for diplomatic communications, and certainly not with one imbued with the feeling of equality. He also made a special note of Macartney's conclusion: "[Ceremonial] is a very serious matter with [the Chinese] … they pressed me most seriously to comply with it; said [the prostration] was a mere trifle, kneld down on the floor and practised it of their own accord to shew me the manner of it, and begged me to try whether I could perform it" (Barrow, 1807, vol. 2: 209).

He was also fully aware of what happened to two other European missions following the Macartney Embassy: The Dutch embassy of 1795, which failed to accomplish any of its goals despite the performance of numerous kowtows; and the Russian Embassy in 1805–1806 as the first European embassy sent to the court of the Jiaqing Emperor. When they made an attempt to follow the "Macartney precedent" of not performing the full kowtow ceremony, the Qing official "was astonished on learning this and called it a 'misrepresentation'" (Amherst, "Notes on the Golovkin Embassy, 1805–06" in BL IOR MSS EUR F 140/36). Hence the Russian ambassador was expelled immediately. This left Amherst with two new precedents and a real dilemma. The stance was quite clear for the Jiaqing Emperor, who had declined to deal with the Russians unwilling to kowtow a few years earlier, he could not yield to one nation on a point he had stood firm on with another. Especially when the British was not invited, and the Qing did not seek to send embassies to Britain either. The so-called "Macartney precedent" actually made the Jiaqing Emperor more resolute in not setting any more awkward precedents, therefore, the second embassy must comply fully with the kowtow ceremony that lay at the core of the Tributary System. To find if there was a possible third route out of the dilemma, Amherst only needed to ask himself one question: What made you different from the Russians who already tried and failed the negotiation?

However, the new expertise held by core members of his embassy only answered the question of why they should not follow the Dutch precedent. In the introductory remarks to his *Memoir* of the Amherst Embassy, Morrison (1820: 8–9) stated that the Chinese custom of the kowtow, if not mutually reciprocated, expressed "in the strongest manner, the submission and the homage of one person or state to another", therefore should be carried out only by those European nations who "consider themselves tributary and yielding homage to China". He also made it clear that trade should be conducted on the basis of "equality and mutual reciprocity". Therefore, when efforts were made to convince Amherst to kowtow by pointing out that the ambassadors of Japan, Siam and other independent countries all kowtowed before the Chinese emperor, Amherst "refused any comparison to be drawn between the King of Great Britain and the feeble states which surrounded the

Chinese Empire" (Letter from Amherst to Canning, 12 February 1817, Ellis, 1817: 118) , and reminded the Qing officials that "these nations could neither be classed in point of civilisation nor power with the English". This point was accepted by the Qing officials who stressed that the British were also being received by the court with far greater esteem than those states, which was demonstrated by delegating mandarins of such high rank to escort the embassy (Staunton, 1824: 81). In response, Amherst stressed that the nine bows he proposed to perform before the Jiaqing Emperor also represented a greater honour than the single bow traditionally paid by a British ambassador to the Russian sovereign. But this point was quickly dismissed as he was told the Russian embassy was expelled from China without an audience due to their refusal of kowtow.

Then came the occasion of the banquet bestowed by the Emperor in Tianjin, where each other's bottom lines were weighed and tested. The banquet's political function to secure British compliance with the performance of kowtow was immediately recognised by Amherst and Staunton as Macartney was put through a similar test. When the ambassador was requested to kowtow before a screen and a yellow-silk-covered table which figured the emperor, Amherst "bowed respectfully nine times" instead (Abel, 1818: 83). This was consistently recorded in his own diary and the Qing court that he "removed the hat three times, and then made a very low and referential bow for nine times" (Huang, 2007: 59). A picture titled "Ceremony of the Kowtow before a yellow curtain" was used as a frontispiece in *Scenes in China,* a book about the Amherst Embassy, to give the public a flavour of how humiliating the requested ceremony was. Later, when Amherst was handed a letter from the emperor in a silk-lined bamboo tube, when kowtow was again suggested by the Qing official to afford him an opportunity of recovering lost ground in the Emperor's favour, Amherst angered the Chinese by merely making "a profound bow" on receiving it (Hibbert, 1970: 68).

The negotiation process showed that despite the language expertise added to the Amherst Embassy, their knowledge of the Tributary System and character of Chinese officialdom was not much improved, as they were using the same old tactics that had been proved unsuccessful by Macartney: by proposing their performance of the kowtow be reciprocated by a mandarin of equivalent rank to Amherst before a portrait of the Prince Regent, or if any Chinese official appointed to London, he would kowtow before the British monarch. But a subtle change between the two embassies was the "emergent discourse of organic nationalism, emerging in Britain post-1815 in the run-up to the First Opium War, and which infiltrated the discourse of the Amherst embassy" (Kitson, 2016: 72). This can be supported by the fact that "there are literally hundreds of pages in the accounts devoted to dissecting the negotiations between the Chinese and the British during Amherst's journey, by riverboat and cart, from Tianjin to Beijing" as recorded by Davis that showed a more adamant stance and even obsession with perfect equality with the British. According to Kitson (2016: 78), when the portraits of the Regent and Princess Caroline was inspected, the Ambassador insisted on clearing the hall as "the Chinese attach such sanctity of the image of their own sovereign, it would not be right to subject these more lively representations to the vulgar gaze".

The following exchange highlighted the clash between the Chinese backward-looking view with the British forward-looking view: the Chinese argument was that they could not make an exception for the Amherst Embassy as this would set a precedent for future diplomatic missions that would eventually lead to the abolition of the ceremony to be fair to all. But this cannot happen as "You know it … [the ceremony] has existed from the highest antiquity, and cannot be altered. Without the performance of this ceremony, the Ambassador and his tribute will be … rejected and cast out" (Morrison, 1820: 48). What a ridiculous logic this was to be used as an open argument! How can a society ever progress if no change can be made for centuries? And how can such a society cope with a changing world? Morrison replied that such ancient rules were no longer applicable to powerful nations – a good host would permit the British to observe their own ceremonies that, in turn, would serve to only increase the esteem of the emperor among foreign nations (ibid: 51). The Chinese insisted that kowtow was essential and non-negotiable, as "there is only one sun, there is only one Ch'ia-ching Emperor; he is the universal sovereign, and all must pay him homage" (Hibbert, 1970: 64). However, they also emphasised that the performance would not relegate Britain to tributary status. Rather, it would have permitted the British the honour of sitting on cushions in the presence of the emperor, thus giving them a privilege reserved for the princes and the highest mandarins, which was never given to envoys from tributary states. This tug-of-war made the kowtow issue a deadlock when the Anglocentric and Sinocentric world views crossed paths.

Amherst then consulted his retinue and found them divided on the subject. Ellis and Morrison being in favour of his complying with the Chinese request, while Staunton held that the ritual was incompatible with personal and national dignity. At the crux of the divergent views was that Staunton interpreted kowtow as political submission while Ellis perceived it as a mere formality of the Chinese court's normal conventions that all former European ambassadors observed. More importantly, both Amherst and Ellis thought its performance was expedient if there was a possibility of the goals of the embassy being discussed. Ellis (1817: 50–51) argued that "it could scarcely be deemed inadvisable to sacrifice the more important objects of the embassy to any supposed maintenance of dignity by insisting upon such a point of etiquette, in such a scene".

Thomas Manning, another interpreter and an independent scholar who came to Canton with the EIC in 1807, was also in favour of kowtow. He was the first Briton who had ever travelled to Lhasa in 1811 and had met the six-year-old ninth Dalai Lama. He made an interesting analogy that "in Tibet the Chinese lord is … like the English in India" (cited in Christine et al., 2020: 153), which in a way is putting the two empires on a par with each other, while stating that he wanted to identify "what there might be in China worthy to serve as a model for imitation, and what to serve as a beacon to avoid". He admitted that he "for the first time …, performed the ceremony of ketese (kowtow) in the presence of a 'Tartar mandarin'". He also explained that his compliance with ceremonial convention was calculated to impress local officialdom to improve his chance of gaining access to China. Although it did not win him the access, he seemed unbothered with this ceremony at all, stating that "if there was an option between one ketese and three, I generally chose to give three", adding that he "knelt down" before Tibet mandarins as well, even though his Chinese servant "wished this mark of respect to be paid only to Chinamen" (ibid: 154).

However, Staunton, taking pride in judging with "local inside knowledge and experience of the Chinese character", and by referring to the two precedents of the Dutch and Russian embassies, concluded that compromise on the court ritual would be more damaging to the Company's interests than non-compliance as it would not guarantee that a positive outcome would follow. On the other hand, Russia's refusal to kowtow did not cause any interruption of trade between the two countries. He insisted that "being granted a mere audience with the emperor would serve no purpose and would result in only a few ceremonial pleasantries, at best, with no scope for serious negotiation on British goals", thereby rendering any such reception as meaningless in practical terms and would be "too dearly purchased by such a sacrifice" (Staunton, 1824: 31–32). Seeing that Amherst and Ellis were not totally convinced, Staunton then suggested the other five EIC representatives should also be consulted. He wrote: "Four of the five gentlemen who accompanied me had resided nine or ten years in China, and possessed such acknowledged talents, judgment, and local experience, as must necessarily entitle their opinions to considerable weight" (Staunton, 1824: 102). This led to the six-to-two vote in his favour, hence Amherst eventually decided to "show deference to an opinion founded on long observation and on local experience" (Gao, 2020: 65). The decisive role Staunton played in reaching the final decision was often used to blame him specifically for the failure of the Amherst Embassy. He was also made the culprit by the Qing court, being expelled from coming to China again as mentioned earlier. This may have planted a seed for the parliamentary debate in 1840 when Staunton gave a swaying speech again. This will be looked at in Chapter 7.

Looking at the week-long program set out in the edict (Appendix 7), it seemed that Staunton was right in judging that there would be "no scope for serious negotiation on British goals" as there was no opportunity to engage with the emperor in any business talks during the three planned receptions. They were all ceremonial occasions that the ambassador would be required to perform numerous kowtows. The program did include a "farewell audience" and being "entertained at a banquet" before departure, which would have made the farewell much grander than the first embassy, but remember, these were also planned for Macartney, but cancelled after the unsatisfactory reception at Rehe. Therefore, seeing that no third route is viable, the Amherst Embassy decided to follow the Russian precedent as at least they did not sell national dignity for nothing in return. This was supported by Tuck's conclusion (2000: pxxxv) that even if the audience had taken place, it would be unlikely that Amherst's negotiating proposals would have received any more sympathetic hearing than the requests made by Macartney. This decision was defended in Staunton's *Memorial* (1856: 71) by quoting the letters from Amherst and Ellis, as well as one signed by sixteen members of the British Factory at Canton in 1817, all supporting his decision in hindsight that it "maintained our national honour" and "promoted our commercial interests".

However, when the Amherst Embassy's fate was announced to the British public that it "has wholly failed" by *The Times* on 10 May 1817, it was still hard to swallow. The public strongly protested against these "foolish and costly embassies", which resulted in nothing but insults to His Majesty's representatives (Hibbert, 1970: 69). The pamphlet published in 1818, *A Delicate Inquiry Into the Embassies to China, and a Legitimate Conclusion from the Premises,* concluded that "the failure of both embassies has been complete", without accomplishing any one object of its professed purposes (no author, 1818: pp. 29–30), while disclosing that "the expense of the first embassy is believed not to have fallen short of a hundred thousand pounds[5]; that of the second, including the loss of His Majesty's ship the Alceste,[6] with all the property embarked in it, may fairly be estimated at near double the amount of the first" (ibid: 11). Although most domestic sentiment praised Amherst's firm actions in upholding British honour and the status of the British sovereign, the *Edinburgh Review* (1818: 29) presented a contrarian view in its review of Ellis's (1817) book. The Chinese Government's right to deny entry into their country of restless and ambitious European visitors "who have played the game of war and ambition, for near three hundred years, in their immediate vicinity" of India was acknowledged (Stevenson, 2021: 293). However, they still attributed the embassy failure to not subscribing to local ceremonies.

Stevenson (ibid: 206) pointed our attention to a more fatal mistake the embassy made to let the British ships sail back to Canton to await the embassy there before receiving official approval from the Jiaqing Emperor. This was considered a more serious offence than the refusal to kowtow as stated in the emperor's imperial decree: "The Embassy's ships were not to be permitted to leave, so that they might be available to take the Mission back by the way it had come" (Appendix 8). It was later found that "the departure of the British ships without imperial approval was a major reason for the subsequent treatment of the embassy. News reached the Select Committee at Canton in late September 1816 that the emperor had made up his mind to refuse any presents and had given directions for the embassy to be dismissed at this time" (Extract from Public Consultations 1816/17, 21 September 1816, in BL MSS EUR F 140/48). Platt (2018: 179) also wrote that it had been the emperor's intention to have a successful meeting, even if it meant compromising on the protocol surrounding the kowtow, stating in an edict three days before Amherst's arrival at Yuanmingyuan that "it is better to meet with them than to send them away", and a detailed week-long program was already prepared for the reception of the embassy. Some analysis that looked beyond the kowtow issue was also made by the British historian Herbert Wood (1940: 139), who believed that regardless of the emperor's grandiose claims, Chinese concerns about British strategic intentions towards China was the main reason for his stand against Amherst. However, due to the decision made by the Amherst Embassy to refuse to kowtow, and the subsequent result of the emperor's refusal to grant the reception, it was still largely believed to be the main reason behind the failure of the mission, particularly because this decision overturned the original instructions from London and Lord Amherst's own judgment.

Given the power status of Britain in Europe at the time, the fate of Amherst mission also gave rise to discussions and debates regarding his refusal to kowtow in Europe. The most worth quoting one was given by Napoleon, when the embassy visited the deposed French emperor on St. Helena on their return voyage. Many were familiar with his famous remarks that "China is a sleeping lion, let her sleep, as when she awakes, it will shake the world", but very few knew it was said during this visit. The meeting was not mentioned in Ellis's (1817) account, but was recorded in a book published in 1822, written by Napoleon's Irish physician who had accompanied him into exile, Barry O'Meara. Napoleon seemed to show better understanding of some of the wrong assumptions underlying the fate of the Amherst Embassy. In his view, the mission had not been sent on behalf of British national honour; rather, it was "an affair of merchandize" sent on behalf of "the tea-merchants in England" (O'Meara, 1822: 44). Therefore, "you must humour them and comply with their customs. They do not seek you. They never have sent ambassadors in return for yours, nor asked you to send any" (ibid: 44). Napoleon, as a former emperor himself, also believed that the ambassador represented his sovereign was a misguided apprehension: "in negotiation as well as in etiquette, the ambassador does not represent the sovereign, and has only a right to experience the same treatment as the highest grandee of the place" (Rockhill, 1897: 637), because "none of the stipulations of affairs which he signs are valid until after a ratification; and so to his rank in etiquette, there never has been an example of sovereign having treated them as equals" (Peyrefitte, 1992: 516). Therefore, he believed that the emperor of China had a right to require the kowtow.

It appeared that kowtow was merely ceremonial in Napoleon's eyes, no more humiliating than any other court ceremony, maybe because he missed the symbolic meaning of kowtow under the Chinese Tributary System, which was more than a ritual to show respect, but to signify that there was but one emperor under the heaven, that all the other sovereigns were his vassals. When O'Meara replied that it did not matter if the British was rejected by the Chinese, they had the Royal Navy, Napoleon said: "it would be the worst thing you have done for a number of years, to go to war with an immense empire like China. You would doubtless, at first, succeed, but you would teach them their own strength. They would be compelled to adopt measures to defend themselves against you ...... and, in the course of time, defeat you". (Abel, 1818: 316). Astounding prophetic words indeed. His prediction of China as a sleeping lion is the most famous, but I feel it is his understanding that "in the course of time" really hits the nail: China would bide her time and does not mind if that "course of time" means a century or two. True, the two embassies failed to wake China up with letters and gifts, but we all know it was the gunboat that finally woke her up. No one would be happy to be woken up from a deep, intoxicating dream, but one can only open their eyes to see what the world has changed into after being woken up.

It took China nearly another century to dislodge the institutional inertia created by the Tributary System and to undo the embedded perception of foreign relationships that the system produced. Its diplomatic ceremonies were refigured through the "Law of Nations" when the ambassadors of the five countries of Britain, France, Russia, U.S and Germany were allowed to bow to meet the Tongzhi Emperor in 1873. The complete defeat of China in the First Sino-Japanese War (1894–1895) gave the final blow to the Chinese world order as this was the first time in Chinese history that it was defeated by a country that once was its tributary state. But the last tributary mission to China was made by Nepal in as late as 1908, and the tradition of performing kowtow by Chinese subjects to their emperor only came to an end in 1912 when the Republic of China was founded. However, it is interesting to note that the Guangxu Emperor, who ruled China from 1875–1908, started to take English lessons from 1891, and it was recorded that the English teachers were allowed to sit to teach while all other Chinese ministers and eunuchs had to kneel before the emperor.

In December 1876, China sent its very first ambassador, Guo Songtao, to the UK. On 7 February 1877, Guo had an audience with Queen Victoria, in which he removed his hat and bowed three times before presenting his credentials to become the first Chinese diplomatic envoy. The Illustrated *London News* commented on Guo's appointment:

> China has at last awakened to a sense of her position amongst nations. Hitherto she has held herself aloof from the rest of the world, indulging in dreams of her former greatness, but now a gleam of light has broken in upon her. The halo of antiquity and her pride, and which still hangs around her institutions, she now sees has mystified and obscured her vision.
>
> (cited in Price, 2019: 119)

During his service of the embassy, Guo realised the strategy of "emulating the strength of foreigners' technology in order to overcome them" (师夷长技以制夷) was to miss the point, as technology was only the tip of the tree branch, even trading is only the tree trunk while the root of the tree was in the governing system, such as the Parliament. Guo also realised the Western Ocean states looked at China in the same way as China looked at them as *Yidi*, even using a phonetic translation to say the West regarded China as "half-civilised", which was exactly the word used by Ellis in his journal (1817) to describe Chinese people: "half-civilised, prejudiced and impracticable". Morrison's (1820: 67) comments may add a footnote to this "half" nature:

> If 'barbarity' or being 'barbarous' expresses something savage, rude and cruel, the present inhabitants of China do not deserve the epithet; if it expresses a cunning selfish policy, endeavouring to deceive, to intimidate, or to browbeat, as occasion may require, connected with an arrogant assumption of superiority on all occasions, instead of cultivating a liberal, candid, friendly intercourse with men of other nations, they are barbarians.

Morrison might have got this impression from dealing with the mandarins since the negotiations had to be done through them. The next section will explore to what extent their conduct actually constituted the most important reason for the failure of the embassy.

6.3 The Minion culture in the Qing court

As explained in the beginning of the chapter, the Qing Empire was on the wane by Jiaqing's time compared with his father's prosperous reign. Both Amherst and Staunton not only attributed this decline to the Jiaqing Emperor, but also blamed him for the failure of the embassy. Amherst claimed that Jiaqing "was less ready to dispense with outward fame of respect than his Father, whose reign was long and victorious … [and so] might attach less consequence to any shew of external homage" (Gao, 2020: 66). As the only member who had participated in both missions, Staunton maintained that "the emperor's violence and precipitation must … be considered as the main cause of what has happened … his conduct throughout has certainly been ungracious in the extreme, and totally unlike that of his predecessor, upon the occasion of the former embassy" (Staunton, 1824: 144). Accounts of the Macartney Embassy had portrayed the Qianlong Emperor as a venerable old gentleman-statesman who was healthy, vigorous, affable and pragmatic, and who had received the British with graciousness and politeness. The Qianlong emperor had, at least, engaged with the British personally, even had a conversation with the young Staunton, which signified an interest in the outside world. Ellis (1817: 122), who did not take the same stand on the kowtow issue with Staunton, agreed with him in that "the rupture must be attributed to the personal character of the Emperor, who is capricious, weak and timid, and the combined effect of these feelings will account for his pertinacity". In an official report presented to the British Government in 1847, Jiaqing's life and reign was described as "blank, as no just, noble, or generous action can be discovered" (Martin, 1847: 285).

Almost on the contrary, modern historiography has revealed that the Jiaqing Emperor was pragmatic, sober, frugal, energetic and intent on instigating a series of new reforms in his reign (Rowe, 2011). Chinese scholar Wang (2014: 244) depicted him as a reforming monarch who "toned down the much celebrated rhetoric of tributary superiority, which has long dominated Chinese thinking about their relationship with the outside world". This was endorsed by the British scholar Kitson (2013: 57) who argued that "the Jiaqing Emperor emerges not as a ruler imprisoned in an ossified ritualistic ceremonialism but one capable of reacting pragmatically to the complex and challenging political events that faced him". Since the Amherst Embassy had never met the emperor, what gave them the strong impression to define him as an embodiment of an oriental despot in the British imagination? Obviously, it was his treatment of the mission, but how did he reach those decisions? Based on the reports he received from the court officials – could they hide the truth from the emperor? If so, for what reason?

Although the embassy was staffed with Britons who had gained a lot of local knowledge in Canton, and despite Staunton's (1824: 206) hope that the presence of Mandarin speakers would enable them to "throw some new and interesting light on the moral character and condition of this singular people", the "China knowledge" they thought they had gained was only sufficient to understand the trading policy. None of them had any direct dealings with the court at Beijing before, so there was no way for them to develop enough insight into two problems that lied at the very heart of the plague that eventually took the empire's life: the minion culture of the Qing court and the practice of Literary Inquisition.

The so-called Literary Inquisition, literally meaning "literary prison" (文字狱) in Chinese, was a cultural phenomenon peculiar to the autocracy system in China, which also bred the minion culture briefly discussed in Chapter 5. It reached its climax during the Qing Dynasty as the

Manchus were deeply worried about the rebellious thoughts of the Han people and were especially sensitive to anything disrespectful about the Manchus to the extent of paranoia. The worst period was between 1774–1788 when scholars were likely to be executed for any slight indication of criticism of the Qing. Apart from suppressing everything that might encourage subversive thoughts, even innocent homophone expressions could be interpreted as treason. One famous case during the Qianlong's reign was when a scholar re-organised the *Kangxi Dictionary* by semantic groups rather than character strokes, but because he forgot to apply "name taboos"[7] to refer to the emperors Kangxi, Yongzheng and Qianlong in the Preface, not only he himself was executed, but also seven of his family members, and a number of officials who have read his work but failed to spot the problem were demoted. This system imposed a firm grip on people's minds, making scholar-officials generally over-cautious and precedent-bound to insure themselves against trouble. "Defensive prevarication, therefore, was the best policy" (Singer, 1992: 58). They dared not initiate any new methods to fit unusual circumstances, but only reiterated former precedents and make new situations fit old conceptions. The reason why precedents mattered so much was because they were made by imperial ancestors, who were the only "human being" above the emperor himself that he would perform kowtow to, thus time-honoured ritual practice codified by their ancestors were sacred and unassailable.

Thomas Percy had written about the excessive honours Chinese paid to their ancestors in his *Pleasing History*. On the one hand, in his comment on the usefulness of a strict adherence to etiquette and ritual, he seemed to admire its consequence in "the wonderful stability of the Chinese empire" and the fact of the empire's "having subsisted about 4000 years". On the other hand, an excessive regard for the past evoked distain: "no people have such blind veneration for antiquity as the Chinese" (Percy, 1761: 182). This could perhaps be understood on a par with worshipping God for citizens of Christian nations who do not worship human beings but only natural law and God, while China was an atheist country that was ruled by man who held absolute power. The mandarins thus considered themselves minions to serve the emperor as they were both submissive and subservient in this system. Hegel's analysis explained the nurturing of a minion culture in the Chinese court: "the head of state in China is a despot, and he leads a systematically constructed government with a numerous hierarchy of subordinate members … the individual has no moral selfhood" (Hegel, 1975: 199). Just as Montesquieu who characterised the principle of despotism as fear, Hegel argued that if the Chinese fulfilled any official or political obligation, it was out of fear for severe penalty rather than their capacity for moral decisions: "it is not their own conscience, their own honour (i.e. the mandarins) which keeps the offices of government up to their duty, but an external mandate and the severe sanctions by which it is supported" (Hegel, 1956: 127), therefore, "they are notorious for deceiving wherever they can" (ibid: 131). In contrast, the absence of political rigidity in Britain nurtured a freedom to inquire, to dispute, and to experiment, believing in unimpeded circulation and exchange of goods, money, people, and ideas. It was the intellectual liberty that goes hand in hand with economic laissez-faire that put the British empire ahead of the rest of the world towards the end of the eighteenth century.

Although Macartney only had a few months' first-hand experience of dealing with the court officials, he had exceptionally sharp observations on how the kowtow ceremony had conditioned mandarins when he saw them giving him a demo: "they are wonderfully supple, and though generally considered as most respectable character, are not very scrupulous in regard to veracity …… Their ideas of the obligations of truth are certainly very lax". Here being supple physically to their master was matched with being unscrupulous and lax with truth. This may be reflected in their hiding the truth from the emperor due to fear of incurring the emperor's displeasure, who had absolute power to demote, punish or even execute his officials. Macartney later had acutely summarised the Qing court character as "a singular mixture of ostentatious hospitality and inbred suspicion, ceremonious civility and real rudeness, shadowy complaisance and substantial perverseness" (Cranmer-Byng, 1962: 223).

During the Amherst Embassy, the emperor's ministers were described with "childish vanity", "insolence", "meanness" and "unblushing falsehoods" by Barrow (1817: 465); and "arrogant, pretentious, rude, devious" and "liars" by Ellis (1830: 29). The characters of Chinese hierarchy, concentration of power and precedent conformity were opposite to political liberty, economic competition and scientific innovation that were the wellsprings of the British wealth and power. As Peyrefitte (1992: 542) put it, China as a mirror "taught them to perceive the West, and as they pondered the characteristics of their own world, they were astonished at the opposite characteristics of Celestial society". But they stopped at being "astonished", without looking deeper into the questions of "why are they like that?" and "why are we so different?" to form a genuine understanding of what had conditioned the Chinese into these qualities, nor did they realise that throughout the course of the negotiations, the mandarins were in an invidious position and were subject to similar, if not greater, stresses and pressures. For Amherst, what weighed heavily on his mind was that if he refused to kowtow, it would almost certainly lead to his expulsion from Beijing, then the grand year-long journey would be not only as a complete failure, but a laughing stock; but if he complied, his name would go down in infamy as the first British ambassador to kowtow before the Chinese emperor. But for the Chinese ministers as his counterparts, the stake was even higher. Unlike Amherst, who was given autonomy to make the final decision by the King, the instructions the Chinese ministers had to follow allowed them little or no room to manoeuvre. Moreover, failure to deliver acceptable outcomes would incur the emperor's displeasure, thus resulting in severe and humiliating punishments, which already had a case on the spot: the two officials who allowed the embassy to proceed beyond Tianjin and their ships to leave for Canton after Amherst had refused to kowtow at the "testing" banquet were disgraced, as "these two men are guilty on these points ...... we shall wait for the Board of Punishment on how to punish them" (Fu, 1966: 406–407).

Fearing such punishments made the intermediary mandarins the direct culprit for the impasse of the negotiations and the ultimate failure of the embassy, but their roles were largely overlooked by the analysis so far. For example, both Amherst's proposals were "refused" because the officials simply dared not submit them to the emperor, whose ultimatum was "kowtow or no audience" (Rockhill, 1897: 636). At one point, the British side thought that agreement was reached for the ambassador to "kneel on one knee three times, and to thrice bow each time" (Staunton, 1824: 67). Amherst then wrote a letter to confirm this with the emperor: "The great affairs of empire being best conducted by precedent, his Royal Highness has instructed me to approach Your Imperial presence with the same outward expression of respect that were received by your dignified father Kien-Lung [the Qianlong emperor], from the former English Embassador, Lord Macartney, that is to say, to kneel upon one knee and to bow the head, repeating this obeisance the number of times deemed respectful". Amherst further emphasised that such a "particular demonstration of veneration from English Ambassador was shown only to Chinese emperors", to show his "profound devotion to the most potent Emperor in the universe" (Lord Amherst to the Emperor of China, August 1816, in Ellis, 1817: 497). It concluded with a request that Amherst be received in an imperial audience to personally deliver the Prince Regent's letter. However, the mandarin later confessed that he had not dared to pass it on to the court at all.

If we look at the situation from the perspective of the mandarins handling the embassy, we can perhaps understand the thoughts on their minds: Why would they risk their career or even life to help the British realise an unjust request? When Amherst informed the Qing official of their final decision of not to kowtow, he did not know that by this time, the official had committed himself to "ensuring the success of the Embassy" and had sent a misleading report to the emperor that the embassy, "despite not having rehearsed the Kowtow, would certainly perform the full ceremonial at the imperial audience" (Tuck, 2000: xxxi). The deception became even more apparent once the embassy arrived at Tongzhou, where the Qing officials sent a "confused and obscure" report, confirming that the "English tribute-bearer is daily practising the ceremony, and manifests the highest possible respect and veneration"

(Imperial edict in the *Peking Gazette*, 4 September 1816, Ellis, 1817: 509). As a final move in desperation, they even made a suggestion that Amherst was free to "make any report he pleased on his return to England", regardless of whether he performed the kowtow or not. The implication that Amherst would be prepared to lie before his sovereign was met with British outrage (Amherst to Canning, 28 February 1817, Ellis, 1817: 141), but this also implied that the Chinese officials were ready to do so when deemed necessary.

After remaining at Tongzhou for a week, the embassy was suddenly told that the emperor had granted them the exemption from performing kowtow and they could leave for Beijing the next day (Abel, 1818: 97). This again turned out to be fabricated by the official, who guaranteed to the emperor "that the English could perform the rites of the occasion of tomorrow's audience" (Fu, 1966: 406). The embassy arrived at Yuanming Yuan on 29 August after an overnight travel around the city of Beijing and was told that the emperor would at once receive them. Amherst said he was so overcome by fatigue and bodily illness, he absolutely needed repose. The emperor then "directed that the Ambassador be taken back to his lodging, and supplied at once with medical aid" (Appendix 8). But after the imperial physician reported back that Amherst was shamming illness, orders came from the emperor to dismiss them. This may sound an overreaction, but since Macartney had also refused to attend the meeting with the first Minister when he arrived at Rehe and was accused for malinger, the Qing court saw this as a reflection of lack of sincerity of the ambassador. It also revealed a lack of trust of course. Morrison and Staunton believed that the court was brutally insensitive to the effects of heat, dust and travel on Amherst and his retinue (Markley, 2016: 93), but they were not aware of the missing information in this real game of "Chinese whispers". What the emperor missed was recorded in his edict dated 30 August, the second day after the embassy left Beijing (Appendix 8):

> We transmitted an edict stating that we were ascending to the palace, and summoned the ambassadors. At first, Ho-shih-t'ai reported that they were unable to walk quickly enough to reach the gate of the palace in time, then he petitioned Us to ascend the throne a second time, stating that the ambassador was sick with diarrhoea and must wait a little while. The third time he reported that the ambassador had collapsed and could not enter the palace for an audience. Thereupon, we ordered the ambassador to return to the hotel. We sent a doctor to cure him, and ordered the vice-ambassador to come for an audience. Then Ho-shih-t'ai reported that the vice-ambassador were also sick, and we had better wait until all recovered, then let them have an audience together.

In the case of Macartney, it was only the meeting with the first Minister, and at least the vice ambassador went there instead. This time, it was to keep the emperor waiting by ascending the throne twice for the audience, and even the vice ambassador shammed illness after being checked by the imperial physician. We can only imagine the emperor's reaction at this point: "the Middle Kingdom is the common sovereign of all nations under heaven. How can we suffer such an insult due to their pride and arrogance? Thereupon we dispatched an edict to expel the ambassadors and order them home. We have decreed no punishment" (Fu, 1966: 406). However, when the emperor later learned that the embassy had travelled the whole night, and one of the reasons why Amherst had refused to appear in audience was because he did not have his ceremonial robe and the credential with him yet, he blamed the mandarin for not reporting these details:

> He could easily have asked for another audience that evening or the next day. He did nothing of the sorts, and allowed me to remain in ignorance until I was proceeding to take my seat on the Imperial Throne. The guilt of Ho Shih-t'ai and his colleagues greatly exceeds the errors of the other two. Had they informed me of the true state of the case I should have postponed the ceremony to a later date. I am astounded at the way in which my stupid officials have mismanaged this business, and I feel that I have completely lost face in the eyes of my Court. All I can do is frankly to acknowledge my mistakes. I shall deal with the four official's punishment after the Board of Civil Office has recommended an appropriate penalty[8]. In the meantime, I record the facts for the information of my officials throughout the Empire and the Mongol Princes (Appendix 8).

The entry to the Qing Archive on 30 August 1816 recorded that "if they had reported this case in time, we could have changed to another day in order to give them an audience so that they might complete their ceremonials before their return" (Fu, 1966, 1: 406–407). From this we can see it is true that even if the audience did take place, it would only mean that the embassy could "complete their ceremonials", as the perceived aim of the mission by the Chinese was to pay homage to the Middle Kingdom as the common sovereign of all nations under Heaven. It could accomplish "nothing except to perpetuate Chinese isolation, exclusionism, and sense of superiority" (Matheson, 1836: 17–19). But it is interesting to note that the edict was instructed to circulate to "the exterior" as well, to let others know the Great Britain also came to pay tribute, and that their dispel was a result of Qing ministers' mishandling of the embassy, not because the ambassador had refused to perform the kowtow.

Upon learning the truth, the emperor also proposed a limited exchange of gifts and accepted "the pictures of their majesties, four large maps, three of which the United Kingdoms, and the books of engravings" as he could not "bear to reject altogether their expressions of veneration and obedience" given the "sincere and entire devotedness" of the British nation, while to have accepted any more would have been "indecorous ... unless he had also determined to receive the ambassador" ("Substance of Imperial Edicts inflicting Punishments on Soo, Ho, and Kwang" in Ellis, 1817: 509). However, as the emperor was due to leave for Rehe, it was too late to recall the embassy and it would have been too costly to invite the embassy to accompany him. Of the presents received by the embassy, Davis recorded a jade *ruyi* and a dozen purses as was given to the Macartney Embassy; and some necklaces of large "court beads". The emperor claimed that in conferring these, he was "giving much and taking little".

If the Jiaqing Emperor's edict is compared with the British records of what actually happened in Beijing, the fact stood out clearly that both the Emperor and the Ambassador were hoodwinked and misled by the mandarins deputed to arrange the details of the ceremony. The officials were too afraid to lose face by having to confess that they were unable to persuade the British embassy to agree to perform the ceremony. Therefore, they lied to both sides until the last minute, when they even attempted to grab the ambassador by his arm to force him to go. Then in order to extricate themselves, they made it appear that the Ambassador had been disrespectful to the emperor. As instructed in the edict, all these details were printed in the *Peking Gazette* (*Jing Bao,* 《京报》) on 4 September 1816 to "proclaim to the interior", in which the Jiaqing Emperor admitted "if, at that time, Ho-she-tay had addressed to me a true report, I, the Emperor, would certainly have issued my commands, and have changed the period of the audience, in order to correspond with their intentions, in thus coming ten thousand lees (miles) to my court" (cited in Gao, 2020: 68). Therefore, the Jiaqing Emperor may be wrongly blamed for the harsh treatment of the Amherst Embassy, and his response should not be understood as simply clinging to ossified ritualism but be considered in the light of all these cover-ups. However, if we borrow Barrow's (1804: 258) diagnose of China as a country worn out by "old age and disease", we can see that by Jiaqing's reign, the disease had gone deeper and its court culture was a main reason to render the embassy a "hudibrastic fiasco" (see Figure 6.1).

This important decree to clarify the mismanagement of the embassy and even to acknowledge the Emperor's mistakes reached the embassy in January 1817, but it was never opened by the British monarch. Waley-Cohen's book (2000: 136) said it had been "sitting unread for over 60 years in a storage room at the Foreign Office until the first Chinese ambassador in London was shown these". This was inaccurate as it was not found by the first ambassador Guo Songtao, but Ambassador Xue Fucheng[9] when he was sent to Britain in 1891. He noted in his diary dated

Figure 6.1 Book cover of the *Hudibrastic History of Amherst's Embassy to China*, by William Augustus Kentish, Illustrated by Robert Cruikshank. Published by London: Davis & Co. Courtesy of the British Library.

on 7 March 1891 that there was a box wrapped in yellow silk that had been kept in the storage room for over 70 years, with no one knowing what was inside. He opened it to reveal "a silk-lined bamboo tube, inside of which was the Jiaqing Emperor's edict, accompanied by translations in Manchurian, Chinese and Latin". Xue thought it was unopened "perhaps because no British could read it" (Xue, 2008: pp. 303–304), which was obviously not true as Staunton went back to the UK in 1818 and offered his substantial collection of Chinese printed books and manuscript dictionaries in establishing the first significant Chinese library in Britain in 1823 when the Royal Asiatic Society was founded. I think the Chinese Emperor's edict, left there to gather dust, may be a gesture to show that the British had decided to turn the page: the Amherst Embassy represented the ending of the "letter and gift" period of interacting with China. In Amherst's own words, he described his reception at the court as one of: "hurry and confusion, of irregularity and disorder, of insult, inhumanity, and almost of personal violence, sufficient to give to the court of the emperor Kia-King the manners, character, and appearance of the roving-camp of a Tartar Horde". (Amherst to Canning, 8 March 1817, in BL IOR G/12/197 (Reel 2) F 285). Not knowing that this letter meant to take blame for the "hudibrastic fiasco", the British were simply not interested in reading another edict perhaps more humiliating than the one issued by his father. With diplomatic efforts rejected and gifts returned, gone was the optimism expressed by Macartney over the possibility of overcoming differences through rational exchange; in its place emerged a discourse that argued for a direct confrontation with China, including the use of force, if necessary, to achieve these aims.

6.4 Redrawing Self and Other: New knowledge produced by the Amherst Embassy

By the time Amherst's mission came to China, the Qing Empire was drifting away from its former prosperity and many of China's assumed superiority over "others" had withered away over time. Its loss of prestige was considerable and clearly observed by the Amherst Embassy, leading to a striking change in the British attitude toward China. As a result of the "Great Divergence" on a global scale, the framework within which the Qing Dynasty had to run was changing drastically, yet the Qing map produced in 1811 named "Perpetual All-under-Heaven's Map of the Unified Qing" still saw itself as presiding from the centre of the universe, infused with the view of world as civilisation and barbarism, and Jiaqing's reign still held onto the unshakable conviction that foreigners were either submissive to China's supremacy, or coveted its wealth.

Amherst's goal was to accomplish those left unaccomplished by the Macartney Embassy: the opening of a port to the north of Canton and a resident minister at Beijing with a Chinese minister to England in return. With its premature dismissal, the mission had no opportunity to impress the Jiaqing Emperor with the new British power in the post-Napoleonic age, the only worthwhile objective left was the opportunity to expand British knowledge of China during its four-month journey from Beijing to Canton, and this had become its biggest legacy. Though much less known today than its famous predecessor, the few scholars (Kitson, 2016; Gao, 2014; Stevenson, 2021) who did research about the Amherst Embassy all argued that it bore more significance in the British understanding and changed views of China. I think its significance is more in the latter. Ellis (1817: 197) echoed this by stating that at the beginning of the Amherst mission, members of the embassy were still divided into "those who landed with an impression that the Chinese were to be classed with the civilised nations of Europe", and others who "ranged them with the other nations of Asia"; by the end of the mission, a general consensus on the backwardness of China had emerged. But Staunton still showed a "divided reaction to China: respect for the decaying grandeur of a cultural and ancient civilisation, and impatience with the failure of the Qing officials to conform to 'modern', European notions of diplomacy, social customs, and international commerce" (Markley, 2016: 94). Davis, who later became a sinologist, in his two-volume work of *The Chinese:*

A General Description of the Empire of China and Its Inhabitants, also offered a mixed opinion of the Chinese people and the Chinese system: "on the whole, the Chinese are among the most good-humoured people in the world, and the most peaceful; and the chief causes of this must be sought in their political and social institutions" (Davis, 1836: 199). Then in his *Sketches of China* (1841), Davis argued that although stagnating, China had a thirst for foreign trade and improved relations, envisioning at least an "incipiently 'modern' China waiting to emerge from Confucian traditionalism" (cited in Markley, 2016: 102). These positive remarks were definitely not prevailing, but a noteworthy difference I found in the accounts of the Amherst Embassy was a candid acknowledgment of the limitations of their perceptions, especially those given by Abel who appreciated the way the embassy's journey was conducted would colour their views of China. He wrote (1818: 205): "I apprehend … that any person travelling through a country in a hurried journey, under a suspicious surveillance, must always be unqualified to pronounce on a question that respects a whole nation". Staunton (1824: 206) also acknowledged that "experience is not always profitable to knowledge – and that our ingenuity in adapting everything to our preconceived notions is such, that our erroneous prejudices are often strengthened, instead of being corrected, by those facts and occurrences, which, had they been dispassionately considered, must have effected their removal".

Since the embassy was allowed to take a different route from that of Macartney's, it gained unprecedented freedom to explore areas that had not previously been visited by a Briton. As said by Staunton (1824: 271), "Although the gates of Pekin had been shut against us, those of Nan-kin at least had yielded to our summons, and thus the original and most ancient capital of the empire, which had been visited, I believe, by no former Embassy, fairly laid open to our curiosity". It was exactly this greater degree of liberty to see the interior China that contributed to the new consensus, as "the widely circulated image in Britain of a backward and declining Chinese empire could be supported for the first time by an abundance of reliable first-hand evidence" (Gao, 2014: 11). As explained earlier, the Jiaqing's court was subject to serious financial problems and frequent rebellions and pirate attacks, which obliged the emperor to give up the extravagant tradition of southern tours along the Grand Canal to the lower Yangtze delta. After the Qianlong Emperor's last visit in 1784, the numerous lavishly decorated buildings on this route, many of which had been purposely built for these imperial tours, remained unattended and their dilapidation became a visible indicator that "there can be little doubt that the prosperity of this empire has been on the decline under the government of the present emperor" (Staunton, 1824: 157). Staunton also read from the *Peking Gazette* (*Jing Bao,* 《京报》) that the Jiaqing Emperor was compelled to abandon even the refurbishment of his own garden for want of available funds. Words such as "decay" and "decline" were common recurring themes in accounts following this embassy, while the unhygienic living conditions and underdeveloped public facilities including roads, boats and vehicles they had to travel in, were particularly highlighted by these British observers.

Ellis portrayed China as a stagnant and dull country whose people suffered from a lack of freedom and progress due mainly to the oppressive rule of the usurping Manchus (Ellis, 1830: 29). However, his book contained little new information or insight into China as he himself concluded (Ellis, 1817: 310): "It has been said, that there is nothing new under the sun, certainly there is nothing new in China; on the contrary, everything is old". Social contact was limited to peasant farmers, shopkeepers, and contacts with Chinese women and insight into Chinese domestic life remained inaccessible. William Havell, the embassy's draftsman who only left a handful of sketches and paintings of China, in contrast to the hundreds of illustrations produced by Alexander of the Macartney Embassy, also suggested that he found little to inspire him, or nothing new since reported by the Macartney Embassy. Their own disappointments in finding fresh aspects of China to report led to the disappointments among British readers, and the lack of change itself contributed to the changing views of China as "a site of space stubbornly inaccessible to the revolution of time" that is "oblivious to any progress in history and lifelessly frozen in its vast time-less immobility" (Zhang, 1998: 29).

The perception gap described in Chapters 4 and 5 during Macartney's mission remained wide if not deepened. During the six months' mission, they maintained a constant intercourse with the officers of the Chinese government and people in the interior of the Chinese empire, where "the British name was as yet little known, and still less esteemed" (Staunton, 1824: 67). For example, they learned that even some educated mandarins who were better informed on European geography and history, thought England was divided into four parts and had four kings, thus similar to those found in maritime Southeast Asia, which traditionally sent tribute to the Qing court (Abel, 1818: 144). They also thought England was dependent entirely on commerce and, although it had a strong navy, the French were a far superior land force, therefore England's importance was not as great as other European nations and it was absurd that her king was "pretending to compete with the Emperor of China", who was the supreme head of all nations (Ellis, 1817: 196). When Amherst met the viceroy of Canton, he asserted in a haughty tone that the British had benefitted from Chinese trade for about 100 years and that Britain could not "dispense with the commodities of China" (Amherst to Canning, 21 April 1817, in Stevenson, 2021: 278), a line from Qianlong's reply to King George III following the first embassy, now became a commonly held belief.

In Davis's (1841: 203) observation, the Manchus were too proud to learn from foreigners, he also noted the coarse manners of their military officers, who he thought were also "illiterate". There was clearly a lack of interest in learning more of the outside world with so many members of the embassy speaking fluent Chinese, offering an unique opportunity for the Chinese to exchange knowledge with the British. In contrast, the British lost no opportunity of studying in order to better exploit the trading opportunities that China offered, believing in "knowledge was power". For example, when Abel, the naturalist, was collecting plants or examining stones during the journey, he was often laughed at by the natives and the escorting soldiers, as if he did so only to satisfy his peculiar curiosity. When Abel spoke to some of these people, he found the British to them were like "inhabitants of another world", because "our features, dress, and habits, were so opposed to theirs, as to induce them to infer that our country, in all its natural characters, must equally differ from their own". "Have you a moon, and rain, and rivers in your country?" were their occasional questions (Abel, 1818: 141). When "ignorance and conceit were perhaps never more strongly combined" (Davis, 1841: 179), it prevented the Chinese from recognising anything foreign as being superior and worth studying.

The consecutive failures of two embassies dimmed the glory of China, which had stepped down from its former throne as an exemplary civilisation. The philosophical aspects once admired by the learned in the Enlightenment era were rendered bland, only the commerce and trade could still provoke the British interests. The China they came to see was no longer the China that once attracted them, but the encounter did help Britain forge its own sense of national identity, with the knowledge it produced functioning like a mirror to better knowing oneself. However, through this mirror, China did not really open its eyes to see that there were other forms of power operating under a different set of systems, while the British did not reflect enough when they saw that there were other forms of power that shaped subjects quite different from their own. Amherst's hostile reception by the Qing court should have provided new intelligence on Chinese officialdom and food for reflection and introspection, instead, the embassy focused on how to claim "success" when they obviously failed the main mission. In Staunton's own words (1856:67), "although this mission has often been stigmatised as a failure, it was practically, perhaps, the most successful of any that had ever been sent to Pekin by any European power; for it was followed by a longer interval of commercial tranquillity and of freedom from annoyance, than had ever been experienced before" with no major stoppages in trade between 1816 and 1839. Staunton believed it was Amherst's defiant stance and firm assertion of British values and honour in his dealings with the mandarins that had achieved this outcome. Although the Amherst Embassy might have been unfairly stigmatised as a failure, to claim the stability as a fruit of this failed mission was far-fetched-just as little difference had been made even by a "successful" mission of the Macartney.

The role a foreign mission can play in influencing the trading situation or China's foreign relations was minimal, it was all depending on China's domestic situation, which always prioritises stability. As Staunton's own writing revealed, the true status of a foreign mission in Chinese eyes was one that was "so little desirable" (Barrow,1821: 420), while Morrison (1815: 425) also expressed a clear view that the Chinese Government would never acquiesce to the demands of a few foreign merchants until forced to do so by an enemy "nearer [to] their gates".

Therefore, Soothill's (1925: 108) analysis was much more tenable in arguing that the Amherst Embassy confirmed the opinion already being reluctantly formed, "that only three possibilities were open to the British – a resort of force, absolute submission to tyranny, or abandonment of the trade". The British government chose to swallow the insult as "abandoning Canton trade was clearly not an option. The use of force seems excessive, not to mention expensive. So, for more than two decades, it was agreed to play by Chinese rules" (Gelber, 2008: 172). Until the 1830s, the China trade was still viewed as a "keystone of that magnificent arch which connects the Anglo-Eastern and Western realms, and affords a medium for the annual transmission of four million sterling of tribute to a small island in the Atlantic, from the territorial revenues of one of the most splendid empires that ever were subjected to the dominion of man" (Martin, 1832: 1–2).

For the Chinese empire, they also failed to reassess the power shift from the exterior forces to see that there were only two options left for them: "to adapt or to perish" (Allison, 2017). The failed Amherst Embassy represented another great missed opportunity for China to move towards real interactions with the West, or even a world-changing moment. As Peyrefitte (1992: xxxii) lamented in his book:

> What if the two worlds had broadened their contacts, mutually enriching each other with what each did best? What if the country that, centuries before all others, had invented printing and paper, the compass and the rudder, gunpowder and firearms, had blended its discoveries with those of the country that had just tamed steam and was about to master electricity? ...... such was the opportunity history offered the Far East and the West. Instead there was a clash of pride, each party imagining itself the centre of the universe and consigning the other to a barbarous periphery.

This failure would continue to plague the Qing Dynasty as it encountered increasing foreign pressures and internal unrest during the nineteenth century. If the opportunity was taken, China could have "awakened" without the world having to "tremble". With the abolition of the EIC's charter, 17 years after Amherst's humiliating dismissal from Beijing, Lord Napier appeared at the Gates of Canton; "on that day began the long and painful process of disillusion, which, through bloodshed and humiliation, was to convince the rulers of China that their attitude of complacent superiority and over-lordship of the world was untenable" (Backhouse and Bland, 1914: 385). History has shown China the high "opportunity cost".

The embassy's observation of the Chinese military also led to the conclusion that "the art of war must be in a very low state" in China (Ellis, 1817: 253). Gao (2014: 58–59) believed that such "important perceptions laid the foundation for future changes in Sino-British relations and led, indirectly to the outbreak of the first Opium War in 1839". What was little mentioned in books about the Amherst Embassy was the small-scale military skirmish that already took place during this mission. Captain Murray Maxwell, who was appointed to escort the Amherst Embassy, arrived off the Pearl River in November 1816 and prepared to sail to Whampoa for his reunion with Amherst. The frigate *Alceste*, which was armed with 46 cannons, was refused permission to enter the river and perfunctorily ordered to halt by a local mandarin, threatening to sink it if it tried to force passage. Maxwell fired the first cannon as a statement that he took personal responsibility for the exchange of fire, this first cannonball was ironically marked "tribute from the King of England to the Chinese" (*United Services Magazine*, 1831, Part II: 533). They attacked the Chinese defences, broke through a blockade of junks and fired on the forts guarding the river mouth, scattering their defenders. The British side suffered no casualties while the Chinese losses were reportedly 47 killed and many wounded. This was unrecorded in China but commended in the British records (*Annual Biography and Obituary*, 1832, Vol. XVI, p. 233). Macartney had once declared this on his return journey that "for a few frigates could in a few weeks destroy all their coast navigation and intercourse from the island of Hainan to the Gulf of Pei-chihli" (Cranmer-Byng, 1962: 211). Gao (2014: 21–22) argued that the Amherst Embassy's experience made it easier to justify a policy of open hostility towards China as they "probably would not have been confident enough to attack such a large and populous country as China had they not become convinced of China's serious decay and growing weakness".

Now looking back, we can see the Amherst Embassy was the very first diplomatic debut of Great Britain as the world's No. 1 hegemon on the global stage, revisiting the former mighty power in the East, the sophisticated civilisation that it had long been meaning to establish equal trading relations with since Queen Elizabeth I back in 1583. From its last attempt a generation ago, the Great Britain was no longer the same power, but the Qing Court remained unchanged, in treating all "others" as tributary kingdoms subject to submission rather than equal and sovereign nations. If there were changes, they were changes for the worse: the changing power balance only gave Qing a stronger sense of defensiveness and assertiveness as they had never faced such a strong rival before. Not surprisingly, even with a star team of 600 members composed of missionaries, diplomats and scholars who were China experts and spoke fluent Mandarin, the Amherst Embassy was still unable to bridge the "communication gap" as there was more than a language barrier in between, but conflicting ideas and world views of how nations should interact with each other. As summarised by Markley (2016: 104), "gaps between Chinese and British ideas of commerce, civility and diplomacy" left the embassy "more sceptical than ever about a dialogue between two equals". Both the Chinese and British thought of themselves as exceptional, each being utterly convinced of their own superiority, the mutual contempt and belief in their own way as the universal way made genuine communication impossible.

With hindsight, we can also see the Amherst Embassy was exactly the midpoint between Macartney's first embassy and the breakout of the First Opium War: 24 years away from both events, coinciding with the evolving image of China from civilised to half-civilised and then uncivilised. Ellis (1817: 429) concluded in his official account that China was undoubtedly "inferior by many degrees to civilised Europe in all that constitutes the real greatness of a nation". As Gao (2020: 78) summarised, "a consensus on the half-civilised image of China was reached by the British observers who participated in the Amherst Embassy and subsequently recorded their opinions of China". The only consensus reached across both sides after the Amherst Embassy was that no more embassies should be dispatched. In the Jiaqing Emperor's letter to Prince Regent dated 11 September 1816, it was stated "henceforward, pray do not trouble to dispatch missions all this distance; they are merely a waste of time and have their journey for nothing. If you loyally accept our sovereignty and show dutiful submission, there is really no need for these yearly appearances at our Court to prove that you are indeed our vassal" (Appendix 7). The British had indeed stopped sending embassies to China as the Amherst report also confirmed the futility of any future diplomatic overtures to achieve British objectives. Its failure accelerated the demystification of China that prepared the way for new hard-line approach to demonstrate British power.

Many scholars, such as Hevia (1995), Gao (2014) and Stevenson (2021) argued that the Amherst Embassy represented a new era in the British relationship with China with a clear set of diplomatic guidelines and notions of international law. I personally do not see much progress made by the embassy in these regards compared with the Macartney Embassy, instead, I see the Amherst Embassy still driven by Britain's ever-expanding demand for commercial growth, which was made quite clear in both its purpose before departure and the China policy adopted after its return. Rather, it was China's reluctance and even hostility to engage in a supposedly mutually beneficial trade agreement that had influenced the development of British notions of international law and foreign intervention, and started a debate on how to adopt new tactics in Britain's management of Chinese affairs and to "open" China.

A legacy of the embassy was that the vessel named after the ambassador, *Lord Amherst*[10], sailed to China in 1832, in a continued mission "to ascertain how far the northern ports of this empire may gradually be opened to British commerce" (Bickers, 2012: 19). It was ordered by the EIC's superintendent at the time, Charles Marjoribanks, who wrote a pamphlet, *Brief Account of the British Character*, assuring the Chinese that "the government of so great an Empire has no thirst for conquest. Its great object and aim is to preserve its subject in a condition of happiness and tranquillity". It was translated into Chinese by Morrison, *Dayingguo Renshi Lueshuo* (《大英国人事略说》), and printed to be distributed as a renewed mission to shape a favourable image of the British. They expected this innovative way to state their case to Beijing if one copy among hundreds could find its way within the walls of the Imperial Palace. However, when it was received by local officials, presented to the Grand Council in Beijing and eventually did land in the hands of the Daoguang Emperor, all the emperor cared to know was how could the Europeans had access to Chinese printing? The emperor's reaction told us that both the priority and attitude of the Qing court towards foreign trade and domestic stability remained unchanged by Daoguang's reign. Consistent policy to isolate its empire from the West, not for seclusion from trade, but more from the western ideas and influence that would penetrate China with exchanges of goods and people, still dominated the Qing mentality. There was a constant distrust of Westerners, who were considered a danger to national security and a threat to Chinese morals, political and domestic harmony.

If the Macartney Embassy had left the gap between the two empires widened as argued in Chapter 5, the effect of the Amherst mission was to change the attitude towards the gap on both sides: from lack of genuine mutual understanding to mutual begrudges. If the Chinese utopia as an exemplary enlightened monarchy was eroded by Macartney's mission, it was further dismantled by the Amherst Embassy. As Kitson summarised (2013: 23), "the allegation that Qing China was politically and economically stagnant, ossified by an inflexible ceremonialism, especially regarding its relations with foreign powers, was apparently confirmed by the accounts of the first two embassies to China". Hevia (1995: 73) even ventured to argue that "China was destroyed in writing well before a single British gun was levelled at a Chinese person". From these accounts, we can see that as England's power was getting stronger and stronger, so did its contempt for China and the Chinese. The dignity of the Great Britain could not tolerate indefinitely the ignorant presumptions of the Chinese, nor the ill-treatment of British subjects at the hands of this arrogant and ramshackle Chinese empire. A new approach was in the making.

Notes

1 From *Lectures on the Philosophy of History,* by Georg Wilhelm Friedrich Hegel (1770–1831), originally given as lectures at the University of Berlin in 1822.
2 This is incorrect. The whole embassy returned to England in September 1794. They even took back a Chinese boy as a companion for the young Staunton to keep learning Chinese. Staunton was appointed a writer to Canton in April 1798 and embarked for China in June 1799. Therefore, it is also incorrect to say that "he has been there for 20 years now".
3 See note 20 in Chapter 4.
4 During the Qianlong Emperor's reception of the Macartney Embassy, he asked if anyone from the embassy can speak Chinese. Staunton, then as a 12-year-old page to the ambassador who learned how to speak the language since age 11 in London and then on the voyage itself, conversed with him in Chinese. The emperor was very delighted and presented the boy with an imperial purse that he was wearing at his side. See Figure 1.7 in Chapter 1. This was considered a special honour as something belonging to the emperor himself. Staunton brought it back to China with him. This was recorded in Anderson's account that they were told about how the emperor thought highly of the young Staunton's talent of speaking six different languages and his appearance, he was presented, with the emperor's own hand, a very beautiful fan, and several small embroidered bags and purses (Wood, 2019: 189).
5 There are different estimates to the cost of the Macartney Embassy. The editor of the abridgment of the late Sir George Staunton's Narrative, 1797, asserted positively that the embassy cost £200,000 (ibid: 31). It was estimated at the cost of £78,000 according to Singer (1992: 6). "This is closer to the £80,000 estimation provided by Barrow in Chapter 5, which includes the gifts but not the cost to the navy of providing the ship".
6 On 18 February 1817, *Alceste* grounded on one of the many hidden reefs in the Java Sea.
7 It is a practice in China's imperial history that the emperors' names need to be either replaced with a different character or written in a special way to avoid a direct reference, which is considered disrespectful.
8 One was deprived of his post of Board President; another was reduced from the rank of Comptroller-General of the Household to that of an official writer of the eighth rank. The other two, both highly placed Manchus, were dismissed from office and sent home.
9 His appointment was recommended by the first ambassador Guo Songtao, so it was not very likely that when he reported back about this finding, Guo would not say anything if he had already known about it.
10 Lord Amherst died in March 1857, aged 84 at Knole House in Kent, the seat of the Dukes of Dorset, where Huang Andong (from Chapter 3) from China was hosted. Amherst's second wife had inherited this property.

References

Abel, C. (1818) *Narrative of a Journey in the Interior of China: And of a Voyage to and from that Country, in the Years 1816 and 1817, Containing an Account of the Most Interesting Transactions of Lord Amherst's Embassy to the Court of Pekin and Observations on the Countries Which It Visited.* London: Longman, Hurst, Rees, Orme, and Brown. Free e-book available at: https://play.google.com/books/reader?id=7kcQAAAAYAAJ&hl=zh_CN&pg=GBS.PA1

A delicate inquiry into the embassies to China, and a legitimate conclusion from the premises, (no author) (1818). London: Thomas and George Underwood & J. M. Richardson.

Allison, G. (2017) *Destined for War*. Melbourne. London: Scribe.

Amherst, W. (1805) 'Notes on policy to be pursued by the British Embassy to China'. in BL IOR MSS EUR F 140/36.

Backhouse, E. and Bland, J.O.P. (1914) *Annals and Memoirs of the Court of Peking*. Boston: Houghton Mifflin.

Barrow, J. (1804) *Travels in China, Containing Descriptions, Observations, and Comparisons, Made and Collected in the Course of a Short Residence at the Imperial Palace of Yuen-min-yuen, and on a Subsequent Journey Through the Country from Pekin to Canton. In which It Is Attempted to Appreciate the Rank that this Extraordinary Empire May be Considered to Hold in the Scale of Civilised Nations*. London, England: A. Straham, or T. Cadell and W. Davies.

Barrow, J. (1807). *Some Account of the Public Life, and a Selection from the Unpublished Writings, of the Earl of Macartney*. Cambridge: Cambridge University Press.

Barrow, J. (1817) *Embassy to China. Chinese Travel, Life and Customs. A Review with Textual Excerpts*. Published by Quarterly Review. London: John Murray.

Barrow, J. (1821) 'Review of 'Narrative of the Chinese embassy to the Khan of the Tourgouth Tartars, in the years 1712, 13, 14, and 15' by the Chinese ambassador, and published by the emperor's authority at Pekin. Translated from the Chinese by Sir George Thomas Staunton', *Quarterly Review*, 25, pp. 414–426.

Berg, M. (2010) 'Britain's Asian century: Porcelain and global history in the long eighteenth century', in Cruz, L., Mokyr, J. (eds) *The Birth of Modern Europe, Culture and Economy, 1400–1800*. Leiden: Brill, pp. 133–156.

Bickers, R. (2012) *The Scramble for China, Foreign Devils in the Qing Empire, 1832–1819*. London: Penguin Books.

Cranmer-Byng, J.L. (1962) *An Embassy to China, Being the Journal Kept by Lord Macartney During His Embassy to the Emperor Ch'ien-lung 1793–1794*. London: Longmans.

Da Qing Renzong Rui (Jiaqing) Huangdi Shilu, (no author) (1964).《大清仁宗睿嘉庆皇帝实录》*[Veritable Records of the Qing Dynasty, Jiaqing's Reign]*. Taipei: Taiwan Huawen Shuju.

Davis, J.F. (1836) *The Chinese: A General Description of the Empire of China and Its Inhabitants*, Vols. I & II. London: Charles Knight & Co.

Davis, J.F. (1841) *Sketches of China; Party During an Inland Journey of Four Months between Peking, Nanking, and Canton, with Notices and Observations Relative to the Present War*. Two volumes. London: Charles Knight & Co.

Ellis, H. (1817) *Journal of the Proceedings of the Late Embassy to China*. London: printed for John Murray.

Ellis, H. (1830) *A Series of Letters on the East India Question. Addressed to the Members of the Two Houses of Parliament by Henry Ellis, Third Commissioner of the Late Embassy to China, Letter I* (2nd ed.). London, England: John Murray.

Fu, L.-S. (1966) *A Documentary Chronicle of Sino-Western Relations (1644–1820)*, 2 vols. Tucson: University of Arizona Press.

Gao, H. (2014) 'The Amherst embassy and British discoveries in China', *History*, 99(337), Oct., pp. 568–587.

Gao, H. (2020) *Creating The Opium War, British Imperial Attitudes Towards China, 1792–1840*. Manchester: Manchester University Press.

Gelber, H. (2008) *The Dragon and the Foreign Devils: China and the World, 1100 B.C. to the Present*. London: Bloomsbury.

Hargrave, J. (2016) 'Marco Polo and the emergence of British sinology', *SEL Studies in English Literature, 1500–1900*, 56(3) (Summer), pp. 515–537.

Hegel, G.W.F. (1956) *Philosophy of History*, translated by Sibree, J. New York: Dover Publications Inc.

Hegel, G.W.F. (1975) *Lectures on the Philosophy of World History: Introduction: Reason in History*, translated by Nisbet, H.B.. Cambridge: Cambridge University Press.

Hevia, J. (1995) *Cherishing Men from Afar, Qing Guest Ritual and the Macartney Embassy of 1793*. Durham and London: Duke University Press.

Hibbert, C. (1970) *The Dragon Wakes, China and the West, 1793–1911*. London: Longman.

Huang, Y.-L. (2007) 'Impression Vs. reality, A study on the guest ritual controversy between Qing China and Britain', *Bulletin of Institute of History and Philology, Academia Sinica*, 78(1), pp. 35–106.

Kentish, W. A. (1840) *Hudibrastic History of Amherst's Embassy to China*, Kentish. London: Davis & Co. Historical Collection from the British Library.

Kitson, P. (2013) *Forging Romantic China, Sino-British Cultural Exchange 1760–1840*. Cambridge: Cambridge University Press.

Kitson, P. (2016) 'The dark gift: Opium, John Francis Davis, Thomas De Quincey and the Amherst Embassy to China of 1816', in Kitson Peter, J., Markley, R. (eds.) *Writing China, Essays on the Amherst Embassy (1816) and Sino-British Cultural Relations*. Cambridge: D.S. Brewer.

Letter from Amherst to George Canning, 8 March 1817, British Library, London: India Office Records (hereafter IOR), G/12/197, f. 281.

Markley, R. (2016) 'The Amherst embassy in the shadow of Tambora: Climate and culture, 1816', in Kitson Peter J., Markley, R. (eds.) *Writing China, Essays on the Amherst Embassy (1816) and Sino-British cultural relations*, pp. 83–104. Cambridge: D.S. Brewer.

Martin, R.M. (1832) *Past and Present State of the Tea Trade*. London: Parbury, Allen & Co.

Martin, R.M. (1847) *China: Political, Commercial, Social*; in an official report to Her Majesty's Government (Vols. 1–2). London: James Madden.

Matheson, J. (1836) *The Present Position and Prospects of the British Trade with China*. London: Smith, Elder, and Co.

McDonough, F. (1994) *The British Empire, 1815–1914*. London: Hodder Education.

McLeod, J. (1817) *Narrative of a Voyage, In His Majesty's Late Ship Alceste to The Yellow Sea, along The Coast of Corea, and Through its Numerous Hitherto Undiscovered Islands, to the Island of Lewchew*. London: John Murray.

Min, E.K. (2004) 'Narrating the Far East: Commerce, civility and ceremony in the Amherst Embassy to China (1816–1817)', *Studies in Voltaire and the Eighteenth Century*, pp. 160–180.

Morrison, R. (1820) *A Memoir of the Principal Occurrences During an Embassy from the British Government to the Court of China in the Year 1816*. London: Free e-book. Available at: https://play.google.com/books/reader?id=Dr1XAAAAcAAJ&hl=zh_CN&pg=GBS.PA1

Morse, H.B. (1926) *The Chronicles of the East India Company Trading to China, 1635–1834*. London: Oxford University Press. Digitalised version available at: https://www.univie.ac.at/Geschichte/China-Bibliographie/blog/2018/05/20/morse-the-chronicles-of-the-east-india-company-trading-to-china-1635-1834/

O'Meara, B. (1822) *Napoleon in Exile, or A Voice from St. Helena*. London: printed for W. Simpkin and R. Marshall.

Percy, T. (1761) *Hau Kiou Choaan: Or Pleasing History*. London: R. and J. Dodsley.

Peyrefitte, A. (1992) *The Immobile Empire*, translated by Rothschild J. New York: Alfred Knopf.

Platt, S.R. (2018) *Imperial Twilight: The Opium War and the End of China's Last Golden Age*. London: Atlantic Books.

Pomeranz, K. (2000) *The Great Divergence.* Princeton: Princeton University Press.

Price, B. (2019) *The Chinese in Britain, A History of Visitors and Settlers.* Gloucestershire: Amberley Publishing.

Rockhill, W.W. (1897) 'Diplomatic missions to the Court of China: The Kotow Question II', *The American Historical Review*, 2(4) (Jul.), pp. 627–643. Published by: Oxford University Press on behalf of the American Historical Association Stable Available at: https://www.jstor.org/stable/1833980

Rowe, W.T. (2011) 'Introduction: The significance of the Qianlong-Jiaqing transition in Qing history', *Late Imperial China*, 32(2), pp. 74–88.

Singer, A. (1992) *The Lion and the Dragon: The Story of the First British Embassy to the Court of the Emperor Qianlong in Peking 1792–94*. London: Barrie & Jenkins.

Soothill, W.E. (2009) *China and the West: A Short History of Their Contact from Ancient Times to the Fall of the Manchu Dynasty*. Yardley: Westholme.

Staunton, G.T. (1810) *Ta Tsing Leu Lee, Being the Fundamental Laws, and a Selection from the Supplementary Statutes, of the Penal Code of China; Originally Printed and Published in Pekin, in Various Successive Editions, under the Sanction, and by the Authority, of the Several Emperors of the Ta Tsing, or Present Dynasty*. London: Printed for T. Cadell and W. Davies.

Staunton, G.T. (1824) *Notes of Proceedings and Occurrences During the British Embassy to Pekin in 1816*. London, England: Henry Skelton (for private circulation only).

Staunton, G.T. (1856) *Memoirs of the Chief Incident of the Public Life of Sir George Thomas Staunton,* BART. London: L. Booth, 307 Regent Street.

Stevenson, C.M. (2021) *Britain's Second Embassy to China, Lord Amherst's Special Mission to the Jiaqing Emperor in 1816*. Acton: Australian National University Press.

Tuck, P. (2000) 'Introduction', in Staunton, G.T. (ed.) *Notes of Proceedings and Occurrences, During the British Embassy to Pekin, in 1816* (Reprint, pp. vii–xlii). London, England: Routledge. (Original work published 1824).

Waley-Cohen, J. (2000) *Sextants of Beijing, Global Currents in Chinese History*. New York: Norton.

Wang, W. (2014) *White Lotus Rebels and South China Pirates: Crisis and Reform in the Qing Empire*. London: Harvard University Press.

Wong, L.W.-C. (2010) 'I Am to Wear a Vice-consul's Coat, with King's Buttons',

The Political Translation of Robert Morrison, *Compilation and Translation Review*, 3(1) (March), pp. 1–40.

Wood, H.J. (1940) 'England, China and the Napoleonic Wars', *Pacific Historical Review*, 9, pp. 139–156.

Wood, F. (ed.) (2019) *Aeneas Anderson in China, A Narrative of the Ill-fated Macartney Embassy 1792–94*. Hong Kong: Earnshaw Books Ltd.

Xue, F. (2008) (《出使英法意比四國日記》) [*Journal of Missions to Britain, France, Italy and Belgium*]. Changsha: Yuelu Publishing House.

Zhang, L. (1998) *Mighty Opposites, From Dichotomies to Differences in the Comparative Study of China*. Stanford: Stanford University Press.

7 From the Tea War to the Opium War

Using a polished bronze as the mirror, we can see if we have dressed properly or not; using people as a mirror, we can see our loss and gain; using history as a mirror, we see the rise and fall of a nation.

– the Tang Emperor Li Shimin

As explained in Chapter 6, the reason why the British agreed to continue to "play by Chinese rules" after the Amherst Embassy was because their primary commercial concern was a steady supply of high-quality tea from China. Tea's ubiquity today makes it hard to recapture its allure for eighteenth century British, to whom tea was not just a drink, but an embodiment of an ancient virtue culture, an exotic novelty to lovers of luxury, an elegant enhancer for social intercourse, an object of curiosity for scholars of botany and medicine, a target of loaded debates between Sinophile and Sinophobia, and of course, a commodity of immense interest to merchants due to its high profit. Its trade "established transglobal connections between two imperial civilisations" (Ellis et al., 2015: 136). The mysterious contexts within which tea was cultivated, harvested and manufactured made it a peculiar element in the fashion for Chinoiserie. Therefore, "tea drinking is a paradigmatic case of a cultural phenomenon in which economics and performativity are inextricably bound up with representation and self-presentation" (Pointon, 1997: 28). Ray (2016: 260–261) summarised it as a botanical exotic that "ornamentalize the body and its social space", "a beverage that had a profound impact upon taste, style, and sociability at the same time that it spurred on imperial ambitions played out in the global corridors of commerce". Since Britain depended on the opium trade to fund its purchase of tea, Davis (1836: 518) noted in the *Quarterly Review* for July 1836 that "it is a curious circumstance that we grow the poppy in our Indian territories to poison the people of China, in return for a wholesome beverage which they prepare, almost exclusively, for us". Ellis et al. (2015: 219) described it incisively as "a system of money laundering by which the profits of the opium trade were superficially cleansed – ethically, morally, politically – through the sanative leaves of

DOI: 10.4324/9781003156383-8

Chinese tea". From the story of tea and opium we can see some peculiar similarities of the main commodities at both ends of the trade scale between China and Britain: they were both "addictive" intakes except that the tea was a gentle, nourishing and healthy panacea while opium was baneful narcotic; they both started as an exotic luxury that were only consumed by the high class, and for the British, "smuggling arguably had a greater impact on the nationwide uptake of tea in the period 1720–1780 than the East India Company itself" and brought the commodity within the reach of working families (Ellis et al., 2015: 177), so both countries had to tackle the rampant smuggling problem when the consumption of tea and opium had grown so rapidly. Most importantly, both tea and opium have a lasting legacy in the two countries identity – Britain as a tea-drinking nation and China's long struggle to rebuild itself from being the "sick man of Asia".

7.1 The story of tea and opium

The eighth-century Chinese sage Lu Yu wrote in his *Classic of Tea* (*Chajing,* 《茶经》, 760–780 BCE) that "tea, used as a drink, was first discovered by the Emperor Shen Nung" (Magic Farmer), a legendary ruler of China dated to 2737–2698 BCE. The most important statement of the new English knowledge of tea was offered by the clergyman John Ovington who published *An Essay upon the Nature and Qualities of Tea* in 1699. This could be called an English version of "ode to tea" by "combining the available commercial, natural, philosophical, medical and moral discourse .... For Ovington, tea itself is civilised and civilizing" (Ellis et al., 2015: 76–77). In Martin's (1832: 196) romantic description, "this innutritious leaf" was "cultivated on the hills of a distant continent, and manufactured by a people almost isolated from the rest of the world", "the introduction of this beverage to England, has materially contributed to improve the morals and health of the nation at large, by superseding in a great measure, the immoderate drinking of spirituous, vinous, and other fermented potations, while its use as a tonic is strongly conductive to health and longevity". These writings elevated and glorified tea by consolidating its association with elite culture, further re-imagining it as a prestigious product in a spiritual dimension.

As mentioned in Chapter 2, the first written record of an Englishman drinking a cup of tea was given by Peter Mundy in 1637, when tea was not on the shopping list of the EIC at the time. It is interesting to note that the Portuguese word for tea is "cha", exactly the same spelling as it is in Chinese, while the French and English word of thé and tea were based on the Fujian pronunciation where tea is produced. In the first advertisement by a London coffee house in 1658, tea was introduced as an "excellent and by all Physicians, approved, China drink, called by the Chinese Tcha, by other nations, Tay alia Tee, is sold at the Sultaness Head Coffee-House, in Sweetings Rents, by the Royal Exchange

London" (Honour, 1961: 51; Price, 2019: 11). The nation's love for tea started to develop after the marriage of princess Catherine of Portugal, to Charles II in 1661. Having been accustomed to drinking tea in her own country, Catherine's passion, and even addiction to tea eventually created a fad for the drink at the royal court. The king and his queen often held tea parties. This was celebrated in the following line in a birthday ode on her Majesty by Waller: (cited in Martin, 1832: 17)

> The best of queens and best of herbs we owe,
> To that bold nation, who the way did show,
> To the fair region – where the sun doth rise,
> Whose rich productions we so justly prize.

The EIC's first invoice of tea was received in 1669, and it was until 1694, when *the Dorothy* became the first English ship to set out from London with a specific instruction to buy tea in China, but imports of tea by the EIC remained small and sporadic throughout the 1690s. (Ellis et al., 2015: 37). By 1702, tea featured more prominently in many China trade itineraries, and by 1725, it displaced silk as the primary object of trade with China (Platt, 2018: 11), thus the largest contributor to the national revenue. With Pitt's Commutation Acts of 1784, tea became the great commercial success story: The gross weight of tea sold in 1784 nearly doubled that of 1783, even though the legislation had only become law halfway through the year. By the 1820s, Britain had identified itself as "a tea-drinking nation" (Kippis, 1825: 515) where tea became closely associated with the British way of life, transcending distinctions of social class, national geography and cultural background. Total imports of tea from China grew from 21b 2 oz in 1664 to nearly 6 million pounds in 1783, and hence to 30 million pounds in the 1830s. Drinking tea became a symbol of elegance and the most conspicuous Chinese import in the English households, leading to the "rapid emergence of ritualised tea-drinking as a national pastime at every level of society" (Porter, 2010: 18). Compared with the maritime silk road between China and Europe where the main commodities traded from China were silk, porcelain and lacquer, the British trade route with China can be better described as the "maritime tea road" as the bedrock of the British trade with China was tea, and no other European nations had such an insatiable appetite for tea than the British.

However, since there was no mass market for English goods in China (also in Indian) to balance the trade, the difference can only be made up by a large export of silver. In 1786, Britain purchased £1,300,000 worth of tea in Canton, and paid out for nearly half of this in silver bullion rather than other export goods (Furber, 1976; Cheung and Mui, 1968). In 1788, when a former EIC director wrote that tea was already the "food of the whole people of Great Britain" (Huw, 2006: 241), Joseph Banks, the botanist and longtime president of the Royal Society, suggested tea transplantation in Bengal and Calcutta to Sir Francis Baring at the EIC, believing that Bengal, "blessed with advantages of soil climate & population", would yield a "tribute" that "binds itself to the mother country by the strongest & most indissoluble of human ties that of common interest & mutual advantage" (cited in Kitson, 2013: 140). It is most interesting that he adopted and applied the word "tribute" to the colonial relationship of Bengal to Britain. This brilliant idea of transplanting tea plant to establish a native tea industry at its colony would have solved Britain's trade deficit problem with China once and for all. As explained in Chapter 5, during Macartney's overland journey through the mountains beyond Hangzhou, he already tried to take some young tea plants to Bengal. Unfortunately, this plan did not work out, as the two botanical gardeners failed to provide detailed notes on the plants in their growing habitat, which rendered the dried specimens virtually useless. Then the specimens collected by the Amherst Embassy were lost in the shipwreck on its return voyage in 1817. By 1830, the number of chests of tea imported each year had risen to approach twenty thousand, an amount before long to be doubled, trebled and quadrupled (Hibbert, 1970: 83). Paying for it became all the more difficult as China's import of British goods, such as raw cotton, was far from enough to counterbalance Chinese exports of tea, silk and porcelain. The trade scale was tipped to an unsustainable level that the British started to balance it out by trading opium. According to Waley-Cohen (2000: 102), opium grown in Britain's Indian colonies could be sold in Canton for three times the initial cost. When exporting opium to China emerged as an effective way of returning the vast amounts of silver bullion, the EIC no longer had an urgent incentive to develop an alternative Indian source of tea. So for nearly two centuries' time, the only place in the world where the British could obtain their tea was from China, until 1839, when the very first Indian tea was sold on the British market. The majority of surviving trade cards from the late eighteenth century made use of a series of stock images representing oriental gardens, pagodas, harbours, junks and Chinese labourers (see Figure 7.1).[1]

During this period of time, tea had been transformed "from a fashionable and expensive luxury ...... into an essential comfort, if not an absolute necessary of life" that had "descended from the palace to the cottage" (Smith, 1826, cited in Kitson, 2013: 78), no longer bearing the exclusive stamp of the exotic. However, it was still a culturally embedded object that was imbricated in extremely complex ways with the prestige of Chinese culture, thus bred some intolerable views of seeing tea as an import from China to become an icon of English identity in the eyes of Sinophobia. In 1756, Hanway wrote an *Essay on Tea,* claiming that tea was a "Chinese drug", an "intoxicating liquor", and a "slow poison", therefore, the consumption of tea was "an epidemic disease" and "universal infection", the "habit reconciles us to tea as it does Turks to

Figure 7.1 Tea Trade Card. Courtesy of the British Library.

opium" and made the British "act more wantonly and absurdly than the Chinese themselves" (cited in Jenkins, 2013: 105–106). One anonymous British pamphleteer in 1777 also condemned tea, along with sugar, butter and other "modern luxuries" as "being the foundation of almost all the poverty, and all the evils which affect the labouring part of mankind ….. It unstrings the nerves, it unbraces the constitution, dissolves nature and destroys the Englishman" (cited in Platt, 2018: 195). Then following the two failed embassies and the resultant reversal of cultural superiority, the British had redefined its national beverage as "British tea", being too proud to acknowledge its Chinese origin to the point that today, many British people thought tea originally came from India. The journey from Chinese tea to British tea was a fascinating way to see the intertwined fate of the two tea-drinking nations that both take pride in tea as a representation of a sophisticated culture and lifestyle, and the fact that the tea tariff in Britain covered one-half the expenses of maintaining the best naval fleet in the world (Fay, 1998) further complicated the intertwined fate of the two empires.

The opium solution soon evolved from being a means to stop silver drain to revenue gain for the British. Until the early nineteenth century, the balance of international trade was decisively in China's favour. By 1828, the balance had shifted when more silver left China than came in. "Chinese exports of tea doubled between 1813 and 1833, and imports of opium quadrupled" (Peyrefitte, 1992: 519). By the 1830s, the imbalance in silver bullion export between Britain and China had been drastically reversed, "with a surplus in the Company's favour of around £38 million and something like 40,000 chests of opium per annum exported into China by the end of that decade" (Kitson, 2016: 62). In this process of rapid growth, smoking opium in China was also quickly transformed "from an elite, sophisticated cultural practice into a more popular pastime" (ibid: 64). For centuries, at least since the early eighth century when the opium-producing poppy had been introduced into China by the Turks and Arabs, opium had been eaten raw as a medicine, but it was not until the early seventeenth century that the Chinese began to mix it with tobacco and smoke it. At first demand for it was small, and even by 1750 fewer than four hundred chests were imported annually. The British policy of using opium instead of silver to pay for Chinese tea was just beginning to take off at the time of the Macartney Embassy in 1792–1793. Macartney received clear instructions that if the emperor asked for Britain's support in cutting down the opium traffic, then he should agree to do so "rather than risk any essential benefit" (Morse, 1926, vol. 2: 239), showing the position of the British government at that time. For the Chinese authorities, the rising opium consumption created not only social and health problems, but also a growing silver drain from the Chinese economy. As early as 1729 an Imperial edict had forbidden the sale and consumption of the drug, and one of the Jiaqing Emperor's first acts was to repeat his father's prohibition, to declare opium contraband, and outlaw its importation and domestic cultivation. However, the Amherst Embassy reported that while opium did not seem to be sold openly in Chinese shops, it was in use, smoked with tobacco, "in all parts of the empire" and was considered "one of the greatest luxuries" (Morrison, 1819: 197; Abel, 1818: 213–214).

As explained in Chapter 4, demands for Chinese goods was also adversely affected by the waning of the European craze for Chinoiserie from its mid-eighteenth century peak, while by the 1820s, there was a consumer fashion for Euroiserie products in China – glass, clocks, furs, which were highly sought after and highly profitable with the label of "Western" attached to them. In 1833, with the abolishment of the EIC's monopoly, the doctrine of free trade was fast becoming the dominant political-economic ideology in Britain, with immediate effect of having far more foreign traders participate in the China trade. When China experienced a complete reversal of its economic prosperity, it was also when the trade war over tea started to evolve into a military war over opium that completely changed modern Chinese and world history. As Morse (1910: Vol. I: 229) summarised, up to 1839, it was China which dictated to the West the terms on which relations should be permitted to exist; after the second Opium War in 1860, it was the West which had imposed on China the conditions of their common intercourse. But, were the two opium wars really fought for the opium?

7.2 The rhetoric war and trade war

It may be impossible to clearly mark the scales of development levels across the spectrum of civilisations, but assuming that there was only a binary division between "civilised" and "barbarous" nations was simply crude and conflict-ridden, especially when both empires adopted such a binary view and each claimed to be the definition of civilisation. With what can we draw the line? In an essay entitled "Civilisation", Mill (1859) put forward reciprocity as the distinguisher as "barbarians will not reciprocate. They cannot be depended on for observing any rules" (cited in Mantena, 2010: 120). Pitts (2010: 67) suggested that the notion of a capacity for reciprocity and mutual respect came to play a central role in the construction of ostensible standards for inclusion in the international society. However, this notion itself is disputable as both empires held a different understanding of what reciprocity means as the principle of country-to-country relations. Even today, dictionaries offer different interpretations of the term: reciprocity means "a situation in which two groups agree to help each other by *behaving in the same way or by giving each other similar advantages*" according to the *Cambridge Dictionary*, while the *Oxford Dictionary* defines it as "the practice of *exchanging things with others for mutual benefit*, especially privileges granted by one country or organization to another". The underlying assumptions are quite different: the former is suggesting relations between two countries are like two companies that want the same things (profit), so they would behave in the same way of pursing profit, while the latter suggests reciprocity is achieved by "exchanging" different things to meet different needs, like a traditional marriage relationship, between a man and a woman who have different things to offer and want different things in return. A healthy and long-lasting marriage relationship is not built on sameness but on Yin-Yang harmony. Therefore, in this sense, reciprocity could also be reached through an exchange of two inequalities under the Tributary System: gain of "face" for the Chinese empire is exchanged with the financial gains for those tributary states. If equality has to be the cornerstone in this debate, then we need to be reminded that although the notion of international law goes hand in hand with sovereign equality, when the phrase was coined by Jeremy Bentham in the 1830s, "international law" was not based on equality between nations, but operated on an "eligible membership" based on "the conviction of Europe's unique moral and political achievements" (Pitts, 2010: 82), or a hierarchical global order linked to the same divisions between "civilised" and "uncivilised". Therefore, even though the traditional Chinese Tributary System was projected to be the opposite of the centrality of international law, both showed the same void at the essence – the lack of equality, and the shared vision of superiority rules over inferiority.

When two versions of empire, trade, and reciprocity collided, the Chinese side seemed to emerge victorious until the Jiaqing Emperor's reign.

When Staunton discovered in Chinese documents in 1814 that the Chinese used the word *Manyi* (southern and eastern barbarians, 蛮夷) to refer to the British in official communications, they filed a "petition" to the local magistrate, arguing that the designation "seemed to be pejorative". The Canton local authorities replied that it was the "general name for foreigners" and there was nothing pejorative about it, but the British as the principal European industrial, financial and naval power now, could no longer accept something simply because it had been accepted by "all others". This was the earliest record found of the British protesting on the naming issue (Chen, 2017: 84). The Macartney Embassy disputed the use of *Gong* (tribute) while the Amherst Embassy started the dispute of *Yi* (barbarian), and as discussed in Chapter 6, the time from the first to the second embassy and then to the breakout of the First Opium War coincided with the evolving images of China from civilised to half-civilised and eventually uncivilised. Actually, in the famous impeachment trial of Warren Hastings that lasted from 1787–1795, aggression and condescension of the West (Europe) towards the East (Asia) was already asserted in the name of civilisation. Along with their industrial and technological superiority, the British became more and more assertive and belligerent. By Queen Victoria's reign, her vision of the global order was also bifocal in separating the "civilised" from the "uncivilised" sphere, believing that reciprocal economic and political relations were only considered appliable among those "civilised" nations. If China had projected a Sino-centric worldview onto the British through its treatment of the two embassies, by now, the British had projected a Euro-centric worldview to the Chinese.

However, since defining civilisation was itself a contested and political process, the distinction between the civilised and uncivilised societies and China's status in this new international law framework dominated scholarly debates in Britain in the second half of the nineteenth century. One way to draw the line was whether the countries adhered to Western standards of law, diplomacy and trade relations (Pitts, 2010). John Quincy Adams castigated China, by shutting out European trade and enclosing themselves behind the high walls of exclusion, had violated the law of nations that imposed a "moral obligation" on countries to facilitate commercial intercourse, thus was "anti-commerce and immoral, an enormous outrage upon the rights of human nature, and upon the first principle of the rights of nations" (cited in Gelber, 2008: 188). In other words, China's refusal to grant an open door policy became a symbol of the nation's "uncivilised" nature. It may surprise many Chinese readers that both Karl Marx and Friedrich Engels had used "semi-barbarian" and "semicivilisation" to describe China in a series of articles (written in English) for the *New York Daily Tribune* in the 1850s. Even though Marx granted the moral high ground to the Chinese in their efforts to ban the importation of opium, he believed the empire's "dissolution must follow as surely as that of any mummy carefully preserved in a hermetically sealed coffin, whenever it is brought into contact with the open air" (June 14, 1853), and that China was a "semi-barbarian" society "contriving to dupe itself with delusions of Celestial perfection" (September 25, September 20, 1858). The harshness of this language is echoed by Engels, who, while denounced British imperialism, described China as "the rotting semicivilisation of the oldest State in the world" (May 22, 1857).

However, a counter argument was put forward by EIC's Court of Directors, who used China's peculiar culture to argue for China's exceptionalism from the universal law of free trade. Robert Montgomery Martin (1832: 214), who later served as Colonial Treasurer of Hong Kong from 1844 to 1845, wrote that "we cannot, in fairness, deny to China the right which our own nation exercises as she sees fit, either by prohibiting, restraining, or subjecting to certain laws and regulations its commercial dealings with other countries. China must be considered free in the exercise of her affairs, without being accountable to any other nation". He viewed China as an empire blessed "within its own territories all the necessaries and conveniences, and most of the luxuries of life; standing, as it proudly asserts, in no need of intercourse with other countries, which openly and arrogantly proclaims its total independence of every nation in the world" (ibid: 1–2). He further argued that "freedom in politics, and freedom in commerce, are two distinct things; ...... and that, although political liberty is essentially requisite in domestic commerce, and highly advantageous in foreign trade, particularly for a manufacturing community such as that of England, yet, that it is not considered paramountly necessary by every nation", thus relations with China can only be improved by "evincing a disposition to respect their regulations" (ibid: 5). This is the type of "local knowledge" China was hoping to be produced by the resident business community in China, to see China as it is, as a difference to respect, not a flaw to correct. However, these "local knowledge" was held to be mere arguments to justify EIC's monopoly and was challenged by the free traders, who pointed to the Qing government's xenophobic and prejudiced policy as an obstacle to remove to allow free communications between the two peoples.

Other people outside the merchants' community pointed out the hypocrisy of the discourse of civilisation as a replacement of an older religious rhetoric of exclusion: "the modern term is more vague, more elastic, more unjust, and it serves to deprive the Chinese of the rights of international law and its mutual obligations, equally with the Feejee Islanders, or other cannibals" (Stanley, 1865: 115). How can it be justly claimed that a nation like China that has enjoyed longstanding sophistication and maintained a regularly administered government for thousands of years, over millions of people is uncivilised? But similarly, given the prior European discourse of civilisation that posited centrally in the British encounter with the "barbarians" in the New World, how can it be justly claimed that Britain itself to be still called *Yi*, the barbarians?

As explained in Chapter 2, the notion of *Yi* also needs to be understood as an evolving and historically contested concept that was based on China's centrality as a civilisation. In the first English Dictionary of the Chinese Language compiled by Robert Morrison in 1815 (vol. 1: 151), the translation of *Yi* was "Foreigners on [in] the east; foreigners generally ...... a foreigner". The first person who translated it as "barbarian" in 1830s was Karl Gutzlaff, the missionary interpreter for the then EIC supercargo, Hugh Hamilton Lindsay, who refused to accept the Chinese explanation that *Yi* only means "foreigner" since the ancient times, and put forward a very telling counterargument that Great Britain possessed colonial territories lying to the east, west, south and north of the Qing empire, thus could not be put on a par with other tributary states. "When you apply the word *Yi* to the subjects of Great Britain, you are humiliating the timian (face) of our country, offending its people, and provoking anger and retaliation" (cited in Liu, 2006: 44). This brought out the true stakes of the dispute, which was about dignity and power of the British Empire. Peter Perring Thoms, who worked as a printer and translator in Macau from 1814, published two essays in the *Monthly Magazine,* protesting the arguments advanced by Lindsay. He pointed out that during his period in Canton in the early 1800s, the word *Yi* was regularly used in the Qing communication system as a general term for Europeans. What government would use "barbarians" in its official document? He also quoted Hoppo's reaction that *Yi* has been in use "for more than thirty years. It did not commence today. If the term is considered ignominious, why did not the former *Barbarian* [the irony and italics intended by Thoms] merchants early indulge their anger, and with hearts dead to the subject, cease to come again to knock heads at the service for an open market?" (Thoms, 1853: 4). In the Preface to his book *The Fan-Gui in China in 1836–7,* Charles Toogood Downing, who travelled to China in the 1830s and worked there as a surgeon, explained that "many persons maybe puzzled to understand the meaning of the word Fan-Gui. Those who have been to China will comprehend it well enough, as they must often have heard it applied to themselves. It literally signifies "barbarian wanderer" or "outlandish demon", but having been so long accustomed to the epithet, and hearing it so often pounced, we are willing to hope that it is now generally used without intention to insult, and may be fairly translated 'foreigner'" (Downing, 1838: 1).

The ending of EIC's monopoly in 1833 escalated the issue of *Yi* when the supercargo was replaced by a resident superintendent of trade as a government official appointed by London. This was of enormous consequences. What chiefly drove the ending of the monopoly was the transference of control over the nation's economic policy from the king's hand to those of parliament, which viewed the EIC as a commercial device that only benefited the largest merchants. So the chief representative of British interests in China now spoke for his country rather than only for the company, thus an insult to the British trade superintendent was now a matter of state. But the Qing did not clearly grasp this distinction. For them, trade had flourished under the existing system for over a century: they saw no need for the change of the Canton System, nor the end of the EIC's monopoly. But the first chief superintendent, Lord William Napier, wanted a complete change as he found it absurd for a representative of the British crown to be treated as an "outside barbarian", who could only approach the Chinese authorities in Beijing by missives labelled "petition" and channelled through the Hong merchants. He ignored the Chinese protocol by making an unannounced arrival in Canton when he arrived in China in July 1834. This greatly disturbed the provincial government who stated that it was a well-known fact that all foreigners must receive a passport before proceeding to Canton. The Chinese had never allowed an official of a foreign government to reside within its territory, and they were not about to change the thousand-year-old tradition for one obnoxious man. Napier refused to follow the Chinese regulation, he was particularly offended when he found out from Morrison that his name was translated into two characters of Lao Bei (劳卑), which means "labour" and "humble"; and his official title, Chief Superintendent of British Trade in China, was translated into *Yimu* (夷目), which literally means "the barbarian eye". Staunton, who had been a *Yimu* himself in Canton in the 1810s and returned to Britain by now, criticised Morrison's translation as it "tends to widen the breach between us and the Chinese" (Staunton, 1836: 90). He contested Morrison by quoting from his own dictionary that had translated *Yi* as "foreigner" and "*Mu*, the eye; that which directs; the head or principal person" (ibid: 37). Staunton thus concluded that the title was fairly translated as the back translation of *Yimu* should be "the head or Foreign Principal".[2]

Indeed, it is the translator's responsibility to find the equivalent, not just in meaning, but also in register and contextual complexities. It is intriguing why Morrison changed his own earlier translation of *Yi* as "foreigner" in his Dictionary to "barbarian". Thoms (1853: 21) suspected that Morrison must have been acting "under authority and not in compliance with his usual judgment" in applying this offensive term. It was especially offensive to the British as the English word "barbarian" was an excessive translation from a loanword of Latin and Greek roots and developed as a colonial discourse for centuries. When the British colonial officials came to China with the new knowledge and pride in their further developed superiority in technology and power, they could not but see the absurdity of being referred to as a "barbarian small island nation" (*ququ daoyi,* 区区岛夷) by the "grand and magnificent Qing" (*yangyang DaQing*, 泱泱大清). This was fully expressed in Napier's virtual declaration of war on September 8, 1834:

> His Majesty, the King of England, is a great and powerful monarch, that he rules over an extent of territory in the four quarters of the world more comprehensive in space, and infinitely more so in power, than the whole empire of China; that he commands armies of bold and fierce soldiers, who have conquered wherever they went; and that he is possessed of great ships of war carrying even as many as 120 guns, which pass quietly along the seas, where no native of China has ever yet dared to show his face (Chinese Repository 3, No. 6, October 1834: 286).

This put the British Empire in direct comparison with the Chinese Empire "in space" and "in power", its "extent of territory in the four quarters" of the physical world was beyond the vision of the Chinese emperor who still believed in his "extent of influence beyond the four seas" in the imagined *Tianxia*. The Napier incident marked an open conflict between mutual otherness triggered by the new translation of *Yi* in English. It appeared 21 times in the *Correspondence Relating to China* that was presented to the Houses of Parliament in 1840 (Basu, 2014: 934), and in the documents dealing with the Napier episode that were translated by the staff at the Superintendent's office in Canton, "Barbarian Eye" and "Barbarian Merchants" appeared altogether 87 times. Medhurst urged the British authorities to impress on the Chinese government that the term *Yi* be permanently discontinued from official use. Such a measure, he hoped, would help remove "the unhappy impression of our inferiority and *obnoxious* character, now so deeply rooted in the Chinese mind" (Medhurst and Thoms, 1852: 14–15, italics in original). His hope became reality in 1858 when there was a special article stated in the *Treaty of Tianjin*: "It is agreed that, henceforward, the character 'I' 夷[barbarian], shall not be applied to the Government or subjects of Her Britannic Majesty in any Chinese official document issued by the Chinese Authorities either in the Capital or in the Provinces" (Liu, 2006: 32). The *Treaty of Tianjin* also specified that "all official communications addressed by the diplomatic and consular agents to the Chinese authorities shall, henceforth, be written in English",[3] and that while the *Treaty* was still accompanied by a Chinese version, which was prepared and provided by the British, "in the event of there being any difference between the English and the Chinese text, the English government will hold the sense as expressed in the English to be the correct sense".

After the ban on the word *Yi* in 1858, it was gradually replaced by "ocean" (*Yang*, 洋), "the west" (*Xi*, 西), and "outside" (*Wai*, 外) to form compounds in designating Westerners and things from the West. Its significance was much more symbolic than the linguistic sense. *Yang* still had both a geographical connotation and a culturally charged meaning, only that it now represented modernity and superiority. However, the hardship caused by the Opium Wars, treaty privileges and Western imperialism led to the increased resentment that ordinary Chinese people felt towards the presence of Westerners – they were called by a new name of *Yang Guizi* (ocean ghosts/foreign devils, 洋鬼子) after those military conflicts, which is still in use today as a nationalist discourse. The evolution from *Yi* to *Yang* then to *Yang Guizi* in Chinse eyes was much more than a reversal of superiority in culture and technology, foreigners were no longer considered "men from afar" that need to be cherished, but a change of sentiment to view them as enemies to fight against.

The proliferation of international treaties and agreements not only left a profound mark on China's understanding of international relations and modernity, but also about the power of language. As pointed out by Hevia (2003: 57), "in the era of the Opium Wars, translation procedures may be understood "as a weapon in combat between British and Qing officials". After the *Treaty of Nanjing* signed following the First Opium War in 1842, *Da Yingguo* (Great Britain)[4] not only became an established name for the Great Britain, but inspired all the other countries to add "da" (great) for their own names: the US as *Da Hezhong guo*, France as *Da Falanxi guo*, even Japan was translated as *Da Riben Diguo* and Korea as *Dahan Minguo*, to show their equal status with the Qing Empire. Article 11 in the *Treaty of Nanking* also stipulated a set of new, modern vocabularies into the Chinese discourse: "It is agreed that Her Britannic Majesty's Chief High Officer in China shall correspond with the Chinese Higher Officers, both at the Capital and in the Provinces under the term 'Communication' [*zhao hui,* 照会]. The Subordinate British Officers and Chinese Higher Officers in the Provinces under the terms 'Statement' [*shen chen,* 申陈] on the part of the former, and on the part of the latter 'Declaration' [*zha xing,* 札行], and the Subordinates of both Countries on a footing of *perfect equality*" (Liu, 2006: 53, emphasis added).

It is just ironical that this treaty affixed on a language of "perfect equality" became the first "unequal treaty" that marked the start of a "century of humiliations" in the modern Chinese history, whose legacy was a series of "unequal treaties". We may argue that the Opium War pushed China from the tribute era to the treaty era, but does the unequal treaties end the unequal treatment and give the British an equal status? The answer is No. The war over the rhetoric of *Yi* and the Britain's winning of it in eventually removing it from the Qing imperial discourse signified a start of *unequal* status of China, as those treaties were not signed to achieve equality, nor to dismantle the Us-Other binaries, but only to reverse it. It was no longer about trade, but about civilisation vs. barbarianism and superiority vs. inferiority, only in an overturned reversal, but with the same inequality at its very heart. If equality can be established through negotiations, it was absent because there was no room for negotiation under the Chinese Tributary System, nor was there any chance for negotiation with gunboats. If the Opium War started as a trade war due to unbalanced trade surplus and unequal trade terms with no channels for negotiations, we can argue its result in unequal treaties was a trade-off of the unequal treatments the British had received for decades. In a way, what Napier wanted to accomplish was the same goal as Lord Macartney – to change the system and be respected for its national standing and treated as an equal partner from a sovereign state. When letters and gifts all failed to start negotiations, and after repeated efforts in knocking the door with commodities as well as science and modern values, the British finally sent their gunboats. So, was the epithet of "Opium War" misleading? How could such an immoral war be justified by those who claimed morality as being civilised? Listening to the debates held in 1840 again will allow us to see further that occasioned the first British military action in China.

7.3 The opium debates

Although the Napier incident in 1834 was often treated as marking the beginning of Britain's pro-war attitude towards China, Gao's book (2020: 141) strongly argued that the voices against a violent policy were still a clear majority, and this period was one of "confused thinking with regard to Britain's China policy, rather than a clear stage in the preparation for a military conflict". It was on 1 October 1839 that the historic decision to send a military expedition to China was made by the Prime Minister Lord Melbourne and Foreign Secretary Lord Palmerston during a secret cabinet meeting held behind closed doors in Windsor. So the war decision did not go through the Parliament, but was leaked out to the press soon after instructions were sent to India in early 1840, provoking immediate interest and sparking an open and vibrant debate that captured the attention of both Britain's political elites and the general public.

Honour (1961: 201) believed it was Gladstone, then a young MP and destined to become Prime Minister decades later, who came up with the infamous name of the Opium War, but Chen's (2017: 127) research attributed the name to the anti-war campaigners in a London newspaper: "History remembers little of the war protests, yet it was the anti-war protesters who ensured that the war was remembered as the Opium War rather than a Chinese war". One thing for sure is that it was an oversimplified label that was emotive but shielded the extremely complex set of causes. This section will first unpack the whole host of factors that led to the decision to wage war before looking at the 1840 debates.

Melancon's book (2003) argued that it was overwhelmed by Britain's own domestic politics. True, when the news of the opium crisis arrived in Britain, it was the Opposition, not the ruling government, which responded first. After reading a newspaper report on 1 August 1839, Lord Ellenborough, former President of the Board of Control, introduced the subject into Parliament with a question to the Prime Minister that same day. He accused the Ministry for having allowed the China trade to be almost totally dependent upon opium, and with the cession of the opium trade, all of Britain's China trade, including the lucrative tea trade, was threatened. The Tories then charged Lord Melbourne's Whig government for neglecting British interests in the Far East, and lost one of Britain's most prized trading partners, for which the Government had to be held responsible. Therefore, it was important to understand that although the parliamentary debate held in April 1840 focused on whether military intervention could be deemed an acceptable and justified method to secure British interests, it was primarily for the Tories to motion yet another no confidence vote in a bid to bring down the Whig government. But they lost the vote with a narrow margin as the key decision-makers were convinced that Britain was legitimately "entitled to demand satisfaction, reparation, and redress" from the Chinese authorities (Hansard, 1840, vol. 55: 1047).

Then let us look at the domestic situation in China. By the early 1800s, the opium trade dominated by British merchants produced millions of Chinese addicts. The opium trade increased steadily: between 1800 and 1821, 4,500 chests were shipped to and sold in China a year. In 1838, the number reached 40,000 chests. The result was a serious outflow of Chinese silver. The world's most populous and richest empire commanding around one third of the world GDP, now being poisoned by British opium. The Qing government finally decided to exterminate the opium trade completely, and in March 1839, the Daoguang Emperor, rejecting proposals to legalise and tax opium, commissioned Lin Zexu to go to Canton to execute the order. Lin wrote to Queen Victoria an open letter (Appendix 9) in an appeal to her moral responsibility to stop the opium trade based on a sense of Confucian righteousness. The official version of the communication, sealed with the Daoguang Emperor's approval, was issued on 3 August 1839, and its English version appeared in the Chinese Repository in February 1840. Lin asked a few people to carefully doublecheck the English translation, in which *Yi* was translated as "foreigner" as we can see from the Appendix. However, it remained unknown whether Queen Victoria ever read the letter. We are tempted to ask the same question as to Queen Elizabeth I's letters to the Wanli Emperor: how would Queen Victoria have responded to it had the letter reached the intended recipient? We may get a sense from her speech to the Parliament on 26 January 1841, when she stated that she "deemed it necessary to send to the coast of China a naval and military force, to demand reparation and redress for the injuries inflicted upon some of my subjects by the officers of the Emperor of China and for the indignities offered to an Agent of my Crown" (cited in Liu, 2006: 55).

When Lin failed to receive a response, he launched strong attacks on both addicts and smugglers. He attempted to get foreign companies to forfeit their opium stores in exchange for tea, but failed. Then Lin ordered confiscation of opium in foreign merchants' possessions including opium stockpiles in warehouses and the thirteen factories and burnt as many as

21,306 chests. He also ordered Chinese troops to board British ships to destroy the opium. He suspended all international trade in Canton and detained the entire foreign community within their factories, demanding that all foreigners sign a "no-opium-trade" bond, the breaking of which was subject to capital punishment. Staunton (1840: 13), who translated the *Ta Tsing Leu Lee*, proclaimed that: "there was absolutely no law authorising the confiscation of goods, under any circumstances, outside the port. The opium, lying in the receiving ships at Lintin, was no more liable to confiscation by any existing fiscal law of the Chinese, than if it had been lying in the river Thames". Charles Elliot, the then Chief Superintendent, accused Lin's actions as insults "against British life, liberty, and property, and … the dignity of the British crown" (cited in Gao, 2020: 149–150).

However, when news of Lin's confiscation order first reached London, there was no reaction. Only in September did London become alarmed, with the arrival of a Canton dispatch relating China's military threats against defenceless British civilians. Public feelings turned to anger and outrage towards the end of 1839 when there were further reports of traders and their families having to seek refuge on board British merchant ships at sea, deprived, at least officially, of food and water supplies from shore. For British politics the issue ceased to be about opium, about which many people sympathised with China, but about any nation who was to persecute a British citizen would face severe consequences. As summarised by Gelber (2008: 157), the cause of conflict lay elsewhere than the opium: "London was outraged by reports of China's affront to the British crown, the denial of state equality, the seizure of property without due process and, above all, the danger to British women and children". Lin's strong measures and cruelty in enforcing the Chinese laws and how his conduct violated international law and Western standards of justice, morality and humanity were used as reasons for the British to justify a war in the name of vindicating its national honour and protecting British citizens overseas. Chen (2016) attributed such claims to be "victim discourse", while Liu (2006) named it "the colonial discourse of injury", but it did provide ample grounds for legitimising Britain's forcible intervention to protect their national interests and honour and defend the principle of free trade and international law.

This brought the three options discussed in Chapter 6 back on the table for a re-evaluation. As Graham pointed out in Parliament, "since one-sixth of the whole united revenue of Great Britain and India depended on our commercial relations with that country", the elimination of Britain's trade with China would be "one of the greatest calamities which could befall the East India Company and the nation" (Hansard, 1840, vol. 53: 670, 674). Now that the second option of playing by the Chinese rule became no longer tolerable, war seems to be the only option left. As Melancon (1999: 874) had insightfully analysed, it was the convergence of the simultaneous economic crisis in China and the political crisis in

London that obliged the Melbourne ministry to reverse its course. However, is Britain really entitled to use force? To fight, or not to fight were pushed to the front of a vibrant and passionate public debate in the spring of 1840 that challenged the legal, constitutional, moral and commercial basis for military intervention.

The opium trade was an ethically complex issue, making it a morally fraught debate. As eloquently put by Platt (2012: xxvii), there was "deeply conflicted emotion in Britain regarding the morality of Palmerston's gunboat diplomacy in China". Gladstone did come up with the fiercest criticism and called it "Palmerston's Opium War", a "most infamous and atrocious", "iniquitous" war that would leave an ineradicable mark on the country's conscience. "A war more unjust in its origins, a war more calculated in its progress to cover this country with permanent disgrace, I do not know, and I have not read of" (Mander, 1877: 12). Thomas Arnold, an English educator and historian, lambasted that "this war with China ...... really seems to me so wicked as to be a national sin of the greatest possible magnitude, and it distresses me very deeply ...... Ordinary wars of conquest are to me far less wicked, than to go to war in order to maintain smuggling, and that smuggling consisting in the introduction of a demoralising drug, which the Government of China wishes to keep out" (cited in Price, 2019: 112). Other members of the Opposition also argued that it was a "war without just cause", as it was fought to "maintain a trade resting upon unsound principles, and to justify proceedings which are a disgrace to the British flag" (cited in Hibbert, 1970: 140). However, it was exactly the same point that was raised by those who were in favour of sending a military force to China "not only to obtain guarantees of Britain's right to trade, but also to demand redress from China for the 'Insult to the British Flag'" (Melancon, 1999: 874). Referring to the flag that Elliot ordered to be taken from the boat and planted in the balcony upon his arrival at the factory at Canton, the young historian and Secretary of State for War, Thomas Macaulay, said the flag "reminded them that they belonged to a country unaccustomed to defeat, to submission or to shame – it reminded them that they belonged to a country which had made the farthest ends of the earth ring with the fame of her exploits in redressing the wrongs of her children" (Hibbert, 1970: 143).

The debates actually carried on into the Second Opium War, when the former Conservative Foreign Secretary, the Earl of Malmesbury, rose to question the ethics of military intervention: "as a nation, we have blood on our hands". It was, in his opinion, not the Chinese who had insulted the British flag, but the diplomats. He questioned what such actions, which were unworthy of a civilised nation, said about the character of the British nation "in the eyes of all civilised nations" (Miller, 2013: 185). It is interesting to see that the most passionate voices from each side were all using national flag, morality, and national character to muster nationalist pride to win over the votes. The other shared weapon used by both proponents and opponents of the government policy was international law. Proponents stated that the Chinese government behaved in defiance of "all international laws recognized by civilised nations for the protection of life and property" (Lindsay, 1840: 7). Opponents stressed that according to international law, an individual must obey the laws of the state in which he resides. The Chinese forbad the importation of opium. British merchants in China had no choice but to comply with that state's wishes. The Government of Britain should not take responsibility for the illegal behaviour of English subjects in China (Bullock, 1840: 64).

The vibrance of the debates showed the ideological divides among British politicians, diplomats and merchants at the time, when "constitutional liberalism" was considered the ideological champion of social, political and economic progress, which can "offer the best route to the moral improvement of the people" (Parry, 1993: 195). It was Britain's "national ideology" in mid-nineteenth century and the benchmark of a civilised nation (Biagini, 2011: 103). In defence, De Quincey marshalled a series of arguments, politically, economically, diplomatically and legally, to justify the necessity and inevitability, of armed conflict with China (North, 2003: 532–572). Many British including Staunton, argued against the Chinese claim for the British having "a deliberate conspiracy to make narcotic slaves of the Chinese empire, it was a greedy, pragmatic response to a decline in sale of other British imports (clocks, watches, furs)" (Lovell, 2011: 25). Davis (1836, Vol. 1: 270) even speculated that if the engineering science of Brunel were allowed to operate on the Yellow River and Grand Canal,[5] "a benefit might be conferred that would more than compensate for all the evil that we have inflicted with our opium and our guns".

What is worth special mentioning is Staunton's remarkable change of attitude towards the war. As someone who had met the Qianlong Emperor and dealt with trade problems as a *Yimu* in China, his fate was interwoven with the fate of China, thus had very mixed feelings. Rightfully, Peyrefitte (1992: xxx) described Staunton as "the witness to three stages": as a page boy of the first embassy, as the vice ambassador for the second mission who mustered a vote against the kowtow, and as a member of parliament who debated and voted for the Opium War. Having been one of the first Englishmen to learn the Chinese language,[6] he had since become the first British sinologist to reveal to the West the other faces of China that were masked by the idealised view presented by the missionaries. In Staunton's eyes, China was an old civilisation that awaits salvation, a land of wealth and opportunity that needs to tap into. As for "the vices of the Chinese national characters, and also the vices of their political and commercial system", he would certainly not defend them as he had "ample opportunities of witnessing these evils" during a considerable portion of his life (Staunton, 1836: 40).

Staunton became a member of the Committee of the House of Commons on the Tea Duties in 1834. In 1835, he argued against the war petition. He described China as an ancient and tranquil country in good order and said that Britain should not intrude, lest the EIC's China tea trade that sustained the company's profitability be disrupted (Chen, 2017: 141). Then in 1836, he again argued that an expedition to extract commercial privileges would insult the British flag and alienate the Chinese government and people (Staunton, 1836: 28). But in the 1840 parliamentary debate, as an honourable member of Parliament for Portsmouth, the city from which he had embarked with the first British embassy, he voted towards the narrow won of 271:262 by giving a swaying speech:

> The question with regard to the opium was not a question of morality or policy, but a question whether there had been any breach of international law. …… and if we submit to the degrading insults of China, the time would not be far distant when our political ascendancy in India would be at an end ……. The stakes of the impending war were incalculable: the British had no right to engage in battle if they were to lose it, and no right to shirk combat if they were to win it.
>
> (Hansard, 1840, vol. 53: 739)

He then concluded, "though very reluctantly, that this war is absolutely just and necessary under existing conditions" (ibid: 745). In his own words in the *Memoir* (1856: 87), he took an "effective part in vindicating the Government policy". He also quoted a letter from Lord Palmerston to thank him for the "excellent and very effective speech, which made a great impression on the House" (ibid: 90). Palmerston himself summarised that the war was "about the country's honour, trade access, and, ultimately, which empire's rules should reign supreme" (cited in Westad, 2013: 41). He was convinced that Britain was now a global power strong enough to impose progress on backward peoples. Palmerston was the statesman who made the famous speech at the House of Commons in 1848 that still resonant in the international arena today: "We have no eternal allies, and we have no perpetual enemies. Our interests are eternal and perpetual, and those interests it is our duty to follow". Like Staunton, he had made it clear to Elliot during the previous three years that he was in no way to offend the Chinese. Now the situation had changed, so no policy should stay eternal. While steering away from the ethical issue of the opium business, he managed to claim moral high ground by strengthening the British determination not to allow its citizens to be subject to an "arbitrary and corrupt" Chinese judicial system. So the government won its vote, and won again in the House of Lords, where the Duke of Wellington, the victor of Waterloo, declared that in half a century of public service he had seen no insults and injuries as bad as those imposed on the British at Canton. The Chinese deserved to be punished.

Palmerston then explained his reasons for use of force in a letter addressed to the Minister of the Emperor of China dated 20 February 1840 (Appendix 10). But the letter was first refused to be taken by the Qing navy at Xiamen, then when it was forwarded to Ningbo, the governor dared not open it and returned it again to the British. A third attempt was made in Tianjin, where the letter was eventually taken and handed over to the emperor. Of course, what the emperor read was the Chinese version that was again rendered carefully to read more like a "petition" from a tributary state rather than a warning before military force is resorted to.[7] In the original English, as we can see, it stated clearly at the outset that "Her Majesty the Queen of Great Britain has sent a Naval and Military Force to the Coast of China, to demand from The Emperor satisfaction and redress for injuries inflicted by Chinese Authorities upon British subjects resident in China, and for insults offered by the same Authorities to the British Crown". He then claimed that he did not dispute China's right to prohibit the sale of opium nor its right to enforce the prohibition, only the methods used by Chinese officials. He ended the letter with a list of demands that included payment for property lost during the crisis of March 1839 and guarantees of future trading rights. "If the Emperor of China refused these demands, the expeditionary force had the authority to exact them by force".

The most interesting thing is this letter was written at almost the same time when Lin Zexu's letter was translated into English: February 1840. If we put the two letters together, we could see how the "wrong assumptions of counterpart" discussed in Chapter 5 still persisted in mutual perceptions between the two empires. The Foreign Secretary Palmerston wrote a letter to "the Minister of the Emperor of China", the first of its kind between two counterparts representing governments, but it was eventually handed over to the emperor as the Minister was nothing but the minion to the emperor, who is the only decision maker for all affairs. Similarly, the letter written by the Qing commissioner Lin Zexu to Queen Victoria in 1839 also showed the Chinese assumption of British government structure, as Lin thought it was the Queen who was managing day-to-day state affairs, in much the same way as the Chinese emperor dictating policy in Beijing. Actually, even today, most Chinese people thought it was the Queen who decided to send gunboats to China, with very few realizing that it was the decision made by the Prime Minister and Foreign Secretary, and even fewer knowing that there was a parliamentary debate after the decision was made. It was simply hard to imagine that the *Magna Carta* was issued as early as 1215 to prevent the king from exploiting his power, and placed limits of royal authority by establishing the principle that the king and his government was not above the law. Then in 1717, following George I's discontinuance of the practice of presiding at the meetings of his cabinet ministers, the ministry was given more power. After George II became the king in 1727, he provided the first Lord of the Treasury, Sir Robert Walpole, with an official residence at 10 Dawning Street, something like the office of Prime Minister came gradually into existence.

There were also some debates regarding the opium policy in China, but it was only between a narrow circle of ruling elites rather than the parliament, let alone reported in media for public participation. Councils were also divided between seeking an accommodation with the British or taking a firm stand and risking war. One faction primarily made up of central government bureaucrats led by Mu Zhang-a, was in favour of legalising the drug and granting some reasonable trade facilities to the foreigner to stop the outward flow of silver, so it was grounded at economic considerations rather than moral concerns. They also recognised that superior British military strength meant that war would almost certainly bring humiliations. The other party, made up of intellectuals of the literati coalition led by Lin Zexu, were opposing the opening of new ports to trade and took an irreconcilable and chauvinists stand, which was also not grounded on moral considerations against opium, but uncompromising stand against foreigners. In *The Inner Opium War* (1992), Polachek set the Opium War in China's domestic political context. Challenging the conventional Chinese view that Lin Zexu and his supporters were selfless patriots who acted in China's best interest, Polachek argued that, for reasons having more to do with their own domestic political agenda, Lin advocated a futile policy of militant resistance to the West. Given the limited knowledge of the outside world available to Lin, he had little chance to properly understand the British and the wishes of the private merchants, let alone the British domestic party politics. The letter he addressed directly to Queen Victoria by "this stiff-necked patriot of the old school, contains, in a few lines, the whole pitiful tragedy of China's collapse before the impact of the West" (Backhouse and Bland, 1914: 395–396). Their support for a trade embargo played a major part in pushing China into war. Kitson (2013: 80) argued with no ambiguity that "Lin's seizure, confiscation and destruction of the merchants' cargoes of opium was the spark that ignited the military conflict between Britain and China known as the first Opium War". Backhouse and Bland (1914: 395) even accused him as "the real cause of the war, because of his attitude of contemptuous insolence and his methods of barbarism were not such as any self-respecting nation could tolerate". Staunton also made it clear that "with regard to the immediate cause of the rupture, that was entirely attributable to the conduct of Imperial Commissioner Lin" (Hansard, 1840, vol. 53: 744). Palmerston believed that Lin's actions had been "unjust and no better than robbery", while Collis (2002: 268) argued that the British, in search of an excuse for war to expand trade, lacked the justification prior to Lin's actions, which "had played straight into his [Palmerston's] hands". In a way, his intervention in the opium crisis converted the

Chinese anti-opium campaign into "an unjust aggression against British lives, liberty, property and national dignity" (Chen, 2016: 239). However, in Chinese history and domestic textbooks, Lin Zexu has always been portrayed as a national hero.[8] In today's China, the logic remained unchanged when the nation was facing an external threat, the peace-makers would be considered as traitors to give in to foreigners while those who fiercely denounced them are considered as patriots.

What this section tries to reveal is the complex interactions and the historical constraints of both sides' decision making, and how it impacted the changing directions of Anglo-Chinese encounters in a historical context. The Opium War's first shots were fired in September 1839 when a skirmish occurred between British and Chinese vessels after Chinese troops were ordered to board British ships to destroy the opium. In April 1840, when the parliamentary debates were unfolding, the sixteen men-of-war, and 4000 British, Irish and Indian troops were already on their way to China to "redress the wrongs" and to vindicate the British honour, which has been grievously injured and wronged by the Chinese arrogance for centuries. In June 1840, two and a half centuries after the first letter was written to the remote fable land from a British monarch, British gunboats arrived in the Chinese waters. The Chinese official narrative always puts 1840 as the start of the Opium War, while in the UK, it normally puts the start time as 1839. This subtle difference in the official narratives of the two countries indicated the vastly different stories being told to the next generations regarding the same war that both empires wanted to claim victimhood.

7.4 Falling into the Thucydides Trap?

A myriad of literature had been produced to identify an array of contributing causes of the war, with the key factors being trade, national honour, domestic politics and the cultural conflicts between the "progressive" Britain and the "backward" China. I agree with Chen's summary that "viewed as a whole, the Opium War historiography proves that the war would not have happened without a combination of factors with coterminous timing" (Chen, 2017: 7). However, there are also scholars who argued that the war was not unavoidable. For example, Hevia (1995: 19–20) believed that if the Qing imperium had been able to rid ritualised foreign relations, the conflict with the West could either have been avoided or its outcome would have been quite different. I do not quite agree. The conflict may have come at a different time and triggered by a different event, but I see it as an accident doomed to happen. Most of the arguments so far still focus on the proximate causes that were limited to what happened between the two empires, but the immediate circumstances often overshadow larger historical forces on a global canvas. Platt (2018: xxvi) had projected the Opium War as the point where the grand eclipse of China crossed the Britain that rose to new nationalist heights through its victories in the Napoleonic Wars and beyond. In this book, I wish to take a grander historical and global angle by adopting the lens of the Thucydides Trap to look at the two empires at both their own historical trajectories in the changing global political, economic and cultural landscape, and the merging trend of globalisation that brought the two to collide. This lens was named after a quote by ancient Athenian historian and military general Thucydides, who posited that the Peloponnesian War between Athens and Sparta had been inevitable because of Spartan fears of the growth of Athenian power. It has been popularised by American political scientist Graham Allison (2017) in describing an apparent tendency towards war when an emerging power threatens to displace an existing great power as a regional or international hegemon. Though fear may not be the underlying cause for the Opium War as it was almost waged against a China not even seeing the challenge evolving into an imminent military threat, I believe it would also help illuminate the very root cause of it: the dynamics between the rising and the ruling power that drove the two on a collision course for war.

China had been Asia's political, economic and cultural hegemon for centuries. I do not think a military conflict would have happened if Queen Elizabeth I's letter was received and replied in a manner even twice as condescending as the Qianlong Emperor. They would have accepted the Tributary System and kowtow rites because they were not strong enough to challenge the China-imposed order at that time. The conflict did not happen between China and other European powers because they came to trade with China, not to challenge it, nor wished to change it, as they adopted the policy of "when in Rome, do as the Romans do". But the British did not just want to trade with China, actually, they had been trading with China for well over a century before the Opium War, but they were not happy to play by the rules set by Imperial China, nor happy to accept that "the system is right because it has always been like this", or "because everyone else is fine with it". Military intervention did not happen immediately following Macartney's embassy because the time was not yet ripe for the tip of the balance of power, as Qing China was still at its pinnacle during the Qianlong Emperor's reign (1736–1796), though the Western world had undergone dramatic changes during the second half of his reign, from the Industrial Revolution in the UK after 1760s to the American War of Independence (1775–1777) and the French Revolution (1789–1799). It is interesting to read Macartney's comment that "our *present* interests, our reasons, and our humanity equally forbid the thoughts of any offensive measures with regard to the Chinese, whist a ray of hope remains for succeeding by gentle ones" (Cranmer-Byng, 1962: 213). This implied that they had thought about the "offensive measures", but those rational considerations listed meant that for now we should bide our time, and the option to play by the Chinese rules was an expediency. As reflections following the Amherst Embassy showed, Britain's most important economic interests actually still pointed to the decision of trying to avoid a crisis. It took another 23 years for the two empires to reach the flash point when their trajectories of ascending and descending crossed paths. Just like "kowtow" was not mentioned in the Qianlong Emperor's letter and "opium" did not make one appearance in the *Treaty of Nanking*, the arguments persistent with the kowtow and opium as the causes for war just scratched the surface.

I also disagree with Hevia's (1995: xii) re-interpretation of the Sino-Western encounter as "one between two expansive imperialisms, the Manchu and British multi-ethnic imperial formations". While Hevia (1995: 241) refuted the old generation scholars such as Tsiang (1936) and Wang (1993), who have argued that the "Sino-Western conflict was a case of cultural misunderstanding, rather than an example of aggressive British imperial expansion", Hevia's argument assumed the two empires collided head-to-head when they were moving in the same expansive trajectory. But by the late Qing, China was more inward-looking than ever to be described as being "expansive", actually, the expansive age was over with the end of Qianlong's reign in mid-Qing, and it became more hierarchical internally than expansional externally. While Britain, on the other hand, was in a constantly upward spiral of economic growth and enhanced military strength since Qianlong's reign, poised to dominate much of the rest of the world after successfully challenging the old powers of Portugal and France in Europe. For China, Britain emerged from a different orbit rather than catching up from behind. I see the collision between them in historic dynamics: conflicts ensued when their trajectories clashed and each attempted to impose its system on the other. The old hegemon believed their way of doing things was the only way while the new power believed their way was better and proved to be the superior way. Mackinder, one of the founding fathers of neo-mercantilist and geopolitical thought, held that "the great wars of history... are the outcomes, direct or indirect, of the unequal growth of nations" (cited in Gilpin, 1981: 93). Gilpin's key argument is that a shift in the power balance weakens the foundations of the existing system, because those gaining power see the increasing benefits and the decreasing cost of changing the system. They would then seek to alter the system through territorial, political or economic expansion until the marginal costs of continuing change are greater than the marginal benefits. They may not seek expansions in all three fronts, as the Opium War indicated, which only aimed to achieve the latter two.

We have staged the debates in the British parliament about whether it was justified to wage war against a sovereign state for commercial interests, however, with hindsight, the purpose was much broader than that. It was a battle for hegemony and a new world order after British merchants expanded their economic connections and interests with

China. Although the advocates for military intervention were coming from the commercial interests, the winning arguments of the debate changed the ultimate objective to imposing "international law" and maintaining "political ascendency" as justified by Staunton's swaying speech, which concluded with the statement that "the British had no right to engage in battle if they were to lose it, and no right to shirk combat if they were to win it" (Hansard, 1840, vol. 53: 739). As "the witness to three stages" who saw first-hand the power shift on both sides, Staunton's judgement was now was the time for Britain to win the war. Therefore, this book argues that the war between the two empires was unavoidable, but in the sense of the Thucydides Trap. According to the power transition theory proposed by Organski (1958), a general trend in history is that after a nation achieves hegemonic power, it will be challenged by a great power. Power transition takes place when the challenger does not think the status quo fits the relative power shifts. We can see this in the seventeenth century Europe when the Portuguese hegemony was challenged by the Dutch, who was later challenged by the British. Although the Opium War was a regional one and did not last very long due to Qing's military weakness, thus not resulting in the same magnitude of catastrophe – its scale of the death toll was not even a fraction of China's internal turmoil that broke out a decade later, the Taiping Rebellion. More importantly, it did not conquer China's territory or seek to overthrow the Qing ruling as it did not aim to do so. These features put the Opium War in a much smaller scale compared with the far lengthier ones listed in Allison's work. However, it shares all the features of the First Sino-Japanese War (1894–1895) that was inlcuded as one of the 16 major cases in the Harvard Thucydide's Trap Project (Allison, 2017: 268–271). Even the example of the First World War can be a mirror to reflect what was happening between the two empires: the military clash was "but a continuation of what had been going on for at least fifteen or twenty years," and had begun "because the former power wished to preserve the existing status quo, whereas the latter, for a mixture of offensive and defensive motives, was taking steps to alter it" (Kennedy: 470).

By the 1830s, we see two completely different empires: Great Britain had already emerged as a full-fledged global power and modern civilisation. Democracy, parliamentary system, philosophy, literature, architecture, industry, modern technology, naval prowess, sophisticated banking and finance, Britain had it all. On the other hand, China became a rickety empire exhibiting an odd mixture of culture splendour with stagnant technology and weak military. As the British strength grew, so did its confidence and pride, and started to show "rising power syndrome" which features "a rising state's enhanced sense of itself, its interests, and its entitlement to recognition and respect" (Allison, 2017: 44), thus followed by "its demands for respect and expectations that arrangements be revised to reflect new realities of power. These were, Thucydides tells us, natural reactions to its changing station" (ibid: xv). From Queen Elizabeth I to Queen Victoria, from Ambassador Macartney to Amherst, then from Chief Superintendent Napier to Elliot, we can observe the roadmap contoured by Allison: A growing sense of self-importance led to an expectation of recognition and respect on an equal footing, and emboldened by its growing strength was its increased demand for settling a long-continued clash of interests, and even vying for a re-established pecking order. I see this roadmap edging towards the so-called Thucydides Trap. In its expansion from England to Great Britain and then the United Kingdom, we can see that Britain was listed in six out of the 12 war scenarios listed in Allison's (2017: 42) case file when he elaborated that Thucydides Trap lied ahead when a rising power confronted a ruling power: twice as the rising power to fight the Dutch Republic (1652–1674) and France (1803–1815), and China just became the next one to challenge. Previous interpretative frameworks that rest on economic and cultural conflicts as well as domestic politics, which unquestionably laid the foundation for a conflict, were still insufficient to fully explain the motivations behind the Opium War by ignoring that it was also about different values and visions to establish a new world order.

But for China, the cost of change outweighed the benefits, it would surely want to preserve the status quo and the Canton System, which was established to demonstrate its dominance and assert China's supremacy. So, "understandably, the established power views the upstart's assertiveness as disrespectful, ungrateful, and even provocative or dangerous" (Allison, 2017: 44). When China refused to change, but showed clear symptoms of a declining power, the newly risen power would seize the opportunity to make the change happen. The economic surge brought by the Industrial Revolution strengthened Britain's determination to stand on equal footing with China. At a time of such irresistible shift of balance of power, what can the ruling power do? Adapt or perish, was the brief answer given by Allison. But the deeply ingrained sense of cultural supremacy made it too difficult for the Chinese to adapt to the new reality or the idea of observing a new rule set by the red-haired barbarian who had long been despised with contempt. As explained in Chapter 2, China believed that it was not just civilised, but being civilisation per se. Now the British also believed that to spread British influence and ideas was to spread civilisation itself. In Britons' eyes, their country was the "greatest power that the world had ever seen" (Parry, 2006: 387) – except by China.

The gravitation towards war is always power and rule. In the *Empire Project*, Darwin (2009: 18) explained why his book began the history of British world-system in the 1830s and 1840s: "The first and most fundamental was the new balance of power and wealth across Eurasia. China's defeat in the first Opium War (1839–42), however partial, signalled that East Asia would be a passive actor in world politics for the foreseeable future. The implications were massive". The key timelines in

Kennedy's (1989: 183) monumental work, *The Rise and Fall of the Great Powers,* also echoed the key events recounted in Chapters 5–7 of this book but condensed to one page: "the turbulence and costs of the 1793–1815 struggle – known to the nineteenth century as 'the Great War' – caused conservatives and liberals alike to opt as far as possible for peace and stability". This happened to be the time between the two British embassies to China. Then he talked about the "spectacular growth of an integrated global economy, which drew ever more regions into a transoceanic and transcontinental trading and financial network centred upon western Europe, and in particular upon Great Britain" after the 1840s. The "decades of British economic hegemony", together with the widespread propagation of ideas about free trade and international law, suggested that a new international order had arisen. For more than a century after this, the British Empire moved towards "the sceptre of the world" by forming a larger and global British "world-system" managed from London. *Treaty of Nanjing* represented a shift in the British control over China's vast trading networks, Hevia (2003: 5) argued that it signified Britain's attempt at establishing a "new world order" in China, based on Western-styled trade relations, legal traditions and diplomacy. I would like to add by highlighting the special significance of the venue for this Treaty to be signed – not the port of Canton where all the trading and conflicts started, but the empire's old capital that was inland along the Yangtse River – meant that the British was able to use its naval force to paralyse China's internal commerce by entering its river course and seizing its junction with the Grand Canal, thus able to bring the dragon throne to terms. Specifically, it was signed aboard the British flagship HMS *Cornwallis,* as war vessels were covered by extraterritoriality as diplomatic mission in international law. The Treaty conceded almost everything Britain had longed for, including the opening of more ports to trade: Shanghai, Fuzhou, Ningbo, Xiamen. A supplementary agreement was made in 1842 and 1843 to apply Western law in British courts if Britons would be tried in China.

This ends my tale of the two empires over the two centuries. But of course, the story carries on, with legacies from these encounters. Recalling Queen Victoria's diamond jubilee celebration in 1897, the British historian Arnold Toynbee claimed that "Here we are on top of the world. We have arrived at this peak to stay there forever. There is, of course, this thing called history. But history is something unpleasant that happens to other people" (cited in Allison, 2017: xi). This was an earlier version of the "end of history" narrative, and China was one of the "other people" in this reference. Of course, it had been proved wrong. History will never end. The Qianlong Emperor may have believed the same one hundred years earlier at the pinnacle of the Qing prosperity. His reign shared many similarities with Queen Victoria: both ruled for over 63 years,[9] and brought their own empires to the height of glory. On a broader historical scale, both the Qing and the British empires were challengers and rose to become a hegemonic power – by defeating the Ming in the East in 1644 and France in the West in 1815 respectively. The Qing dismantled Ming China's *Hua-Yi* distinction to justify its own legitimacy. After residing over the re-established China-and-the-Rest distinction for two centuries, it also faced an emerging challenger from beyond the "four seas". The British king even tried to put himself in a brotherly position with the Chinese emperor when the two embassies were sent to establish equal diplomatic relations, starting the tug-of-war between Qing's vertical "world" order built on the notion of *Tianxia* and the new, horizontal global order that the British sought to create to expand their mercantile growth and imperial influence.

It was during Qianlong's reign when Queen Victoria's grandfather King George III sent the first British embassy to China. The time lapsed was almost exactly a century in between: Qianlong reigned from 1735–1799 while Victoria from 1837–1901. The Pax Britannica was ended by the outbreak of the First World War in 1914. Almost a century later in 2013, China's new leader Xi Jinping came up with the new vision of realising the China Dream of national rejuvenation, which was mentioned nine times in his inauguration speech. It set the timeframe for 2049, a centennial goal for China to achieve its rejuvenation, about two centuries after the Opium War. The interlude of two centuries was long enough for the West to regard China's rise as a "new" challenge, while is it short enough for China itself to view its national rejuvenation as simply returning to its "old" rightful position of prominence in the world, and a cultural status and prestige that it had enjoyed for many, many centuries until 1840. Understanding the Opium War from a grander historical and global context expands the established analysis about its causes, particularly when looking back from today's China that is rising again on its way to regain its former glory and starts to confront today's hegemon established by the US with Pax Americana, which will also be over 100 years by 2049. Hence China is now considered the new threat as the big power that refuses to be taken into the American orbit, though not wish to change it, but refuses to *be changed* this time. However, in the context of today's world rivalries, where not just the nuclear weapon is of mutual assured destruction, I do not think China and the US are falling into the Thucydides Trap, as it is quite clear that the war option would lead to a lose-lose outcome, even if it was just a trade war.

7.5 Postscript

If the two empires indeed fell into the Thucydides Trap as argued above, the Qing certainly did not see this coming as they came to terms with the British development in a very passive manner. They did not realise that this small island had cast its long imperial shadow on its neighbouring vassal states as early as Qianlong's reign. In 1793, the British India was known to the Qing court as a loanword from its Tibetan name of Phe-rang or Phyi-gling (披楞 in Chinese), but they never made the connection between this Phyi-gling that bordered with the Kingdom of Gorkha (present day Nepal, then a vassal state of China) with the "red-haired state" trading in Canton. The connection between Phyi-gling and England surfaced only after Lord Macartney's embassy had left, when they interrogated one captive from Nepal, but this was never confirmed in written records. When the Opium War broke out in 1840, the Qing court started to establish the speculations of connection between the two from the report sent from Gorkha again, but it was not until 1846 when a letter of credence from Gorkha reached Tibet, and with the help of two French Jesuits to translate, did they finally confirm that Phyi-gling and England were one same country. In the letter's Chinese version, Phyi-gling was translated as England (*Yingjili*, 英吉利) for the first time. In the same year, Britain sent two requests simultaneously to discuss border demarcation at Tibet and trading rights at Canton through the Qing Minister in Tibet and the Viceroy of Guangdong and Guangxi respectively, finally crystalising the connection between the two to the Qing government. Just as it took centuries for the West to realise that the Cathay described by Marco Polo in the thirteenth century was indeed China as confirmed by Matteo Ricci in 1607, it also took China decades to ascertain that the Phyi-gling in 1793 was another name for England.

China then learnt a bitter lesson about how powerful England was through the Opium War, however, it is completely erroneous to interpret the Daoguang Emperor's questions in 1842 as not even knowing "the most basic information about its antagonists", including where England was, as stated in Lovell's book *The Opium War* (2011: 114; also its Chinese translation by Liu, 2020: 305). Although the Chinese knowledge of England was still rather limited at the time, the first treatise on the British composed by a Chinese person already appeared in 1832, by Xiao Lingyu (萧令裕), who produced *An Account of England* (《记英吉利》). This account gave detailed and specific data on British ships, including how many guns they could carry, how they aimed by using telescopes and could accurately reach targets miles away. He was also aware that those guns and ships were instrumental to Britain's quest for economic power and imperial expansion, and he even wrote about India as a British colony, something not commonly understood in China at that time. What was particularly intriguing was his description of how Britain had conquered those colonies with its navy, received a regular share of their annual wealth in the form of "tribute and taxes", and how its expansion into India butted heads with the Qing in Tibet (Platt, 2018: 226–227). This posed the British Empire as a direct rivalry to the Qing not only along the coast, but also on the continental frontier. Most importantly, he clearly understood that although the British could grow crops at home, their "national custom was to seek profit overseas", but he disputed the belief that "the English sell opium to corrupt China". He wrote: "the fashion for opium dates back only to the early 1800s and the English have been industriously making textiles and trading them at Canton for a great many decades now. Their woollen fabrics can be found everywhere; it is not as if they have only sold opium from the start. And if people in China did not smoke opium, then the English would not be able to sell it" (ibid: 228). Perhaps the most important lesson that can be learned from his book was his clear awareness about the gap in military strength by the 1830s. Xiao argued that "our navy had no means to resist the pirates, yet the pirates themselves were quite fearful of the foreign ships" (ibid: 228–229). However, with the knowledge of the British weapons being vastly superior to China's, and the British expansion in Asia, Xiao shared the thoughts with most of the Qing officials that the trade with China was of such vital importance to the British that they would never do anything to risk losing it. This book was studied carefully by Lin Zexu and Wei Yuan and referenced in Wei's seminal book *Haiguo Tuzhi* (*Illustrated Treatise on Maritime Countries,* 《海国图志》) when published in 1843, which renewed and magnified its influence. Wei's famous strategy of "emulating the strength of foreigners' technology in order to overcome them" (*Shi Yi changji yi zhi Yi,* 师夷长技以制夷) was developed from Xiao's ideas. Here, we can see *Yi* was recognised as superior in technologies that China needs to learn from.

If we establish the context for the Daoguang Emperor to ask those questions to his Military Minister – after seeing the report mentioning the number of "white, red and black barbarians" among the captives, we will see of course he knew where England was on the map; he was even aware of its empire status of having vassal states. What was beyond his knowledge and imagination was the nature of a sea power, as China had been a continental empire constrained by an "orthodox agrarian worldview that was firmly rooted to the soil" (Gungwu, 2013: 44). The Chinese world map did not visualise Napier's claim that Britain "rules over an extent of territory in the four quarters of the world". That is why the emperor was more likely to feel baffled or even deceived by the small size of this "barbarian island" on the map, and interrogated to find out "how big on earth its realm was" to have soldiers of many different races fighting for it? According to the *Qing Historical Archive* (*Qing Shi Lu,*《清实录》, scroll 370, 6 April 1842), Daoguang Emperor also asked the following questions: "How many vassal states does it have? Are there routes over land connecting England and Xinjiang? Do they have regular interactions? Does it border with Russia? Do they have trade connections?" ("究竟該國地方周圍幾許？所屬國共有若干？……又，英咭唎至回疆各部有無旱路可通? 平素有無往來？俄羅斯是否接壤？有無貿易相通?") Answers to these questions were provided in Wang Wentai's *Hongmao Fan Yingjili Kaolue*

(*A Study of the Red-haired Foreigners Called English,* 《红毛番英吉利考略》) published in 1844: there was a northern route via Russia, middle route via Xinjiang and southern route via Tibet, all leads to England. Due to the astonishingly massive expansion of the British empire since 1815, "the amount of territory controlled by Britain increased by an average of about 100,000 square miles per year during the period from 1815 to 1870" (McDonough, 1994: 15), it is not surprising that the Chinese emperor could not keep up with the speed of its expansion. As a matter of fact, this was the grand question that captivated many generations of historians to answer, including Ferguson's (2003: xiii) whole book on *Empire*: How did an archipelago of rainy islands off the north-west coast of Europe come to rule the world? In fact, they created an "informal empire", a term that has been given authority by Dr C. R. Fay in the *Cambridge History of the British Empire* (1940, II: 399) to describe the extensive reach of British interests into regions and nations which were not formal parts of the Empire, or colonies directly ruled by the British. Not even realising there was a "Thucydides Trap" looming ahead, China fell into the status of being "semi-colonised" for the first time in its history.

The other character of the British Empire that baffled the Daoguang Emperor was that its traders were so much supported by the state. The idea that foreign trade should be done between private merchants on both sides to trade freely, and a foreign state would go to war for trade, for the sake of its merchants was inconceivable to the Chinese court (Wang, 2003: 51). As explained earlier, continental empires would go to war for territory, and in Chinese minds, no state resources would go to help merchants as they belonged to a very low social class. Chen (2017: 5) argued that it was "the institution of the Canton one-port system – not China's 'all under heaven' (*Tianxia*) ideology nor the Tributary System, as scholars have wrongly argued, that dictated the Qing's relations with and knowledge of Europeans, especially the British". I think this was also "wrongly argued" as it failed to understand that the Canton system was merely a product of the Tributary System which again was bred by the *Tianxia* ideology. In British eyes, the system was set up to restrict foreign trade, but for China, it was to keep foreigners and foreign influence under control, as what mattered for the Chinese empire was not trade but maintaining internal stability and security of the ruling, which could be jeopardised by foreign forces through trading with and even joining hands with Han Chinese rebels. The different views towards trade between a continental empire of China and a sea power of Britain means that for China, any activity across the borders represents a country-to-country relation thus ties into national security, while for the British, it ties into national interest which is inseparably united with commerce.

While we all know the significance of the Opium War as a turnaround event in the bilateral relations, it is probably hard to imagine that two months before the *Treaty of Nanking* was signed to bring the war to an end, a pagoda was installed in London's Hyde Park as an entrance to its Chinese Exhibition, whose opening on 23 June 1842 was attended by Queen Victoria. In design this entrance is characteristically Chinese, and over the doorway was inscribed, in Chinese characters, "Ten Thousand Chinese Things" (万唐人物). It was reported in the *Illustrated London News:*

> The display allows one to appreciate their pagodas, their bridges, their arts, their sciences, their manufactures, their trades, their fancies, their parlours, their drawing rooms, their clothes, their finery, their ornaments, their weapons of war, their vessels, their dwellings, and the thousand etceteras which make up their moving and living world. The beauty, rarity, novelty, and extreme singularity of these curiosities are very striking.

From these reports and the number of visitors it received, we can see despite the Sinophobic propaganda and the anti-Chinese sentiments leading to the Opium War, the majority of the British public continued to show interest in Chinese art and objects.

Then in 1848, the Chinese junk *Qiying*, named after the imperial commissioner who signed the humiliating *Treaty of Nanking* and *Treaty of the Bogue* following the Opium War, arrived in London and rapidly became one of the most popular visitor attractions. It was bought by British businessmen in the now British Colony of Hong Kong and sent back to England, as the first Chinese junk that had ever appeared in British waters. Numerous medals were struck to commemorate this, featuring an image of the *Qiying* at sea at the front, with its reverse showing: "THIS REMARKABLE VESSEL IS A JUNK OF THE LARGEST CLASS, AND IS THE FIRST SHIP CONSTRUCTED BY THE CHINESE WHICH HAS REACHED EUROPE, OR EVEN ROUNDED THE CAPE OF GOOD HOPE". *The Times* also reported the *Qiying*'s visit: "There is not a more interesting Exhibition in the vicinity of London than the Chinese Junk: one step across the entrance, and you are in the Chinese world; you have quitted the Thames for the vicinity of Canton". In a way, the junk brought the "romance of China" to London, and the public lined up to pay fifty cents to tour the vessel and peruse its displays. Apart from viewing the remarkable curiosities, visitors could hear traditional Chinese music and see displays of spear fighting. When Queen Victoria visited the *Qiying* with the Prince of Prussia and others, she was very impressed and wrote at length in her diary about the visit.[10] She described the junk in detail and gave special mention to the mandarin of third rank, who was in fact one of the crew dressed up as a mandarin to greet the visitors.

In May 1851, the "Ten Thousand Chinese Things Exhibition" was brought to London to coincide with the Great Exhibition of the Works of

Industry of All Nations held in the iconic building of glass and cast iron, the Crystal Palace in Hyde Park. This privately sponsored exhibition had greatly compensated the disappointing Chinese collection as there was no official input from China to join the Great Exhibition. The *Illustrated London News* reported this new attraction as "a pleasing addition has been made to the Chinese Collection consisting of a Chinese lady, named Pwan-ye-Koo, with small lotus-feet only 2 ½ inches in length, a Chinese professor of music, his two children (a boy and a girl), the femme de chamber of the lady, and an interpreter" (Price, 2019: 93). Like the Mandarin on the *Qiying*, this "family" was a fabrication for a selling point, actually hiring a local Chinese woman to "play" the part of wife and mother (Moon, 1974). Not knowing this, Queen Victoria invited them to the Osborne House on the Isle of Wight, which was reported by *Illustrated London News*. In her diary, the Queen described the family's visit in detail, including the women's bound feet. She also drew a sketch of the women which she pinned into her diary, however, this kind of interest in "Chinese things" was more in the form of their exoticness, rather than admiring its sophisticated culture as her predecessors.

A peculiar incident happened at the end of the opening ceremony that marked a reversed admiration: the "Mandarin of the Chinese junk" was reported to be the first Chinese man to kowtow to Queen Victoria. According to the *Punch* magazine and *London Times,* he was "unable any longer to control his feelings", made his way through foreign diplomatists, Ministers of State, and the distinguished circle with which Court etiquette had surrounded the throne, and, advancing close to Her Majesty, saluted her by an "elaborate salaam, consisting of a sudden act of prostration on his face".[11] The other reports in The *Household Narrative of Current Events* added that "her Majesty acknowledged the obeisance, and saluted the Mandarin in return; and at her request he was placed between the Archbishop of Canterbury and the Comptroller of the Household". This was such a significant scene that his figure was captured in all the major paintings and art works produced to commemorate the opening ceremony, including the one painted by Henry Courtney Selous that is now on display at V&A South Kensington. As described in Chapter 3, when the first Chinese visitor Shen Fuzong arrived in Europe in 1682, he also performed the reverential kowtow bows before the King of France, but as a demonstration of the Chinese ritual ceremony, along with other demonstrations to show how to use a paintbrush to write characters and chopsticks to eat. Now, this crewman (dressed up as a Mandarin) kowtowed before the Queen as he would do in front of a Chinese emperor, but as he would never have a chance to meet the emperor in China given his humble social position, he could not help but throwing himself down in the Chinese obeisance in meeting the Queen. This symbolic gesture, which had once wounded the British pride and even argued by some to be the reason for the Opium War, now performed by a Chinese person voluntarily to the British monarch, may be interpreted to be another symbolic gesture marking a reversal of the relationship between the two empires.

Charles Dickens also made use of the occasion of the Great Exhibition to starkly juxtapose the innovative British grandeur displayed at the Crystal Palace with the backwardness of the Chinese Celestial Empire. England and China, he wrote, were the "two countries that displayed the greatest degree of progress and the least … England, maintaining commercial intercourse with the whole world; China, shutting itself up, as far as possible, within itself". In his eyes, the "stupendous" naval anchors made the Chinese junk seem like nothing but a "floating toyshop", the visible representation of a stagnant country where "thousands of years have passed away, since the first Chinese junk was constructed on this model; and the last Chinese junk that was ever launched was none the better for that waste and desert of time". Dickens contrasted Britain's massive steam locomotives, vast and vaunting suspension bridges and the huge printing presses that produced *The Times* every morning with the tinkling teacups, dainty little pagodas, and joss sticks of the "flowery Empire", although printing was one of its four classic inventions. This was also commented by Macartney during his mission, who had observed that "their printing, such as I saw, is merely a wooden cut", "from the necessary accuracy of the process, and the tediousness of the execution, it would seem that new publications are not very frequent, and that knowledge is not so rapidly disseminated in China as in England" (Cranmer-Byng, 1962: 240). However, I wonder how would Dickens comment on today's China, attempting to sell its cost-effective high-speed rail to the UK, who was once the inventor of the world's first steam locomotives. The way Dickens took pride in how printing and knowledge dissemination was much faster in England then is mirrored in China's high-speed rail today, mocking the outdated railway system in the UK.

Looking at Chinese history, it is not hard to reach the conclusion that the internal causes for dynastic decline always far outnumber the external. As incisively put by Du Mu in the year 825, an essayist in the Tang Dynasty, who commented on the demise of the six states and the following first dynasty of Qin: "Alas, it was the Six States and not Qin that destroyed the Six States; and it was Qin itself and not the world who exterminated it". The fact that the Qing navy had to use cannons made from the Ming Dynasty during the Opium War tells us that the defeat of China was owed less to the British rise than of its own decline since Qianlong's reign. The Great Exhibition offers an interesting glimpse of the reversal between the two empires that will be summarised in the Conclusion of the book.

Notes

1 The Chinese characters on the two tea boxes were scrambled imitations and looked like the original character of 茶 putting sideways.

2 *Yimu* was already used in the Ming Dynasty to refer to a similar role held by the Portuguese (Wan, 2011: 666).

3 The full text of the Treaty can be found at: https://worldjpn.grips.ac.jp/documents/texts/pw/18580626.T1E.html

4 Morrison started to use *DaYing Diguo* as the Chinese translation of the "Great British Empire" in 1819, and *Daying Bowuguan* for the British Museum, but China believed only the grand and magnificent Qing deserved the title of "great" in its name (Da Qing).

5 Isambard Kingdom Brunel was an English civil engineer who is one of the greatest figures of the Industrial Revolution. He built dockyards, the Great Western Railway, and a series of steamships including the first propeller-driven transatlantic steamship and the largest ocean-going iron ship ever built in 1843.

6 As described in Chapter 3, Thomas Hyde was "the first Englishman to learn the Chinese language", but Staunton was the one who learned the language to the level of communication who impressed the Qianlong Emperor during the Macartney Embassy, when no one from England can function as an interpreter between the two languages.

7 This kind of self-censorship still lingers in today's official translation. Discussions of China on foreign media will only be selectively translated into Chinese on mainstream media. Although faithfulness is the No. 1 tenant for a translator's job, disrespectful discourse would not be able to pass the censorship at the editorial level and may reflect negatively on the translators themselves as if it was sinful to utter any offensive words to the Chinese government even if they were only translating other people's views.

8 In 1985, on his bi-centennial birth anniversary, a statue was erected with inscriptions of "National Hero" in Fujian. Another statue was erected in New York in 1997, the year when Hong Kong was returned to China. His character and deeds were inscribed in a manner conforming to the official discourse of the authority.

9 As explained in Chapter 5, Qianlong relinquished the throne to his son Jiaqing in 1796 but continued to "instruct" Jiaqing until his death in February 1799, an extra three years as the de-facto emperor.

10 Her diary is fully available online at http://www.queenvictoriasjournals.org/home.do

11 Available at: http://news.bbc.co.uk/1/hi/magazine/7457066.stm

References

Abel, C. (1818). *Narrative of a Journey in the Interior of China: And of a Voyage to and from that Country, in the Years 1816 and 1817, Containing an Account of the Most Interesting Transactions of Lord Amherst's Embassy to the Court of Pekin and Observations on the Countries Which It Visited.* London: Longman, Hurst, Rees, Orme, and Brown. Free e-book available at: https://play.google.com/books/reader?id=7kcQAAAAYAAJ&hl=zh_CN&pg=GBS.PA1

Allison, G. (2017) *Destined for War.* Melbourne, London: Scribe.

Backhouse, E., and Bland, J.O.P. (1914) *Annals and Memoirs of the Court of Peking*. Boston: Houghton Mifflin.

Basu, D.K. (2014) 'Chinese xenology and the Opium War: Reflections on sinocentrism'. *The Journal of Asian Studies*, 73(4) (November), pp. 927–940.

Biagini, E.F. (2011) 'The politics of Italianism: Reynolds's newspaper, the Indian Mutiny, and the radical critique of liberal imperialism in Mid-Victorian Britain', in Crook, T., Taithe, B., Gill, R., (eds.) *Evil, Barbarism and Empire: Britain and Abroad, c.1830–2000*, pp. 99–125.

Bullock, T.H. (1840) *The Chinese Vindicated, or, Another View of the Opium Question; Being in Reply to a Pamphlet by Samuel Warren.* London: W. H. Allen & Company. Free e-book available at: https://play.google.com/books/reader?id=3yhYAAAAcAAJ&hl=zh_CN&pg=GBS.PA1

Chen, L. (2016) *Chinese Laws in Imperial Eyes: Sovereignty, Justice, and Transcultural Politics.* New York: Columbia University Press.

Chen, S.C. (2017) *Merchants of War and Peace: British Knowledge of China in the Making of the Opium War.* Hong Kong: Hong Kong University Press.

Cheung, H. and Mui, L.H. (1968) 'Smuggling and the British tea trade before 1784', *American Historical Review*, 74, pp. 44–73.

Chinese Repository (1832–1851) Available at: https://www.univie.ac.at/Geschichte/China-Bibliographie/blog/2010/06/19/chinese-repository-1832–1851/

Collis, M. (2002) *Foreign Mud.* New York: New Directions.

Cranmer-Byng, J. L. (1962) *An Embassy to China, Being the Journal Kept by Lord Macartney During His Embassy to the Emperor Ch'ien-lung 1793–1794.* London: Longmans.

Darwin, J. (2009) *The Empire Project, The Rise and Fall of the British World-System 1830–1970.* Cambridge: Cambridge University Press.

Davis, J. (1836) *The Chinese: A General Description of the Empire of China and Its Inhabitants*, 2 vols. London: Charles Knight.

Davis, J. (1836) 'The Chinese', *Quarterly Review*, 112 (June), pp. 489–521.

Downing, C.T. (1838) *The Fan-Gui in China in 1836–7.* London: Henry Colburn Publisher.

Ellis, M., Coulton, R. and Mauger, M. (2015) *Empire of Tea: The Asian Leaf that Conquered the World.* London: Reaktion Books, Limited.

Fay, P.W. (1998) *The Opium War, 1840–1842: Barbarians in the Celestial Empire in the Early Part of the Nineteenth Century and the War by Which They Forced Her Gates Ajar.* Chapel Hill: University of North Carolina.

Furber, H. (1976) *Rival Empires of Trade in the Orient, 1600–1800.* Minneapolis: University of Minnesota Press.

Gao, H. (2020) *Creating the Opium War, British Imperial Attitudes Towards China, 1792–1840.* Manchester: Manchester University Press.

Gelber, H. (2008) *The Dragon and the Foreign Devils: China and the World, 1100 B.C. to the Present.* London: Bloomsbury.

Gilpin, R. (1981) *War and Change in World Politics.* Cambridge: Cambridge University Press. 10.1017/CBO9780511664267

Gungwu, W. (2013) *Anglo-Chinese Encounters since 1800: War, Trade Science and Governance.* Cambridge: Cambridge University Press.

Hansard, Corrected report of speech on China Trade (April 7, 1840) Corrected report of speech on Opium Trade, April 4, 1843. Available at: https://api.parliament.uk/historic-hansard/commons/1840/feb/18/china#S3V0052P0_18400218_HOC_6

Hansard's Parliamentary Debates (1840) House of Commons, vol. 53–55.

Hevia, J. (1995) *Cherishing Men from Afar, Qing Guest Ritual and the Macartney Embassy of 1793*. Durham: Duke University Press Books.

Hevia, J. (2003) *English Lessons: The Pedagogy of Imperialism in Nineteenth-century China*. Durham: Duke University Press.

Hibbert, C. (1970) *The Dragon Wakes, China and the West, 1793–1911*. London: Longman.

Honour, H. (1961) *Chinoiserie, The Vision of Cathay*. London: John Murray.

Huw, B. (2006) *The Business of Empire. The East India Company and Imperial Britain, 1765–1833*. Cambridge: Cambridge University Press.

Jenkins, E.Z. (2013) *A Taste for China: English Subjectivity and the Prehistory of Orientalism*. Oxford: Oxford University Press.

Kippis, A. (1825) *The New Annual Register, or General Repository of History, Politics, Arts, Sciences, and Literature, for the Year 1824*. (Classic Reprint) 2018, Forgotten Books.

Kitson, P. (2013) *Forging Romantic China, Sino-British Cultural Exchange 1760–1840*. Cambridge: Cambridge University Press.

Kitson, P. (2016) 'The dark gift: Opium, John Francis Davis, Thomas De Quincey and the Amherst Embassy to China of 1816', in Kitson, P.J., Markley, R. (eds.) *Writing China, Essays on the Amherst Embassy (1816) and Sino-British Cultural Relations*. Cambridge: D.S. Brewer, pp. 56–82.

Lindsay, H.H. (1840) *Is the War with China a Just One?* London: James Ridgway Piccadilly.

Liu, L.H. (2006) *The Clash of Empires, the Invention of China in Modern World Making*. Cambridge, MA and London, England: Harvard University Press.

London Times (1851) 2 May 1851, The Opening of the Great Exhibition. Available at: http://www2.iath.virginia.edu/exist/cocoon/london/monuments_all.xq?id=times/1times51.502

Lovell, J. (2011) *The Opium War, Drugs, Dreams and the Making of China*. Oxford: Picador.

Mander, S.S. (1877) *Our Opium Trade with China*. London: Simpkin Marshall & Co.

Mantena, K. (2010) 'The crisis of liberal imperialism', in Bell, D. (ed.) *Victorian Visions of Global Order*. Cambridge: Cambridge University Press, pp. 113–135.

Martin, R.M. (1832) *Past and Present State of the Tea Trade*. London: Parbury, Allen & Co.

McDonough, F. (1994). *The British Empire, 1815–1914*. London: Hodder Education.

Medhurst, W.H. and Thoms, P.P. (1852) *Remarks on the Significance With their National Philosophy, Ethics, Legislation, and Administration, to Which Is Added an Essay on Civilisation and Its Present State in the East and West*. London: Smith, Elder & Co.

Melancon, G. (1999) 'Honour in opium? The British declaration of war on China, 1839–1840', *The International History Review*, 21(4), pp. 855–874. doi: 10.1080/07075332.1999.9640880

Melancon, G. (2003) *Britain's China Policy and the Opium Crisis, Balancing Drugs, Violence and National Honour, 1833–184*. London and New York: Routledge.

Mill, J.S. (1859) *Dissertations and Discussions: Political, Philosophical and Historical*. London: John W. Parker and Son, West Strand.

Miller, H. (2013) *Politics Personified: Portraiture, Caricature and Visual Culture in Britain, c. 1830–1880*. Manchester: Manchester University Press.

Moon, K.R. (1974) *Yellowface: Creating the Chinese in American Popular Music and Performance, 1850s–1920s*. New Brunswick, New Jersey and London: Rutgers University Press.

Morrison, R. (1815) *A Dictionary of the Chinese Language*. Macau: Printed at the Honourable East India Company Press.

Morse, H.B. (1910) *The International Relations of the Chinese Empire*. London: Longmans, Green, & Co.

Morse, H.B. (1926) *The Chronicles of the East India Company Trading to China*, 1635–1834. London: Oxford University Press. Digitalised version available at: https://www.univie.ac.at/Geschichte/China-Bibliographie/blog/2018/05/20/morse-the-chronicles-of-the-east-india-company-trading-to-china-1635-1834/

North, J. (ed.) (2003) 'Opium and the China Question' and 'Postscript on the China and the Opium Question'. *The Works of Thomas De Quincey*, Volume 11: Articles from Tait's Magazine and Blackwoods Magazine. London: Pickering and Chatto.

Organski, A.F.K. (1958) *World Politics*. New York: Alfred A. Knopf.

Parry, J. (1993) *The Rise and Fall of Liberal Government in Victorian Britain*. New Haven and London: Yale University Press.

Parry, J. (2006) *The Politics of Patriotism, English Liberalism, National Identity and Europe, 1830–1886*. Cambridge: Cambridge University Press.

Peyrefitte, A. (1992) *The Immobile Empire*, translated by Rothschild, J. New York: Alfred Knopf.

Pitts, J. (2010) 'Boundaries of Victorian International Law', in Bell, D. (ed.) *Victorian Visions of Global Order*. Cambridge: Cambridge University Press, pp. 67–88.

Platt, S.R. (2012) *Autumn in the Heavenly Kingdom*. New York: Alfred Knopf.

Platt, S.R. (2018) *Imperial Twilight: The Opium War and the End of China's Last Golden Age*. London: Atlantic Books.

Pointon, M. (1997) *Strategies for Showing: Women, Possession, and Representation in English Visual Culture, 1665– 1800*. Oxford: Oxford University Press.

Polachek, J. (1992) *The Inner Opium War*. Cambridge, MA: Council on East Asian Studies, Harvard University.

Porter, D. (2010) *The Chinese Taste in Eighteenth-century England*. Cambridge: Cambridge University Press.

Price, B. (2019) *The Chinese in Britain, A History of Visitors and Settlers*. Gloucestershire: Amberley Publishing.

Qing Shi Lu (1842)《清实录》*[Historical Archive]*, Digitalised version available at: https://ctext.org/wiki.pl?if=gb&chapter=137738

Ray, R. (2016) 'Ornamental exotica, Transplanting the aesthetics of tea consumption and the birth of a British exotic', in Batsaki, Y., Cahalan, S., Tchikine, A. (eds.) *The Botany of Empire in the Long Eighteenth Century*. Washington DC: Dumbarton Oaks Research Library and Collection, pp. 259–281.

Smith, W. (1826) *Tsiology: A Discourse on Tea*. London: published by WM. Walker.

Stanley, H. (ed.) (1865) *The East and the West: Our Dealings with Our Neighbours*. London: Hatchard and Co.

Staunton, G.T. (1836) *Remarks on the British Relations with China, and the Proposed Plans for Improving Them*. London: E. Lloyd. Free e-book available at: https://play.google.com/books/reader?id=vZVdAAAAcAAJ&hl=zh_CN&pg=GBS.PA1

Staunton, G.T. (1840) 'Corrected report of the speech of Sir George Staunton, on Sir James Graham's Motion on the China Trade'. In *The House of Commons*, April 7, 1840. London: Simpkin, Marshall.

The Household Narrative of Current Events (1851) Available at: http://www.djo.org.uk/household-narrative-of-current-events/year-1851/page-114.html

Thoms, O.O. (1853) *The Emperor of China v. the Queen of England: A Refutation of the Arguments Contained in the Seven Official Documents Transmitted by Her Majesty's Government at Hong Kong, Who Maintain That the Documents of the Chinese Government Contain Insulting Language*. London: P.P. Thoms.

Tsiang, T.F. (1936) 'China and European expansion'. *Politica*, 2, pp. 1–18.

Waley-Cohen, J. (2000). *Sextants of Beijing, Global Currents in Chinese History*. New York: Norton.

Wan, M. (2011) 《明代中外关系史论稿》 *[China's Foreign Relations in the Ming Dynasty]*. Beijing: China Social Sciences Press.

Wang, T.T. (1993) 'The Macartney Mission: A bicentennial review', in Bickers, R.A. (ed.) *Brief Reviews of Books – Ritual and Diplomacy: The Macartney Mission to China, 1792–1794*, pp. 43–56. Papers Presented at the 12 Conference of the British Association for Asian Studies, Marking the Bicentenary of the Macartney Mission to China. London: The British Association for Chinese Studies and Wellsweep Press.

Westad, O.A. (2013) *Restless Empire, China and the World since 1750*. London: Vintage Books.

Conclusion: The two great reversals – Historical implications on the modern-day interactions between a post-Brexit UK and a globalising China

History never repeats itself, but it does often rhyme.

– Mark Twain[1]

In 1986, Queen Elizabeth II became the first and only reigning British monarch who visited China. She presented her ancestor's 1596 letter to the Ming Emperor as a special gift to the then chairman of China Li Xiannian and mentioned it in her speech that "Some 390 years ago my forebear, Queen Elizabeth I, wrote to the Wan Li Emperor expressing the hope that trade might be developed between England and China. The messenger met with misfortune and that letter never arrived. Fortunately, postal services have improved since 1602, your message inviting us here arrived safely, and it has given me great pleasure to accept it".[2] The Queen had initially planned to take the 1602 letter to China (Figure 1.1 in the book), in a correspondence from Buckingham Palace to the Lancashire Archive dated 8 October 1986, it stated: "it is a fascinating story and the present Queen Elizabeth is very pleased to have learnt about it before her own visit to the Emperor's successors. What a pity that a copy has already gone to the Chinese National Archives[3] since it would have been even better if the Queen herself had been able to arrange for the late delivery of Her Majesty's predecessor's message".[4] What struck me is the wording of "her own visit to the Emperor's successors"; it seems the People's Republic of China founded in 1949 to mark the end of the "century of humiliations" was still seen as the same empire and the new Communist Party leader was considered the "Emperor's successors". On the one hand, the continuity between the Imperial China and modern China is an enchanting topic that the authoritarian regime of modern China often invites associations with the Chinese emperor. When Xi Jinping came to power in 2013, *The Economist* published a feature story titled "Let's party like it's 1793", with a cover image of Xi dressed like the Qianlong Emperor, but with images of a modern China embroidered in his dragon robe, holding a champagne glass in one of his hands,[5] ready to trade with the rest of the world. We can appreciate the astounding words

DOI: 10.4324/9781003156383-9

that Peyrefitte (1992: 553) finished his book with: "Qianlong and Macartney are not dead but live among us still, reincarnated in this century. Perhaps they are immortal". On the other hand, if we reflect on Macartney's famous remark on the Qing China as an "old, crazy First rate man-of-war" that "can never be rebuilt on the old bottom", the China that welcomed Queen Elizabeth II in 1986 was a completely rebuilt China that had survived foreign invasions, civil wars, disastrous economic policies and thrived in the economic boom thanks to its opening-up, by itself to the outside world. It is a China embracing the world and becoming part of the world, though many Chinese nationalists today still look at the world as if there are only two countries: the "middle country" (Zhongguo, 中国) and the "outside country" (Waiguo, 外国). Interestingly, in very loosely defined yet commonly referenced terms, there are also only two kinds of countries in the world, i.e., "developed" and "developing" countries. China still considers itself a developing country because it is in the process of developing and changing quickly, while the Western economy is less dynamic as it has completed the stage of development. This is a fascinating reversal as two centuries earlier, the British Empire was the developing one that challenged Qing China, the developed civilisation.

Looking back from today, this "see-saw of history" (Dawson, 1967: 30) between the two empires allows us to see two great reversals in the bilateral relations: first was the reversal of "otherness" when China first regarded the British as barbarous, then being regarded by the British to be uncivilised. From the early days of contact, Europeans had gazed into the mirror of China to understand "self and other". In the eighteenth century, the idea of China "was central to the making of modernity and the formation of the modern Western human self" (Kitson, 2013: 5; Hayot, 2009; Porter, 2010). It had served as a positive inspiration to many European thinkers who imagined the Confucian China as a model society of enlightenment. When China's door was forced open with gunboats, its international status was reduced from an admirable wealthy power with cultural superiority to a backward "sick man of Asia" by the mid-nineteenth century, when Great Britain became the new "land of wealth and power" and a model society that gave Chinese people "an overpowering desire to brave the seas in order to study the civilisations of the West and ascertain the secrets of their strength and prosperity" (Tyau, 1920: 14). This was accompanied by the Chinese claim of universal supremacy giving way to the British claim of universal values. However, when the British became strong enough to emerge as the prevailing global power and a mighty hegemon, its view of the world order with equality at the core of their doctrine of diplomacy and international relations, also became a hierarchal one with itself at the superior position.

The other reversal is the contemporary one that is happening today when China transformed from being a closed-off country to an advocate of globalisation and the world's No. 1 trading nation with modern technology. In May 1851, between the two Opium Wars, the Great Exhibition was staged in London, with a prime motive to use this prodigious display of the industrial and scientific dynamism of the British Empire to make clear to the world its role as industrial leader. The Queen wrote that the inauguration of the Great Exhibition was the "greatest day in our history". It set the precedent for the World Expo that became popular in the nineteenth century. It was until 2010 when China (Shanghai) hosted its first World Expo, the year when China's GDP became the world's second largest. In a way, these two World Expos represented the two reversals in terms of economic prowess between the two countries. Between the two reversals, we can see the recurrent themes of honour and humiliation; perplexity and complexity; open door to international trade and close door for national security. It is now China's turn to knock the door of the West, with commodities, investment, and even 5G technology. Here by saying "knock the door of the West" I do not mean to say the door was always intentionally closed to China, but refer to the recent bans in the US and UK targeted at Chinese companies such as Huawei. For them, the knock may come as a wake-up call, when China is now trying to sell its most cutting-edge world-leading technologies to the Western countries. In Bickers (2012: 399) words, "a globalised China is not new; but a powerful global China is unprecedented", to this the western reaction can be summarised by the news headline title, "West can't believe nor accept China's progress".[6] Even their countermeasures adopted ring a bell: back then, in order to reduce Britain's dependency on tea from China, they brought tea cultivation and production to Indian plantations that were owned and managed by the British; today, they are aiming to form a Democracy-10 alliance to reduce their reliance on 5G technology from the authoritarian China. It seems the psychological pattern has played out once again, to the extent that not only a global divide of "us and them" is sustained, but even in terms of "friends and enemies"?

This book has traced how China was imagined, admired, studied and re-examined, criticised and then despised by the British along with the rise of the British Empire during the two centuries from the seventeenth to the mid-nineteenth century. As perceptively summarised by Westad (2013: 15), "these two centuries is the story of China's encounter with capitalist modernity and of how Chinese shaped that modernity and were shaped by it in roughly equal turns". However, for the subsequent two centuries of Chinese tumult, the ascendant West has almost forgotten that for much of the previous millennium, it was China that had been more advanced, by many measures of economic development and cultural achievement. Imperial China harvested admirations and envy from "the crisis-riven seventeenth-century Europe" before "stagnation and inertia that left China outside of history altogether and the Chinese peculiarly insensible to otherwise irresistible forces of historical change" (Porter, 2010: 181–182). Now, it is China's turn again to move back closer to the centre of the world stage as a prominent, if not predominant power, with similar "irresistible forces of historical change". If we look at the seemingly inexorable rise of China through a rear-view mirror of history, we can see why "the rise – or more accurately re-emergence – of China as a world power has already begun to occasion, in the West, complex and dramatically ambivalent responses that resonate unmistakably with those evoked by the emergence of China" (Porter, 2010: 11).

So, what is the British response to the Chinese impact? Over four centuries on from the earliest letter correspondence, Britain is still trying to forge a satisfactory relationship with China. We can see the trajectory of China's movement from splendour to decay then to regeneration. When China rises again, the West all want a piece of its wealth, but do not know how to deal with its authoritarian government. It feels like a "familiar stranger". When Xi Jinping's "China Dream" was set to regain its former glory, it is called a dream of "national rejuvenation", using the sentiment-loaded "Chinese nation", rather than the ideology-charged "socialist country" as a new vision. It was inspired by the strong desire to end the stigma from the "century of humiliations", and we can also see the legacy of Macartney's "mission of humiliations" in the British dealing with China today. In fact, reminiscences are everywhere, with two ready examples being the state visits exchanged between the UK and China in the 2010s.

In November 2010, when the then British Prime Minister David Cameron took the largest ever delegation to China for the start of the "golden era" of bilateral relations, the poppy he was wearing caused a little standoff. *The Guardian* reported that "Chinese officials apparently asked the UK delegation not to wear Remembrance Day poppies because they were a symbol of China's humiliation at the hands of Europe in the Opium Wars. To comply would have been good manners". A good sign for some hard-won mutual respect and understanding was shown by the Chinese nationalist media *Global Times*, which finished the report about the controversy with an interview with a scholar from the Chinese Academy of Social Sciences. He explained the British tradition of wearing a poppy for the Frist World War, with no other political connotations, nor any connections with the Opium War, so "we should respect their tradition and not take offence".[7]

As explained in Chapter 5, as the first Chinese word entering the English language, the word "kowtow" remains etched in the political discourse in the UK today, it was repeatedly used in various China-related contexts and media criticism of the government's "soft" stance of developing relations with China, from David Cameron's Golden Era to Boris Johnson's initial decision to allow Huawei's role in the British 5G network. When Xi paid his first state visit to the UK in 2015, we can read "to kowtow or not" in the British news headlines when some critics believed the UK needed "to redeem the honour and cultural superiority of the British, which had been compromised in the earlier encounter between Lord Macartney and the Qianlong Emperor" (Liu, 2006: 217); we can still see the Hong Kong issue as a constant obstacle and a new flash point standing between the two countries; and we can still hear the echo of the 1840 Parliamentary debate over sending gunboats to China in the 2020 debate over Huawei's participation in the UK's 5G network. Humiliation is the mirror narrative that was played by both sides, neither want their compatriots to experience the humiliations again, nor want them to forget the lessons they learned from the Anglo-Chinese history. However, if the 1793 mission of humiliation is picked up by the British media to remind its political leaders today, the "century of humiliations" have been constantly taught at schools to all Chinese people, thus not a distant memory but embedded knowledge in its political history and incorporated into the very heart of its relations with the West.

As put in the very beginning of Chapter 1, when the history of Anglo-Chinese relations is studied, it often starts with the Opium War in China and the Macartney Embassy in the UK. Each chose the humiliating incident as the start of the turbulent history of Anglo-Chinese relations that was marked with arrogance and antagonism, because it was the other party that was on the morally wrong side. The "century of humiliations" is part of the patriotism education today to picture China as a victim, it left an indelible mark in people's memory as inscribed on the Monument to the People's Heroes at the heart of the Tian'anmen Square: "Long Live people's heroes over the years since 1840 who had fallen in the fights against internal and external enemies and for the independence of Chinese nation and happiness of Chinese people". As Platt (2018: xxii) summarised, "the Opium War had stood for the essence of everything modern China has tried to leave behind: weakness, victimhood, shame". The ruined Yuanming Yuan park as a reminder of the plunder by rapacious nations has become a must-visit for school trips to incite strong patriotic feelings. It may be hard for a Westerner to imagine the profound political symbolism of the repatriation of the zodiac bronzes, the most easily recognised looted "national treasures" from Yuanming Yuan during the Second Opium War, back to China. Kleutghen (2011: 165) elaborated its symbolism as "global icons of Chinese nationalism", "the divine tripods of contemporary Chinese government", and "a critical benchmark against which China measures its redemption from national humiliation and political legitimacy on the international stage".

In the UK, in the public-facing National Army Museum that would also receive school visits, the following was put for the exhibition of Opium War: "Between 1839 and 1842, British forces fought a war in China that benefitted drug smugglers. Their subsequent victory in the conflict opened up the lucrative Chinese trade to British merchants". The narrative also traced the root causes to the kowtow issue: "Relations were already strained by the hostile attitude adopted by Chinese officials in negotiations with the British. The Chinese were suspicious and refused to enter into full diplomatic relations. This was because British officials had shocked the Chinese by refusing to kow-tow before the Emperor in accordance with protocol".[8] Then in the souvenir shop of the Cutty Sark Museum in London, what caught my eyes was a tin of Chinese tea branded "gunpowder green tea", which has been "hugely popular in Britain since the eighteenth century and was one of the original teas brought over from China by the *Cutty Sark*. Sourced from Hunan Province, the tealeaves are pan-fried, resulting in the leaves curling up into tight pellets that bear an uncanny resemblance to the gunpowder shots of the eighteenth century, hence the name. When brewed, the delicate tealeaves will unfurl, delivering a beautifully soft and balanced green tea flavour – deliciously refreshing".[9] This name association is indeed "uncanny" for me, as this type of tea is known as "pearl tea" in Chinese, both for its tiny round shape and highly rated value. No Chinese person would associate its elegant movement when unfurling in the water and its "deliciously refreshing" pleasant flavour with gunpowder, while in England, the way the name has been kept for successful commercialisation makes one wonder if there was much historical reflection with remorse. On the other hand, when China regained the pre-eminence it had held for centuries on the global stage and self-confidence in its own culture, the ambience to prompt historical reflections and to learn from the West is also diminishing.

This points to another reversal in the learning direction: when China saw itself as the definition of civilisation, it saw no need to send people abroad to learn from the rest of the world, while the British were very keen on learning everything about China as discussed in Chapters 3–6, gaining much more knowledge about China than the other way round. During the Macartney Embassy, they were not able to find one single British who can understand Chinese to be the interpreter; by the time when the *Treaty of Nanking* was signed, there was not a single Chinese who can translate the English treaty as the interpreters in Canton only speak Pidgin English, so both the official English version and the Chinese translation were provided by the British side. Then the water-shed event of the Opium Wars turned it around and started a new era of *Xi Xue Dong Jian*[10] (Western learning spreading to the East, 西学东渐) in China with the maxim of "Chinese essence and Western utility" (*Zhongti Xiyong*, 中体西用). This made it possible for the debut of *Xi Xue* in China, which has no English equivalent till today. As the mirror image of Sinology in the West, I would like to translate it as Occidentalogy (the study of the West done by Chinese), as this is the first time for Chinese from the Celestial Empire to actively pursue the Western learning. Tongwen Guan (同文馆), or School of Combined Learning, was established in 1862, following the setup of the General Office of Managing Foreign Affairs (Zongli Geguo Shiwu Yamen, 总理各国事务衙门) in 1861. Then the first four batches of 120 Chinese students were sent abroad to learn from the West from 1872 to 1875. Even the last Emperor Xuantong had an English tutor[11] from 1919 to1924, when he still lived inside the Forbidden City as a non-sovereign monarch.

Interestingly, the British disillusion of China was mirrored years later when the first generation of Chinese students arrived in the UK in the beginning of the twentieth century, when London was reputed as "the metropolis of the world's greatest empire", that "possessed everything which human vanities could crave for – honour, fame, wealth". As Tyau (1920: 19–20) vividly described in his book *London through Chinese Eyes*:

> London – the emporium of the world's commerce! London – the vortex of the world's politics! London – the idol city of loyal Britons, the fountain head of a language which bids fair to be the universal language of the globe! London – the heart of a world empire, the nerve centre of territories and dominions on which the sun never sets! Aided and coloured by a fertile imagination, I pictured London as the embodiment of all the wealth and luxury that were so vividly portrayed in the 'Arabian Nights'.

However, the author admitted that "I was soon disillusioned", when he realised that it was just as "Peking was painted by Marco Polo in his remarkable Travels". Yet, the difference is after this period of disappointment of seeing London as nothing like his dream land, the author said "my respect for it increased none the less with the lapse of years" (ibid: 23). As his book title suggests, *London through Chinese Eyes* became a symbol of rule of law, liberalism, democracy, and press freedom, which allowed "the affairs of the state or the policies of the government may be discussed or criticised" (ibid: 62). These reflections are still highly relevant to contemporary China today, where these are still lacking. In a way, Beijing today has changed so much, yet with so much remaining unchanged. The key to solving today's problems can often be found from history, as the world history per se is the outcome of competition between different systems.

The education system is another example of the reversal. China's rigorous examination system for officialdom was once considered a model for the West to learn from during the mid-seventeenth century, which sustained the imagined perfect meritocracy, even the EIC adopted this model in 1806 in establishing a competitive exam of its own. A century later in 1905, the Chinese imperial exam was abolished as a result of the Westernization Movement started in the 1860s. The backward-looking rigidities of Chinese education system was considered an impediment to progress in China. Since the imperial examinations were principally confined to knowledge of the language and study of classical Confucian texts, its reliance on the rote learning of ancient dogma and its failure to engage with contemporary scientific and technological advancement made the Chinese people and the country non-progressive. Rationality and scientific enquiry based on experiment and observation was alien to the Chinese. The Westernization Movement after the Second Opium War stimulated China's "thirst for and understanding of the West, or European and American thought, culture and technology, which eventually far outstripped the efforts of the foreign China experts" (Bickers, 2012: 397). The knowledge "see-saw" was reversed in that the average Chinese people's knowledge about the West is a lot more than the other way round, not to mention the Chinese students, visiting scholars, and immigrants to the West outnumbering Westerners to China. The West is so used to being the centre of modern civilisation that it shows a similar pattern of complacency, being blind to what is happening in China today. Therefore, the mutual perception gap is never filled, at first due to language barriers which were almost insurmountable obstacles as the Chinese law forbid foreigners learning the language, then because of the power shift that gave rise to Orientalism. Equality is never truly established between the two: they either "look up" or "look down", never "look into" the other. If we can really learn something from history, the first lesson would be that there is a thin line between arrogance and ignorance. It is time to end the perennial Self-Other dichotomy and transform the relationship between the two from a see-saw shift of rise and fall against each other to a Yin-Yang nexus of enhancing each other.

Unfortunately, the see-saw shift continues, and in a much more compressed timeframe. Since China's economy had long overtaken the UK and now close to that of the US, the wave of learning from the West is subsiding and a return to China's own tradition is surging. This can be seen in the revival of Confucianism, after long neglect in the West and being attacked in China's own New Culture Movement (1915–1920) and the Cultural Revolution (1966–1976), it is coming back and "echoes in interesting ways its involvement in European debates in an earlier age", when it offered "an important critique of and alternative to Western individualism" (Clarke, 2003: 223–224). Another example is the rapidly evolving education and training market in China. The top performer of the industry was a private company "New Oriental Education", whose business focused on English teaching and exam preparations for students to study abroad. It was listed in the NYSE in 2006, with its success story even made into an award-winning film *American Dreams in China* in 2013. By 2019, it was overtaken by Beijing Offcn Education & Technology as the top player, which specialises in the National Admission Examination for Civil Service, a modern version of the imperial examination to gain entry into the government sector. Then in 2021, a new government regulation that banned private tutoring on and off campus caused an earthquake in the industry. While the Chinese lawmaker proposed removing English as "core subject"[12] in May 2021, a new policy was already announced in Shanghai in August that "English out, Xi Jinping Thought in at Shanghai schools".[13] There was no public hearing or discussions before the policy was announced, and anyone who suggested China would benefit from Western curricula and ideas were heavily criticised for being unpatriotic (Price, 2019: 11). The pattern of *Zhongti Xiyong* (Chinese essence and western utility) is still discernible in China today as the *ti-yong* (essence-utility) rationale serves conceptually to selectively adopt Western practical technical skills to serve its economic development, but not ideologies that is suspected to have subversive potential to its own political identity. The need for a system change was hereby denied.

The old standing off between the Chinese and Western operating systems also continues to shift position. As Bell (2007: 9) summarised, "liberal internationalism was powered by the twin engines of international law and international commerce, its adherents believing that when combined and properly directed, the two could generate a transformation in international 'morality', ushering in a new, more harmonious age". Although sharing two key concepts of "morality" and "harmony" with Confucianism, these twin "international" engines are completely different cornerstones from the Chinese system that is built on state control and concentric hierarchy. While the Tributary System had long been dissolved into the ash heap of history along with the decline of the Qing, international relations scholar Susan Strange (1999: 345) has boldly put forward a term of "Westfailure System", which is "failing Capitalism, the Planet and global (and national) civil society". Of course, we will not anticipate a revival of the antiquated Tributary System, but we are witnessing China's challenge to the Western universalism of its political model, claimed by the famous "end of history"[14] narrative. We all have to agree that history is far from reaching the end, but if there *is* an end, must it be one side prevailing the other like the Chinese saying made famous by Mao Zedong – "either the east wind prevails over the west wind, or the west wind prevails over the east wind"[15]? When there is a second reversal, it forms a circle, but aren't we supposed to move forward along the "long course of river of history" rather than being stuck in a circle? Perhaps we can draw inspirations from the first stanza of Kipling's (1889) *Ballad of East and West*:

> East is East, and West is West,
> and never the twain shall meet,
> Till Earth and Sky stand presently at God's great Judgement seat;
> But there is neither East nor West,
> Border, nor Breed, nor Birth,
> When two strong men stand face to face,
> though they come from the ends of the earth!

After the periods of Pax Sinica, Pax Britannica and Pax Americana, the twenty-first century is when the two strong men stand face to face, not looking up or looking down at each other, but into the eyes and contemplating. This is the time when border should become bridge while breed and birth become what is exchanged over the bridge. Through the exchanges, it will nurture inner drives to make changes to oneself, at least that is how change would work for China. China cannot *be changed*, it can only *change itself*; the most amazing success story so far is when China opened itself to the outside world, at an opportune time to catch the new wave of globalisation, which changed the economic balances and power dynamics so swiftly that it became known as the "Fourth Industrial Revolution".

In a way, globalisation has played a central role in China's rise, similar to the role played by the Industrial Revolution to the British rise. Both enabled the two to surge upward at astonishing rates and send worldwide repercussions. Morris (2011) argued that the Industrial Revolution created the "great divergence" between the West and the East, mainly by using new steam-powered engines. The substantial head start gained from the Industrial Revolution enabled Britain to become the "workplace of the world", it accounted for almost a quarter of the world's manufacturing output and trade by 1880 (Kennedy, 1989). A century later, China's opening up since the 1980s has paved its way of becoming the "world factory", and by 2021, its miraculous economic development has projected it to account for nearly 30 per cent of the global manufacturing output. The volume of world trade, and the comparative advantage of China's manufacturing means it benefits more from globalisation than other countries. It is now China's turn to build factories and sell low-cost commodities to all over the world. In the 1830s and 1840s, the expansion of overseas trade took on a new urgency for the British: "New markets were needed for the swiftly rising production of textiles and ironware, to avert depression, unemployment and strife in industrial districts. British's domestic tranquillity required the growth of its trade" (Darwin, 2009: 36). Now China is facing a similar issue to the then Britain and pursuing similar solutions – looking for new markets for its expanded capacity and using employment and economic prosperity to maintain domestic stability, there was also an urge to rewrite some of the established rules. Its Belt and Road Initiative has a clear road map to make the whole world its market. Some observers already commented that "the dramatic shift of power from East to West which occurred in the Renaissance period is in the process of being reversed" (Clarke, 2003: 223).

I still remember the deep impression the line left on me when I first visited the British Museum of Science and Industry: "I sell here, Sir, what all the world desires to have – Power". This most powerful double entendre was said by Matthew Boulton in 1776, when power was not only transforming England, but the whole world order, setting off the collapse of a centuries-old world order maintained by agrarian and regional empires. Britain became the first empire with a global reach and vision, forming a stark contrast to the inward-looking vision of China that is still evident today: If you watch BBC news, the headlines would be dominated by breaking news stories happening all over the world, even if in a distant land of a small nation like Myanmar. While in China, even if a war is breaking out in a neighbouring country, there is simply no way for "international news" to clinch the prime-time headlines, which is always reserved to the head of state and domestic news.

So, globalisation has smoothed transactions but not erased the fundamental ideological differences. Notwithstanding the tremendous change in configurations of global power we witness today, there is also so much that has remained unchanged or even unchangeable. China's ongoing quest to strike a balance between foreign trade and foreign influence, between embracing globalisation and retaining autonomy and a distinctive national identity, and between the so-called two extremes of "self-conceited and self-deprecation", or between confidence in oneself and openness to others, in many ways represents a more sophisticated continuation of past struggles, as trade terms are more negotiable than clashing ideas. The equilibrium is thus fragile and hard to achieve. More often than not, it ends up in China's complex love-hate relationship with the West, reflected in a paradox of rejection and emulation: the government rhetoric is often mixed with a deep mistrust and hostility with willingness to engage with the West; while the emerging middle class and new rich are allowed to embrace western technology, pursue a Western lifestyle, send their children abroad to private schools and universities, and flaunt the latest gadgets and luxuries, but not embrace the freedom and democratic norms. For example, you can queue to get a newly released model of an Apple smart phone on the same day as the US but cannot use Google and Youtube – another example of the government's stance of *Zhongti Xiyong*. When the ancient Great Wall is now used to attract foreign tourists rather than defending against foreign invaders, the Great Fire Wall of China is erected to protect its "essence" from being attacked. The old border of civilisation and barbarism has evolved into a segregation between outsiders and insiders to ward off potentially dangerous foreign influence that could pose threats to domestic stability and national security. China is even nicknamed the "walled country" (墙国), a homophone of the "strong country" (强国) that it aims to develop into. But can a walled country be a strong country at the same time?

The virtual Great Wall reminds us of the similar difficulties experienced by the Macartney and Amherst Embassies to those encountered by diplomats and the businessmen from both countries at the present time. For example, careful omissions if not deliberate distortions in translation are still common practice in China today, such as selected Chinese translations of western media commentaries on current affairs and book publications. China may have transformed dramatically in the twenty-first century, but it still plays by rules that differ from those of the Western world, and even gained a new name of the "China Model", making it a formidable international contender. In the marketplace today where Chinese businesspeople dressed in Western suits can negotiate across linguistic barriers in English, and even in modern office buildings designed by Western architects, it still yields to authority in Beijing that shows no intention of changing its state-controlled system in defiance of the clamour of foreigners. Two centuries later, they may be feeling the same as Bickers (2012: 397) remarked, "Foreigners felt imprisoned in the Canton factories, then confined in the five treaty ports. They felt constrained no matter how many open cities or rivers there were. The foreign traders only ever saw new restrictions; never saw their horizons broadened but only new barriers to overcome".

Exactly one hundred years ago in 1922, Bertrand Russell wrote:

> Chinese problems, even if they affected no one outside China, would be of vast importance, since the Chinese are estimated to constitute about a quarter of the human race. In fact, however, all the world will be vitally affected by the development of Chinese affairs, which may well prove a decisive factor, for good or evil, during the next two centuries. This makes it important, to Europe and America almost as much as to Asia, that there should be an intelligent understanding of the questions raised by China, even if, as yet, definite answers are difficult to give. (Russell, 1922: 1)

Today, the puzzling questions of China are even more difficult to answer, and affecting a lot more people outside China, many of whom do not have the "receptive and reflective disposition". China continues to fascinate as much as it frustrates the West. It is a story kept on being told and retold by different people and even today, there is still "a Tale of Two Chinas":

> China is superior, China is inferior;
> China is modern, China is antiquated;
> China is hard, China is soft;
> China is hostile, China is friendly;
> China is the bully, China is the victim;
> China is a threat, China is an opportunity;
> You can accomplish anything in China,
> You can accomplish nothing in China.

China's vision today has moved from realising its own China Dream to building "a community of shared future for mankind", refusing to adopt the notion of a "zero sum game" in international relations. What may emerge from a renewed encounter is not just to embrace the differences, but to draw inspirations from them and make them mutually enhancing. Four centuries ago, it was a great way for the British to present itself as China's "neighbour on the sea" when China's notion of neighbours was restricted to those who shared land borders with it. In the globalised world today, we are not just neighbours but also partners, and we do not just exchange ideas and commodities, but create new ideas and develop new products together. As explained in the Introduction, this book is written for the commemoration of the 50th anniversary of formal diplomatic relations established between the UK and China. On a historical canvas, it has traced the persistence of transcultural exchanges and trade between the two empires. Standing together today in the new challenging terrain beyond Orientalism and Occidentalism, we are writing answers for future historians, who will be writing for its centennial celebration in another 50 years. Will today's reflection about "us" and "other" generate a new thinking about "we" in the future? Will we enter a new phase of East-West nexus in which the encounter of ideas will eventually reach the Yin-Yang harmony? Only time can tell.

Notes

1 There is no substantive evidence that Twain ever uttered this aphorism, he died in 1910. In 1970, the two known close matches appeared in print, and both attributed it to him. The line is too good to resist and rhymes with my own conclusion of the book.
2 Source: https://www.latimes.com/archives/la-xpm-1986-10-13-mn-3171-story.html
3 A colloquium was held from 7–10 October 1985 in Beijing to celebrate the 60th anniversary of the establishment of the National Archives of China. Dr. Geoffrey Martin, then Keeper of Public Records, presented a copy of the letter to the Archives Director in Beijing.
4 The gifts exchanged during the Queen's visit offered an interesting echo to the Macartney Embassy: apart from this historic letter, the Queen also gifted a limousine of Rolls Royce, the make for royalty and heads of state. This is reminiscent of the King's carriage gifted to the Qianlong Emperor by the first embassy. Interestingly, the Chinese government has gifted back a model of the Qin bronze chariot (秦陵铜车马) that were unearthed in 1980 at the Mausoleum of the First Chinese Emperor, Qin Shi Huang, along with some silk materials, representing the ancient civilisation and what fits for a Chinese emperor.
5 Source: https://www.economist.com/weeklyedition/2013-05-04
6 Daily Express, 4 July 2021. Available at: https://www.dailyexpress.com.my/read/4459/west-can-t-believe-nor-accept-china-s-progress/
7 The interview can be seen at: https://world.huanqiu.com/article/9CaKrnJpeuD
8 Source: https://www.nam.ac.uk/explore/opium-war-1839-1842
9 Source: https://shop.rmg.co.uk/products/cutty-sark-gunpowder-green-tea-by-twinings
10 The first stage refers to the spreading of Western learning by missionaries spearheaded by Matteo Ricci during the Ming China, but that was when China was being receptive of Western learning, not actively pursuing it.

11 His name is Reginald Fleming Johnston. After he came back to the UK, Johnston was appointed Professor of Chinese in the University of London in 1931, a post based at the School of Oriental and African Studies. He published the book *Twilight in the Forbidden City* in 1934 and bequeathed his library to SOAS in 1935, one of the finest collections of Chinese and East Asian books in the country, consists of over 16,000 volumes.

12 Source: https://www.globaltimes.cn/page/202103/1217396.shtml

13 Source: https://asia.nikkei.com/Business/Education/English-out-Xi-Jinping-Thought-in-at-Shanghai-schools

14 The "end of history" is a political and philosophical concept popularised by Francis Fukuyama, whose essay *The End of History?* was published months before the fall of the Berlin Wall in 1989 that centers around the idea that now that its two most important competitors, fascism and communism, have been defeated, there should no longer be any serious competition for liberal democracy and the market economy. This does not mean that Fukuyama believes that a modern liberal democracy is the perfect political system, but rather that he does not think another political structure can provide citizens with the levels of wealth and personal liberties that a liberal democracy can.

15 The original line was from the classic novel of *Dream of the Red Chamber* by Cao Xueqin, 1791.

References

Bell, D. (ed.) (2007) *Victorian Visions of Global Order, Empire and International Relations in Nineteenth-Century Political Thought*. Cambridge: Cambridge University Press.

Bickers, R. (2012) *The Scramble for China, Foreign Devils in the Qing Empire, 1832–1819*. London: Penguin Books.

Clarke, J.J. (2003) *Oriental Enlightenment: The Encounter between Asian and Western Thought*. London: Routledge.

Darwin, J. (2009) *The Empire Project, The Rise and Fall of the British World-System 1830–1970*. Cambridge: Cambridge University Press.

Dawson, R. (1967) *The Chinese Chameleon: An Analysis of European Conceptions of Chinese Civilisation*. Oxford: Oxford University Press.

Hayot, E. (2009) *The Hypothetical Mandarin: Sympathy, Modernity and Chinese Pain*. New York, USA: Oxford University Press.

Kennedy, P. (1989) *The Rise and Fall of the Great Powers*. London: William Collins.

Kitson, P. (2013) *Forging Romantic China, Sino-British Cultural Exchange 1760–1840*. Cambridge: Cambridge University Press.

Kleutghen, K. (2011) 'Heads of state: Looting, nationalism, and repatriation of the zodiac bronzes', in Delson, S. (ed.) *Ai Weiwei: Circle of Animals*. New York: Prestel, pp. 162–185.

Liu, L.H. (2006) *The Clash of Empires, The Invention of China in Modern World Making*. Massachusetts and London, England: Harvard University Press.

Morris, I. (2011) *Why the West Rules for Now, The Patterns of History and What They Reveal about the Future*. London: Profile Books.

Peyrefitte, A. (1992) *The Immobile Empire*, translated by Rothschild, J. New York: Alfred Knopf.

Platt, S.R. (2018) *Imperial Twilight: Shortlisted for the Baillie Gifford Prize.* London: Atlantic Books.
Porter, D. (2010) *The Chinese Taste in Eighteenth-Century England.* Cambridge: Cambridge University Press.
Price, B. (2019) *The Chinese in Britain, A History of Visitors and Settlers.* Gloucestershire: Amberley Publishing.
Russell, B. (1922) *The Problem of China.* London: George Allen & Unwin Ltd.
Strange, S. (1999) 'The Westfailure system', *Review of International Studies*, 25, pp. 345–354.
Tyau, M.C.T.Z. (1920) *London Through Chinese Eyes.* London: The Swarthmore Press, Ltd.
Westad, O.A. (2013) *Restless Empire, China and the World since 1750.* London: Vintage Books.

Appendix 1

Queen Elizabeth I's 1583 letter to the Ming Emperor Wanli, discussed in Chapter 1

Source: Richard Hakluyt's book *The Principall Navigations, Voiages, Traffiques and Discoueries of the English Nation* (1589–1600). Imprinted at London by George Bishop, Ralph Newberie and Robert Baker. Vol. 2, p. 245.

Original Sixteenth Century Text

A letter written by her Majestie to the King of *China*, Februarie 1583.

Elizabeth by the grace of God (1) Queene of England, etc. Most Imperial and invincible prince, our honest subject John Newbery the bringer hereof, who with your favour hath taken in hand the voyage which nowe hee pursueth to the parts and countreys of your Empire, not trusting upon any other ground then upon the favour of your Imperiall clemencie and humanitie, is moved to undertake a thing of so much Difficultie, being perswaded that hee having entered into so many perils, your Majestie will not dislike (2) the same, especially, if it may appeare that it be not Damageable unto your royall Majestie, and that to your people it will bring some profite: of both which things he not doubting, with more willing mind hath prepared himself for his Destinated voyage unto us well liked of. For by this means (3) we perceive, that the profit which by the mutual trade on both sides, al the princes our neighbours in the West (4) do receive, your Imperial majestie and those that be subject under your dominion, to their great joy and benefit shal have the same, which consisteth in the transporting outward of such things whereof we have plenty, and in bringing in such things as we stand in need of. It cannot otherwise be, but that seeing we are borne and made to have need one of another, and that wee are bound to aide one another (5), but that your imperial Majestie wil wel like of it, and by your subjects too like indevor wil be accepted (6). For the increase whereof, if your imperial Majestie shall added the securitie of passage, with other privileges most necessary to use the trade with your men, your majestie shal doe that which belongeth (7) to a most honourable and liberal prince, and deserve so much of us, as by no continuance or length of time shal be forgotten.

Which request of ours we do most instantly desire to be taken in good part of your majestie, and so great a benefit towards us and our men, we shall endevor by diligence to requite (8) when time shal serve thereunto. The God Almighty long preserve your Imperial majestie.

Translation into modern English

Elizabeth, by the grace of God (1), Queen of England, etc. Most imperial and invincible Prince, our honest subject, John Newbery, the bringer of this letter, who with our favour has taken in hand the voyage which he now pursues to the parts and countries of your empire, not trusting upon any other ground than upon the favour of your imperial clemency and humanity, is moved to undertake a thing of so much difficulty. Being persuaded that he has entered so many perils, your Majesty will not dislike (2) his undertaking, especially if it may appear to be of no damage to your royal Majesty, and that it will bring some profit to your people, both of which he has no doubt.

With a most willing mind, he has prepared himself for his destined voyage, a voyage we like very well. By these means (3), we perceive that the profit from the mutual trade of both sides will benefit all our neighbouring princes in the West (4) along with your imperial Majesty and those subjects under your dominion to their great joy. The benefit they shall all share consists in the exporting of such things we have in abundance and in the importing of things we have need of.

It cannot be otherwise that by seeing we are born and made to have need of one another (5), and bound to aid one another, that your imperial Majesty will like it well, and that your subjects will endeavour to accept it (6). For the increase of such trade, if your imperial Majesty shall add the security of passage along with the other necessary privileges for trade between us, your Majesty shall do that which belongs (7) to the most honourable and liberal of princes and deserve so much from us. Such acts which will never be forgotten.

This request of ours, we do instantly desire to be taken in good part by your Majesty and, with such a great benefit to us and our men, we shall endeavour with diligence to reciprocate (8) in future.

The God Almighty long preserve your imperial Majesty.

Notes

Up to and just beyond, the sixteenth century was the time of the "suspended sentence" (not a legal term). The clause and phrase complexity of the sentence reflected a way of thinking. Such suspended sentences have been compared to a person dressing for a formal photograph who cannot stop adjusting their clothes and general appearance! The main clause may be at the end of the long line of subordinate clauses and phrases, or it may be at the beginning with the key piece of information at the end. Either way, the essential information, the chief subject matter, is suspended while all the other detail is added. With such subordination, and the use of non-finite verbs, it can be difficult to translate these sentences into modern English, which now aims to avoid such complexity. A translation would have to add finite verbs and independent clauses where there were none in the original and remove unnecessary conjunctions and adverbs. This letter contains examples of the suspended sentence. I have tried to simplify them where I can.

I assume both these texts were first written in Latin and then translated into English. Certainly the 1596 text was translated from Latin. This may account for some of the length and awkwardness of parts of the texts. Also, such awkwardness for the modern reader can be accounted for in the nature of the text. The letter is an example of formal and conventional diplomacy and as such it is loaded with impersonal politeness and courtesy, hence the hyperbole! I've divided the letter into paragraphs to make the reading clearer and I have cut much of the redundant hyperbole, such as in "most necessary" – the meaning of "necessary" does not require a superlative adjective to proceed it, it conveys its own "necessity"!

The irregular spellings may not have appeared in the original letter. The printer would add letters (he/hee, we/wee, imperial/imperiall) and use contraction or annotation (and/&) to justify the line prior to printing. As it is a printed copy of the original, it may not carry the same edited scrutiny with regards to spelling and case. Also, worth noting, during the sixteenth century, standard English was in the process of being codified. It was expanding, or elaborating, its range of meanings while minimising, or codifying, its range of forms using dictionaries and grammars. However, it wasn't until the eighteenth century that this process of codifying the language stabilised, at this point in the sixteenth century the spellings and grammatical and syntactic forms still maintain an element of flexibility. Printing and mass publication, of course, are also essential parts of the codifying process – imagine the variety evident in hand-written manuscripts!

Here are some specific notes on various words and phrases:

1 "by the grace of God" – free and unmerited favour of God – manifested in the royal inherited line of descent. Elizabeth is understood to be queen by divine right. Maybe an interesting comparison with China's "son of heaven"?
2 "not dislike" – negated negative verb, a double negative. During this period, they were not considered logically. A double or triple negative stressed the negation. You could ask why they did not simply write "you will like"? We must assume they are being polite and not assuming what the reader will like or dislike. It is perhaps a blend of the two. Jane Austen is famous for using this form with

adjectives, writing that a certain character is "not unkind" – she will not say he is "kind", she is presenting a subtle criticism.

3 "by these means" – with your help.

4 "our neighbouring princes in the West" – presumably other rulers of states in Europe wishing to trade with China. Interesting that they had perceived themselves geographically at this time as the "West" and China and Asia as the "Orient".

5 "it cannot be otherwise" – suggestion of destiny, providence? Human beings, especially those from China and England, naturally help those in need. The persuasion is greater here as both sides will profit and benefit from cooperation.

6 "your subjects will endeavour to accept it" – "indevor"/"endevor" – same meaning, both spellings were current. This suggests that whatever the King decides and acts upon, his subjects will "endeavour" to do the same, i.e. help John Newbery and his crew.

7 "belongeth"/"belongs" – this and all the other examples in the letter show the change of inflection in the third person singular form of the verb. It began to change in the seventeenth century – the "-eth" has now gone.

8 "requite"/"reciprocate" – The English will do the same for Chinese travellers and traders in the future, following on from this initial contact and cooperation.

*Translated and annotated by Frank Pearson.

Translation into Chinese

Qin, Guojing and Gao Huanting (1998), *The Qianlong Emperor and Lord Macartney*. Beijing: Forbidden City Publishing House, pp. 19–20.

天命英格兰诸国之女王伊丽莎白，致最伟大及不可战胜之君主陛下：

呈上此信之吾国忠民约翰•纽伯莱，得吾人之允许而前往贵国各地旅行。彼之能作此难事，在于完全相信陛下之宽洪与仁慈，认为在经历若干危险后，必能获得陛下之宽大接待，何况此行于贵国无任何损害，且有利于贵国人民。彼既于此无何怀疑，乃更乐于准备此一于吾人有益之旅行。吾人认为：我西方诸国君王从相互贸易中所获得之利益，陛下及所有臣属陛下之人均可获得。此利益在于输出吾人富有之物及输入吾人所需之物。吾人以为：我等天生为相互需要者，吾人必需互相帮助，吾人希望陛下能同意此点，而我臣民亦不能不做此类之尝试。如陛下能促成此事，且给予安全通行之权，并给吾人在与贵国臣民贸易中所需之其他特权，则陛下实行至尊贵仁慈国君之事，而吾人将永不能忘陛下之功业。吾人极愿吾人之请求能为陛下之洪恩所允许，而当陛下之仁慈及于吾人及吾邻居时，吾人将力图报答陛下也。愿上天保佑陛下。

Appendix 2

Queen Elizabeth I's 1596 letter to the Ming Emperor Wanli, discussed in Chapter 1

Source: Richard Hakluyt's book *The Principall Navigations, Voiages, Traffiques and Discoueries of the English Nation* (1589–1600), Imprinted at London by George Bishop, Ralph Newberie and Robert Baker. Vol. 3, pp. 853–854.

Original Sixteenth Century Text

Letter from Queen Elizabeth to the King of China, 11th July 1596.

Elizabeth by the grace of God Queene of England, France, and Ireland, the most mightie defendress of the true & christian faith against all that falsely professe the name of Christ, etc. (1) To the most high and sovereign Prince the most puissant (2) Governour of the great kingdome of China, the chiefest (3) Emperour in those parts of Asia and of the lands adjoining, and the great monarke of the orientall regions of the world; wisheth (4) health and many joyfull and happy yeeres, with all plenty and abundance of things most acceptable. (5) Whereas (6) our honest and faithfull subjects which bring these letters unto your Highnesse, Richard Allot & Thomas Bromefield, marchants of oure citie of London in our foresaid kingdome of England, have made most earnest suit unto us, that we would commend their desires and indevours of sayling to the regions of your Empire for traffiques (7) sake: whereas also the same of your kingdome so strongly and prudently governed, being dispersed and published over the face of the whole earth, (8) hath invited these our subjects not onely to visite your Highnesse Dominions, but also to permit themselves to be ruled and governed by the lawes and constitutions of your kingdome during the time of their aboad in those partes of the world, as it becommeth marchants, who for exchange of marchendize are desirous to travell unto regions so farre distant and not hitherto sufficiently knowen unto these nations of the world, having this regard onely, that they may present their wares and certaine examples or musters (9) of diverse kinds of marchendizes, where with the regions of our dominions do abound, unto the view of your Highnesse and of your subjects, & that they may indevoure to know whether here be any other marchandize with us fit for your use, which (according to the honest & lawfull custome of traffique in all countries) they may exchange for other commodities, whereof in the parts of your Empire there is great plenty both naturall and artificiall: We yielding (10) unto the most reasonable requests of these honest men, because we doe suppose that by this most just intercourse of traffique, no inconvenience nor losse, but rather most exceeding benefite will rebound unto the Princes and subjects of both kingdoms, while by the carrying foorth of those commodities wherewith we abound, and the bringing home of others which we want, wee may on either side at most easie rates helpe and inrich one another; Doe crave (11) of your sovereign Majestie, that these our subjects, when they shall come for traffiques sake unto any the stations, portes, places, townes or cities of your Empire, they may have full and free libertie of egresse and regresse, and of dealing in trade of marchandize with your subjects, may by your Highnesse clemency most firmely enjoy all such freedoms, immunities, and privileges, as are usually granted to the subjects of other Princes which exercise traffique in your dominions: and we on the other side will not onely performe all the offices of a well-willing Prince unto your Highnesse, but also for the greater increase of mutuall love (12) and commerce between us and your subjects, by these present letters of ours doe most willingly grant unto all and every your subjects (if it shall seeme good unto your Highnesse) full and entire libertie unto any of the partes of our dominions to resort, there to abide and traffique, and thence to returne. All and every of which premisses we have caused to be confirmed by annexing hereunto our royall seale. God most mercifull and almighty, the Creator of heaven and earth, continually protect your kingly majestie. Given in our palace at Greenwich the 11 of the moneth of July, in the yeere of Christ 1596, and the eight and thirtie yeere of our reigne.

Translation into modern English

Elizabeth, by the grace of God, Queen of England, France, and Ireland, the mightiest defender of the true and Christian faith against all who falsely profess the name of Christ, etc. (1) To the highest and sovereign prince, the most powerful (2) governor of the great kingdom of China, the chief (3) Emperor in those parts of Asia and of the adjoining lands, and the great monarch of the oriental regions of the world, we wish (4) health and many joyful and happy years, with all plenty and abundance of most acceptable things. (5)

(6) Our honest and faithful subjects, who bring these letters to your Highness, Richard Allot and Thomas Bromefield, merchants of London, the capital city of our kingdom, have earnestly entreated us to commend their intentions and endeavours in sailing to the regions of your empire for the purpose of trade (7). As your kingdom is so strongly and well governed, and so widely known across the face of the whole earth, (8) it has inspired

these our subjects not only to visit your Highness's dominions but also to submit to, and be ruled and governed by, the laws and constitutions of your kingdom during the time of their stay there. This is consistent with merchants who, for the exchange of merchandise, will travel to distant regions that are little known to us in this part of the world.

They only have this purpose, that they may present their diverse products and examples and specimens (9) of merchandise in the regions of your dominions, to your Highness and to your subjects. They will endeavour to know whether any other merchandise that we have will be useful to you. According to the honest and lawful customs of trade in all countries, they may exchange these goods for both natural and manufactured commodities that are plentiful in your empire.

We agree (10) to the modest requests of these honest men because we assume that by this just communication of trade there will be no inconvenience or loss but rather extraordinary benefits for the princes and subjects of both kingdoms. By exporting the commodities that we have in abundance and importing those which we want, we may, with low rates, help and enrich each other.

We do request (11) of your sovereign Majesty that these our subjects, when they arrive to engage in trade at any of the stations, ports, places, towns, or cities of your empire, they may have full and free liberty of entry and departure and in dealing and trading in merchandise with your subjects. May they, by your Highness's clemency, most firmly enjoy all such freedoms, immunities and privileges that are usually granted to the subjects of other princes who engage in trade in your dominions. We, for our part, will not only perform all the offices of a ready and willing prince to your Highness, but also those for the increase of mutual respect (12) and commerce between us and your subjects. These present letters of ours do willingly grant to all and everyone of your subjects (if this is acceptable to your Highness) full and complete liberty to visit any part of our dominions, to live and trade there and, afterwards, depart.

All these propositions we confirm by attaching here our Royal Seal.

God most merciful and almighty, the creator of heaven and earth, continually protect your kingly Majesty.

Given in our palace at Greenwich, on 11th July, in the year of Christ 1596, and the 38th year of our reign.

Notes

As with the earlier letter, there are numerous suspended sentences and bewildering complexities. This is due in part to formal bureaucratic prose, as well as the translation from the initial Latin text. The hyperbole ("most", "most exceeding") is conventional diplomatic politeness and is largely redundant. As with the previous letter, I've divided the text into paragraphs for some clarity.

I've highlighted several lexical, semantic, and grammatical points for annotation.

1. "defender of the true faith", "falsely profess" – Elizabeth was head of the Church of England, a Protestant church and conflicted with the Catholic church in Rome and particularly Spain, and with many sects of Protestantism that believed they represented the "true faith" and that the Church of England was too close to Catholicism. Heretical Catholics were tortured and burnt to death during this period. It is interesting writing this in Preston (Lancashire). Preston was a rare remaining centre of Catholicism during this time, and Catholic believers were known as recusants. A recusant rejects formal authority and a Catholic recusant rejected the authority of the Church of England, for which they were persecuted. When I went to school in the 70s, Catholic schools were named after Catholic martyrs who were tortured and executed during this period – Edmund Campion, John Fisher, John Southworth, and the Catholic school I attended, Cuthbert Mayne. Most have now gone or been renamed. It is a simple statement, but it is loaded with the weight of history!
2. "puissant" – meaning "having ability through power and authority" – now archaic or poetic, though it sounds good!
3. The use of graded adjectives is common, especially the superlative form "-est". In many cases it is redundant in modern English, for example, "chiefest", as "chief" already carries the ultimate meaning and doesn't require a superlative suffix.
4. Third person singular form of the verb – change of inflection from "eth" to "-s". Also, I have added the subject "we" as it has got lost in the suspended sentence.
5. "things most acceptable" – early English often placed the adjective, or adjective phrase, after the noun. This form is now obsolete – used occasionally as a poetic form.
6. "Whereas" – this was a conventional preamble in a formal document, now redundant.
7. "traffique" – Old French word for trade, now obsolete.
8. "earth"/"world" – interesting contrast in terms. "Earth" means more the physical, material globe, whereas "world" has an etymology suggesting the globe as perceived through a human perspective. In Germanic, "weor" meant man and "old" meant age or time, hence "weorold" – "the time or age of man"; "world" is historical, "earth" is geological.
9. "muster" – Old French for "specimen" or "sample" – now obsolete.
10. "yield"/"yeeld" – "to submit". Not obsolete though now an archaic use. Its meaning in this context is to give way to persuasion, as the Queen is unlikely to "submit" to anyone!

11 "crave" – "require", "ask for earnestly, courteously, humbly" – now archaic.
12 "love" – here used as a formal term for regard, or respect, now an archaic use, though still evident in the closing formula of a letter. Similarly, "desire" was used then to express a wish or request, whereas now it usually associated with personal emotions. It is unlikely that either "love" or "desire" would appear in such diplomatic letters between the UK and China today!

*Translated and annotated by Frank Pearson.

Translation into Chinese

Qin, Guojing and Gao Huanting (1998), *The Qianlong Emperor and Lord Macartney.* Beijing: Forbidden City Publishing House, pp. 20–21.

天命英格兰、法兰西及爱尔兰之女王，使基督之名不被滥用的真实基督教信仰之最强有力保护者伊丽莎白，致至尊主权国君，伟大中华王国之最强力主宰者，亚洲各部与及附近诸岛屿最主要之皇帝陛下：

愿陛下安康，多寿多喜，百事顺利。持此信致陛下之吾国忠实臣民理查•阿伦及汤麦司•布伦菲，系我英格兰王国伦敦城之商人。彼等坚决恳求吾人准许彼等取海道前往贵国贸易。盖贵国治理坚固而贤明，其声誉传遍天下，是以此等我臣民不仅欲参见陛下，且愿于彼等身居贵国期间，遵循贵国之法令。此等商人，为交换货物故，愿前往远方我等不熟知之国，以图将我国所丰有之货物以及各类产品，展示于陛下与贵国臣民之前。则彼等能得知何种我国货物能于贵国有用，可否以各国现行之合法关税交换得贵国富有之产品与制品。吾人对于此般忠心臣民之合理请求，不得不为认可。因吾人实见公平之通商，无任何不便与损失之处，且极有利于我两国之国君及臣民。以其所有，易其所无，各得其所，何乐不为？令求至尊之陛下，凡我国人来贵国某处、某港、某地、某镇或某城贸易时，务请赐以自由出入之权，俾得与贵国人交易，在陛下仁慈治下，使其得享受自由特典及权利，与其他国人在贵国贸易所享受者，一无差等。则吾人在他方面不独对于陛下尽具事上国之道，且为我两国国君及臣民之互爱与贸易起见，愿对于贵国人民之入境贸易者，到处予以自由，加以保护（如陛下以为善者）。所有此等条件，吾人皆以固以国玺。愿至慈悲与至强之上帝及天地之创造者永远保护尊王陛下。

耶稣降生后1596年，我王在位第38年6月11日

授于格林威治宫

Appendix 3

Queen Elizabeth I's 1602 letter to the Ming Emperor Wanli, discussed in Chapter 1

The original Mediaeval English text

Source: Lancashire Archives

ELIZABETH BY THE GRACE OF GOD QUEEN of England, France and Ireland Defendor of the faith ets. To the great, mighty, and Invincible Emperour of Cathaia. greeting. Wee haue receaued Dyuers, and sundry relac~ons both by our owne Subiects, and by others, whoe haue visited some parts of your Ma.ts Empire, and Dominions, wherby they haue reported unto us as well your Inuincible greatness, as your kind vsage of Strangers, that resorte unto yo~r Kingdomes with trade of merchandise, w~ch hath wrought in us a desire, to fynd oute some neerer waye of passage by Seas from us, into your cuntrey, then the usuall frequented course that hitherto hath byn houlden by compassing the greatest part of the world, By which neerer passage, not only opportunity of entercourse of traffique of merchandize may be offred between ye Subiects of both or Kingdomes, but also a mutuall league, and amity may growe, and be continued, between yor Mats and us, or Cuntries, and Dominions being in their distance of scituations, not so farr remote, or severed, as they are estranged, and unknowen the one to the other, by reason of the long and tedious course of Navigacon hitherto used – from theis party unto yor. To which ende wee have heretofore many yeares past, and at sundry tymes synce made choice of some of or Subiects, being a people by nature enclyned to great attempts, and to the discouery of Contries, and Kingdomes unknowen and sett them in hand wth the fynding out of some neerer passage by Seas into yor Mats Contries, through the North. Or East parts of the World, wherin hitherto not preuayling, but some of their Ships neuer returning back agayne, nor being heard of synce their departure hence, & some of them retourning back agayne being hindered in their entended voyage by the frozen Seas, and intolerable cold of those Clymayes; wee haue yet once more of o r earnest desire to try the uttermost yt may be done to pforme at length a neerer discouery of yor Contrye, prepared and sett fourth two small

Shipps under ye direction of our Subiect & Seruant George Waymouth being ye principall Pylott of this present voyage, a man for his knowledge & Experience in navigacon, specially chosen by us to this attempte, Whom if it shall please god so to prosper in his passage, yt either he, or any of his company shall aryue in any port of your Kingdome, wee pray yor Matie in fauor of us, who haue soe desired ye attaining this meanes of accesse unto you, & in regard of an enyerprize pformed by hym, & his company wth so great difficulty, & danger, yt you will use them wth that regard yt may gyue them encouragemt to make this their newe discouered passage, wch hitherto hath not byn frequented, or knowne by any to become a usuall frequented trade from theis pts of ye world to yor Matie. By wch meanes yor contry may hereafter be serued wth the natyue comodityes of theis parts of speciall seruice, & use both for yor Matie and Subiects and by returne, and enterchange of your contrey comodities, wee & our Subiects may be furnished wth thinges of lyke seruice and use out of wch mutuall benefit amity, and frendshipe may growe, and be established between us, wch wee for our part will not lett hereby to offer unto you for the honorable report wch we haue heard of yor Matie and because in yis first discouery of the waye to yor contrey, it seemed to us not convenient to ymploy Shipps of that burthen wch might bring them any great quantity of or natyue comodities wherby they might be pestered, wee had resolue to use small shipps as fittest for an unkowen passage, laden for ye most part wth such necessaries, as were of use for their discouery. It may please yor Matie by the pticukers of such things, as are brought in theis shipps to understand yt of goods of those kyndes, or kingdome is able to furnish yor Matie most amply & also of sundry other kynds of merchandize of like use, wherof it may please yor Matie to be more pticulerly enformed by the said George waymuth, & his company, of all wch upon signifcaco unto us by yor Matie Lres (Ed. = Largesse?) to be returned by or said Subiect, yt our visiting of yor Kingdomes wth our shipps, & merchandize shalbe acceptable, & kindly receiued, wee will in the next fleet, wch wee shall send unto you, make it more fully appeare what use, & beneftt, or amity, & entercourse may bring yor Matie & contre. And in the meane tyme do commend yor Matie to the protection of the Eternall God, whose providence guideth, and pserueth all Kinges, and Kingdomes. From our Royall Pallace of Greenwiche the fourthe of May ano Dni 1602 and of or Raigne 44°. Elizabetth R.

Translation into modern English provided by the Lancashire Achieves is included in Chapter 1

Translation into Chinese

天命英格兰、法兰西及爱尔兰之女王，国教守护者伊丽莎白致候于伟大而不可战胜之中华皇帝陛下：

吾臣民有游于陛下之国土者，彼等奏言所云，特述陛下雄伟大能，并种种恩待诸异邦之游商于陛下国土者。陛下此等恩慈，使吾等决意觅一航线通于贵邦，其较今日通行于天下者则短矣。此既可益吾两国商贸之长盛，亦当利吾两国臣民之永好。持念于斯，故往昔也，吾亦数遣臣民能为先行者，自北而出，求此航道。然彼等去不再返，音尘永绝，盖大洋冰封、寒极难抗也。

然吾等决意复行前举，经兹筹备，特遣船二艘，交臣民乔治·威茅斯指挥出洋，彼乔治·威茅斯者以航海有年、经验渊深，而聘为首席领航。谨愿陛下慈恩照拂彼辈，赐予彼辈鼓舞以寻得此一未曾有之航线。以此胜因，吾两国之商贸，既可收互惠互利之效，而吾两国臣民之谊，亦可得增修睦好。然因系初航，复探险于未知之海，彼辈非有必须之资不能存命，故吾人议定，暂不能以丰盛之物进上于陛下，谨请陛下留心此船队所携之吾国样品，其类多有，凡陛下所求，吾等必可为陛下供最充足之用。下次舰队以何物进上，则谨请陛下讯于彼乔治·威茅斯者。

吾等谨付陛下于永恒上帝之守护下，上帝指引并守护一切诸王、诸国土。我主耶稣纪元第1602年、吾王治世第44年5月4日，于格林威治宫。

伊丽莎白女王

Translated by Xi MA. (no other translated version available so far, published for the first time)

Appendix 4

King George III's letter to the Qianlong Emperor, 1792, discussed in Chapter 5

English original

Source: H. B. Morse (1926). *The Chronicles of the East India Company Trading to China, 1635–1844,* Vol. II, London; Oxford University Press. pp. 244–247. FO 1048/1. Kew: The National Archives.

His Most Sacred Majesty George the Third, by the Grace of God King of Great Britain, France and Ireland, Sovereign of the Seas, Defender of the Faith and so forth, To the Supreme Emperor of China Kien-long worthy to live tens of thousands and tens of thousands thousand years, sendeth Greeting.

The natural disposition of a great and benevolent Sovereign, such as is Your Imperial Majesty, whom Providence has seated upon a Throne for the good of Mankind, is, to watch over the peace and security of his dominion, and to take pains for disseminating happiness, virtue and knowledge among his subjects, extending also the same beneficence with all the peaceful arts, as far as he is able, to the whole human race.

Impressed with such sentiments from the beginning of Our Reign when We found Our People engaged in War We granted to Our enemies, after obtaining Victories over them in the four quarters of the World the blessings of Peace upon the most equitable condition. Since that period not satisfied with promoting the prosperity of Our own subjects in every respect, and beyond the example of any former times We have taken various opportunities of fitting out Ships and sending in them some of the most wise and learned of Our Own People, for the discovery of distant and unknown region, not for the purpose of conquest, or of enlarging Our dominion which are already sufficiently extensive for all Our wishes, not for the purpose of acquiring wealth, or even of favoring the commerce of Our Subjects, but for the sake of increasing Our knowledge of the habitable Globe, of finding out the various production of the Earth, and for communicating the arts and comforts of life to those parts where they were hitherto little known; and We have since sent vessels with the animals and vegetables most useful to Man, to Islands and places where it appeared they had been wanting.

We have been still more anxious to enquire into the arts and manners of Countries where civilization has been perfected by the wise ordinances and virtuous examples of their Sovereigns thro a long series of ages; and above all, Our ardent wish had been to become acquainted with those celebrated institution of Your Majesty's populous and extensive Empire which have carried its prosperity to such a height as to be the admiration of all surrounding Nations.

–

And now that We have by prudence and Justice avoided the calamities of War into which discord and ambition have plunged most of the other Kingdoms of Europe, and that by engaging Our Allies in Hindostan to put an end to hostilities occasioned by the attack of an ambious Neighbour, even when it was in Our power to destroy him, We have the happiness of being at peace with all the World, no time can be so propitious for extending the bounds of friendship and benevolence, and for proposing to communicate and receive those benefits which must result from an unreserved and amicable intercourse, between such great and civilized Nation as China and Great Britain.

Many of Our subjects have also frequented for a long time past a remote part of Your Majesty's dominion for the purpose of Trade. No doubt, the interchange of commodities between Nation distantly situated tends to their mutual convenience, industry and wealth, as the blessings which the Great God of Heaven has conferred upon various soils and climates are thus distributed among his Creatures scattered over the surface of the Earth.

But such an intercourse requires to be properly conducted, so as that the new Comers may not infringe the laws and Customs of the Country they visit, and that on the other hand they may be received on terms of hospitality and meet the Justice and protection due to Strangers. We are indeed equally desirous to restrain Our Subjects from doing evil or even of shewing ill example in any foreign Country, as We are that [they] should receive no injury in it.

There is no method of effecting so good a purpose, but by the residence of a proper Person authorized by Us to regulate their conduct and to receive complaints against them whenever they should give occasion for any to be made against them, as well as any they might consider as having just cause to make of ill treatment towards them.

By such means every misunderstanding may be prevented, every inconveniences removed, a firm and lasting friendship cemented and a return of mutual good offices secured between our respective Empires.

All these consideration have determined Us to depute an Embassador Extraordinary and Plenipotentiary to Your Court, and willing to make choice for this purpose of a Person truly worthy of representing Us and of appearing before Your August Presence We have fixed upon Our right trusty and well-beloved Cousin and Counsellor the Right Honorable George Lord Viscount Macartney, Baron of Lissanoure and one of Our most honorable Privy Council of Our Kingdom of Great Britain, Knight of the most honorable order of the Bath and of the most ancient and royal order of the White Eagle, and Fellow of Our Royal Society of London for the promotion of natural knowledge, a Nobleman of high rank and quality, of great virtue, wisdom and ability, who has filled many important offices in the State of trust and honor, has already worthily represented Our Person in an Embassy to the Court of Russia, and has governed with mildness, justice and success, several of Our most considerable possession in the Eastern and western Parts of the World, and appointed to the Government General of Bengal, to be Our Embassador Extraordinary and Plenipotentiary to Your Imperial Majesty with credentials under Our Great Seal of Our Kingdoms and Our Sign Manual, to whom We entreat Your Majesty to grant a gracious reception, as well as a favorable attention to his Representation.

And in order to avoid every possibility of interruption in this amicable communication which we wish to establish and maintain with Your sublime Person and Court, and which might happen after the departure of Our said Embassador Extraordinary whose presence may be necessary to Our Affairs elsewhere or in case of his death or ocassional absence from Your Capital, We have appointed Our trusty and well beloved Sir George Staunton, Bart., honorary Doctor of Laws of Our University of Oxford, and Fellow of Our Royal Society of London for the promotion of natural knowledge, whom We have appointed Our Secretary of Embassy under the direction of Our Embassador as a Gentleman of wisdom and knowledge who hath already served us with fidelity and zeal as a Member of Our honorable Council and Colonel of Militia in some of Our Dominion in the West Indies, and appointed by Us Our Attorney General in the same, and hath since exercised with ability and success the Office of Commissioner for treating and making Peace with Tippoo Sultaun, one of the most considerable Princes of Hindostan, to be also Minister Plenipotentiary to Your August Person, with Credentials likewise under Our Great Seal, and for whom, in case of the death departure or occasional absence of Our said Embassador Extraordinary, We entreat in like manner Your Majesty's gracious reception and attention to his Representation in Our name.

We rely on Your Imperial Majesty's wisdom and Justice and general benevolence to Mankind so conpicuous in Your long and happy reign that You will please to allow Our Ambassador and Representative at Your Court to have the opportunity of contemplating the example of Your virtues and to obtain such information of Your celebrated institution as will enable him to enlighten Our People on his return; He, on Our part being directed to give, as far as Your Majesty shall please to desire it, a full and free communication of any art, science, or observation, either of use or curiosity, which the industry ingenuity and experience of Europeans may have enabled them to acquire:

And also that You will be pleased to ① allow to any of Our Subjects frequenting the Coasts of Your dominion, and conducting themselves with propriety a secure residence there, and a fair access to Your Markets, under such laws and regulation, as Your Majesty shall think right, and that their lives and properties shall be safe under Your Imperial protection: ② that one Man shall not suffer for the crime of another, in which he did not participate, and whose evasion for Justice he did not assist, but that every measure shall be taken on the part of your Government as Our Embassador is instructed strictly to direct to be taken on the part of Our People to seize and bring to condign Punishment, any of Our Subjects transgressing the laws or good order of Your Empire, or disturbing the Peace and friendship subsisting between Us.

We have particularly instructed Our Embassador to take every method in his Power to mark Our regard and friendly disposition to Your Imperial Majesty, and it will give Us the utmost satisfaction to learn that Our wishes in that respect have been amply complied with and that as We are Brethren in Soverignty, so may a Brotherly affection ever subsist between Us.

May the Almighty have you in his holy protection!
Given at Our Court at St. James's in London
And in the 32nd Year of Our Reign.
Imperator Augustissime
Vester bonus grater et Amicus
Georgius R
Augustissimo Principi
Kien Long
Sinarum Supremo Imperatori

Appendix 5

The Qianlong Emperor's Letter to King George III, 1793, discussed in Chapter 5

English translation version 1

Source: E. Backhouse and J. O. P. Bland (1914). *Annals and Memoirs of the Court of Peking*. Boston: Houghton Mifflin. pp. 322–331.

You, O King, live beyond the confines of many seas, nevertheless, impelled by your humble desire to partake of the benefits of our civilisation, you have dispatched a mission respectfully bearing your memorial. Your Envoy has crossed the seas and paid his respects at my Court on the anniversary of my birthday. To show your devotion, you have also sent offerings of your country's produce.

I have perused your memorial: the earnest terms in which it is couched reveal a respectful humility on your part, which is highly praiseworthy. In consideration of the fact that your Ambassador and his deputy have come a long way with your memorial and tribute, I have shown them high favour and have allowed them to be introduced into my presence. To manifest my indulgence, I have entertained them at a banquet and made them numerous gifts. I have also caused presents to be forwarded to the Naval Commander and six hundred of his officers and men, although they did not come to Peking, so that they too may share in my allembracing kindness.

As to your entreaty to send one of your nationals to be accredited to my Celestial Court and to be in control of your country's trade with China, this request is contrary to all usage of my dynasty and cannot possibly be entertained. It is true that Europeans, in the service of the dynasty, have been permitted to live at Peking, but they are compelled to adopt Chinese dress, they are strictly confined to their own precincts and are never permitted to return home. You are presumably familiar with our dynastic regulations. Your proposed Envoy to my Court could not be placed in a position similar to that of European officials in Peking who are forbidden to leave China, nor could he, on the other hand, be allowed liberty of movement and the privilege of corresponding with his own country; so that you would gain nothing by his residence in our midst.

Moreover, our Celestial dynasty possesses vast territories, and tribute missions from the dependencies are provided for by the Department for Tributary States, which ministers to their wants and exercises strict control over their movements. It would be quite impossible to leave them to their own devices. Supposing that your Envoy should come to our Court, his language and national dress differ from that of our people, and there would be no place in which to bestow him. It may be suggested that he might imitate the Europeans permanently resident in Peking and adopt the dress and customs of China, but, it has never been our dynasty's wish to force people to do things unseemly and inconvenient. Besides, supposing I sent an Ambassador to reside in your country, how could you possibly make for him the requisite arrangements? Europe consists of many other nations besides your own: if each and all demanded to be represented at our Court, how could we possibly consent? The thing is utterly impracticable. How can our dynasty alter its whole procedure and system of etiquette, established for more than a century, in order to meet your individual views? If it be said that your object is to exercise control over your country's trade, your nationals have had full liberty to trade at Canton for many a year, and have received the greatest consideration at our hands. Missions have been sent by Portugal and Italy, preferring similar requests. The Throne appreciated their sincerity and loaded them with favours, besides authorising measures to facilitate their trade with China. You are no doubt aware that, when my Canton merchant, Wu Chaoping, was in debt to the foreign ships, I made the Viceroy advance the monies due, out of the provincial treasury, and ordered him to punish the culprit severely. Why then should foreign nations advance this utterly unreasonable request to be represented at my Court? Peking is nearly two thousand miles from Canton, and at such a distance what possible control could any British representative exercise?

If you assert that your reverence for Our Celestial dynasty fills you with a desire to acquire our civilisation, our ceremonies and code of laws differ so completely from your own that, even if your Envoy were able to acquire the rudiments of our civilisation, you could not possibly transplant our manners and customs to your alien soil. Therefore, however adept the Envoy might become, nothing would be gained thereby.

Swaying the wide world, I have but one aim in view, namely, to maintain a perfect governance and to fulfil the duties of the State: strange and costly objects do not interest me. If I have commanded that the tribute offerings sent by you, O King, are to be accepted, this was solely in consideration for the spirit which prompted you to dispatch them from afar. Our dynasty's majestic virtue has penetrated unto every country under Heaven, and Kings of all nations have offered their costly tribute by land and sea. As your Ambassador can see for himself, we possess all things. I set no value on objects strange or ingenious, and have no use for your country's manufactures. This then is my answer to your request to appoint a representative at my Court, a request contrary to our dynastic usage, which would only result in inconvenience to yourself. I have expounded my wishes in detail and have commanded your tribute Envoys to leave in peace on their homeward journey. It behoves you, O King, to respect my sentiments and to display even greater devotion and loyalty in future, so that, by perpetual submission to our Throne, you may secure peace and prosperity for your country hereafter. Besides making gifts (of which I enclose an inventory) to each member of your Mission, I confer upon you, O King, valuable presents in excess of the number usually bestowed on such occasions, including silks and curios-a list of which is likewise enclosed. Do you reverently receive them and take note of my tender goodwill towards you! A special mandate.

English translation version 2

Source: Cranmer-Byng, J. L. (1962). *An Embassy to China, Being the journal kept by Lord Macartney during his embassy to the Emperor Ch'ien-lung 1793–1794.* London: Longmans. pp. 337–341.

AN EDICT

We, by the Grace of Heaven, Emperor, instruct the King of England to take note of our charge.

Although your country, O King, lies in the far oceans, yet inclining your heart towards civilization you have specially sent an envoy respectfully to present a state message, and sailing the seas he has come to our Court to kotow and to present congratulations for the Imperial birthday, and also to present local products, thereby showing your sincerity.

We have perused the text of your state message and the wording expresses your earnestness. From it your sincere humility and obedience can clearly be seen. It is admirable and we fully approve. As regards the chief and assistant envoys who have brought the state message and tribute articles, we are mindful that they have been sent from afar across the sea, and we have extended our favour and courtesy to them, and have ordered our ministers to bring them to an Imperial audience. We have given them a banquet and have repeatedly bestowed gifts on them in order to show our kindness. Although the officers, servants and others, in charge of the ships more than six hundred in number, returned to Chou-shan [Chusan. – Ed.) and did not come to the capital, yet we have also bestowed gifts on them generally so that all should receive favours equally.

As to what you have requested in your message, O King, namely to be allowed to send one of your subjects to reside in the Celestial Empire to look after your country's trade, this does not conform to the Celestial Empire's ceremonial system, and definitely cannot be done. Hitherto, whenever men from the various Western Ocean countries have desired to come to the Celestial Empire and to enter the Imperial service we have allowed them to come to the capital. But once having come, they were obliged to adopt the costume of the Celestial Empire, they were confined within the Halls, and were never allowed to return home. These are the fixed regulations of the Celestial Empire, and presumably you also know them, O King. Now, however, you want to send one of your subjects to reside at the capital. But he could neither behave like a Western Ocean man who comes to the capital to enter our service, remaining at the capital and not returning to his native country, nor could he be allowed to go in and out, and to have regular correspondence. So it would really serve no purpose.

Moreover, the territories ruled by the Celestial Empire are vast, and for all the envoys of vassal states coming to the capital there are definite regulations regarding the provision of quarters and supplies to them and regarding their movements. There never has been any precedent for allowing them to suit their own convenience. Now, if your country retains someone at the capital his speech will not be understood and his dress will be different in style, and we have nowhere to house him. If he is to resemble those Western Ocean men who come to the capital to enter the Imperial service we must order him, without exception, to change his dress to that of the Celestial Empire. However, we have never wished to force on others what is difficult to do. Besides, if the Celestial Empire desired to send someone permanently to reside in your country surely you would not be able to agree to it? Furthermore, there are a great many Western Ocean countries altogether, and not merely your one country. If, like you, O King, they all beg to send someone to reside at the capital how could we grant their request in every case? It would be absolutely impossible for us to do so. How can we go as far as to change the regulations of the Celestial Empire, which are over a 100 years old, because of the request of one man-of you, O King?

If it is said that your object, O King, is to take care of trade, men from your country have been trading at Macau for some time, and have always been treated favourably. For instance, in the past Portugal and Italy and other countries have several times sent envoys to the Celestial Empire with requests to look after their trade, and the Celestial Empire, bearing in mind their loyalty, treated them with great kindness. Whenever any matter concerning trade has arisen which affected those countries it has always been fully taken care of. When the Canton merchant Wu Chao-p'ing [Wayqua.-Ed.] owed money to foreign ships we ordered the Governor-General to advance the money out of the Treasury and to pay his debts for him at the public expense, and to have the debtor-merchant severely punished. Presumably your country has also heard about this. Why, then, do foreign countries need to send someone to remain at the capital? This is a request for which there is no precedent and it definitely cannot be granted. Moreover, the distance between Macau, the place where the trade is conducted, and the capital is nearly ten thousand *li*, and if he were to remain at the capital how could he look after it?

If it is said that because you look up with admiration to the Celestial Empire you desire him to study our culture, yet the Celestial Empire has its own codes of ritual which are different from your country's in each case. Even if the person from your country who remained here was able to learn them it would be of no use since your country has its own customs and regulations, and you would certainly not copy Chinese ones.

The Celestial Empire, ruling all within the four seas, simply concentrates on carrying out the affairs of Government and does not value rare and precious things. Now you, O King, have presented various objects to the throne, and mindful of loyalty in presenting offerings from afar, we have specially on the Yamen to receive them. In fact, the virtue and power of the celestial Dynasty has penetrated afar to the myriad kingdoms, which have come to render homage, and so all kinds of precious things from "over mountain and sea" have been collected here, things which your chief envoy and others have seen for themselves. Nevertheless we have never valued ingenious articles, nor do we have the slightest need of your country's manufactures. Therefore, O King, as regards your request to send someone to remain at the capital, while it is not in harmony with the regulations of the Celestial Empire we also feel very much that it is of no advantage to your country. Hence we have issued these detailed instructions and have commanded your tribute envoys to return safely home. You, O King, should simply act in conformity with our wishes by strengthening your loyalty and swearing perpetual obedience so as to ensure that your country may share the blessings of peace.

Besides giving both the customary and extra gifts, as listed separately, to the chief and assistant envoys, and to the various officials under them as well as to the interpreters, soldiers and servants, now, because your envoy is returning home we have issued this special edict, and confer presents on you, O King – elaborate and valuable things all, in accordance with the usual etiquette. In addition we have bestowed brocades, gauzes, and elaborate curios; all precious things. These are listed separately.

Let the King reverently receive them and know our kind regard for him.

This is a special edict.

Appendix 6

The Qianlong Emperor's last letter to King George III, 1796, discussed in Chapter 5

English translation

Source: Backhouse E. and J. O. P. Bland (1914). *Annals and Memoirs of the Court of Peking*. Boston: Houghton Mifflin. pp. 331–334.

Chu Kuei (Viceroy of Canton) memorialises Us that the King of England has forwarded a memorial with tribute. Two years ago, on the occasion of the tribute mission from the King coming to Peking, We conferred upon him many valuable presents, so he has now dispatched a further memorial with offerings of tribute, thus indicating his loyal sincerity. We raise absolutely no objection to the fact of his having omitted to send a mission on this occasion, and are graciously pleased to accept his offerings. In addition, We bestow upon him the following mandate: Your nation is inaccessible, lying far beyond the dividing seas, but you sent a mission with a memorial and tribute to pay homage at our Court, and We, in recognition of your loyal sincerity, conferred upon you our mandate and valuable gifts, as evidence of our satisfaction. Now, O King, you have again prepared a memorial and offerings, which have been conveyed by your barbarian vessels to Canton and transmitted to Us. Your reverent submission to Our person in manifest. Our Celestial dynasty, which sways the wide world, attaches no value to the costly presents which are offered at Our Court: what We appreciate is the humble spirit of the offerers. We have commanded Our Viceroy to accept your tribute in order that your reverence may be duly recognised.

As regarding Our sending of a punitive expedition to Nepal, Our Commander-in-chief marched at the head of a great army into that country, occupied the chief strategic points, and terrified the Ghoorkas into grovelling submission to Our majestic Empire. Our Commander-in-chief duly memorialised Us, and We, whose Imperial clemency is world-wide, embracing Chinese and foreigners alike, could not endure the thought of exterminating the entire population of the country. Accordingly, we accepted their surrender. At that time Our Commander-in-chief duly informed us of your having dispatched a mission into Tibet, with a petition to

Our Resident, stating that you had advised the Nepalese to surrender. But at the time of your petition Our troops had already gained a complete victory and the desired end had been attained. We were not obliged to trouble your troops to render assistance. You allude to this matter in your present memorial, but are doubtless ignorant of the precise course of events in Nepal, as your tribute mission was on its way to Peking at the time of these occurrences. Nevertheless, O King, you entertained a clear perception of your duty towards Us, and your reverent acknowledgement of Our dynasty's supremacy is highly praiseworthy.

We therefore now bestow upon you various costly gifts. Do you, O King, display even more energetic loyalty in future and endeavour to deserve for ever Our gracious affection, so that we may conform to Our earnest resolve to pacify distant tribes to manifest Our Imperial clemency.

Chu Kuei is to hand this mandate to your Agent, for transmission to yourself, in order that you may be encouraged to display still greater gratitude and reverent submission hereafter, in acknowledgment of Our indulgence.

It is contrary to Our dynastic ordinances for Our officials to enter into social relatiosn with barbarians, and Chu Kuei acted therefore quite properly in returning the presents which were sent to the former Viceroy and Superintendent of Customs at Canton.

Appendix 7

The Jiaqing Emperor's Imperial Mandate to the King of England, 1816, discussed in Chapter 6

English translation

Source: Backhouse E. and J. O. P. Bland (1914). *Annals and Memoirs of the Court of Peking*. Boston: Houghton Mifflin. pp. 382–385.

Imperial Mandate to the King of England: Whereas your country, though lying far beyond the wide seas, was sincerely desirous of attending the blessings of civilisation, in the 58 year of Ch'ien Lung (Qianlong), when my sainted father was on the Throne, you sent a special mission to pay homage. At that time your Ambassador performed the ceremony required of him with the greatest respect and committed no breach of decorum or etiquette. It was his high privilege, therefore, reverently to receive the gracious kindness of His late Majesty. He was admitted into his presence and was given a banquet and many presents.

You have now sent another mission bearing a memorial and offerings of your produce. Your respectful homage has met with my appreciation, and I was glad of the coming of your mission. I examined into the details of the ceremonial adopted on the previous occasion, and bade my Court arrange for your Envoy's reception by myself, and to provide a banquet and presents, in exact accordance with the ceremonial prescribed by His late Majesty. On the mission's arrival at Tientsin, I ordered that a banquet should be given there in my name. To my great surprise your Ambassador, on returning thanks, failed to conform with the prescribed etiquette. Nevertheless, I bore in mind that a lowly official of a distant nation could hardly be expected to show familiarity with our ceremonial usage, and I was please to pardon his remissness.

I commanded my officials to inform your Envoy, on his approaching the metropolis, that his predecessor, your former Ambassador, in the 58th year of Ch'ien Lung (Qianlong), did duly perform the whole prescribed ceremony, including the genuflexion and kotow. How, then, could any deviation from this course be permitted on the present occasion? Your Envoy replied to my Minister that he would certainly perform both genuflexion and kotow at the time of his audience, and promised that there should be no violation of etiquette. My Ministers duly informed me, whereupon I issued a decree commanding your Ambassador to attend for audience on the 7th day of the 7th Moon. On the 8th day I arranged for a banquet in the Hall of Perfect Rectitude and Enlightenment, when the bestowal of presents was to take place, after which he was to be regaled with a further entertainment in the Garden of Universal Joy. On the day following, the 9th, he was to be received in farewell audience and to be taken over the grounds of the Summer Palace. On the 11th he was to proceed to the gate of the Main Hall of the Forbidden City, there to receive my mandate and gifts for presentation to yourself, after which he was to be entertained at a banquet by my Board of Ceremonies. On the 13th he was to be ordered to take his departure.

My Minister informed your Ambassador of the dates and details of the above programme. On the 7th, the date fixed for audience, the mission had reached my Palace gate, and I was about to take my seat on the Imperial Throne, when your Chief Ambassador suddenly announced that he had been attached by a sudden illness and was unable to move. Admitting that this might possibly be the case, I merely commanded the presence of the two subordinate Envoys, but they also simultaneously excused themselves on the plea of sickness. Such gross discourtesy is utterly unprecedented; nevertheless, I administered no severe reproof, but confined myself to ordering their immediate departure from Peking. As the mission was not received in audience, your memorial, strictly speaking, should not have been presented, but I remembered that your country is afar off, and that the feelings were praiseworthy which led you to memorialise Us and send tribute. Your Envoys are alone to blame for their gross breach of respect; I fully recognise the spirit of reverent submission which animated you. I have consequently accepted the whole of your tribute, including maps, pictures, and portraits, and I duly acknowledge your devotion. Moreover, in my return, I confer upon you a white jade and a green jade sceptre, a Court necklace, two pairs of large pouches to be worn at the girdle and eight small ones, that my bounty may be made manifest.

You live at such a great distance from the Middle Kingdom that these Embassies must cause you considerable inconveniences. Your Envoys, moreover, are wholly ignorant of Chinese ceremonial procedure, and the bickering which follows their arrival is highly displeasing to my ear. My dynasty attaches no value to products from abroad; your nation's cunningly wrought and strange wares does not appeal to me in the least, nor do they interest me. For the future, O King, if you will keep your subjects in order and strengthen your national defences, I shall hold you in high esteem, notwithstanding your remoteness. Henceforward, pray do not trouble to dispatch missions all this distance; they are merely a waste of time and have their journey for nothing. If you loyally accept our sovereignty and show dutiful submission, there is really no need for these yearly appearances at our Court to prove that you are indeed our vassal. We issue this mandate to the end that you are may perpetually comply therewith.

A different version is published in *Asiatic Journal*, 1819, vol. 8, p. 342 and in Fu (1966: pp. 404–405).

Appendix 8

The Jiaqing Emperor's Imperial Decree issued following the departure of the Amhurst Embassy, 1816, discussed in Chapter 6

English translation

Source: Backhouse E. and J. O. P. Bland (1914). *Annals and Memoirs of the Court of Peking*. Boston: Houghton Mifflin. pp. 386–389.

On the occasion of the tribute Mission from England landing at the port of Tientsin, I commanded Su-leng-e and Kuang Hui to give a banquet in my name and to compel the members of the Mission to return thanks for the same by the three genuflexions and nice prostrations. If these obeisances were duly performed the Mission was to be conducted to Peking, but in the event of any failure to observe the proper ceremonial, or if it were clumsily rehearsed, the officials above named were to memorialise and await my further commands. The Embassy's ships were not to be permitted to leave, so that they might be available to take the Mission back by the way it had come.

My orders have been wilfully disregarded. The Mission has been allowed to come up to Peking, and the ships have taken their departure without leave from me. Herein lies a gross dereliction of duty on the part of these two officials.

Furthermore, I commanded Ho Shih-t'ai and Mukdenga to proceed to T'ungchou, where they were to direct the Mission to rehearse the ceremony. For this I gave them till the 6th day of the 7th Moon, by which time, if the Mission had acquired proficiency in the requisite etiquette, they were to be brought on to the capital; if not, the tribute Mission was to be denounced and my decision requested forthwith. On the 5th instant I received a vaguely worded memorial from Ho Shih-t'ai and his colleagues, and on the 6th the Mission was escorted into Peking. At 1:30 p.m, on that day I took my seat on the Throne in the Hall of Diligent Government and summoned Ho Shih-t'ai and Mukdenga to an audience. First I inquired as to the rehearsal of the ceremony at T'ungchou. Hereupon the two officials removed their hats and with repeated kotows confessed that no rehearsal had taken place at all! I asked them why, this being the case, they had not carried out my instructions and denounced the Mission to the Throne. Ho Shih-t'ai answered: "When the audience takes place tomorrow I will guarantee that the ceremonial will be performed in full". For this blundering they are responsible, and just as much to blame as the first two officials. On the morning of the 7th I partook of breakfast, and at 6:30 a.m. Issued a decree saying I was about to proceed to the Throne Hall, where I would receive the Mission in audience. To this Ho Shih-t'ai at first replied: "The Mission is delayed on the road; so soon as it reaches the Palace gates I will inform Your Majesty". In a little while he reported further, saying: "The Chief Ambassador has had a severe gastric attack; it will be necessary to postpone the audience, giving him time to recover". At last he reported: "The Ambassador is too sick to appear at audience at all".

I directed that the Ambassador be taken back to his lodging, and supplied at once with medical aid, after which I desired the immediate attendance of the Deputy Ambassador. To his Ho Shih-t'ai replied that the Deputy Ambassador had also been attacked by sickness, and that both would attend together one the Chief Ambassador's recovery.

China is lord and sovereign of the world; was it possible for Us to submit calmly to such a wanton display of irreverent arrogance? Therefore I issued a decree, commanding the expulsion of the Mission from China. Nevertheless, I inflicted no punishment upon the Ambassadors; I bade Kuang Hui escort them back to Canton and see to it that they set sail from there. It has only now been reported to me by the Grand Council that the Mission had had an all night's journey from T'ungchou to the ante-chamber of the Imperial Palace at Yuan Ming-yuan, and that the Ambassador, whose Court dress had not arrived, had strongly protested at the idea of appearing before His Imperial Majesty the Emperor in travelling clothes. Why did Ho Shih-t'ai not inform me of these facts? If it was because he overlooked them at the moment, he could easily have asked for another audience that evening or the next day. He did nothing of the sorts, and allowed me to remain in ignorance until I was proceeding to take my seat on the Imperial Throne. The guilt of Ho Shih-t'ai and his colleagues greatly exceeds the errors of the other two. Had they informed me of the true state of the case I should have postponed the ceremony to a later date. I am astounded at the way in which my stupid officials have mismanaged this business, and I feel that I have completely lost face in the eyes of my Court. All I can do is frankly to acknowledge my mistakes.

I shall deal with the four official's punishment after the Board of Civil Office has recommended an appropriate penalty. In the meantime, I record the facts for the information of my officials throughout the Empire and the Mongol Princes.

Appendix 9

Lin Zexu's letter to Queen Victoria, 1839, discussed in Chapter 7

English Translation version 1

Source: published in Chinese Repository 8, no. 10 (February 1840).

Letter to the queen of England, from the high Imperial Commissioner Lin, and his colleagues. From the Canton press.

Lin, high imperial commissioner, a president of the Board of War, viceroy of the two Keäng provinces, &c., Tang, a president of the Board of War, viceroy of the two Kwang provinces, &c., and E, a vice-president of the Board of War, lieut.-governor of Kwangtung, &c., hereby conjointly address this public dispatch to the queen of England for the purpose of giving her clear and distinct information (on the state of affairs) &c.

It is only our high and mighty emperor, who alike supports and cherishes those of the Inner Land, and those from beyond the seas – who looks upon all mankind with equal benevolence – who, if a source of profit exists anywhere, diffuses it over the whole world – who, if the tree of evil takes root anywhere, plucks it up for the benefit of all nations – who, in a word, hath implanted in his breast that heart (by which beneficent nature herself) governs the heavens and the earth! You, the queen of your honorable nation, sit upon a throne occupied through successive generations by predecessors, all of whom have been styled respectful and obedient. Looking over the public documents accompanying the tribute sent (by your predecessors) on various occasions, we find the following: "All the people of my country, arriving at the Central Land for purposes of trade, have to feel grateful to the great emperor for the most perfect justice, for the kindest treatment", and other words to that effect. Delighted did we feel that the kings of your honorable nation so clearly understood the great principles of propriety, and were so deeply grateful for the 1 From The Chinese Repository, vol. VIII, no 10 (February 1940): 497–503. 2 heavenly goodness (of our emperor): – therefore, it was thatwe of the heavenly dynasty nourished and cherished your people from afar, and bestowed upon them redoubled proofs of our urbanity and kindness. It is merely from these circumstances, that your country – deriving immense advantage from its commercial intercourse with us, which has endured now 200 years – has become the rich and flourishing kingdom that it is said to be! But, during the commercial intercourse which has existed so long, among the numerous foreign merchants resorting hither, are wheat and tares, good and bad; and of these latter are some, who, by means of introducing opium by stealth, have seduced our Chinese people, and caused every province of the land to overflow with that poison. These then know merely to advantage themselves, they care not about injuring others! This is a principle which heaven's Providence repugnates; and which mankind conjointly look upon with abhorrence! Moreover, the great emperor hearing of it, actually quivered with indignation, and especially dispatched me, the commissioner, to Canton, that in conjunction with the viceroy and lieut.-governor of the province, means might be taken for its suppression! Every native of the Inner Land who sells opium, as also all who smoke it, are alike adjudged to death. Were we then to go back and take up the crimes of the foreigners, who, by selling it for many years have induced dreadful calamity and robbed us of enormous wealth, and punish them with equal severity, our laws could not but award to them absolute annihilation! But, considering that these said foreigners did yet repent of their crime, and with a sincere heart beg for mercy; that they took 20,283 chests of opium piled up in their store-ships, and through Elliot, the superintendent of the trade of your said country, petitioned that they might be delivered up to us, when the same were all utterly destroyed, of which we, the imperial commissioner and colleagues, made a duly prepared memorial to his majesty; – considering these circumstances, we have happily received a fresh proof of the extraordinary goodness of the great emperor, inasmuch as he who voluntarily comes forward, may yet be deemed a fit subject for mercy, and his crimes be graciously remitted him. But as for him who again knowingly violates the laws, difficult indeed will it be thus to go on repeatedly pardoning! He or they shall alike be doomed to the penalties of the new statute. We presume that you, the sovereign of your honorable nation, on pouring out your heart before the altar of eternal justice, cannot but command all foreigners with the deepest respect to reverence our laws! If we only lay clearly before your eyes, what is profitable and what is destructive, you will then know that the statutes of the heavenly dynasty cannot but be obeyed with fear and trembling! We find that your country is distant from us about sixty or seventy thousand miles, 2 that your foreign ships come hither striving the one with the other for our trade, and for the simple reason of their strong desire to reap a profit. Now, out of the wealth of our Inner Land, if we take a part to bestow upon foreigners from afar, it follows, that the immense wealth which the said foreigners amass, ought properly speaking to be portion of our own native Chinese people. By what principle of reason then, should these foreigners send in return a poisonous drug, which involves in destruction those very natives of China? Without meaning to say that the

foreigners harbor such destructive intentions in their hearts, we yet positively assert that from their inordinate thirst after gain, they are perfectly careless about the injuries they inflict upon us! And such being the case, we
2 That is, Chinese miles, or from 20,000 to 23,000 British statute miles. 3
should like to ask what has become of that conscience which heaven has implanted in the breasts of all men? We have heard that in your own country opium is prohibited with the utmost strictness and severity: – this is a strong proof that you know full well how hurtful it is to mankind. Since then you do not permit it to injure your own country, you ought not to have the injurious drug transferred to another country, and above all others, how much less to the Inner Land! Of the products which China exports to your foreign countries, there is not one which is not beneficial to mankind in some shape or other. There are those which serve for food, those which are useful, and those which are calculated for re-sale; but all are beneficial. Has China (we should like to ask) ever yet sent forth a noxious article from its soil? Not to speak of our tea and rhubarb, things which your foreign countries could not exist a single day without, if we of the Central Land were to grudge you what is beneficial, and not to compassionate your wants, then wherewithal could you foreigners manage to exist? And further, as regards your woolens, camlets, and longells, were it not that you get supplied with our native raw silk, you could not get these manufactured! If China were to grudge you those things which yield a profit, how could you foreigners scheme after any profit at all? Our other articles of food, such as sugar, ginger, cinnamon, &c., and our other articles for use, such as silk piece-goods, chinaware, &c., are all so many necessaries of life to you; how can we reckon up their number! On the other hand, the things that come from your foreign countries are only calculated to make presents of, or serve for mere amusement. It is quite the same to us if we have them, or if we have them not. If then these are of no material consequence to us of the Inner Land, what difficulty would there be in prohibiting and shutting our market against them? It is only that our heavenly dynasty most freely permits you to take off her tea, silk, and other commodities, and convey them for consumption everywhere, without the slightest stint or grudge, for no other reason, but that where a profit exists, we wish that it be diffused abroad for the benefit of all the earth! Your honorable nation takes away the products of our central land, and not only do you thereby obtain food and support for yourselves, but moreover, by re-selling these products to other countries you reap a threefold profit. Now if you would only not sell opium, this threefold profit would be secured to you: how can you possibly consent to forgo it for a drug that is hurtful to men, and an unbridled craving after gain that seems to know no bounds! Let us suppose that foreigners came from another country, and brought opium into England, and seduced the people of your country to smoke it, would not you, the sovereign of the said country, look upon such a procedure with anger, and in your just indignation endeavor to get rid of

it? Now we have always heard that your highness possesses a most kind and benevolent heart, surely then you are incapable of doing or causing to be done unto another, that which you should not wish another to do unto you! We have at the same time heard that your ships which come to Canton do each and every of them carry a document granted by your highness' self, on which are written these words "you shall not be permitted to carry contraband goods"; this shows that the laws of your highness are in their origin both distinct and severe, and we can only suppose that because the ships coming here have been very numerous, due attention has not been given to search and examine; and for this reason it is that we now address you this public document, that you may clearly know how stern and severe are the laws of the central dynasty, and most certainly you will cause that they be not again rashly violated! 4 Moreover, we have heard that in London the metropolis where you dwell, as also in Scotland, Ireland, and other such places, no opium whatever is produced. It is only in sundry parts of your colonial kingdom of Hindostan, such as Bengal, Madras, Bombay, Patna, Malwa, Benares, Malacca, and other places where the very hills are covered with the opium plant, where tanks are made for the preparing of the drug; month by month, and year by year, the volume of the poison increases, its unclean stench ascends upwards, until heaven itself grows angry, and the very gods thereat get indignant! You, the queen of the said honorable nation, ought immediately to have the plant in those parts plucked up by the very root! Cause the land there to be hoed up afresh, sow in its stead the five grains, and if any man dare again to plant in these grounds a single poppy, visit his crime with the most severe punishment. By a truly benevolent system of government such as this, will you indeed reap advantage, and do away with a source of evil. Heaven must support you, and the gods will crown you with felicity! This will get for yourself the blessing of long life, and from this will proceed the security and stability of your descendants! In reference to the foreign merchants who come to this our central land, the food that they eat, and the dwellings that they abide in, proceed entirely from the goodness of our heavenly dynasty: the profits which they reap, and the fortunes which they amass, have their origin only in that portion of benefit which our heavenly dynasty kindly allots them: and as these pass but little of their time in your country, and the greater part of their time in our's, it is a generally received maxim of old and of modern times, that we should conjointly admonish, and clearly make known the punishment that awaits them. Suppose the subject of another country were to come to England to trade, he would certainly be required to comply with the laws of England, then how much more does this apply to us of the celestial empire! Now it is a fixed statute of this empire, that any native Chinese who sells opium is punishable with death, and even he who merely smokes it, must not less die. Pause and reflect for a moment: If you foreigners did not bring the opium hither, where should our Chinese people get it to re-sell? It is you foreigners who involve our simple natives in the pit of death, and are they alone to be permitted to escape alive? If so much as one of those deprive one of our people of his life, he must forfeit his life in requital for that which he has taken: how much more does this apply to him who by means of opium destroys his fellow-men? Does the havoc which he commits stop with a single life? Therefore it is that those foreigners who now import opium into the Central Land are condemned to be beheaded and strangled by the new statute, and this explains what we said at the beginning about plucking up the tree of evil, wherever it takes root, for the benefit of all nations. We further find that during the second month of this present year, the superintendent of your honorable country, Elliot, viewing the law in relation to the prohibiting of opium as excessively severe, duly petitioned us, begging for "an extension of the term already limited, say five months for Hindostan and the different parts of India, and ten for England, after which they would obey and act in conformity with the new statute", and other words to the same effect. Now we, the high commissioner and colleagues, upon making a duly prepared memorial to the great emperor, have to feel grateful for his extraordinary goodness, for his redoubled compassion. Any one who within the next year and a half may by mistake bring opium to this country, if he will but voluntarily come forward, and deliver up the entire quantity, he shall be absolved from all punishment for his crime. If, however, the appointed term shall have expired, and there are still persons 5 who continue to bring it, then such shall be accounted as knowingly violating the laws, and shall most assuredly be put to death! On no account shall we show mercy or clemency! This then may be called truly the extreme of benevolence, and the very perfection of justice! Our celestial empire rules over ten thousand kingdoms! Most surely do we possess a measure of godlike majesty which ye cannot fathom! Still we cannot bear to slay or exterminate without previous warning, and it is for this reason that we now clearly make known to you the fixed laws of our land. If the foreign merchants of your said honorable nation desire to continue their commercial intercourse, they then must tremblingly obey our recorded statutes, they must cut off for ever the source from which the opium flows, and on no account make an experiment of our laws in their own persons! Let then your highness punish those of your subjects who may be criminal, do not endeavor to screen or conceal them, and thus you will secure peace and quietness to your possessions, thus will you more than ever display a proper sense of respect and obedience, and thus may we unitedly enjoy the common blessings of peace and happiness. What greater joy! What more complete felicity than this! Let your highness immediately, upon the receipt of this communication, inform us promptly of the state of matters, and of the measure you are pursuing utterly to put a stop to the opium evil. Please let your reply be speedy. Do not on any account make excuses or procrastinate. A most important communication. P. S. We annex an abstract of the new law, now about to be put in force. "Any foreigner or foreigners bringing opium to the Central Land, with design to sell the same, the principals shall most assuredly be decapitated, and the accessories strangled; and all property (found on board the same ship) shall be confiscated. The space of a year and a half is granted, within the which, if any one bringing opium by mistake, shall voluntarily step forward and deliver it up, he shall be absolved from all consequences of his crime". This said imperial edict was received on the 9th day of the 6th month of the 19th year of Taoukwang, at which the period of grace begins, and runs on to the 9th day of the 12th month of the 20th year of Taoukwang, when it is completed.

English translation version 2, published in Ssu-yu Teng and John K. Fairbank (1954). China's Response to the West. Harvard University Press. pp. 24–27.

English translation version 3, published in Dun J. Li (ed.) (1969).*China in Transition*, 1517–1911. New York: Van Nostrand Reinhold Inc., U.S. pp. 64–67.

Appendix 10

Letter from Lord Palmerston to the Minister of the Emperor of China, 1840, discussed in Chapter 7

English Original

Source: Morse, Hosea Ballou (1910). *International Relations of the Chinese Empire, The Period of Conflict (1834–1860),* Vol. 1, Appendix A, pp. 621–6. London: Longmans, Green & Co.

THE UNDERSIGNED, Her Britannick Majesty's Principal Secretary for Foreign Affairs, has the honour to inform the Minister of The Emperor of China, that Her Majesty The Queen of Great Britain has sent a Naval and Military Force to the Coast of China, to demand from The Emperor satisfaction and redress for injuries inflicted by Chinese Authorities upon British subjects resident in China, and for insults offered by the same Authorities to the British Crown.

For more than a 100 years, commercial intercourse has existed between China and Great Britain; and during that long period of time, British Subjects have been allowed by the Chinese Government to reside within the territory of China for the purpose of carrying on trade therein. Hence it has happened that British Subjects, trusting in the good faith of the Chinese Government, have fixed themselves in Canton as Merchants, and have brought into that city from time to time property to a large amount; while other British Subjects who wished to trade with China, and who could not for various reasons go thither themselves, have sent commodities to Canton, placing those commodities in the care of some of their fellow Countrymen resident in China, with directions that such commodities should be sold in China, and that the produce of the sale thereof should be sent to the Owners in the British Dominions.

Thus there has always been within the territory of The Emperor of China a certain number of British Subjects, and a large amount of British Property; and though no Treaty has existed between the Sovereign of England and the Emperor of China, yet British Subjects have continued to resort to China for purposes of trade, placing full confidence in the justice and good faith of The Emperor.

Moreover, of late years the Sovereign of Great Britain has stationed at Canton an officer of the British Crown, no wise connected with trade, and specially forbidden to trade, but ordered to place himself in direct communication with the local Authorities at Canton in order to afford protection to British Subjects, and to be the organ of communication between the British and the Chinese Governments.

But the British Government has learnt with much regret, and with extreme surprise, that during the last year certain officers, acting under the Authority of The Emperor of China, have committed violent outrages against the British Residents at Canton, who were living peaceably in that City, trusting to the good faith of the Chinese Government; and that those same Chinese officers, forgetting the respect which was due to the British Superintendent in his Character of Agent of the British Crown, have treated that Superintendent also with violence and indignity.

It seems that the cause assigned for these proceedings was the contraband trade in Opium, carried on by some British Subjects.

It appears that the Laws of the Chinese Empire forbid the importation of Opium into China, and declare that all opium which may be brought into the Country is liable to confiscation.

The Queen of England desires that Her Subjects who may go into Foreign Countries should obey the Laws of those Countries; and Her Majesty does not wish to protect them from the just consequences of any offences which they may commit in foreign parts. But, on the other hand, Her Majesty cannot permit that Her Subjects residing abroad should be treated with violence, and be exposed to insult and injustice; and when wrong is done to them, Her Majesty will see that they obtain redress.

Now if a Government makes a Law which applies both to its own Subjects and to Foreigners, such Government ought to enforce that Law impartially or not at all. If it enforces that Law on Foreigners, it is bound to enforce it also upon its own Subjects; and it has no right to permit its own Subjects to violate the Law with impunity, and then to punish Foreigners for doing the very same thing.

Neither is it just that such a Law should for a great length of time be allowed to sleep as a dead letter, and that both Natives and Foreigners should be taught to consider it as of no effect, and that then suddenly, and without sufficient warning, it should be put in force with the utmost rigour and severity.

Now, although the Law of China declared that the importation of Opium should be forbidden, yet it is notorious that for many years past, that importation has been connived at and permitted by the Chinese Authorities at Canton; nay, more, that those Authorities, from the Governor downwards, have made an annual and considerable profit by taking money from Foreigners for the permission to import Opium; and of late the Chinese Authorities have gone so far in setting this Law at defiance, that Mandarin Boats were employed to bring opium to Canton from the Foreign Ships lying at Lintin.

Did the Imperial Government at Peking know these things?

If it did know these things, it virtually abolished its own Law, by permitting its own officers to act as if no such Law existed. If the Chinese Government says it did not know of these things, if it says that it knew indeed that the Law was violated by Foreigners who brought in opium, but did not know that the Law was violated by its own Officers who assisted in the importation, and received fixed Sums of money for permitting it, then may Foreign Governments ask, how it happened that a Government so watchful as that of China should have one eye open to see the transgressions of Foreigners, but should have the other eye shut, and unable to see the transgressions of its own officers.

If the Chinese Government had suddenly determined that the Law against the importation of Opium should be enforced, instead of remaining, as it long had been, a dead letter, that Government should have begun by punishing its own Officers who were the greatest delinquents in this matter, because it was their special duty to execute the Law of their own Sovereign. But the course pursued by the Chinese Government has been the very reverse; for they have left unpunished their own officers, who were most to blame, and they have used violence against Foreigners, who were led into transgression by the encouragement and protection afforded to them by the Governor of Canton and his inferior Officers.

Still, however, the British Government would not have complained, if the Government of China, after giving due notice of its altered intentions, had proceeded to execute the Law of the Empire, and had seized and confiscated all the opium which they could find within the Chinese territory, and which had been brought into that territory in violation of the Law. The Chinese Government had a right to do so, by means of its own officers, and within its own territory.

But for some reason or other known only to the Government of China, that Government did not think proper to do this. But it determined to seize peaceable British Merchants, instead of seizing the contraband opium; to punish the innocent for the guilty, and to make the sufferings of the former, the means of compulsion upon the latter; and it also resolved to force the British Superintendent, who is an officer of the British Crown, to become an instrument in the hands of the Chinese Authorities for carrying into execution the Laws of China, with which he had nothing to do.

Against such proceedings the British Government protests, and for such proceedings the British Government demands satisfaction.

A large number of British Merchants who were living peaceably at Canton, were suddenly imprisoned in their houses, deprived of the assistance of their Chinese servants, and cut off from all supplies of food, and were threatened with death by starvation, unless other persons, in other places, and over whom these Merchants so imprisoned had no authority or control, would surrender to the Chinese Government a quantity of Opium which the Chinese Authorities were unable themselves to discover or to take possession of, and a portion of which was at the time not within the territories and jurisdiction of China. Her Majesty's Superintendent, upon learning the violence which was done towards these British Merchants, and the danger to which their lives were exposed, repaired, though with some risk and difficulty, to Canton, in order to enquire into the matter, and to persuade the Chinese authorities to desist from these outrageous proceedings. But the Imperial Commissioner did not listen to Her Majesty's Officer; and in violation of the Law of Nations, and in utter disregard of the respect which was due by him to an officer of the British Crown, he imprisoned the Superintendent as well as the Merchants, and, continuing to deprive them all of the means of subsistence, he threatened to put them all to death by starvation, unless the Superintendent would give to other persons, not in Canton, orders which he had no power or authority to give, for delivering to the Chinese Authorities a fixed quantity of Opium.

The Superintendent, in order to save the lives of his imprisoned fellow Countrymen, gave at last the orders required of him, and the parties to whom these orders were addressed, although by no means bound to obey them, and although a great part of the property demanded, did not belong to them, but was only held by them in trust for others, yet complied with these orders, wishing no doubt to rescue the British Merchants in Canton from death, and trusting that the Queen of Great Britain would at a future time cause them to be indemnified for their loss.

The British Government cannot condemn the steps which were taken by Her Majesty's Superintendent under the pressure of an over-ruling and irresistible force, to rescue from the barbarous fate which awaited them, so many of Her Majesty's Subjects for whose special protection the Superintendent had been appointed, and the British Government highly applauds the readiness with which the persons to whom the orders were directed surrendered the Property demanded, and showed themselves willing to submit to the destruction of their Property, in order to prevent the destruction of the lives of so many of their fellow countrymen. But the British Government demands full satisfaction from the Government of China for these things. In the first place it requires, that the Ransom which was exacted as the price for the lives of the Superintendent, and of the imprisoned British Merchants, shall be restored to the persons who paid it, and if, as the British Government is informed, the goods themselves, which were given up to the Chinese Authorities, have been so disposed of, that they cannot be restored to their owners, in the same state in which they were given up, then the British Government demands and requires that the value of those goods shall be paid back by the Government of China to the British Government, in order that it may be paid over to the Parties entitled to receive it.

In the next place, the British Government demands satisfaction from the Government of China for the affront offered to the Crown of Great Britain, by the indignities to which Her Majesty's Superintendent has been subjected; and the British Government requires that in future the officer employed by Her Majesty to watch over the commercial interests of Her Subjects in China, and to be the organ of communication with the Government of China, shall be treated, and shall be communicated with by that Government, and by its officers, in a manner consistent with the usages of civilized Nations, and with the respect due to the Dignity of the British Crown.

Thirdly. The British Government demands security for the future, that British Subjects resorting to China for purposes of trade, in conformity with the long-established understanding between the two Governments; shall not again be exposed to violence and injustice while engaged in their lawful pursuits of Commerce. For this purpose, and in order that British Merchants trading to China may not be subject to the arbitrary caprice either of the Government at Peking, or its local Authorities at the Sea-Ports of the Empire, the British Government demands that one or more sufficiently large and properly situated Islands on the Coast of China, to be fixed upon by the British Plenipotentiaries, shall be permanently given up to the British Government as a place of residence and of commerce for British Subjects; where their persons may be safe from molestation, and where their Property may be secure.

Moreover, it appears that the Chinese Government has hitherto compelled the British Merchants resident at Canton to sell their goods to certain Hong Merchants, and to no other persons, and the Chinese Government, by thus restricting the dealings of the British Merchants, has become responsible for the Hong Merchants to whom these dealings were confined. But some of those Hong Merchants have lately become insolvent, and the British Merchants have thus incurred great pecuniary losses, which they would have avoided, if they had been allowed to trade with whomsoever they chose. The British Government therefore demands that the Government of China shall make good to the British Creditors the Sums due to them by the insolvent Hong Merchants.

The British Government moreover has recently heard of further acts of violence committed by the Chinese Authorities against British Subjects; and it may happen that before this Note reaches the Chinese Minister, other things may have been done in China, which may render necessary further demands on the part of the British Government. If this should be, the British Plenipotentiaries are authorised to make such further demands; and the Undersigned requests the Chinese Minister to consider any additional demands so made, as being as fully authorised by the British Government as if they had been specified in this note.

Now as the distance is great which separates England from China, and as the matter in question is of urgent importance, the British Government cannot wait to know the answer which the Chinese Government may give to these demands, and thus postpone till that answer shall have been received in England, the measures which may be necessary in order to vindicate the honour and dignity of the British Crown, in the event of that answer not being satisfactory.

The British Government therefore has determined at once to send out a Naval and Military Force to the Coast of China to act in support of these demands, and in order to convince the imperial Government that the British Government attaches the utmost importance to this matter, and that the affair is one which will not admit of delay.

And further, for the purpose of impressing still more strongly upon the Government of Peking the importance which the British Government attaches to this matter, and the urgent necessity which exists for an immediate as well as a satisfactory settlement thereof, the Commander of the Expedition has received orders that, immediately upon his arrival upon the Chinese Coast, he shall proceed to blockade the principal Chinese ports, that he shall intercept and detain and hold in deposit all Chinese Vessels which he may meet with, and that he shall take possession of some convenient part of the Chinese territory, to be held and occupied by the British Forces until everything shall be concluded and executed to the satisfaction of the British Government.

These measures of hostility on the part of Great Britain against China are not only justified, but even rendered absolutely necessary, by the outrages which have been committed by the Chinese Authorities against British officers and Subjects, and these hostilities will not cease, until a satisfactory arrangement shall have been made by the Chinese Government.

The British Government in order to save time, and to afford to the Government of China every facility for coming to an early arrangement, have given to the Admiral and to the Superintendent, Full Powers and Instructions to treat upon these matters with the Imperial Government, and have ordered the said Admiral and Superintendent to go up to the Mouth of the Peiho River, in the Gulph of Pechelee, that they may be within a short distance of the Imperial Cabinet. But after the indignity which was offered to Her Majesty's Superintendent at Canton, in the course of last year, it is impossible for Her Majesty's Government to permit any of Her Majesty's Officers to place themselves in the power of the Chinese Authorities, until some formal Treaty shall have been duly signed, securing to British Subjects safety and respect in China; and therefore the Undersigned must request that the Chinese Government will have the goodness to send on board the Admiral's Ship the Plenipotentiaries whom the Emperor may appoint to treat upon these matters with the Plenipotentiaries of The Queen of England. Those Chinese Plenipotentiaries shall be received on board the Admiral's Ship, with every honour which is due to the Envoys of The Emperor, and shall be treated with all possible courtesy and respect.

The Undersigned has further to state, that the necessity for sending this Expedition to the Coast of China having been occasioned by the violent and unjustifiable acts of the Chinese Authorities, the British Government expects and demands, that the expenses incurred thereby shall be repaid to Great Britain by the Government of China.

The Undersigned has now stated and explained to the Chinese Minister, without reserve, the causes of complaint on the part of Great Britain; the reparation which Great Britain demands, and the nature of the measures which the British officer commanding the Expedition has been instructed in the first instance to take. The British Government fervently hopes that the wisdom and spirit of Justice for which The Emperor is famed in all parts of the World, will lead the Chinese Government to see the equity of the foregoing demands; and it is the sincere wish of Her Majesty's Government that a prompt and full compliance with those demands may lead to a speedy re-establishment of that friendly intercourse which has for so great a period of time subsisted between the British and Chinese Nation, to the manifest advantage of both.

The Undersigned, in conclusion, has the honour to state to the Minister of The Emperor of China that he has directed Her Majesty's Plenipotentiaries to forward to His Excellency the present Note, of which he has transmitted to the Plenipotentiaries a copy; with instructions to cause a Translation of it to be made into the Chinese language, and to forward to the Chinese Minister the Translation at the same time with the original Note.

The Undersigned avails himself of this opportunity to offer to His Excellency the Minister of The Emperor of China the assurances of his most distinguished consideration.

PALMERSTON.

Index

Printed in the United States
by Baker & Taylor Publisher Services